Each of these specific '  -
trated with actual cases.

The Dynamics of Nonviolent Action examines the complex operation of this technique against a violent, repressive opponent.

Groundwork which may precede the struggle is explored, as well as basic requirements for effectives. Then the focus turns to the initial impact of the nonviolent challenge.

Repression is probable. Determined, yet nonviolent, continued resistance is needed to fight it. The opponent's repression may rebound by "political *jiu-jitsu*", weakening his power by loss of support and increased resistance.

Three main mechanisms by which nonviolent action may produce victory are examined: conversion (the rarest), accomodation, and nonviolent coercion. Massive noncooperation may paralyze and disintegrate even an oppressive system.

All these elements of the dynamics of nonviolent struggle are illustrated with examples.

The resisting group itself is also changed: it gains in self-respect, confidence and power.

Empowerment of the struggle group, the accompanying strengthening of the non-State institutions, ability to defeat repressive elites, and the extension among the populace of a nonviolent struggle capacity, contribute to long-term social changes by redistributing power.

The Methods of Nonviolent Action

part two of:

Extending Horizons Books

A study prepared
under the auspices of
Harvard University's Center
for International Affairs

The Politics of Nonviolent Action

Gene Sharp

With the editorial assistance of Marina Finkelstein

Porter Sargent Publishers, 11 Beacon St., Boston, Ma. 02108

Copyright © 1973 by Gene Sharp
All rights reserved.
Library of Congress Catalog Number 72-95483
ISBN 0-87558-071-8

Fourth Printing, 1980

CONTENTS

Chapter Two

NONVIOLENT ACTION: AN ACTIVE TECHNIQUE OF STRUGGLE

PART TWO: THE METHODS OF NONVIOLENT ACTION
POLITICAL JIU-JITSU AT WORK

Chapter Three

THE METHODS OF NONVIOLENT PROTEST AND PERSUASION

Chapter Four

THE METHODS OF SOCIAL NONCOOPERATION

Chapter Five

THE METHODS OF ECONOMIC NONCOOPERATION:
(1) ECONOMIC BOYCOTTS

Chapter Six

THE METHODS OF ECONOMIC NONCOOPERATION: (2) THE STRIKE

Chapter Seven

THE METHODS OF POLITICAL NONCOOPERATION

Chapter Eight

THE METHODS OF NONVIOLENT INTERVENTION

PART THREE: THE DYNAMICS OF NONVIOLENT ACTION

Chapter Nine
LAYING THE GROUNDWORK FOR NONVIOLENT ACTION

Chapter Ten
CHALLENGE BRINGS REPRESSION

Chapter Eleven

SOLIDARITY AND DISCIPLINE TO FIGHT REPRESSION

Chapter Twelve

POLITICAL JIU-JITSU

Chapter Thirteen

THREE WAYS SUCCESS MAY BE ACHIEVED

Chapter Fourteen

THE REDISTRIBUTION OF POWER

PART TWO:

The Methods of Nonviolent Action: Political Jiu-Jitsu at Work

INTRODUCTION
TO PART TWO

Nonviolent action "works" in very special ways which must be grasped if the technique itself is to be understood, evaluated intelligently, and applied most effectively. These ways diverge significantly from popular assumptions about conflict and struggle—in particular the assumption that violence can be effectively met only with violence.

Nonviolent action is designed to operate against opponents who are able and willing to use violent sanctions.[1] There is no assumption in this technique that such opponents will, when faced with nonviolent action, suddenly renounce their violence, or even that they will consistently restrict their use of violent repression.

However, the use of nonviolent means against violent repression creates a special, asymmetrical, conflict situation, in which the two groups rely on contrasting techniques of struggle, or "weapons systems"—one on violent action, the other on nonviolent action. To have the best chance of success, the nonviolent actionists must stick with their chosen technique. An extensive, determined and skillful application of nonviolent action will cause the opponent very special problems, which will disturb or frustrate the effective utilization of his own forces. The actionists will then be able to apply something like *jiu-jitsu* to their opponent, throwing him off balance politically, causing his repression to rebound against his position, and weakening his power. Furthermore, by remaining nonviolent while continuing the struggle, the actionists will help to improve their own power position in several ways.

It is sometimes assumed that the nonviolent technique inevitably leads to high public exposure and high vulnerability to punishment. Therefore, it is concluded, only a minority of persons is likely to use it. It is true that where nonviolent actionists are few in number and lack the support of majority opinion, the actionists may well be in an exposed and vulnerable position. (The use of violence in such a case would make them even more exposed and vulnerable.) However, the situation is very different where nonviolent actionists are acting in support of general public opinion and themselves constitute a large part of the population. In that situation there is less exposure, and the chances of any one person's being singled out for punishment may be disproportionately reduced. But the opponent is unlikely to submit meekly.

There should, in fact, be no dismay or surprise at repression: it is often the result of the opponent's recognition that the nonviolent action is a serious threat to his policy or regime. Nonviolent actionists must be willing to risk punishment as a part of the price of victory. The severity and chances of repression will vary. This risk is not unique to nonviolent action, however. There are also risks when both sides use violence —some similar to and some different from those faced by nonviolent actionists. One difference is that in violent action risks are incurred in the course of attempting to injure or kill the opponents, while in nonviolent action, this is not the case. Some people erroneously understand that to mean that the nonviolent group is helpless. This is not true. This difference in the treatment of the opponent should not lead to feelings of impotence or frustration, especially if the nonviolent actionist understands that remaining nonviolent makes it more possible for him to gain increased control over the opponent, reduce the violence against the nonviolent group, and increase the chances of winning.

The fact is, of course, that repression does not necessarily produce submission. For sanctions to be effective, they must operate on people's minds, produce fear, and create willingness to obey. However, lack of fear, or some overriding loyalty or objective, may cause the actionists to persist despite repression. (This is also true in military struggle.) When the nonviolent actionists so persist, the opponent's problems may be aggravated in a number of ways. Most of his usual means of repression have been designed to deal with violent disobedience and violent rebellion. Because the dynamics and mechanisms of violent and nonviolent struggle differ, however, very different effects will result from repression against nonviolent actionists. For example, men imprisoned in a nonviolent struggle—whether Gandhi, King, Dubček, or students sitting-in at lunch counters—are widely regarded as still in the "front lines," and not as removed from the battle. Instead of trying to avoid provoking repression, nonviolent actionists may seek to exhaust the opponent's means of repression—such as by filling the jails—and thus to demonstrate his incapacity to rule even with such means. Repression against nonviolent action *may* be effective, of course. But depending on conditions, it also *may not*. If it is not, the opponent may be in difficulties. There will also be other sources of his troubles, however.

The opponent facing nonviolent action may be in a very awkward position if his own policies are hard to justify, if the nonviolent action involves the optimal combination of quality of behavior and number of actionists, and if, in face of repression, the nonviolent group is able to maintain a disciplined and determined persistence in its intended course. If the defiance is widespread or especially daring, the opponent cannot really ignore it without appearing to be helpless in face of defiance and thereby risking its spread. Yet repression may not only *not* strengthen his position, but may in certain circumstances set in motion forces which may actually weaken it further. These problems may make him wish that the rebels had chosen violent rather than nonviolent means, for violence does not pose the same kind of enforcement problems.

The opponent's difficulties in coping with nonviolent action do not depend on his being surprised by the nonviolence or on unfamiliarity with the technique. The opponent's knowledge of the operation of nonviolent struggle, for example, does not on its own give him the capacity to defeat the actionists: as in military conflicts, both sides may seek to utilize for their own ends knowledge of the technique of struggle they are using. With more knowledge, the opponent may become more sophisticated, and perhaps less cruel. But the nonviolent group also may learn how to struggle more skillfully and effectively.

The opponent's difficulties in dealing with nonviolent action are primarily associated with the special dynamics and mechanisms of the technique, and their tendency to maximize the influence and power of the nonviolent group while undermining those of the opponent. For example, partly because extremely brutal repression against a nonviolent group is more difficult to justify, the opponent's repression may be more limited than it would be against a violent rebellion. Furthermore, overreacting in repression may, instead of weakening the resisters, react against sources of the opponent's own power, and thus weaken *his* power position. The opponent may therefore prefer that the rebels use violent, rather than nonviolent, action and may deliberately seek to provoke the resisters to violence, perhaps by severe repression intended to break the nonviolent discipline or by spies and *agents provocateurs.*

If the nonviolent actionists nevertheless maintain their discipline and continue the struggle, and if they involve significant sections of the populace, the results of their behavior may extend far beyond individual example and martyrdom. They may effectively block the opponent's will and make it impossible for him to carry out his plans, even with the aid of repression. The arrest of leaders may simply reveal that the nonviolent movement can carry on without a recognizable leadership. The opponent may make new acts illegal, only to find that he has opened new opportunities for defiance. He may find that while he has been attempting to repress defiance at certain points, the nonviolent actionists have found sufficient strength to broaden their attack on other fronts to the extent of challenging his very ability to rule. Instead of mass repression forcing cooperation and obedience, he may find that the repression is constantly met by refusal to submit or flee; repression may repeatedly be demonstrated to be incapable of inducing submission. Furthermore, in extreme cases his very agencies of repression may be immobilized by the massive defiance; there may be too many resisters to control, or his own troops may mutiny. All these possible effects are examples of a process which may be called "political *jiu-jitsu."*

The nonviolent actionists deliberately refuse to challenge the opponent on his own level of violence. Violence against violence is reinforcing. The nonviolent group not only does not need to use violence, but they must not do so lest they strengthen their opponent and weaken themselves. They must adhere to their own nonviolent "weapons system," since nonviolent action tends to turn the opponent's violence and repression against his own power position, weakening it and at the same time strengthening the nonviolent group. Because violent action and nonviolent action possess quite different mechanisms, and induce differing forces of change in the society, the opponent's repression—given a maintenance of nonviolent discipline and of persistence in the nonviolent group—can never really come to grips with the kind of power wielded by the nonviolent actionists. Gandhi has compared the situation with that of a man violently striking water with a sword: it was the man's arm which was dislocated.[2]

This is part of the reason why it is important for the actionists to maintain nonviolent discipline even in face of brutal repression. By maintaining the contrast between the violent and nonviolent techniques, the nonviolent actionists can demonstrate that repression is incapable of cowing the populace, and they can undermine the opponent's existing support. This can lead to weakening of his ability or will to continue with the repression and to defend his objectives and position.

To sum up: Repression of a nonviolent group which nevertheless persists in struggle and also maintains nonviolent discipline may have the following effects. As cruelties to nonviolent people increase, the opponent's regime may appear still more despicable, and sympathy and support for the nonviolent side may increase. The general population may become more alienated from the opponent and more likely to join the resistance. Persons divorced from the immediate conflict may show increased support for the victims of the repression. Although the effect of national and international public opinion varies, it may at times lead to significant political and economic pressures. The opponent's own citizens, agents, and troops, disturbed by brutalities against nonviolent people, may begin to doubt the justice of his policies. Their initial uneasiness may grow into internal dissent and at times even into such action as strikes and mutinies. Thus, if repression increases the numbers of nonviolent actionists and enlarges defiance, and if it leads to sufficient internal opposition among the opponent's usual supporters to reduce his capacity to deal with the defiance, it will clearly have rebounded against him. This is political *jiu-jitsu* at work.

Whether or not this is achieved hinges on the capacity of the nonviolent actionists to continue their struggle by the use of *their own* "weapons system." These "weapons," or specific methods of opposition, are also capable of altering the selected social, economic, or political relationships, whether or not changes in the balance of forces are also produced by political *jiu-jitsu*. There are a multitude of such methods, which collectively constitute the technique of nonviolent action; it is to a classification of these to which the focus of this study now shifts.

Such a classification is useful in a number of ways. For one thing, it assists us in understanding better the nature of the nonviolent technique, while also revealing very clearly the important distinctions and classes which exist within it. Some methods are basically symbolic actions, some involve a withdrawal of particular types of cooperation, others are largely direct interventions in a conflict situation. Classification also reveals the very large number and variety of methods of action the technique encompasses;[3] the present listing is certainly not exhaustive. The terminological refinement and definition of specific methods will also make possible future comparative analyses of the operation of different methods, or of the same method in different situations. In addition, a detailed classification provides something of a checklist of the main methods of nonviolent action thus far practiced.[4] Such a listing may assist actionists in the selection of methods most appropriate for use in a particular situation. It may also give groups faced with nonviolent opposition an idea of the methods which may be used against them, possibly reducing nervousness and brutalities. In addition, the list may give researchers and persons evaluating the political potentialities of the nonviolent technique a greater grasp of its armory of methods of struggle.

The broad classification of the particular methods of action under the general categories of *protest and persuasion, noncooperation* and *intervention* ought not to be regarded as rigid, but simply as generally valid. In particular circumstances one method may more correctly fall into a different category than the one under which it is classified in this study. In some situations one method may in the course of action develop into another, so there is no clear dividing line between them. Or two distinct methods may in a particular case be so closely combined as to be inseparable, even for analytical purposes.

Neither should the listing of specific methods be regarded as complete for all time. Doubtless some have been missed altogether, and a number of unlisted variations exist on those methods which are included. Perhaps more important, new forms of nonviolent action may be deliberately developed or improvised in the course of struggle. The "reverse strike," for example, in which people do without pay additional work they are not expected to do, is probably only about twenty years old. The examples of the specific methods offered in these chapters should be regarded as only illustrative. They are not intended to be representative, either geographically or historically, and they include both "successful" and "unsuccessful" cases. They do, however, indicate something of the widely differing historical, political and cultural conditions under which the technique of nonviolent action has already been used. Further research could doubtless provide additional examples from many cases not even mentioned in this study.

Which methods will be used in a particular case, and how many of them, will vary widely depending on such factors as 1) the traditions of the people involved; 2) the extent and depth of the knowledge of, and experience with, methods of nonviolent action possessed by the general population, the direct participants in the struggle and their leaders; 3) the general social and political situation; 4) the degree of repression which the general population, the actionists and the leaders are prepared to suffer; 5) the nature of the opponent's objectives; 6) the resources at the opponent's disposal (including his administrative system, agents of repression, and so on);7) the degree of ruthlessness the opponent is prepared to use; 8) the degree of the opponent's dependence on members of the nonviolent opposition; 9) the numbers of participating actionists and the degree of support they receive from the population; 10) the quality of the actionists and leaders; 11) the nature of the grievance; and 12) the physical details of the specific situation in which action is contemplated.

Let us now turn to an examination of our first category of the methods of this technique: nonviolent protest and persuasion.

NOTES

1. Cases in which *both* sides use nonviolent means are discussed in Chapter Eleven.
2. M. K. Gandhi, **Non-violent Resistance,** p. 57; Ind. ed.: **Satyagraha,** p. 57.
3. The terms "method" and "form" are used interchangeably here, although generally "method" is used and recommended. There are precedents for the use of these terms in the way we apply them here. Joan Bondurant **(Conquest of Violence,** p. 36) uses the phrase "forms of nonviolent action" to describe the phenomena discussed in these chapters. Carl von Clausewitz **(On War,** [New York: Barnes and Noble, 1956, and London: Routledge & Kegan Paul, 1956], vol. I, pp. 125 and 166, and vol. II, p. 409) refers to those types of action in war which are in their relationship to the over-all struggle roughly comparable to these "forms" in nonviolent struggles as "methods." Despite the vast differences between military and nonviolent struggles there is sufficient

similarity in the role of the respective "methods" or "forms" in the over-all conflict to justify, and for clarity even require, the use of the same or similar terminology.

4. This catalog of methods of nonviolent action has no precedent in the literature. There are, however, separate listings of various types of strikes and of economic boycotts in the literature, and these are cited in the appropriate chapters. But for nonviolent action as a general technique, earlier listings were extremely limited. See, for example, Shridharani, **War Without Violence,** pp. 28-62 (fifteen methods, at least two of which "negotiations and arbitration" and "self-purification" are not classified within the technique here), and Lindberg, Jacobsen and Ehrlich, **Kamp Uden Vaaben,** p. 10 (seven methods, including sabotage which is excluded here, some of which are here discussed in whole chapters).

3

The Methods
of Nonviolent Protest
and Persuasion

INTRODUCTION

Nonviolent protest and persuasion[1] is a class which includes a large number of methods which are mainly symbolic acts of peaceful opposition or of attempted persuasion, extending beyond verbal expressions but stopping short of noncooperation or nonviolent intervention. Among these methods are parades, vigils, picketing, posters, teach-ins, mourning and protest meetings.

Their use may simply show that the actionists are *against* something; for example, picketing may express opposition to a law which restricts dissemination of birth control information. The methods of this class may also be applied *for* something; for example, group lobbying may support a clean-air bill pending in the legislature or overseas aid. Nonviolent protest and persuasion also may express deep personal feelings or moral condemnation on a social or political issue; for example, a vigil on Hiroshima Day may express penance for the American atomic bombing of that Japanese city. The "something" which the nonviolent protestors may be concerned with may be a particular deed, a law, a policy, a general condition, or a whole regime or system.

The act may be intended primarily to influence the *opponent*—by arousing attention and publicity for the issue and thereby, it is hoped, support, which may convince him to accept the change; or by warning him of the depth or extent of feeling on the issue which is likely to lead to more severe action if a change is not made. Or the act may be intended primarily to communicate with the *public,* onlookers or third parties, directly or through publicity, in order to arouse attention and support for the desired change. Or the act may be intended primarily to influence the *grievance group*—the persons directly affected by the issue—to induce them to do something themselves, such as participate in a strike or an economic boycott. A method of nonviolent protest and persuasion such as a pilgrimage may also be associated with some other type of activity, such as collections of money for famine victims. Certain mild methods of this class are intended to persuade in order to produce a stronger action by someone else: leafleting may be aimed at inducing participation in an economic boycott, and fraternization within the context of resistance may be intended to help induce later mutiny by occupation soldiers, for example.

In summary, within the context of this class of methods, emphasis may be placed on being for or against something; the grievances may be diverse; the group to whom the act is primarily directed may vary; the types of influence will differ; the intended result may range widely; the act may be an independent one or closely combined with some other method (or methods) of nonviolent action.

Behavior in such demonstrations clearly extends beyond personal verbal expressions of opinion, either by reason of the corporate nature of the act or the form of action or, in a few cases, the circumstances which give an individual act a corporate significance. Yet the methods of nonviolent protest and persuasion usually remain (unless combined with other methods) expressions in action of a point of view, or an attempt in action to influence others to accept a point of view or to take a certain action. This is distinguished from the social, economic, or political pressures imposed by noncooperation or nonviolent intervention. There are political circumstances in which some of the forms of nonviolent protest, such as marches, for example, are illegal. Under such circumstances their practice would merge the method with civil disobedience and possibly other forms of political noncooperation.

The impact of these methods of nonviolent protest and persuasion, which depend on influencing the attitudes of someone, will vary considerably. It is possible that where a particular method is common, its impact on any one occasion may be less than may be the case where the method has hitherto been rare or unknown. The political conditions in which it occurs are also likely to influence its impact, with dictatorial conditions making an act of nonviolent protest less possible, more dangerous and rarer; hence if it does occur, the act may be more dramatic and gain greater attention than it would where the act is common or carries no penalty. Demonstrations of protest and persuasion may precede or accompany acts of noncooperation or nonviolent intervention, or may be practiced in their absence.

What, then, are the specific methods of nonviolent action which may be classified as nonviolent protest and persuasion? Fifty-four methods are included in this listing; they are grouped here in ten subclasses.

FORMAL STATEMENTS

Normally, written or oral statements, whether by an individual, group or institution, are simply verbal expressions of opinion, dissent or intention, and not acts of nonviolent protest and persuasion as defined above. However, certain circumstances may give such statements a greater than usual impact and such an act may then fall within this class. Whether this happens or not will depend on the political situation in which the statement is issued, the status of the person or body issuing the statement, the nature of the statement itself, the degree of conformity and nonconformity in the political society, and the risk taken in issuing such a statement. As with many if not all acts of nonviolent action, such statements may be primarily for, or against, some issue, regime, system, policy or condition. They take various forms, and on the basis of these we distinguish six specific methods. These statements are primarily addressed to the opponent or to the person or body which is being supported or opposed, but secondarily they may influence some wider public.

1. Public speeches

Some public speeches may become significant acts of nonviolent protest. They may be spontaneous in some unexpected situation, they may be formal addresses, or they may be sermons delivered during religious services. In 1934, for example, when the Nazis were simply a minority in a coalition cabinet headed by Hitler as Chancellor, the non-Nazi Vice-Chancellor was Franz von Papen. In a dramatic, rather untypical act, Papen in a speech to students at the University of Marburg on June 17, 1934, expressed his alarm at the course of events since Hitler's accession to the chancellorship and called for an end to Nazi terror and a restoration of some freedoms, especially freedom of the press.[2] Coming from the Vice-Chancellor himself, this was an unexpected act of opposition which, despite censorship, received widespread support within Germany and major publicity abroad.

In Berlin on November 11, 1941, a sixty-five-year-old Roman Catholic priest, Provost Lichtenberg, declared in a sermon in St. Hedwig's Cathedral that he wished to share the fate of the Jews and be deported to the East in order to be with them to pray for them.[3] His wish was granted. Another incident on November 18, 1943, was recorded in his diary by Joseph Goebbels, Nazi Propaganda Minister: "During the burial of victims of the last bomb attack on the Bulgarian capital, the Bishop of Sofia delivered a speech in which he attacked the Bulgarian Government rather severely."[4]

2. Letters of opposition or support

Letters as a method of this class may take several forms. These include primarily private letters to a certain person or body, conveying a particular political viewpoint or declaration of intention. These letters may be from individuals or from groups; or similar or identical letters may be sent by many people. At times private letters may deliberately or otherwise become public knowledge. Or the letter may be published as an "open letter"—written to a particular person but intended equally or primarily to influence the general public which reads it.

Letters usually gain sufficient significance to be classed as a method of nonviolent protest because of the status of the signer or signatories, because of the number of persons signing the letter or sending identical or similar letters, or because the political situation has heightened the significance of such an act. In the Netherlands in December 1941, for example, over four thousand physicians signed and sent a letter to *Reichskommissar* Arthur Seyss-Inquart asking that plans to set up a compulsory National Socialist organization of physicians be abandoned.[5] And in occupied Norway *Reichskommissar* Josef Terboven received, in May 1941, a letter signed by representatives of forty-three organizations and associations, citing a series of specific actions by the Quisling regime in support of their general charge that "the acting ministers have in a series of cases issued decrees and made decisions that are in open conflict with international law, Norwegian law, and the general Norwegian understanding of justice . . ."[16] Also in Norway in 1942 (as described in detail in the previous chapter), in addition to individually written form letters to the Church and Education Department from Norwegian teachers rejecting membership in the new fascist teachers' organization, tens of thousands of signed letters of protest were sent to the department by the parents of the pupils.[7]

Among other examples, Bulgarian protest against Nazi antisemitic measures during World War II might be cited. For example, when the anti-Jewish "Law in Defense of the Nation" was introduced, opposition "was expressed in floods of letters and telegrams addressed to parliament, cabinet ministers, statesmen, and social and political leaders." In addition to such letters from individuals, the Union of Bulgarian Writers sent a letter to the government and parliament asking that the bill not be made law, for it would "enslave part of the Bulgarian people and would blemish Bulgaria's modern history." Similar objections came from the Executive Council of the Union of Bulgarian Writers and the Executive Council of Bulgarian Doctors.[8]

To come to more recent history, on August 22, 1968, delegates of the Extraordinary Fourteenth Congress of the Communist Party of Czechoslovakia sent a letter of support to Alexander Dubček, First Secretary of the Party, who was then in Moscow.[9] On the same day, the Ambassador to Prague of the German Democratic Republic (East Germany) refused to receive a letter from the Czechoslovak National Assembly addressed to the parliament and government of the German Democratic Republic, protesting the presence of their troops in Czechoslovakia.[10] Two days later, on August 24, the Presidium of the Central Council of the Czechoslovak Trade Unions wrote to Aleksandr Shelepin, the Chairman of the All-Union Central Council of Soviet Trade Unions, asking that Soviet trade unionists demand an immediate withdrawal of Soviet and Warsaw Pact troops.[11] Similar letters were sent to officials and citizens of the Soviet Union, among them an open letter to the President of the Academy of Sciences of the Soviet Union from the Chairman of the Czechoslovak Academy of Sciences.[12]

3. Declarations by organizations and institutions

One of the forms such declarations have taken has been that of pastoral letters and similar official church statements. During World War II, in Vichy France, for example, in August and September 1942, protest declarations against the deportation of Jews were read by priests from their pulpits in Toulouse and in the Lyons diocese.[13] On February 16, 1941 a pastoral letter was read in the majority of Norwegian pulpits (and widely circulated in printed form), protesting fascist violations of principles of government under law and interference by Quisling's government with the priests' duty of silence regarding confessions of parishioners. The letter exhorted the regime "to end all which conflicts with God's holy arrangements regarding justice, truth, freedom of conscience and goodness and to build entirely on God's law of living." [14] In February 1943 the Dutch Reformed Church and the Roman Catholic Church in the Netherlands, in a similar declaration and pastoral letter, urged their listening congregations toward civil disobedience and the refusal of collaboration as religious duties. [15] Goebbels was later to call this "an exceptionally insolent pastoral letter." [16] Anti-Nazi pastoral letters were also read on a number of occasions in churches in Germany itself. [17]

Public declarations of support for the Dubček regime and of opposition to the Soviet-led invasion of Czechoslovakia were widespread and important in the early days of the occupation. They were among the factors which made it impossible for a collaborationist regime to be created at the time. The first day after Warsaw Pact troops crossed the borders, the Presidium of the National Assembly addressed a declaration to the governments and parliaments of the five invaders, denouncing the act and demanding "immediate withdrawal." [18] A whole series of bodies issued formal statements in support of the Dubček regime and in opposition to the invasion. [19]

4. Signed public statements

A declaration directed primarily to the general public, or to both the public and the opponent, and released with the signatures of supporters is a method of nonviolent protest and persuasion. The signatures may be those of persons from particular organizations, occupations or professions, or of people from various parts of the society.

Thus, in St. Petersburg, following the events of "Bloody Sunday" (January 9, 1905), sixteen members of the Academy of Sciences publicly declared their belief that events had created a need for a change in government. They were joined by 326 leading university professors and lecturers in circulating the "Statement of the 342," which affirmed that Russia would enjoy the benefits of education only after "freely elected representatives of the people are given the power to make laws and keep a check on the administration." This was endorsed by 1,200 of the country's most noted scholars, and has been called "an outstanding, and perhaps the most effective, action in stirring the educated to a sense of the urgent need for change . . ."[20]

About fourteen hours after the invasion of Czechoslovakia, a statement supporting the legal constitutional and political authorities and denouncing the invasion as an "illegal act" was issued with signatures of fourteen members of the Czechoslovak Government. Certain other officials had already been seized by the Russians.[21]

5. Declarations of indictment and intention

Certain written statements of grievance or future intentions to produce a new situation, or a combination of both, are seen to be of such a quality or to meet such a response that the document itself becomes influential in influencing people's loyalties and behavior. The American Declaration of Independence is one such document; it was adopted by the Second Continental Congress on July 4, 1776. Another is the South African "Freedom Charter" adopted at the Congress of the People at Kliptown, Johannesburg, South Africa, on June 25-26, 1955. Dr. Albert Luthuli, leader of the South African National Congress, has written that "nothing in the history of the Liberatory movement in South Africa quite caught the popular imagination as this did, not even the Defiance Campaign."[22] During this period the anti-*Apartheid* movement was committed to nonviolent means. After a moving list of the social and political objectives of these opponents of *Apartheid,* the document concluded: "These freedoms we will fight for, side by side, throughout our lives, until we have won our liberty."[23]

6. Group or mass petitions

Group or mass petitions are written requests or suplications seeking the redress of a specific grievance, signed by a large number of individuals or by a smaller number of individuals acting on behalf of organizations, institutions or constituencies. (Petitions from individuals normally do not fall within "nonviolent protest and persuasion," since they are usually simply personal efforts to persuade. Exceptions may occur, however.) Of the multitudes of examples, we offer here a few of the less known in order to illustrate some of the diversity in the use of this method. Examples of petitions go back at least as far as the Roman Empire. In one instance, in the years A.D. 183-185, during the reign of Emperor Commodus, son of Marcus Aurelius, the peasant tenants of one of the imperial estates of Africa sought relief from the amount of compulsory work required of them by petitioning the Emperor directly; they sent their petition to Rome by a plenipotentiary who was a Roman citizen. They expressed confidence in the Emperor and hatred for their oppressors (the farmer-general and the procurators) and appealed to the Emperor for relief. The tenants asked protection of the *Lex Hadriana* and insisted on their rights. This petition was successful, though others were not.[24]

Another example from ancient history is the petition to the Roman Emperor Septimius from the village of Aga Bey in Lydia (Asia Minor). In their position the peasant tenants of an imperial estate sought two objectives, one of which was relief from municipal duties which had been imposed on them even though they did not reside in cities, as well as other forms of relief. The peasants threatened the Emperor with a work stoppage by means of a mass "flight" from the estate. (That method is described in Chapter Four.) Relief from the municipal duties was granted.[25]

M. Rostovtzeff describes another petition of the same period, this one in A.D. 201. The petition was from the *navicularii* of Arelate, who probably transported men and supplies by sea from Gaul to the East during the second Parthian expedition. The petition from the *navicularii* complained bitterly of "the vexations and exactions to which they were subjected in performing their service to the state," Rostoztzeff reports. It is likely, he adds, that repeated complaints, coupled with threats of a strike, induced Septimius to revise, complete, and even extend some of the privileges granted to this important group.[26]

A millennium and a half later the American colonists repeatedly petitioned the British officials for relief from their grievances, sometimes in the form of addresses from colonial assemblies, sometimes as petitions from merchants. In November 1766, for example, 240 merchants of the city of New York petitioned the House of Commons for major changes in the trade and navigation system.[27] As part of a struggle among the poor back-country people in North Carolina against the group which was in power in that province, two hundred sixty inhabitants of Anson County signed a petition to the colony's Assembly, listing the grievances from which they sought relief and saying that "we . . . have too long yielded ourselves slaves to remorseless oppression."[28]

African slaves in the Province of Massachusetts Bay also petitioned, addressing the Governor (General Gage), the Council, and the House of Representatives on May 25, 1774. They asserted that in common with all other men they had a right to their freedom. Therefore they asked for legislation to grant that freedom, "our Natural right," and particularly that their children should be set at liberty when they reached the age of twenty-one years.[29]

In more modern times petitions have been used both by nationalists objecting to foreign rule, as in Finland and Egypt, and in grievances
against Communist governments. For example, in 1898, five hundred thousand Finns (out of a total population of three million) signed a petition
protesting a new Russian law drafting Finnish youths into Russian army
units and subjecting them to five years of military duty.[30] Despite British
prohibition, two million signatures were gathered for a petition in Egypt
aimed at achieving a popular mandate for a national delegation which
sought the right to participate in the Versailles peace conference after
World War I.[31]

In the German Democratic Republic (East Germany) on July 7,
1953, 1,500 workers at the Zeiss factory at Jena signed a petition demanding the release of Eckhardt Norkus (who had been sentenced to three
years in prison after an arbitrary arrest following the June rising) and the
release within three days of every striker against whom a criminal charge
could not be proved.[32]

A "Memorandum" signed by several dozen of the elite of Hungary's
Communist writers and artists in early November 1956 requested the Central Committee of the Communist Party to stop officials from applying
"anti-democratic methods which cripple our cultural life," and expressed
the view that ". . . the only basis for eliminating difficulties and wrong
opinions . . . is a free and sincere and healthy and democratic atmosphere
imbued with the spirit of popular rule."[33] As with the other methods
in this chapter, illustrations could go on indefinitely.

COMMUNICATIONS WITH A WIDER AUDIENCE

Several of the methods of this class are designed primarily to communicate ideas, viewpoints and information to a wider audience. The objective may be to influence the opponent group, gain sympathy and support from third parties, or gain converts, members, or assistance for the
nonviolent group. Persuasion is the aim at least as often as protest. Both
visual and oral forms are included in these six methods.

7. Slogans, caricatures and symbols

Among the very common forms of nonviolent protest are slogans, caricatures and symbols. They may be written, painted, drawn, printed,
mimed, gestured, or spoken. From the summer of 1941 to May 1942 a
resistance group of Jewish youths in Berlin, the Baum Group, carried out
such activities without a single arrest, Professor Ber Mark reports.

Going out with buckets of paint and brushes at night was a very risky business. Still, the young fighters went eagerly to post the leaflets and paint the slogans on the walls. The group considered such acts as a test of one's revolutionary ardor, and as the best way to strengthen the revolutionary daring and the spirit of self-sacrifice of the members.[34]

Painted symbols on walls, rocks or fences are often used to express protest. During the Nazi occupation, for example, H VII for the exiled Norwegian King Haakon VII, were so displayed. The nuclear disarmament symbol and the Nazi swastika may also be seen in various countries.[35] In Munich in early 1943 young student members of the *Weisse Rose* (White Rose) resistance group wrote "DOWN WITH HITLER" on walls.[36] In occupied Poland, a group of young boys called "The Little Wolves" in 1942 used indelible paint to decorate German trucks and automobiles, German residences, and even the backs of Germans themselves with inscriptions, such as "POLAND FIGHTS ON," which appeared in Warsaw every morning. Caricatures and posters were also displayed. According to one Polish commentator: "The mischievous and diabolically efficient little pack did much to sustain the psychological atmosphere of contempt for the Germans and fostered the spirit of resistance."[37] After the Russian invasion of Czechoslovakia, in August 1968, one of the slogans that was written on walls widely in Prague was "LENIN, WAKE UP! BREZHNEV HAS GONE MAD."[38]

8. Banners, posters and displayed communication

Written, painted or printed communications such as banners, posters and displayed signs are similar enough to be classed together, but the range of variations is fairly large. During President Wilson's address to Congress on December 4, 1916, five members of a woman suffragist organization, Congressional Union, unrolled a yellow sateen banner from the Visitors' Gallery saying, "MR. PRESIDENT, WHAT WILL YOU DO FOR WOMAN SUFFRAGE?"[39] In India during the struggle in 1930–31, sidewalks and even paved streets served as blackboards for notices of the Indian National Congress.[40] During the *Ruhrkampf*, German resistance fighters tore down French occupation proclamations and posters, replacing them with their own.[41] In Rotterdam in 1942 signs plastered on walls urged the people to show respect for Jews on the street who were wearing the required yellow star.[42] During the Moncton Commission's visits to Northern Rhodesia and Nyasaland in 1960 to review for the

British government the future of the Federation of Rhodesia and Nyasaland (which was hated by black Africans as an instrument of European control), posters urging a boycott of the commission frequently appeared in towns and cities.[43]

On the night of August 23–24, 1968, the Warsaw Pact occupation troops went throughout Prague tearing down resistance posters and patriotic appeals to the citizens to resist, and putting up their own proclamations. The paper *Svoboda* reported that this was: "To no avail! New ones were up by morning. Prague is like one huge poster. 'Occupiers go home!' "[44] One tall smokestack in the Prague-Vrsovice railroad depot was decorated with the sign "FRIENDSHIP, NOT OCCUPATION."[45] On the morning of August 25, the Prague city buses began their routes bearing the signs: "U.N.: S.O.S." Shop windows in the center of the city had been turned into huge display areas for the posting of notices. A car drove by carrying the sign: "THEY OCCUPIED CHARLES UNIVERSITY."[46]

9. Leaflets, pamphlets and books

The publication and distribution of leaflets, pamphlets or books which have as their main purpose the expression of a point of view in opposition to, or in support of, particular or general policies, or to the regime as a whole may in political conditions of repression and struggle become a method of nonviolent action. The distribution of leaflets is perhaps the most common method of communication used by dissenting groups, but under conditions of censorship, books may also be involved. (Literature which calls for active resistance, as distinct from making a general case, is classified below as a separate method, under political noncooperation, because of the content and consequences of such calls.)

For example, the centennial celebration of the Declaration of Independence in Philadelphia was invaded by a group of woman suffragists who distributed leaflets to the assembly and chairman containing a Declaration of Women's Rights.[47] In the section of Nazi-occupied Poland known as the *General Gouvernement,* the underground in 1942(?) counteracted a new Nazi propaganda campaign to acquaint Poles with all types of German achievements by preparing exact duplicates with the original contents radically altered into a biting satire which cited a series of Nazi cruelties and executions.[48] Protest letters which had been sent by Norwegian organizations to *Reichskommissar* Joseph Terboven in early 1941 were printed in Norway from texts broadcast back to Norway from England, and circulated throughout the country in thousands of copies. [49] They were reported to have had a strong and stimulating influence.

In 1941 and 1942 the Baum Group of Jewish resisters in Berlin had as one of their five fields of activity the publication and distribution of various leaflets, brochures and pamphlets which they sent to private homes and offices, distributed to workers, and posted at night on walls.[50] In Munich the student *Weisse Rose* group published several anti-Nazi leaflets and distributed them in Munich and several other South German cities. The leaflets usually were placed in letter boxes, and finally, in 1943, were openly distributed in the University of Munich.[51] In April and May 1959, the Direct Action Committee Against Nuclear War carried a mass leaflet distribution in the Norfolk area of England.[52] Leaflets demanding that the Warsaw Pact armies leave Czechoslovakia, asserting loyalty to the legal governments, and urging resistance were widespread in the early days of the occupation.[53] An "Appeal to the Warsaw Pact Soldiers!" urged them to "leave our territory as friends and do not interfere with our internal development."[54] The Russians also waged a leaflet campaign, distributing them by helicopter and motor vehicles; the resisters' Czechoslovak Radio reported that the fraudulent leaflets over the names of Czechoslovak representatives had been distributed by the occupation forces.[55]

Books, too, may be important in arousing and expressing opinions in times of conflict and in contributing to wider actions and changes. Such influences may occur whether the book is officially allowed or has been prohibited under censorship. In the latter case, books have circulated in manuscript, typescript, or in printed editions published illegally within the country or smuggled in from without. One such book was N.G. Chernyshevsky's *What Is To Be Done?*, a novel which expressed important ideas of revolutionary populism. It was written in prison in 1862 and 1863. It was approved by the censor without reading it, as he thought other officials had already examined it. Published in serial form in the journal *Sovremennik*, it "moulded a whole generation of Populist students and revolutionaries. It became a blueprint of life for the young intelligentsia." It pointed to activities which revolutionaries should undertake, and the need for firm opposition to despotism.[56] A multitude of books have wielded considerable influence in social, economic, religious or political conflicts.

10. Newspapers and journals

Journals and newspapers, both legal and illegal, constantly recur throughout the history of social and political conflicts as media for advancing the views and causes which their publishers espouse. The very existence of such publications is at times illegal, and in such cases this method merges with civil disobedience and the general class of political noncooperation.

The publication and distribution of illegal newspapers and journals played a very important role in the Russian revolutionary movement in the nineteenth and early twentieth centuries.[57] Illegal newspapers and news sheets were also widely published and circulated in Norway during the Nazi occupation,[58] as was the case in other countries such as Denmark,[59] the Netherlands,[60] and Poland.[61] Where politically possible, articles and advertisements in regular papers and journals may also be used to communicate views.

11. Records, radio and television

Under certain conditions records, radio and television themselves become instruments of nonviolent protest and persuasion. Phonograph records may convey ideas through music, speeches or declarations. Much of the American rock music of the 1960s conveyed dissent and dissatisfaction, as did Bob Dylan's song *Blowin' in the Wind*.

In that song Dylan poignantly asked:

— how often can any man turn away as if he hadn't noticed;

— how many times must the cries of suffering be heard before a man pays attention;

— how much time must pass with people in their present conditions before they experience freedom? [62]

Recorded songs with explicit political lines and objectives have been distributed by various political groups for some decades. In 1968 newly released phonograph records were available in Prague on the morning of August 24, carrying the statement of the Extraordinary Fourteenth Party Congress which had been issued on August 22; that declaration, addressed to the citizens of the country, condemned the invasion, rejected Soviet justifications, and demanded release of all detained officials and withdrawal of the foreign troops: "Socialist Czechoslovakia will never accept either a military occupation administration or a domestic collaborationist regime dependent on the forces of the occupiers."[63]

Although radio broadcasts to the populations and resisters in occupied countries were widespread during World War II, Czechoslovakia in 1968 provided the most advanced use to date of radio and television broadcasts originating *within* the occupied country. The clandestine radio network, some of which was able to continue operating for a full two weeks, not only conveyed information about what was happening, but broadcast declarations of opposition to the invasion. The radio also called for specific acts of resistance, warned against violence and urged peaceful discipline in the struggle, opposed collaboration, cautioned against rumors, and took over certain emergency administrative functions. Television broadcasts (which were made from private apartments and other locations away from the regular studios where they would have been subject to Soviet controls) continued into the first days of September.[64]

12. Skywriting and earthwriting[65]

These are words or symbols communicated to people over large distances by writing them in the unusual media of the sky or earth. Skywriting by airplane was used on October 15, 1969, to place a large nuclear disarmament symbol in the sky over the rally against the war in Vietnam, which was then taking place on the Common in Boston, Massachusetts.[66] Earthwriting was used by a California rancher, Edwin Frazer, who lived near San Diego, when his milder protests against sonic booms from planes based at the nearby Miramar Naval Air Station had been ignored. In huge letters in his back pasture he ploughed the word QUIET. (It didn't work either.)[67] Variations could be achieved by planting contrasting crops, trees and the like in the desired pattern, or by arranging such materials as rocks or shrubs in the form of a word or symbol on hillsides or mountains.

GROUP REPRESENTATIONS

Groups may make representations for or against some policy, etc., in a variety of ways. Four of the five methods listed in this category involve the physical presence of those making the representations; in one method this is not the case.

13. Deputations

Protest and disapproval may be expressed by a group of self-selected individuals or of representatives of one or various organizations who go to meet with an official (or his representative) who is particularly responsible for the grievance. On occasion, deputations may seek consideration or adoption of a new policy or measure.

In a district near China's imperial capital in about 1890, taxpayers responded to repeated malpractice by the tax collector (who arbitrarily regulated the exchange rate between copper cash and silver in his favor) by sending a deputation to the capital with documents prepared by a local committee. The first delegation was a failure and the members received fifty blows of the bamboo and a fine. The second deputation was successful; the tax collector was fired and banned from future government employment.[68]

After Tsar Nicholas II had autocratically enacted a law which incorporated the Finnish army into the Imperial Russian army and had declared in a manifesto, on February 15, 1899, his "right" to enact laws for Finland regardless of the views or decision of the Finnish Diet, a deputation of five hundred men carried a protest petition with 523,000 signatures (nearly half the adults of the country) to the Tsar. He refused to receive them.[69]

On November 1, 1958, a London organization called the Geneva Committee of Parents sent a delegation of women to Geneva to see the representatives at the forthcoming test ban conference to press for a permanent end to nuclear testing.[70] Following a demonstration in which between three and four hundred African students marched to the Kremlin on December 18, 1963, a deputation of Ghanaian students went to the Ministry of Education to protest against racial discrimination in Moscow. It was received by the Minister of Education and the Minister of Health.[71]

On August 24, 1968, the Presidium of the Prague City Committee of the Communist Party sent a delegation to the Soviet Embassy to demand the release of Comrade Bohumil Simon, a member of the newly elected Presidium of the Central Committee and the leading secretary of the Prague City Committee. After initial denial of all knowledge of Simon, the Soviet attaché later made assurances that he was all right and that everything was being done to achieve his release.[72]

14. Mock awards[73]

Satirical "awards" may be presented to opponents in order to publicize grievances and perhaps also to appeal to the recipient of the "honor" to correct the grievance. For example, in Massachusetts in November 1969, while hearings on industrial pollution were in progress, the Boston Area Ecology Action campaign presented to the Boston Edison Company a "Polluter of the Month" award. Numerous complaints had previously been made against this electric company on charges of excessive pollution of the atmosphere from its generating plants.[74]

15. Group lobbying

Lobbying in the sense of personal visits to a parliamentary representative by his constituent in an effort to influence his voting in the parliament or assembly is normally simply a verbal expression of opinion. When done as a group action, however, lobbying becomes a form of corporate nonviolent action, because in addition to persuasion of the legislator, the gathering of a fairly large group of people in order to lobby itself becomes a demonstration. This may take the form of *small group lobbying* when a series of individuals or groups in moderate numbers on one occasion, or over a period of time, or on several occasions visit their representatives in an effort to influence them. For example, in the spring of 1966, under the sponsorship of the Friends Committee on National Legislation, persons and groups visited their congressmen and senators in Washington each Wednesday for several weeks to discuss U.S. policy in Vietnam.[75] Or lobbying may be organized to focus on getting very large numbers on a particular day. This is *mass lobbying.* For example, the Anti-*Apartheid* Movement held a "mass lobby" of members of the House of Commons in London on March 8, 1965. Its supporters urged Members of Parliament to press for a firm official stand against South Africa by such means as an arms embargo, collective economic sanctions, and other measures.[76]

16. Picketing

Picketing is an effort to persuade others to do or not to do a particular act, or a method of protest by means of one's physical presence at a place significantly related to the matter in question. The picketing may be conducted by standing, sitting, or walking back and forth. Placards may or may not be carried, and leaflets may or may not be distributed. The pickets may or may not try to talk with others as a means of promoting their end.

Especially in the West, picketing has been widely associated with strikes, largely in an effort to ensure that strikebreakers did not accept the jobs of the strikers or that strikers did not return to their jobs before an agreed settlement. As Lloyd G. Reynolds, a writer on labor economics, put it:

> The device which unions have developed to keep workers out of a struck plant is the picket line. Strikers patrol back and forth in front of the plant entrance, advertising the existence of a strike by placards and word of mouth. Workers entering the plant are greeted with

pleas not to go to work. As a worker leaves the plant at the end of the shift, a picket may walk alongside him for a few steps and urge him not to come to work the next day. Under experienced direction picketing is an effective method of peaceful persuasion, though it can also degenerate into physical conflict. . . . picketing necessarily involves moral pressure if it is to be fully effective. It is not merely a method of reasoning with the would-be strike-breaker, but is intended also to shame him and perhaps alarm him.[77]

In such circumstances the picketing may also be a means of informing the public of the existence of the strike and the issues at stake, and of seeking to enlist their sympathy and support.

Picketing may also be associated with the boycott and political non-cooperation. This was especially the case in India during the nonviolent struggles for freedom. In 1930 the law courts were picketed by the nationalists, the litigants being urged to go instead to the *Panchayats* (village-five or town-five tribunals revived by the India National Congress); government schools and colleges were picketed, and the students were urged to attend "national institutions" which were independent of the British government; shops selling boycotted goods were picketed to discourage purchases of the boycotted items; government buildings were picketed, Indians holding government jobs being urged to give them up in the cause of India's freedom; opium and liquor shops were picketed, usually by women urging the prospective customer not to buy.[78]

Picketing may also be a means of protesting against particular policies, acts, or general policies of the government, or those of the body whose office, headquarters, or the like is being picketed. For the first time in the country's history the White House was picketed on January 10, 1917, and for several days thereafter by woman suffragists who sought to point to President Wilson's lack of commitment to votes for women. In March of that year nearly one thousand women picketed the White House.[79] When President Eisenhower arrived at the San Francisco Civic Auditorium in October 1958, he was greeted by a picket line of two hundred persons from the Northern California Committee for the Abolition of Nuclear Weapons.[80] In some northern U.S. cities, writes Arthur Waskow, white parents have picketed school boards trying to end *de facto* segregation in the school system.[81]

Even picketing may, of course, be illegal (as may most of the methods). Its exercise has been restricted even in parliamentary democracies —it was, for example, in Britain for nearly twenty years prior to 1946. The Trade Disputes and Trade Union Act of 1927, enacted after the British General Strike of 1926, contained a section which, writes Julian Symons, "limited the right to picket, in terms so vague that almost any form of picketing might be liable to prosecution."[82] (It was repealed in 1946.)

In countries with considerable civil liberties, picketing is often used as a means of public protest against the policies of both the government and foreign governments. Embassies, consulates, courts, legislatures, government departments, agencies, and so on may all be the focal point for protests involving picketing. Picketing varies considerably in a number of respects, such as how long the action is continued, the degree to which it is intended to be persuasive or obstructive, and the numbers involved—ranging from a token group to mass picketing. In a particular situation, picketing may be combined with other methods, such as strikes, boycotts and fasts.

17. Mock elections

The final method of making group representations described here is the mock election. An opposition group may, as a means of protest, hold extralegal elections or direct popular balloting on a topical issue. Special "polling" places at which to "vote" may be established, or the "votes" may be collected in some other way, such as by house-to-house calls. This method may be used by large minorities or by majorities when restrictions on the operation of the regular constitutional electoral system prevent the opposition from participating, either fully or in any form at all. Or minorities with full access to the regular electoral system may also, or instead, use the mock election when they feel that they need additional means of reaching the public about the issue which concerns them.

This approach was used in Mississippi in 1963 and 1964. Civil rights groups set up "freedom registration" for any Mississippian who wanted to register, regardless of the legal restrictions which were widely used to disfranchise Negroes. (Only seven percent or 23,000 of all voting-age Negroes were legally registered to vote in regular elections at the time.) About 83,000 people did "freedom register" and cast their "freedom ballot" for governor and lieutenant governor, choosing among official Democratic and Republican candidates and a civil rights slate. "More than a dramatic gimmick to attract national attention," wrote James Farmer, former head of the Congress of Racial Equality, "the mock election proved a superb educational device for instructing Mississippi Negroes in the ways and means of voting."[83] Arthur Waskow has pointed out that if they had been cast for the minority candidate in a regular gubernatorial election, that many votes could have changed the result, and that therefore the mock election "proved how considerable their own [the Negroes'] strength might be if they were ever able to enter the regular political system."[84]

Denied a place on the regular ballot, the predominantly Negro Freedom Democratic Party staged its own "election" in the autumn of 1964, inviting all Mississipians to vote and listing all the regular candidates plus the Freedom Democratic Party candidates—who won among the nearly eighty thousand "voters." Three "newly elected" F.D.P. congresswomen then unsuccessfully challenged the seating of regularly elected congressmen in the U.S. House of Representatives, charging the denial of voting rights in Mississippi, where forty-three percent of the citizens of voting age were barred from participation.[85]

SYMBOLIC PUBLIC ACTS

There are many ways in which the viewpoint of nonviolent actionists or their grievances may be expressed in symbolic behavior. These forms of action have been popular over the years, and the specific methods listed here do not exhaust the possibilities.

18. Displays of flags and symbolic colors

The display of the flag of a national, religious, social or political group, or the colors of such a group, or the flag or colors with some other type of symbolism is a common type of nonviolent protest. Such displays are often motivated by or arouse deep emotions.

On the visit of Emperor Franz Josef to the capital of Hungary on June 6, 1865, inhabitants of Pesth at first displayed only a very few flags of the Empire, as they opposed Austrian domination and sought home rule for Hungary. At the urging of the pro-Austrian governor, Palffy, the whole city was beflagged, which pleased the Emperor when he left the Agricultural Exhibition he had visited—until he realized that the flags were the green, white and red official flag of independent Hungary.[86]

Black flags have been used as symbols of protest and disapproval on numerous occasions: in India in 1928 by nationalists who were refusing to cooperate with the visiting British parliamentary Simon Commission,[87] in Ceylon in 1957 by the minority Tamils,[88] and in Pakistan in condemnation of the incorporation of Kashmir with India.[89]

In India the nationalists observed Independence Day on January 26, 1930, with the hoisting of the national flag at numerous demonstrations and celebrations.[90] In December 1956 students at Jena University in

East Germany in solidarity with Hungarian revolutionaries displayed the national colors of Hungary in the hall selected for their winter dance.[91]

Flags also played an important role in the 1963 Buddhist campaign against the Diem regime in South Vietnam, with government objections to the display of the Buddhist flag being important in the genesis of the conflict. On September 9 of that year students at the Chu Van An boys' high school, in the largely Chinese Cholon section of Saigon, tore down the government flag and hoisted the Buddhist flag, after which more than one thousand students were arrested.[92] In the first days of the August 1968 Czech resistance, flags and national colors were displayed in symbolic resistance. The morning of August 21, only hours after the invasion, crowds carried Czechoslovak flags in the streets of Prague, flags decorated the statue of St. Wenceslas, and the students carried a bloodstained flag into Wenceslas Square. Four days later flags throughout the city of Prague were flying at half-mast.[93]

Flags indicating political views are sometimes displayed in unusual ways. The morning of January 19, 1969, a Viet Cong flag was discovered flying from the top of the 240-foot central spire of Notre Dame Cathedral in Paris. The flag was fifteen feet by six feet; a helicopter from the Paris Fire Department was required to remove it.[94]

19. Wearing of symbols

Political dissent may be expressed by wearing on one's person some item of clothing, a color, a badge, a flower, or the like. For example, in France during the winter of 1792 the "red cap of liberty" became fashionable among the *sans-culottes*.[95] In World War II red, white and blue caps—imitations of the R.A.F. roundel—were worn by students in Denmark as symbols of opposition to the Nazi occupation,[96] while red caps were worn in Norway for the same purpose.[97] Occasionally, non-Jews in Germany and France wore the yellow star out of sympathy after it had been made compulsory for Jews.[98] In the Netherlands sympathy was shown by the wearing of yellow flowers in the lapel.[99] Symbols worn in Norway ranged from a flower on King Haakon's seventieth birthday to paper clips in the lapel ("keep together"), with considerable variations.[100] In the early days after the Russian invasion, Prague citizens wore the patriotic colors as tricolor bands on their lapels and elsewhere on their clothing.[101]

A related form of protest used in South Vietnam involves not wearing of some object, but the altering of one's appearance as a form of symbolic protest. During the 1963 Buddhist struggle against the Diem regime, the Foreign Minister, Vu Van Mau, resigned his post and "shaved his head in protest against the violent policy of that regime," Thich Nhat Hanh reports. "After that many professors and students did the same. The movement among students and professors was deeply influenced by that act."[102]

The way one who wears an article of clothing, or whether or when one wears it, may also symbolically convey a certain viewpoint. For example, at the inaugural session of the States General on May 5, 1789, when the French king replaced his hat, followed as usual by the clergy and the nobles, instead of remaining bareheaded (according to ancient custom) deputies of the Third Estate also "defiantly placed their hats on their heads." [103]

20. Prayer and worship

Prayer and worship may be so conducted that the participants by their religious act express moral condemnation and even political protest. This may be made clear by the content of the prayer or worship service, the immediate situation (as when an order to disperse has been given or demonstrators are arrested), the place in which the prayer is made, or the day on which it is made.

On learning of the planned British closure of the port of Boston in Massachusetts Bay Province on June 1, 1774 (an act taken in retaliation for resistance in that city), the Virginia House of Burgesses on May 24 resolved that June 1 be set aside as a "day of fasting, humiliation and prayer." Arthur Schlesinger writes: "Governor Dunmore, suspecting rightly that the fast was intended to prepare the minds of the people to receive other and more inflammatory resolutions, dissolved the House two days later."[104]

In occupied Poland in 1942 the Germans destroyed all monuments which commemorated Polish heroes or patriotic events. "By common consent all Poles made conspicuous detours around the spots where these monuments had been located. Prayers would even be offered up at these spots, to the outrage of the German officials."[105]

In South Africa during the 1952 Defiance Campaign prayer constituted an important part of the movement, as Leo Kuper reports:

> Thus, in July at Uitenhage, during the trial of ten resisters, hundreds knelt and prayed, led by an old African woman in a red shawl. At East London, some 250 singing and praying Africans gathered out-

side the Magistrates Court while eighty-five of their fellow campaigners were charged with not being in possession of night passes . . . about 1,000 Africans gathered outside the courtroom in Port Elizabeth, and sang hymns and prayed for the accused. In August, again at Port Elizabeth, some 5,000 Africans prayed for the success of the campaign, after welcoming 250 volunteers released from prison.[106]

Albert Luthuli reports that in 1959 African women demonstrating at Ixopo, when ordered by the police to disperse, "fell down on their knees and began to pray! The police hung around helplessly."[107]

In Trafalgar Square in London, on November 12, 1961—Remembrance Sunday for the war dead—a public service of worship with an anti-war, pro-nuclear-disarmament orientation was held with about one thousand participants, under the joint auspices of Christian Action and the Christian Group of the Campaign for Nuclear Disarmament.[108]

Six civil rights workers knelt and prayed on the steps of the city hall in Albany, Georgia, in August 1962.[109] Public prayers were made on several occasions during the 1963 campaign in Birmingham, Alabama; on Sunday evening, May 5,

A little before sunset the crowd of about two thousand Negroes came out [of the new Pilgrim Baptist Church] and faced the police. They knelt in silence as one of the ministers prayed solemnly: "Let them turn their water on. Let them use their dogs. We are not leaving. Forgive them, O Lord."

Perhaps for a moment this touched something in Bull Connor, for he let the Negroes cross the police line and spend fifteen minutes in a small park near the city jail, where they prayed and sang hymns within hearing of the hundreds of demonstrators inside. Afterward, they returned to the church, where it was announced that the children would definitely march on Monday.[110]

During the 1963 Buddhist struggle against the Diem regime, Father Cao Van Luan, a Roman Catholic and rector of the Hué University, led students to the Buddhist Tu Dam pagoda to pray, in symbolic protest against the government.[111] In June 1966, Buddhists in Hué and Quan-tri, South Vietnam, erected altars in the middle of streets and conducted religious observances there, even though government troops wished to have full use of the streets to facilitate control of the city.[112] Thich Nhat Hanh describes the carrying of family altars into the streets to oppose tanks as an act "no less tragic than the self-immolation of the Venerable Thich Quang Duc." It was, he said, the use of "traditional values to oppose inhumanity and violence.''[113] This also has elements of psychological intervention. That year prayer ceremonies were conducted throughout Vietnam in opposition to the war. These are described as having a "tremendous effect.''[114]

On June 30, 1966, in the U.S. Senate Visitors' Gallery, after the Senate had adjourned twelve members of the Society of Friends held a silent Quaker Meeting for prayer and worship in protest against the recess of that body while the bombing of North Vietnam was being intensified. Their two-and-a-half-hour Meeting and wait-in were combined with trespass for refusing to leave when ordered, for which they were arrested.[115]

During the Great October Strike of the 1905 Russian Revolution, young schoolchildren on one occasion made their political protest in a related but rather different way:

> Tsarskoe Selo, a small city almost completely dominated by the imperial residence, had its day also: local secondary school boys went out on strike and were joined by the pupils of the girls' secondary school; and the primary school children registered their feelings by refusing to say their morning prayers and, when the prayers were read to them, responding with the favored Russian form of disrespect, whistling.[116]

21. Delivering symbolic objects

The delivery of an object which symbolizes a grievance or an objective to the official or office associated with the issue has been used in various ways to advance the views of the protesters. For example, in Chicago a few years ago when "The Woodlawn Organization" (T.W.O.)—a neighborhood organization in a black slum area—sought action from Mayor Daley to deal with bad conditions in their district, they piled rats on the steps of City Hall, Saul Alinsky reports.[117] In protest against Soviet nuclear weapons tests, Committee of 100 supporters in London in October 1961 brought hundreds of bottles of milk, each labeled "DANGER—RADIOACTIVE" in red letters, and left them in front of the Soviet Embassy.[118]

President Kennedy in 1963 had not yet fulfilled his 1960 campaign promise to eliminate discrimination in federally assisted housing (made in his "stroke of the pen" statement, in which he promised to issue and sign such an executive order). James Farmer writes that there was reliable information that an executive order on the subject, drafted by his staff, had lain unsigned in the President's office since 1961. The Congress of Racial

Equality then joined the wider campaign on the issue. Farmer writes: "We figured JFK's pen had run dry, and we sent thousands of bottles of ink to the White House."[119]

22. Protest disrobings

One of the rarer old—but newly reactivated—forms of nonviolent protest is the public removal of clothes as a means of expressing one's religious dissapproval or political protest. During the Quaker "invasion" of the intolerant Massachusetts Bay Colony in the seventeenth century, Lydia Wardel entered Newbury Church naked as a protest.[120] Members of the Sons of Freedom sect of the Doukhobors in British Columbia, Canada, have been credited with "uncounted nude parades" and in some cases individual women have disrobed in front of their own burning homes, to which they set fire as a protest against alleged government interference or prosecution of their husbands for resistance activities, including demolitions.[121] When Prime Minister John Diefenbaker was attending a political rally at Trail, British Columbia, on May 28, 1962, Doukhobor women whose husbands were awaiting trial for terrorist acts interrupted the meeting, tearfully protesting "unfair treatment" of their group, and took off their clothing as part of their protest.[122]

One of several cases of protest disrobing in the United States in recent years by young people in the antiwar and social protest movements took place at Grinnell College, in Grinnell, Iowa, on February 5, 1969. The students staged a "nude-in" during a speech by a representative of *Playboy* magazine, in protest against the magazine's "sensationalism of sex."[123]

23. Destruction of own property

An unusual method of nonviolent protest is the voluntary destruction of *one's own* property in order to demonstrate the intensity of one's feelings of opposition. Where there is danger from the act of destruction, all persons are removed to safety in advance so that there is no physical harm to anyone.

Early American colonial patriots publicly destroyed letters when they disliked their political contents. When New York merchants in July 1770 decided to break with the general policy of nonimportation of British goods, they sent letters of their decision to Philadelphia and Boston. "When a copy of the letter reached Princeton, James Madison and his fellow-students garbed in black gowns, solemnly witnessed the burning of the

letter by a hangman while the college bell tolled funereal peals."[124]
"At Boston, a meeting of the trade at Faneuil Hall voted unanimously
that the New York letter, 'in just indignation, abhorrence and detestation,
be forthwith torn into pieces and thrown to the winds as unworthy of the
least notice,' which was accordingly done."[125]

In support of the movement for economic sanctions against England,
the merchants in Charleston, South Carolina, promoted an association
for the nonconsumption of India teas, whether or not duty had been paid
on them, beginning on November 1, 1774. At the instigation of the merchants, schoolboys collected tea from private houses and it was publicly
burned on November 5, Gunpowder Plot Day—the anniversary of an attempt to blow up the Houses of Parliament in London.[126] In Providence,
Rhode Island, on March 2, 1775, the day after the total halt to the use
of tea became effective, a bonfire was made of three hundred pounds of
tea which had been collected from the inhabitants.[127]

In the Province of Massachusetts Bay in February 1775, Colonel Les-
lie, a British officer, sailed from Boston to Marblehead to seize artillery
which colonists had taken to Salem for safekeeping.

> He landed his detachment successfully on a Sunday morning; but,
> when the alarm reached the nearest meeting-house, the congregation
> turned out and took up a position upon some water which barred his
> route. They refused to lower the draw-bridge on the plea that there
> was no public right of way across it; and when Leslie attempted to
> lay hands on a couple of barges, the owners proceeded to scuttle them.
> The soldiers drew their bayonets, and inflicted some wounds . . .[128]

A segment of the Doukhobor religious group in Canada has a long
record of burning their own homes in protest against government regulation or government repression for (sometimes more violent) acts of resistance.[129]

In 1918 and 1919 woman suffragist members of the Women's Party
publicly burned copies of President Wilson's speeches in Washington, D.C.,
on the gounds that he advocated freedom and democracy while not, in
their opinion, doing everything possible to give women the vote at home.[130]

Other examples of symbolic acts include the burning of imported
cloth during the nonviolent Indian struggles (as a symbol of renunciation
of dependence on foreign countries and of determination to build a free,
self-reliant India)[131] and the destruction of the statue of Stalin in Budapest during the Hungarian Revolution.[132]

In some cases this method may include destruction of documents provided by and technically owned by the government or some organization, which persons are required or expected to keep their possession or carry for long periods of time—for most practical purposes such items thereby become the property of such persons. Examples are passes, party membership cards, passports, identity cards, and conscription registration and classification cards. For purposes of this classification the item in question is seen as *de facto* the property of the person who has it in his possession, although *de jure* it belongs to the government, party or other body.

For example, in 1960 following the launching by the Pan Africanist Congress of the campaign against the pass laws in South Africa, the rival African National Congress called for the burning of passes. "We did not desire to leave our shackles at home," wrote Albert Luthuli. "We desired to be rid of them. I burned my Reference Book, others burned theirs and the bonfires began to grow in number."[133]

On October 15, 1965, during an antiwar rally outside the Army Induction Center in New York City, a youth burned his draft card while Federal agents looked on.[134] *The New York Times* reported that during anti-Vietnam war rallies throughout the country on August 16, 1967, five young men burned draft cards as a protest in Philadelphia, sixty-seven did so at the Arlington Street Church in Boston, and in Los Angeles at least eight burned their cards. In the latter city several veterans were reported to have burned their certificates of discharge. Many other draft cards were turned in undamaged throughout the country to offices of Selective Service or U.S. Attorneys.[135]

24. Symbolic lights

Torches, lanterns and candles are often carried in protest parades and marches and have sometimes also been used in other types of protest activities. For example, in South Africa on June 26, 1953, the anniversary of the launching of the 1952 Defiance Campaign, the African National Congress leader Chief Albert Luthuli appealed to Africans and their allies to light bonfires or candles or lanterns outside their homes "as a symbol of the spark of freedom which we are determined to keep alive in our hearts, and as a sign to freedom-lovers that we are keeping the vigil on that night."[136]

Three days after burning himself in opposition to the Soviet invasion, Jan Palach died on January 19, 1969. Young people then marched in a candlelight ceremony in Wenceslas Square, Prague, where the self-immolation had taken place. They quietly carried black flags and the

Czechoslovak red, white and blue flag to the fountain in the square where the burning had happened, in front of the National Museum which still bore scars of Soviet bullets. Alvin Schuster reported in *The New York Times:*

> Hundreds of somber people, many of whom had placed candles and wreaths on the fountain, surrounded it in silence. Others gathered around the statue of Wenceslas, fifty yards away, the site of an informal memorial to those killed in the August invasion. It, too, was aglow with candles.[137]

25. Displays of portraits

The public display of pictures of resistance heroes or persons who otherwise symbolize the objectives of the movement is sometimes used as a means of communicating to others one's political loyalties. During the Indian 1930-31 struggle, photographs of the national leaders—Gandhi, Nehru and others—were widely sold and displayed in homes and shops.[138] Similarly, in Czechoslovakia in August 1968, buildings in Prague displayed portraits of President Svoboda and of Dubček, First Secretary of the Czechoslovak Communist Party.[139]

26. Paint as protest

During the East German Rising, on June 17, 1953, the night shift at the Stralsund shipyard covered the name of a new lugger, *Walter Ulbricht,* with thick black paint, and the ceremony scheduled for the next day to launch that new boat for the herring fleet had to be canceled.[140] In 1962 in Eisenbach, East Germany, someone altered a huge picture of Walter Ulbricht by painting a rope around his neck.[141]

27. New signs and names

Erecting signs where there have been none or replacing old street names with new ones of symbolic significance are among the forms which this method may take. (Complete removal of all street, highway, town, and railroad station signs, or their replacement with erroneous ones, is not simply symbolic but an act of noncooperation, and hence is classified under political noncooperation.) In occupied Poland in 1942, for example, "The Little Wolves" group of youthful resisters stole many of the "FOR GERMANS ONLY" signs which were displayed at the best cafés, cinemas, and hotels in Warsaw, and also prepared many copies. One morning the signs appeared on hundreds of the city's lamp posts and trees—where the Germans had frequently hung Polish patriots.[142] On orders of a branch of the underground government, the Poles renamed most of the country's streets. "Overnight, on the walls, on street corners and lamp posts, inscriptions and placards appeared bearing new names, the heroes or statesmen of this war whom the Poles admired: Niedzialkowski Avenue, Rataj Drive, Roosevelt Street, Churchill Boulevard." Patriots all used the new names, and the name someone used was a clue to his political opinion (unless he were an agent working with the Germans).[143]

28. Symbolic sounds

Oral or mechanical sounds may be used to convey ideas in a conflict situation. The tolling or simple ringing of bells has often been used in this way, as in the example cited above in which James Madison and other Princeton students witnessed the burning of a letter they did not like, "while the college bell tolled funereal peals."

A very different case occurred at the end of May 1917, when major mutinies of the French army had already taken place, even those units which were nominally obeying orders were often highly discontented. "Throughout the Zone of the Armies the units which could be persuaded to march forward to the trenches were baaing in imitation of lambs led to the slaughter, and their officers were helpless to prevent it."[144] Between 9:00 and 9:15 A.M. on August 26, 1968, bells and sirens were sounded throughout the whole of Czechoslovakia, reported *Lidova Demokracie,* as

> a protest of the citizens of a sovereign state against a forcible occupation, against barbarism and the brute force of the occupiers. The wail of the sirens mingled with the majestic tolling of church bells. The Bishop of Ceske Budejovice, Dr. Josef Hlouch, called upon all the clergy of his diocese to support the negotiations of our statesmen in Moscow by the tolling of these bells. In the streets of Prague, even the cars of foreign visitors sounded their horns.

This Russian reaction was also reported:

> The demonstration apparently frightened the occupation troops. At the main railroad station, Soviet officers with drawn pistols threw themselves on an engineer and tried to force him to stop the locomotive whistle. During the demonstration, a young woman was shot at Klarov. She was taken to a hospital, but she died.[145]

29. Symbolic reclamations

Certain types of acts may be carried out to demonstrate a creative alternative to the disputed existing use or ownership of the territory in question. Among the forms this may take are the planting of seeds, plants or trees, the cultivation of neglected or seized land, and the construction of a building whose intended use runs counter to existing and future policies for the area. For example, in October 1962 demonstrators of the Committee of 100 in Britain, protesting nuclear weapons, planted seeds at the edge of the R.A.F. V-bomber base at Honington, England, as a symbol of their desire to reclaim the land for constructive civilian use.[146]

30. Rude gestures

There are many variations of rude gestures and behavior which convey insults. They may rarely be used in situations of political, and even international, conflict. One example comes from the Sino-Soviet conflict. According to Edmund Stevens, in January 1967

. . . each morning an entire platoon of Chinese soldiers would march out on the ice and lowering their trousers train their buttocks towards the Soviet side, the ultimate in Chinese insults. This exercise continued until one morning just as the Chinese assumed their positions the Russians set up large portraits of Mao facing in their direction. The Chinese hastily covered themselves and retired in confusion. There were no repetitions.[147]

PRESSURES ON INDIVIDUALS

Several methods may be used in attempts to put pressures on individual members of the opponent group, whether officials or ordinary soldiers, for example. These acts may be directed against specific persons or groups of persons, or may be intended to apply pressure on individuals who are part of a large body, such as an occupation army. The ones included here are not exhaustive. Certain other methods in this chapter, such as picketing, may also be used for that purpose, as may social boycotts and fasts, which are described in later chapters.

31. "Haunting" officials

As a means of reminding officials of the "immorality" of their behavior in repressing a nonviolent resistance movement and of the determination and fearlessness of the population, volunteers may sometimes follow and "haunt" officials everywhere they go, thus constantly reminding them of the population's determination. For example, as Joan Bondurant has reported, during the 1928 Bardoli campaign in India: "Volunteers followed officials everywhere, camping on roads outside official bungalows. When arrested, they were replaced by others until authorities tired of the process." [148]

32. Taunting officials

Instead of the predominantly silent and dignified behavior used in the above method, people may mock and insult officials, either at a certain place or by following them for a period. In the summer of 1942, for example, in Honan, China, under Kuomintang rule, tax collectors and soldiers seized grain from unwilling peasants who were facing a severe famine, having refused to accept either money or farm tools instead. As a result,

> in many villages, more soldiers had to be called in before the tax-collectors dared remove all the grain. As they dragged it away, the peasants would follow like a pack of monkey scarecrows, bitterly mocking, and sometimes threatening, without a trace of "virtue and obedience." [149]

33. Fraternization

An alternative to a social boycott of the soldiers and police of the opponent is to fraternize with them, in the process subjecting them to intense influence and direct or indirect propaganda or both. [150] The objectives may be 1) to become personal friends with the soldiers and convince them that no personal hostility or desire to injure them is involved in the resistance; 2) to convince them that the objectives of the regime which they serve are unjust and immoral and that those of the nonviolent actionists are just and right; 3) to persuade the soldiers (or other agents of repression) to reduce the efficiency with which they carry out orders against the resisters and the population, or, eventually, to mutiny and refuse to carry them out; or 4) to provide information for the population and the resistance movement on the opponent regime's plans. Such fraternization is accompanied by noncooperation with the regime and disobedience of its regulations.

For example, during the 1956 Hungarian Revolution, even in a situation where both violent and nonviolent methods of resistance were being used, Hungarians made deliberate efforts at fraternization and at influencing Soviet soldiers, both by personal conversation and leaflets in Russian. These efforts seem to have had a degree of success. One journalist reported that as a result of Hungarians talking with Russian soldiers, "something like a bond of sympathy was arising."[151]

There were many direct attempts to influence Russian soldiers in the early stages of the invasion and occupation of Czechoslovakia in August 1968. A Czech journalist reported, in *Rude Pravo,* participating in conversations with a Soviet captain, a Soviet lieutenant colonel, two Russian ambulance attendants, a Czech captain, a Czech citizen, and Czech ambulance attendants. It was "a lively discussion":

> We presented our arguments [about the invasion], and when we parted we all said: "We shall not say *au revoir*, we shall not wish you luck, and we shall not even shake your hands." This was perhaps the ultimate argument. I actually saw tears in the eyes of the Soviet captain. There was even a small spasm in the lieutenant colonel's face. The soldiers who had earlier just listened stood about hanging their heads. As we were leaving, the captain followed us a few steps and said: "We shall all reflect about what we discussed here. I am afraid that you are right about a number of things. It is a terrible tragedy. And you can print this if you want to." "If that is really so," I said, "perhaps we shall shake hands after all some day."[152]

Within four days it proved necessary to rotate invasion troops and bring in replacements.[153]

34. Vigils

A vigil is an appeal normally addressed not to one or a few persons, but to many people. Like picketing, a vigil consists of people remaining at a particular place as a means of expressing a point of view. It differs from picketing, however, in that it is frequently maintained over a longer period of time, sometimes around the clock, and is associated with a more solemn attitude, often of a pleading or religious character. It often involves late hours and loss of sleep.

In 1917, for example, women in the Netherlands maintained a vigil for weeks outside the building where a new constitution for the country was being drafted, seeking a clause granting woman suffrage. The clause was not inserted, but woman suffrage was determined to be an issue on which a simple majority vote of the legislature could rule.[154] Other examples include the constant vigil for fourteen months at barricades preventing volunteers (including untouchables) from using a road passing a Hindu temple in 1924-25 at Vykom in South India, as described in Chapter Two;[155] the South African "black-sash" women, who in 1955 and 1956 stood, mute and still, outside government offices in protest against efforts to change the South African constitution in the direction of greater regimentation;[156] the nine-week day-and-night vigil outside the Aldermaston Atomic Weapons Research Establishment in England conducted from July to September 1958 by the Direct Action Committee Against Nuclear War;[157] the year-long silent "Appeal and Vigil" maintained from July 1, 1959, outside the germ warfare plant at Fort Detrick in Frederick, Maryland, by pacifists and others who protested against germ warfare research and preparations conducted there;[158] and the attempt by Western exponents of unilateral nuclear disarmament to hold an antinuclear weapons vigil with banners in Red Square, Moscow, on July 13, 1962.[159]

DRAMA AND MUSIC

Nonviolent protest and persuasion may be expressed also in acting and music. Variations are possible on the methods described here.

35. Humorous skits and pranks

Political humor may become a method of nonviolent action when expressed in some social form such as a humorous prank or a skit, or, conceivably, a play of political satire. In such cases the humor or satire ceases to be simply verbal political dissent (as often expressed in dictatorial countries in political jokes passed from one person to another) and becomes an act of public political protest.

It has been impossible to find documentation for the following, but the story is told that in Austria, prior to the peace treaty and while Soviet troops still occupied sections of Vienna and the countryside, students tied a suitcase to the arm of a statue of Stalin.

In late 1956 students at Jena University in East Germany included humorous skits which parodied the amateur theatricals used to further Communist propaganda in the cabaret program at their winter dance; these skits were received with high applause. One concerned a hunter and his dog. The dog was muzzled, the hunter said, as a protection against malignant wasps and the extremely short lead on the dog was a "bond of friendship." The hunter shot the dog for running away, but he said he had shot the wasps which had been attacking the dog; the hunter replied to criticisms of his earlier beating of the dog by calling them accusations of "over-critical harsh tongues." Someone then described the hunter as "a protector true" of dogs, whose work would be venerated by future generations.[160]

36. Performances of plays and music

Under certain political conditions, the performance of certain plays, operas, and other music may be a form of nonviolent political protest. For example, in early January 1923, in the opening stages of the *Ruhrkampf* against the French and Belgian occupation, "the performance of *Wilhelm Tell* at the municipal theater in Essen developed into a demonstration of the national will to resist, and finally occupation troops invaded the theater and dispersed the audience."[161]

Another example took place in January 1943 in Trondheim in Nazi-occupied Norway. It was three months after executions in the city by the Nazis, and as part of the citizens' protest, the city's theaters offering light plays were still empty despite official efforts to fill them. But when the musician Ingeborg Gresvik gave two concerts the same day at the church called *Fruekirka* (where Nazi permission was not required), the lines of people wanting to attend blocked two of the city's main streets; over 2,500 people were seated in the church itself to hear the heavy and somber piano music. The *Ballade* by the Norwegian composer Grieg was an example of the music played. As a Norwegian author put it, "the program must be regarded as a Norwegian cultural demonstration."[162]

37. Singing

Under appropriate conditions, singing may constitute a method of nonviolent protest—for example, singing while an unwanted speech is being made, singing national or religious songs and hymns, rival vocal programs to compete with boycotted ones organized by the opponent, singing while engaged in a march, civil disobedience, or some other act of opposition, and singing songs of social and political satire and protest.

In the midst of the Finnish disobedience movement against the Tsar's autocratically imposed, and from the Finns' view unconstitutional, new conscription law of July 1901 (which conscripted Finns into the *Russian* army), *Kagal* (the secret society directing the disobedience movement) called for noncooperation. Everyone was to refuse to cooperate: youths should refuse to report for induction, doctors should refuse to examine recruits, communes should refuse to elect members to draft boards, and the preachers should refuse to announce the military conscriptions from their pulpits. When most of the ministers disobeyed *Kagal*'s call and instead obeyed their archbishop's order to make the conscription announcements, "the parishioners drowned out the voice from the pulpit by singing hymns."[163]

In Denmark during the Nazi occupation, while the Danes boycotted concerts of German military music, they set up rival programs of community singing of traditional Danish songs.[164]

A Red Army officer who was among Jewish prisoners from the Soviet at the Sobibor extermination camp in eastern Poland reports two instances in which the inmates asserted defiance by singing. The officer, Alexander Pechersky, reports that on September 24, 1943, the morning after their arrival at the camp, *Oberscharführer* Franz ordered the Russian Jews to sing Russian songs:

> "We don't know which songs we're allowed to sing," I said.
> The kapo (a prisoner with the status of a policeman) translated my words.
> "Sing what you know," Franz replied.
> "Sasha, what shall we sing?" Tsibulsky turned to me. He was a Jew from Donbas, tall and with a round face.
> *"Yesli Zaftra Voina."* (If War Comes Tomorrow.)
> "What's the matter with you? They'll kill us."
> "I say sing. We don't know any other songs." Tsibulsky began:
> > "If war comes tomorrow
> > Tomorrow we march
> > If the evil forces strike—"
> All the others chimed in:
> > "United as one
> > All the Soviet people
> > For their free native land will arise."
> The guards came running out of the barracks when our column passed. In this camp of death and despair the Soviet song rang out like a clap of spring thunder. We felt refreshed and exhilarated, as though we had received happy tidings, a promise of victory, and liberation.[165]

After a large number of South African resistance leaders were arrested in early December 1956, a large crowd gathered outside the Drill Hall in Johannesburg on the first day of the Preparatory Examination: "Just before the proceedings began, [wrote Albert Luthuli,] the huge crowd began *Nkosi Sikelel' i Afrika,* the African National Anthem. It sounded like an angelic choir: to us the sound seemed to come from above."[166] In May 1963 more than three thousand Negro children converged on the downtown area of Birmingham, Alabama. "Groups of them trooped in and out of stores, singing 'Ain't gonna let nobody turn me 'round' and 'I'm on my way to freedom land.'"[167]

In Prague at eight in the morning on August 21, 1968, after the night invasion, in one corner of the Old Town Square a group of citizens sang the national anthem while others argued with a Soviet captain, urging him to go home. Thirty-five minutes later a column of Czechoslovak vehicles passed through Wenceslas Square headed for the Old Town Square; the vehicles carried people who were singing the Slovak national anthem: "There is lightning over the Tatras, and terrible thunder . . ."[168]

Satirical political songs, as well as folk poetry and wise sayings, were used as means of education and protest in the Buddhist struggles in South Vietnam, especially in 1963. Thich Nhat Hanh writes:

> Political satirical songs are easy to learn by heart and can be circulated very quickly. They were widely used during the struggle against Ngo Dinh Diem [who was ousted as head of the government in 1963]. There were hundreds of them. The most famous was *Nghe ve, nghe ve, nghe ve Nhu Diem,* a song dealing with corruption of that regime.[169]

Singing songs of satire and protest is not, however, a modern innovation, much less a Vietnamese one. They go back at least as far as the early fourteenth century, when they occurred in France, and probably much further. Alejandro Planchart, an authority on medieval music, refers to this as "one of the most troubled times in the history of France," a time of widespread corruption among clergy and nobility, the Hundred Years' War, the papal exile in Avignon, and the schism in the church.

> In contrast to the luxury of the courts famine swept the countryside and pillage was rampant. Thus besides the love songs of the court poets we have the thundering of the political pieces with their scathing attacks upon all-pervading corruption.[170]

Political protest music survives in a number of manuscripts, the most famous of which is *Le Roman de Fauvel;* the words are from a satirical poem written by Gervaise de Bus between 1310 and 1314. *Fauvel* is a symbolic animal, an ass, whose name is composed of the initials of *flaterie, avarice, vilanie, variété, envie,* and *lascheté.* The original poem was later modified with additions from other texts, and various musical accompaniments and arrangements were created for it. Some of these were in the form of motets, in which two different texts were sung simultaneously with a different instrumental melody. In one of these, while the first singer is condemning corruption in clerical life, the second is singing a comment on secular affairs, while the instrumental melody *Ruina* underlies both. The text of the second singer includes this passage:

> Presiding today in the thrones of the world are deceit and pillage. The soldiers of Hercules have stopped. The discipline of the church perishes. Arms push hymns out of the smallest corner. Rapaciousness and craftiness reign at home, growing rich on the blood of the small. The cornerstone lacks foundation. To what purpose? More often to proclaim: ruin is near![171]

PROCESSIONS

Some of the best-known methods of nonviolent protest and persuasion are forms of processions, i.e., people walking or marching. Five ways this is commonly done are included here.

38. Marches

The march as a form of nonviolent protest and persuasion is practiced when a group of people walk in an organized manner to a particular place which is regarded as intrinsically significant to the issue involved. The duration of the march may vary from an hour or two to several weeks, or even longer. Posters and banners may or may not be carried, and leaflets may or may not be distributed to bystanders. In May 1765, fifty thousand English weavers convened at Spitalfields and marched by three different routes to Westminster, London, to petition for relief against competition from French silk.[172] Marches occurred several times during the 1905 Russian Revolution. During the Great October Strike of 1905, striking railroadmen in Tashkent marched on the governor-general's home and were turned back by troops without bloodshed.[173] Following the "October Manifesto" (in which the Tsar granted civil liberties, gave voting rights to groups hitherto excluded from them, and established the principle of *Duma* consent to laws and *Duma* supervision of officials), in many cities throughout the Russian Empire people marched to the residence of the governor or to the municipal *Duma* to celebrate and to make further demands, especially for the release of political prisoners.[174] Other examples include the several marches of three thousand persons which proceeded simultaneously to foreign consulate buildings in Seoul in 1919 to demonstrate to the world that the Koreans were opposed to Japanese rule.[175] Gandhi's 1930 Salt March to the beach at Dandi to commit civil disobedience by making salt,[176] and the six thousand mile march (December 1, 1960 to October 8, 1961) from San Francisco to Moscow by pacifists urging unilateral disarmament.[177]

An "Agreement for the Deportation of the First Batch of twenty thousand Jews to the East German Territories" was signed by a Bulgarian and a German official on February 22, 1943. But revolutionary groups in Sofia appealed to the Bulgarian people, urging them to stand before Jewish homes and crowd into the Jewish quarters, refusing to allow the Jews to be deported. On May 24, 1943, writes Matei Yulzari, the Jews of Sofia organized a protest in which many non-Jewish Bulgarians also participated:

> It started from the Jewish synagogue in one of the suburbs, where the gathering was addressed by Rabbi Daniel Zion and several young men. The crowd started an impressive march, which was intended to join the demonstration of the university students and make its way to the royal palace to protest against the outrages to which the Jews were subjected. Clashes with the police were followed by numerous arrests.
>
> This mass demonstration alarmed the authorities and they did not carry out the second stage of their deportation plan—deportation to Poland, where the Jews of Europe found their death. Fearing internal unrest, the Fascist government and the king were forced to give up their plan to send the Jews of Bulgaria to their doom in the death camps.[178]

In Oriente province of Cuba in late 1956, during the Batista regime, the bodies of twenty-nine Cuban youths are reported to have been delivered, badly mutilated, as government reprisals for the November uprising. Later there were other murders and countermurders in Santiago. On January 2, 1957, soldiers in Santiago seized William Soler, a fourteen-year-old boy; his badly tortured body was dumped in an empty lot the next night. Robert Taber writes:

> At ten o'clock in the morning [of January 4], some forty women dressed in black left the Church of Dolores . . . and moved in slow procession, praying in unison and fingering their rosaries, down Calle Aguilera . . . At their head marched the mother of William Soler, and with her the mothers of other youths slain by police and soldiers . . . Over their heads they carried a large white banner with the black inscription: *Cesen los asesinatos de nuestros hijos.* (Stop the murder of our sons.)
>
> As they moved on past the park and through the shopping dis-

trict, other women joined them. There were two hundred by the time they had passed the first block, then eight hundred, then a thousand. At every step more women left the shops to join the procession, pressing slowly forward through the narrow, cobbled street. A few policemen stood by, helpless, at the intersections. Men watched from the doorways and many wept with shame as the women passed by, the only sound of their murmured litany and the funereal tapping of their heels.

At one intersection, a jeep load of soldiers suddenly appeared, training a machine gun on the procession, blocking the way. The women waited, silently. The demonstration continued to grow until it overflowed into nearby streets, blocking all traffic.

When the soldiers tried to break up the manifestation, pushing their way into the dense crowd, the women simply opened aisles for them to pass through, and then closed ranks again. The mothers refused to be provoked into any overt act of physical resistance, but stood in quiet dignity until the soldiers gave up their futile efforts and, shamefaced, turned away. Then the women began, still silently, to disperse. Part of the procession continued on to the city hall and to the offices of several newspapers to leave petitions, demanding an end of the terror and the restoration of civil law. Then these women, too, went quietly home.

The mothers' protest march in Santiago had significance because it was the first public act to signal the beginning of organized civic resistance on a broad and effective scale in Cuba, under the aegis of the *fidelista* movement.[179]

39. Parades

A parade as a demonstration of protest or persuasion involves a group of people walking in an organized manner as a means of calling attention to their grievance or point of view. The parade is distinguished from the march in that, although it has a point of termination, that point is not of intrinsic significance to the demonstration. Banners, leaflets, posters, and the like may or not be used in conjunction with the parade. This type of demonstration may or may not be accompanied by bands providing music and by other types of activities.

The first parade for woman suffrage in Washington, D.C., was held in 1913 by the National American Woman Suffrage Association, with between eight thousand and ten thousand participants, including many senators and representatives with their wives. As it dispersed, the parades were assaulted by opponents, which resulted in a major press and political uproar.[180] Parades were often used during the Indian nonviolent struggles; for example, the parades of Muslims in Bombay on June 3, 1930, to demonstrate their support for the civil resistance movement.[181] An example from the West is the four-hour protest parade in London on November 4, 1956, against the invasion of Egypt.[182]

Six thousand supporters of the People's United Party paraded through the streets of Belize on August 24, 1958, in support of their demand for immediate self-government for British Honduras.[183] In South Africa, in June 1957, several thousand professors, lecturers and students at Capetown University paraded through the streets of Capetown in protest against the Universities' Apartheid Bill, which made multiracial university education illegal in the country.[184]

There are many possible variations on the parade. For example, during the boycott of tea (as part of the nonimportation campaign against the Townshend duties) the merchants of Marblehead, in the Province of Massachusetts Bay, on October 19, 1769 ceremoniously carted through the streets a chest of tea purchased from a Boston importer and then returned it to its starting point in Boston.[185] During the 1960 Japanese campaign against the revision of the United States-Japanese Security Pact, the student group *Zengakuren* developed other variations of the parade: "Zig-zag demonstration (snake-like parade), French style of demonstration (hand-in-hand parade), centripetal demonstration (parades starting from many points and finally centralizing at the Center . . ."[186]

40. Religious processions

A religious procession as a method of nonviolent action has the general characteristics of a march or a parade, plus certain religious qualities, which may take such forms as carrying religious pictures or symbols, singing religious songs, and significant participation by clergy and monks. The degree of religious as compared to other motivations may vary. In mid-nineteenth century China, following a serious flood in Kiangsu, a member of the gentry in Kao-yu district aroused the city's people to demand relief from the government, in defiance of the governor's memorial to the contrary. "The people gathered, refused to open their shops for trade, carried statues of the gods about the streets, and disturbed the yamen [government officials]."[187]

The several columns of petitioning Russians, led by Father Gapon, headed toward the Tsar's Winter Palace, on January 9, 1905, clearly took the form of a religious procession. According to carefully laid plans, several columns of workers with their families started from various points in St. Petersburg, to converge on Palace Square at 2 P.M. All these columns were "to advance as if in a Procession of the Cross, a dignified progression of devotees following their clergy, carrying icons and singing hymns . . ." One of these, led by Gapon himself, began marching about noon, after worship and prayers:

> In orderly train, they followed their leader along the Peterhof Chaus-sée, holding aloft icons, religious standards, the Russian national flag, and portraits of the Tsar and the Tsarina. As they marched they sang such favorite hymns as "Our Father" and "Save, O Lord, Thy People." It was a decorous procession, and police along the route cleared the way for them, as was customary for religious processions, while the crowds who gathered to watch them made the customary signs of respect to religious and national symbols.[188]

According to official figures, well over a hundred of these demonstrators died from bullet wounds from the Tsar's troops and well over three hundred were wounded.[189] This action alienated the peasants from the Tsar and aligned most of the intelligentsia and even conservatives against the regime.

41. Pilgrimages

The pilgrimage as a form of moral condemnation has deep moral and religious qualities. It involves one or more persons walking 1) as a means of bringing a message to people, 2) as penance for some deed or policy which has been committed or pursued by the people or government, and 3) as a means of self-dedication to a program for altering the status quo. Often the pilgrimage will involve walking to a particular point of significance to the underlying beliefs or to the policy in question.

Such a pilgrimage usually lasts at least several days, and perhaps for months. Banners and posters are not usually used, although leaflets might be. At times some type of transportation may be combined with the walking. An example of a pilgrimage in the sense in which it is defined here is Gandhi's walking tour of the Noakhali district of Bengal in early 1947, undertaken in an effort to persuade Hindus and Muslims to halt their murderous rioting and to live together peacefully.[190]

42. Motorcades

A modern Western variation of the parade or march is the motorcade, which takes the form of the march or parade except that the participants drive cars at a very slow speed. The cars usually bear posters or banners. The motorcade may also be combined with a parade or march of people on foot. An example of this method is the motorcade organized by various pacifist groups which toured through Boston in November and December 1959, stopping at selected points to distribute leaflets and to urge people to support peace and disarmament.[191]

HONORING THE DEAD

Several methods of nonviolent protest and persuasion involve paying respect to the memory of deceased persons. The person so honored may be a hero from previous decades or centuries, or those remembered may have recently died in the course of participating in the struggle. One of these methods, a "mock funeral," is used to suggest that some cherished principle or social condition has been destroyed or is in danger, or to suggest that certain policies imperil human lives.

43. Political mourning

The same symbols which are used in mourning the death of an individual are often used for expressing political opposition and regret at particular events and policies. Public mourning was important during the American colonists' struggle against the Stamp Act in 1765. When the tax stamps for Pennsylvania, New Jersey and Maryland arrived by ship at Philadelphia on October 5, for example, all the ships in the harbor flew their flags at half-mast, and the city's bells tolled throughout the day.[192] When the Act was to go into effect, on November 1, the day was generally observed in the colonies as a day of mourning, again with the tolling of bells. In Boston, for example, the "Loyal Nine," or "Sons of Liberty," ensured that the day's protest was conducted in perfect order.[193]

During the Hungarian Protestants' resistance to Austrian attempts to destroy the autonomy of Hungary's Protestant churches, many arrests of pastors and bishops took place in February and March 1860, and church meetings were repeatedly broken up. Students went to the towns where these churchmen were to be tried and, dressed in black, conducted silent demonstrations.[194]

Sometimes the mourning may begin for the dead and gradually turn to political protest, as in this example from an eyewitness in Warsaw in November 1939:

At the corner of Marshall and Jerusalem Boulevards, in the heart of Warsaw and close to the Central Railroad Station, the paving stones had been uprooted and a huge mass grave dug for unknown soldiers. It was covered with flowers and surrounded by burning candles. A crowd of mourners knelt beside it, praying. I learned later that this unceasing vigil had been kept up since the burials had taken place three months ago.

During the next few weeks I continued to see the mourners by the side of the grave from dawn to the curfew hours. Gradually the ceremonies that took place ceased to be only a devotion to the dead;

they became tokens of political resistance as well. In December, the Nazi Gauleiter for Warsaw, Moser, realized the significance the grave had assumed and ordered the bodies disinterred and buried in a cemetery. But even after this measure, mourners would still come to kneel in prayer at this corner and candles would be lighted as if the spot had been hallowed by a presence the shovels of the Nazi soldiers could not expel.[195]

In Argentina, beginning in 1943, opponents of Perón's dictatorship demonstrated by wearing various black symbols of mourning: neckties, armbands, ribbons on lapels and coats, veils, headcloths, or small black handkerchiefs pinned on women's dresses. The numbers doing this rapidly multiplied, and this is credited with giving antiregime forces considerable encouragement.[196]

After the killings of Africans at Sharpeville, South Africa, when demonstrators defied the pass laws, Albert Luthuli called for an observance of March 28, 1960, as "a national day of mourning."

On this day I asked people to stay at home, and treat it as a day of prayer. The response was good, and in some centres it was magnificent. Moreover, it was multi-racial and went far beyond our usual allies.[197]

Luthuli for some days wore a black tie and black crepe as emblems of mourning.[198]

At the beginning of the 1963 Buddhist struggle against the Diem regime, following the killing of eight demonstrating Buddhists in Hué, the ancient Annamese capital, the predominantly Buddhist population wore white for mourning, in a situation in which the mourning seemed intended both for the dead and as opposition to the government which was discriminating against the Buddhists.[199]

44. Mock funerals

Political protest has also been expressed in the form of a "funeral" for some principle which the demonstrators cherish and which they accuse the opponent of violating. Or it may take the form of a mock funeral procession in which the participants seek to symbolize the seriousness of their protest both by restrained and serious demeanor and by including some of the paraphernalia of a real funeral procession, such as the use of black and the carrying of caskets.

Such a protest was held in Newport, Rhode Island, amid great tensions, at the time when the Stamp Act was officially to go into effect on

November 1, 1765. The event is described by Edmund S. and Helen M. Morgan, who quote from a contemporary newspaper:

> On November first, in order to forestall any possible riot, the Sons of Liberty attempted to divert popular feeling into an orderly demonstration, by staging "a grand funeral of Freedom." A procession of mourners marched through the streets to the burying ground following a coffin marked "Old Freedom." Upon arrival at the place of interment, according to the description in the *Mercury,*
>
> "A Son of LIBERTY emerging from the horrid Gloom of Despair, addressed himself thus: 'Oh LIBERTY! the Darling of my Soul! —GLORIOUS LIBERTY! admir'd, ador'd, by all true Britons!—LIBERTY dead! it cannot be!'—A groan was then heard, as if coming from the Coffin; and upon closer attention, it proved to be a Trance, for old FREEDOM was not dead—The Goddess Britannia had order'd a guardian Angel to snatch Old FREEDOM from the Jaws of frozen Death, to the Orb of the rising Sun, to remain invulnerable from the attacks of lawless Tyranny and Oppression."
>
> After this agreeable diversion the afternoon was spent in rejoicing, with bells ringing and the courthouse ornamented with flags.[200]

Similar mock funerals were also held on the same occasion in Portsmouth, New Hampshire, Baltimore, Maryland, and Wilmington, North Carolina.[201]

In November 1961 on the day following the detonation of a Soviet superbomb, antitest demonstrators in Oslo, Norway, walked in a mock funeral procession with burning torches and black flags to the Soviet Embassy.[202] In March 1965 after a religious service in a small church at Lowndesboro, Alabama (near which Mrs. Viola Liuzzo was murdered), civil rights demonstrators took ten caskets in a funeral procession of automobiles to the state capital of Montgomery. The caskets symbolized the ten persons killed to date because of participation in the civil rights struggle in Alabama. The caskets were carried from the cars to a point near the capitol building, where prayers were said, and a black-clad woman brought flowers.[203]

45. Demonstrative funerals[204]

Under conditions of political unrest, memorial services and funerals —especially funeral processions for persons killed by political opponents or those who died of other causes in the course of the struggle—may express protest and moral condemnation. This may take place whether the person or persons killed were prominent opposition leaders or unknown demonstrators, whether the killers were a private individual or secret group on the one hand, or the police or troops of the regime on the other. Rarely, the occasion is the death of a person who has committed suicide as a protest. (This is not here regarded as a method of nonviolent action.) This method will usually take the form of a dignified walking procession.

There are a number of examples of this. During American colonial resistance to the Townshend Acts, on February 22, 1770, some boisterous school children in Boston were scolded by an "infamous Informer" named Richardson for placing a crude effigy in front of the door of an importer who was violating the boycott policy. Richardson failed to destroy the effigy, and a pelting exchange of rubbish between the children and Richardson, his wife and another man ended with Richardson's shooting several times into the crowd; he wounded one boy and killed Christopher Snider, eleven years old. Christopher Snider's funeral, reports Schlesinger, was made the occasion for a great demonstration, and he became the "little hero and first martyr to the noble cause."[205]

In the autumn of 1905 Prince Trubetskoi suddenly died; he had been a moderate liberal who led the delegation which, on behalf of the Third *Zemstvo* Congress, in June had urged the Tsar to establish the promised national assembly, the *Duma*. The Prince's death was used, by the revolutionaries and other opponents of the government, in the struggle against the regime. In St. Petersburg, Social Democrats organized six hundred students and workers to accompany the body, along with other deputations, when it was taken to the railroad station to be sent to Moscow for burial. In Moscow the funeral "was transformed into a great political demonstration," with many opponents of the regime speaking to crowds and organizing special memorial services to present much more extreme opinions than those held by the deceased Prince.[206] Later in the revolution, reports Harcave, whenever antigovernment demonstrators "were killed in the encounters, elaborate funerals would be arranged to honor them as martyrs." The Moscow funeral of Nicholas Bauman, a Bolshevik, on October 20, 1905, was one of the most dramatic, when "over one hundred thousand workers, students, *intelligents,* and even soldiers in uniform followed the cortège for nearly eight hours through the Moscow streets in what was clearly an anti-government demonstration."[207]

In late September 1917, Thomas Ashe, an imprisoned Irish nationalist, died after being forcibly fed for a week during a hunger strike of a number of prisoners. Edgar Holt describes the funeral:

> The funeral of Thomas Ashe on September 30, 1917, was the clearest sign of the resurgence of the Easter Week spirit that had yet been given. . . .
>
> In all, some 20,000 to 30,000 people followed the hearse together with several bands; for the most part the crowds watched in silence. . . .
>
> The Dublin police took no action as the forbidden uniforms [of the Citizen Army and the Irish Volunteers, of which Ashe had been a member] were flaunted before them. . . .
>
> The British authorities took no action over the funeral and burial of Thomas Ashe. But they were shocked by his death and at once made a number of changes in the treatment of Sinn Fein [nationalist party] prisoners.[208]

During the *Ruhrkampf* in 1923 the funeral procession for thirteen workers at a Krupp factory who were shot by occupation soldiers the Saturday before Easter became a demonstration of national mourning.[209]

News of the murder in the fall of 1940 of Rudi Arndt, who was a Jewish resistance leader in the Buchenwald concentration camp, by the S.D. *(Sicherheits-Dienst,* Security Service) did not reach Berlin underground circles until early in 1941. Herbert Baum then called a memorial meeting in his own home to honor Rudi Arndt, and later organized a memorial ceremony at the Jewish cemetery on the Weissensee. Professor Ber Mark describes these as both "tremendously effective" in that they raised the prestige of Baum's resistance group and "heightened the yearning for resistance." Some other Jewish leaders had thought that "such large gatherings were too risky"; normally attendance for an underground cell was limited to seven.[210]

In 1960 *Zengakuren* demonstrators against the United States-Japanese Security Pact held incense-burning demonstrations for the martyrs of their struggle.[211] Following the murder in May 1963 of Dr. Gregory Lambrakis, independent member of the Greek Parliament and strong opponent of nuclear weapons, a dignified and orderly procession at his funeral was formed by an estimated quarter of a million people to demonstrate respect for Lambrakis and solidarity with his political ideals.[212] (This murder was the basis for the novel and film *Z.)*

Following police firings into demonstrating crowds in East Berlin, on June 17, 1963, the body of the young man who was the first fatality was carried on a stretcher through the Petersstrasse with a wreath across his body, while onlookers threw flowers as the cortège passed.[213]

The funeral parlor of the Strasnice crematorium in Prague was the scene on August 26, 1968, of the funeral of a twenty-seven-year-old young man, a simple bystander who had been shot by a Soviet soldier. A group of weeping young people entered the parlor, carrying a Czechoslovak flag and a banner which read: "WE ARE COMING TO BURY THE VICTIM OF YOUR 'LIBERATION.'" Some of them spoke, swearing they would never forget those days and the victims. Then, reports a Prague newspaper, "the mother's heart-rending voice mingles with the strains of the national anthem: 'Do not leave me, my son . . .'"[214]

At least a half million people attended the funeral of Jan Palach in Prague on January 25, 1969, to honor the young student who had burned himself as an expression of his devotion to Czechoslovak freedom. At noon the day before the funeral, all of Prague stopped work for five minutes. Thousands of people, many weeping and many with flowers, filed past the coffin which lay in state in Charles University at the foot of a statue of Jan Hus. Hus, a Protestant reformer, had been burned at the stake for heresy in 1415.

Soviet troops were kept out of sight for the funeral, and Czechoslovak troops which had been called out to keep order were not needed. The government had not wanted the funeral to develop into civil disobedience to give the Russians the excuse to bring back tanks to Prague. The service began in Charles University; the procession then moved slowly through the streets of the Old Town to "Jan Palach Square," where the national anthem was played. Crowds stood in the cold drizzle for hours. National flags with black sashes were hung from windows. The students' own commentary on the funeral was broadcast from Radio Prague and other stations. Throughout the country, memorial services were held in factories, universities and public halls. A correspondent wrote: "This was the Czechoslovakia [which] the Russian leaders both fear and wish to crush—a quiet, disciplined people whose slightest gesture nevertheless cries out for freedom and self-respect."[215]

46. Homage at burial places

A visit to a person's burial place by a large number of people together or by a series of individuals and small groups may express political protest and moral condemnation when the dead has been in some way associated with the cause of the current struggle or when the dead has been killed by the opponent. For example, in St. Petersburg on October 4, 1861, a procession of students opposed to the tsarist regime carried a wreath to the tomb of Granovsky, the historian and friend of Alexander Herzen, the founder of Russian Populism.[216] On November 17, 1861, student revolutionaries from the University of Petersburg called "the Terrorist Section of the People's Will" sought to mark the fifth anniversary of the death of Dobrolubov, the comrade of Chernyshevsky (the great Russian Populist leader) by placing a wreath on his grave, but were prevented by the police and Cossacks.[217] During the Nazi occupation of Czechoslovakia on the "anniversaries of Thomas Garrigue Masaryk's birth and death, people used to go . . . in thousands to his grave at Lany near Prague to put flowers on his grave," writes Josef Korbel. "They also would go to the monument of Jan Hus in the center of the old city of Prague and do the same."[218] In France the bodies of hostages executed by the Nazis were dispersed among inaccessible cemeteries, apparently to avoid large-scale visiting of their graves.[219]

On December 4, 1956, one month after the second attack on Budapest by Soviet troops, Hungarian women, many black-veiled, walked to the tomb of Hungary's Unknown Soldier in Heroes' Square, in Budapest, where they heaped flowers on the tomb to pay tribute to the recent dead. The women sang the old national anthem and recited Sándor Petöfi's poem "Up, Hungarians!"[220] which contains these lines:

Up, Hungarians! It's your country calling.
Now's the moment, now or never!
Shall we be slaves? Shall we be free?
That's the question—what's your answer?
In God's great name we swear, we swear,
No more shall we be slaves—no more![221]

(Petöfi, poet-hero of the 1848 rebellion, died in battle with the Russians in 1849.)

PUBLIC ASSEMBLIES

When people have been concerned to express their viewpoint to a larger public or to an opponent, one of the most common ways they have chosen is to gather together in some type of assemblage or meeting.

47. Assemblies of protest or support

Opposition to the policies or acts of an opponent, or support for certain policies, may be expressed by public assembly of a group of people at appropriate points, which are usually in some way related to the issue. These may be, for example, government offices, courts, or prisons. Or people may gather at some other place, such as around the statue of a hero or villain. Depending on the particular laws and regulations and on the general degree of political conformity, such an assemblage may be either legal or illegal (if the latter, this method becomes combined with civil disobedience).

Students of the University of St. Petersburg, both protesting and seeking details of the rumored but unannounced new regulations which would virtually eliminate all freedom within the university, on September 24, 1861, assembled in the courtyard seeking to speak with the Curator. When the Curator told them he was no longer in office, the students marched in long orderly files across the bridge over the River Neva toward his home—in what Venturi says was the first demonstration in St. Petersburg. [222]

Following a protest by the Pesth county council against the dissolution of the Hungarian Parliament by Emperor Franz Josef, the council was ordered dissolved; then, having ignored the order and continued to meet, it was evicted from its council chambers by Austrian soldiers in August 1861. A supporting crowd of Hungarians gathered, first outside the chambers and then, after a march through the streets, at the home of the chairman of the council, who declared: "We have been dispersed by tyrannic force—but force shall never overawe us." [223]

In one case during the *Ruhrkampf* a crowd of thousands gathered outside a court to express solidarity with arrested resisters. [224] In Norway solidarity with arrested noncooperating teachers was expressed by children who gathered at railway stations the prison train carrying the teachers would pass on its way to the ship which would take them to a prison camp in northern Norway. [225] In Berlin in 1943—as described in Chapter Two—about six thousand non-Jewish wives of arrested Jews assembled outside the gate of the improvised detention center near the Gestapo headquarters demanding release of their husbands. [226] And in the entry for March 6, 1943, Goebbels wrote in his diary: "Unfortunately there have been a number of regrettable scenes at a Jewish home for the aged, where a large number of people gathered and in part even took sides with the Jews." [227]

In 1956 a massive demonstration against applying the South African pass system to women was held in Pretoria, the administrative capital, with women of all races from every part of the country taking part. They sang: "Strijdom, you have struck a rock!" [228]

In Algiers on August 31, 1962, a crowd of twenty thousand gathered in a square to protest the quarrel raging between the leaders of the newly independent country and approved a resolution calling for a general strike for an indefinite period in case of civil war.[229]

48. Protest meetings

Another method of protest and persuasion is to conduct protest meetings. These may vary considerably in size and nature, ranging from open-air street meetings to small local meetings, from the well-organized fairly formal protest meetings to the mass open-air protest meetings of thousands. As most of the people attending such meetings are already agreed on the need to protest, the speeches are usually of secondary importance and the protest itself consists of people assembling together as a means of expressing their views. Protest meetings are associated with a wide variety of causes and opposition groups. The meeting may be an end in itself or associated with other methods of action.

Mass meetings played a significant role in the American colonists' struggles in the 1760s and 1770s, often merging with the established town meeting system in which each enfranchised man had a voice and a vote. In protest against the customs' seizure of John Hancock's sloop *Liberty,* charged with illegal importation of Madeira wine, the Sons of Liberty in Boston, for example, called a meeting at the Liberty Tree on June 13, 1768. This was adjourned to Faneuil Hall, where a legal town meeting could be held, and thence to South Church because of the large numbers attending. The meeting adopted a petition to Governor Bernard seeking the rights of Englishmen under the British constitution, which, they claimed, had established that "no man shall be governed by laws, nor taxed, but by himself or representative legally and fairly chosen, and to which he does give his own consent. In open violation of these fundamental rights of Britons, laws and taxes are forced on us, to which we not only have not given our consent, but *against* which we have firmly remonstrated."[230]

Mass meetings, such as those in Philadelphia, Boston, and New York in October, November and December,[231] were also very important in the struggle in 1773. On December 16, for example, two thousand persons met in New York despite bad weather and resolved to establish a Committee of Correspondence to communicate with the other provinces.[232] A meeting of eight thousand people in Philadelphia in late December directed the captain of a tea ship arriving during the boycott of tea not to enter the vessel at the customhouse but to leave for England at once.[233]

After the tsarist regime had, during the 1905 Revolution, conceded the reestablishment of immunity rights on the premises of universities and other higher schools, student leaders, in cooperation with socialists and liberals, in early September 1905 turned their buildings into political meeting places. As many as ten thousand persons—students, workers, intelligentsia—met in a single evening in the lecture halls, laboratories and auditoriums of the universities in St. Petersburg and Moscow; smaller meetings were held elsewhere.[234] On October 14, 1905, in St. Petersburg, as a general strike got under way, the halls and courtyards of the University and the Academy of Arts were filled with mass meetings attended by about fifty thousand persons, and the city's high schools were also overflowing with striking workers and their supporters.[235]

In May 1917 improvised meetings were often held by mutinying French troops, rebelling against the vast and hopeless slaughter of the soldiers. When the troops of the 370th Infantry Regiment were notified in the morning that shortly after midnight they were to be sent to the front lines, some of the soldiers made inflammatory speeches urging the men to refuse to board the trucks which would take them to the trenches. By 11 P.M. the troops were drunk on wine they had looted and were milling in the streets of Soissons (sixty-five miles northwest of Paris). Two trucks, belonging to other regiments, then appeared filled with soldiers waving red flags and shouting *"À bas la guerre!"* The trucks stopped and became platforms for antiwar speakers.

> In wine-thickened voices the speakers ranted about the butchery of war, about the peace offers spurned by a French government in the grip of the profiteers, about the politicians who callously sent troops to their death merely to prevent the inevitable encroachment of a truly socialist system. Instead of the 370th Regiment moving forward to attack the Chemin des Dames, it might be better employed in cleaning out the nest of vipers who were the government in Paris!
>
> For a moment the men around the trucks were silent, and then there began an ominous roar. "We march on Paris!" "Get the deputies out of Parliament!" *"À bas la guerre!"* In another moment the drunken mob of five hundred men was surging down the cobblestone streets toward the railroad station.[236]

In the early 1940s, when fewer than four hundred Negroes in New Orleans, Louisiana, were registered to vote, mass outdoor meetings were called to hear victims of police brutality describe their experiences, and to protest the repeated instances of such brutalities. These meetings, called by a Negro labor leader, were on occasion attended by police representatives, and assurances of investigations and action were often forthcoming.[237] The open-air meetings against *Apartheid* and in support of the resistance held throughout South Africa in 1952 before and during the Defiance Campaign are also examples: mass open-air meetings in Sophiatown, Capetown, Port Elizabeth, East London, Pretoria and Durban held on April 6, 1952, while the whites were celebrating the three hundred years of their presence in the country,[238] as well as the meeting held in Durban on November 9, 1952, in support of the Defiance Campaign.[239]

In China in 1957, during the "Hundred Flowers Blossoming" period, eight thousand students in Peking held a rally on May 4 to celebrate the thirty-eighth anniversary of the student May Fourth Movement—claimed by the Communists to have been Socialist-inspired. Students used the meeting, however, to charge the Communists with "suppression of freedom and democracy in all the country's educational institutions" and called for nationwide agitation against the regime.[240]

Protest meetings were widely used in England in 1961-62 by the Committee of 100, on both a small and a large scale. The North-West Committee of 100, for example, in November 1962 held a "public assembly" at the Victoria Monument in Manchester in support of its policies.[241] In London, on October 29, 1961, the Committee held a mass forum in Trafalgar Square on the need for and nature of civil disobedience attended by about five thousand people.[242] On Sunday, February 25, 1962, at the time of the prosecution of six of its leaders for organizing civil disobedience, the Committee of 100 held a public assembly, again in Trafalgar Square, where it presented its case against the government, including statements by some witnesses which had been disallowed in the court.[243]

49. Camouflaged meetings of protest

Under certain political conditions gatherings of protest may be held under the (sometimes undisguised) pretense that the gathering is for some other more legal and approved purpose. (Sometimes everyone may be aware of the pretense.) This may happen when the regime is a relatively moderate type of tyranny, neither liberal enough to allow open meetings of protest nor tyrannical enough to act ruthlessly against persons attending a gathering which is ostensibly legal and approved, although the real purpose of the gathering may be well understood. Camouflaged meetings of protest may take various forms. For example, the meeting may occur under the auspices of an organization which has some totally different and quite innocent purpose, such as sport, amusement, art or religion. Or the gathering may take the form of a social affair. For example, on several occasions in France in 1847 and 1848, when meetings of open protest were not permitted, camouflaged meetings of protest were held under the pretense that they were banquets. The *Gauche Dynastique* and their moderate republican allies sought to mobilize public opinion to force government action against famine conditions by launching, in Paris and the provinces, a successful "campaign of banquets," beginning on July 9, 1847. The last of the banquets, which had been planned by others in 1848, was forbidden by the government, a ban which helped to precipitate the 1848 Revolution.[244]

Political banquets were also widespread during the 1905 Revolution in Imperial Russia. They began in October 1904 on the call of the Council of the Union of Liberation (liberals) at a time when many types of meetings were illegal. As part of a wider political campaign, the Liberationists set November 20—the fortieth anniversary of the Judicial Statutes, which had established a modern system of courts—as the date for the banquets. A surviving paraphrase of the original text of the plan called on Liberationists to "organize banquets on that day in Petersburg, Moscow, and as many other cities as possible, at which must be adopted constitutional and democratic resolutions much more decisive in tone than could be expected from a congress of *zemstvo* and municipal leaders." [245] That is, at the banquets their members would propose resolutions calling for a popularly elected national assembly to create a democratic constitution. Similar banquets attended by the intelligentsia were also held on that date in other cities, including Kiev, Saratov, Odessa, Kaluga, Rostov-on-Don, Baku, Kostroma, Tiflis, Nizhny Novgorod and Tashkent.

[Later,] ingenious liberals found additional occasions, for banquets —the anniversary of the founding of the Medico-Surgical Academy in St. Petersburg, perhaps, or the sesquicentennial of the opening of the University of Moscow. Almost any anniversary provided the excuse for a banquet; and a banquet, the opportunity for long and impassioned antiregime speeches and strongly worded resolutions . . . .

The opposition had never been so outspoken, nor had the attack on the regime and its policies ever been so open.[246]

Such banquets continued in December and into 1905 following "Bloody Sunday."[247]

50. Teach-ins

A teach-in and a protest meeting have certain features in common. In each case the topic for discussion is one on which there is considerable controversy. A teach-in, however, differs from a public protest meeting in that various political viewpoints are represented both among the speakers and those attending, and the speakers may be high-level specialists on the subject or otherwise regarded as especially able to provide, not only a capable presentation of their own attitude to the issue, but important factual and background information relevant to the issue. Teach-ins may thus have a larger number of speakers and extend for longer periods of time than ordinary meetings. Their aim, also, is not simply protest—although the holding of a teach-in on a topic of important public controversy recognizes the existence of differing views on the issue and provides a platform for all of these. An important aim of a teach-in is to provide the opportunity for people to hear various viewpoints and obtain relevant information in order to be able to make up their own minds. Confrontation of opposing viewpoints, questioning of the speakers, and discussion from the floor constitute important aspects of a teach-in. Teach-ins were widely held throughout the United States[248] and England in 1965, when the teach-in was a fresh and unusual method: in Washington, D.C., on May 15[249]; at the University of California at Berkeley, on May 21[250] at the University of Minnesota on June 4[251]; and at Oxford University in mid-June 1965.[252]

WITHDRAWAL AND RENUNCIATION

The final subclass of methods of nonviolent protest and persuasion includes those forms in which the people briefly, or in a very limited way, withdraw from certain usual behavior or renounce some honor they hold. These forms already possess limited characteristics of noncooperation, especially of methods of social noncooperation. However, the element of noncooperation is predominantly symbolic, and these methods are intended to express protest and to persuade.

51. Walk-outs

A group of persons, a delegation, or even an individual may express his political objections by walking out of a conference, assembly, meeting, or discussion before it has been adjourned. In 1920, for example, there was considerable opposition among Russian trade unionists, including members of the Communist Party, to the extension of government control over trade unions and their activities. This opposition was expressed by a walkout when the enlarged plenum of *Tsektran* (the Joint Central Transport Committee) met in December; the "communist representatives of the water transport workers together with a large number of railwaymen left the conference room as a protest."[253] On at least two occasions the normally subservient Field Marshal Wilhelm Keitel, then Chief of the German High Command, walked out on Hitler. In April 1940, for instance, he walked out of the conference chamber when Hitler rebuked him in front of others after Keitel had opposed the transfer of the administration of occupied Norway from the German commander-in-chief there to *Gauleiter* Josef Terboven, who then became *Reichskommissar*. [254] And following Hitler's angry repudiation of his memorandum opposing a war with the Soviet Union, and his offer of resignation in late August 1940, Keitel again "walked out of the room without a word."[255]

52. Silence

Corporate silence has also been used as a method of expressing moral condemnation. The silence may be a main method for expressing the attitude, or it may be an auxiliary method combined with another, for example, a march or stay-at-home demonstration. There are several German examples among those cited here.

During the Kapp *Putsch* in Berlin in 1920, Berliners would have nothing to do with the few apologists for the usurpers. When one pro-Kapp enthusiast climbed on the Potsdamer Bridge and spoke against the legitimate regime, calling the President "King Ebert," icy silence was all he evoked from the crowd.[256] On September 27, 1938, Berliners who believed that war over Czechoslovakia was imminent received the parade of armored troops down the Wilhelmstrasse for review by Hitler with clear hostility; they either scattered and refused to watch or stood "in utter silence."[257]

On June 16, 1953, a column of at least two thousand protesting East Berlin workers passed the new Soviet Embassy on the Unter den Linden in silence.[258] After the crushing of the rising, workers at the Zeiss factory at Jena met the speeches and pleas of Socialist Unity Party representatives with "a wall of sullen, obstinate silence."[259]

Aware of unrest and revolt in Poland, Hungarians on October 22, 1956, held a silent demonstration outside the Polish Embassy.[260] Later, during the Hungarian Revolution of 1956 "silent hour" demonstrations were observed between 1 and 2 P.M. in many parts of Budapest; after notification by poster, leaflet or word of mouth, many people hurried home to be off the streets during that hour, or went into doorways at the apppointed time.[261] In England, the last mile of the eight thousand-strong first Aldermaston March in 1958 was observed in silence, as the marchers approached the nuclear weapons research establishment.[262]

In 1962, in response to a leaflet call for the women of Madrid to show solidarity with tens of thousands of striking workers in the Asturias mines, the Basque provinces, and other parts of Spain, women went to Madrid's historic central square, the Puerta del Sol, to show "silent support." Singly or in pairs they walked around the plaza on that day, May 15, 1962. The secret police quietly arrested seventy of them—many very prominent women and wives of important public figures. The next day they were fined from one thousand to twenty-five thousand pesetas.[263]

When a militant Cuban at the Twenty-third Congress of the Communist Party in Moscow advocated taking all risks to defeat the Americans in Vietnam, his speech was greeted with silence rather than applause.[264]

During the 1964 free speech controversy at the University of California at Berkeley, one night (about October 1) a crowd of students opposed to the free speech movement heckled and molested student demonstrators and threw eggs and lighted cigarette butts at them. The demonstrators responded with simple silence, and after forty-five minutes of provocations the hecklers left.[265]

Silence was a main characteristic of the mourning for Jan Palach, the student who in January 1969 burned himself to protest the Russian occupation. The student action committee said: "In the circumstances, a complete silence will be the best way of showing our real feelings."[266] The funeral itself was described as "marked by perfect silence and order." "Bells from scores of churches tolled over the quiet city."[267]

53. Renouncing honors

One method of communicating one's views to others has been the renunciation of special honors which had been conferred by, or new ones which were offered by, the government against which the campaigns were conducted. This may involve the voluntary renunciation of titles of honor, medals and honorary offices, and resignation from prestigious societies closely identified with the opponent's cause. Such renunciation may be regarded as a means of self-sacrifice for the cause and weakening the authority of the government.

During the Indian nonviolent struggles, for example, Sikh soldiers in large numbers returned their war medals, and thousands of other Indians relinquished their titles.[268] The famous poet Rabindranath Tagore surrendered his title of British knighthood.[269] During the Korean national demonstration against Japanese rule in 1919-22 some Koreans who had been given titles of nobility by the Japanese also resigned them.[270] Bertrand Russell returned the Carl von Ossietzky peace medal awarded in 1963 by the East German Peace Council because the East German officials refused to release Heinz Brandt who had been long imprisoned by both the Nazis and the Communists. (Brandt was later named "Prisoner of the Year" by Amnesty International.)[271]

54. Turning one's back

Silent disapproval may be emphasized by turning one's back (whether standing or sitting) to the person or persons who are or represent the opponent. For example, in his proclamation of a day of fasting and prayer in 1771 Governor Hutchinson of Massachusetts Bay had included a call for thanks for the "Continuance of our Privileges," the radicals took this as an open insult because of the implication of support for British policies. The proclamation was to be read in the churches, but, Philip Davidson writes, "Dr. Pemberton alone of the Boston pastors read the proclamation—and he did so simply because the Governor was a member of his congregation—and he did so with evident embarrassment, for many of the members turned their backs or left the building."[272]

After the dramatic days of the June 16-17 East German Rising, on June 18, 1953, East Berlin strikers returned to their factories but refused to work. "They squatted in front of their lathes and benches and turned their backs on Party officials."[273]

These latter methods have shown symbolic withdrawal of cooperation with the opponent. The overwhelming majority of the methods of nonviolent action, however, are more substantial forms of action in which people refuse to begin new cooperation of some type with an opponent, or in which they withdraw some type of cooperation which they have previously been providing. It is to these methods to which our attention now turns.

NOTES

1. This is a modification of previous titles I have given to this class. The title of "nonviolent protest and persuasion" has been adopted at the risk of clumsiness in order to be more accurate. Adam Roberts has pointed out that my previous title "nonviolent protest" was misleading since many of these methods are often used to persuade instead of protest. In fact, the same method may in different situations be used for both purposes.

2. William L. Shirer, **The Rise and Fall of the Third Reich** (New York: Simon and Schuster, 1960, and London: Secker and Warburg, 1962), p. 218.

3. Gerard Reitlinger, **The Final Solution: The Attempt to Exterminate the Jews of Europe, 1939-1945** (New York: A. S. Barnes & Co., 1961), p. 90.

4. Louis P. Lochner, ed., **The Goebbels Diaries, 1942-1943** (Garden City, New York: Doubleday & Co., 1948), p. 517.

5. Warmbrunn, **The Dutch Under the German Occupation, 1940-1945**, p. 154.

6. Magne Skodvin, "Norwegian Nonviolent Resistance During the German Occupation," in Roberts, ed., **Civilian Resistance as a National Defense**, p. 142; Br. ed.: **The Strategy of Civilian Defence**, p. 142, and Thomas Chr. Wyller, **Nyordning og Motstand: Organisasjonenes Politiske Rolle Under Okkupasjonen** (Oslo: Universitetsforlaget, 1958), pp. 29-33. Other comparable letters by Norwegian organizations are also described by Wyller.

7. Gene Sharp, **Tyranny Could Not Quell Them** (pamphlet; London: Peace News, 1959 and later editions). It is potentially significant that the receipt by a German language paper in Poland in October 1942 of a single unsigned postcard from a Jew expressing outspoken hostility because of the sufferings of the Jews caused considerable disturbance and the "Propaganda Division feared that it was the beginning of a flood of postcards . . ." Raul Hilberg, **The Destruction of the European Jews** (London: W. H. Allen, 1961), p. 332.

8. Matei Yulzari, "The Bulgarian Jews in the Resistance Movement," in Yuri Suhl, ed., **They Fought Back: The Story of the Jewish Resistance in Nazi Europe** (New York: Crown Publishers, 1967), p. 276.

9. Littell, ed., **The Czech Black Book**, p. 81.

10. *Ibid.,* p. 91.

11. *Ibid.,* pp. 149-150.

12. *Ibid.,* pp. 163-164.

13. Hilberg, **The Destruction of the European Jews**, p. 409.

14. Bjarne Høye and Trygve M. Ager, **The Fight of the Norwegian Church Against Nazism** (New York: Macmillan, 1943), pp. 24-25.

15. Werner Warmbrunn, **The Dutch Under German Occupation, 1940-1945**, pp. 160-161.

16. Lochner, ed., **The Goebbels Diaries**, p. 278.

17. See *ibid.,* pp. 20 and 374; also p. 388 for another French case.

18. Littell, ed., **The Czech Black Book**, p. 41.
19. Among the bodies which issued statements in support of the Dubcek regime and in opposition to the invasion were the Association of Anti-Fascist Fighters, the Presidium of the Union of Czechoslovak Journalists, the Central Trade Union Council, the National Assembly, the Extraordinary Fourteenth Party Congress, the Presidium of the Prague City Committee of the National Front, the All-Unit Committee of the Communist Party in the main administration of the State Security, the editors of **Rude Pravo** (the official Party paper) and other papers, the Central Labor Union Council, and the Central Committee of the Trade Union Organizations, the Presidium of the Central Trade Union Council, the University Committee of the Communist Party, the Presidium of the Central Committee of the Communist Party, and the Czechoslovak Writers Union. *Ibid.,* 32-34, 42-44, 48-49, 80-81, 90-91, 150-51, 158-60, 170-71, 191-92, and 203-04.
20. Harcave, **First Blood,** p. 101. For other public declarations see pp. 104-105.
21. Littell, ed., **The Czech Black Book,** p. 47.
22. Albert Luthuli, **Let My People Go: An Autobiography** (New York: McGraw Hill Co., 1962, and London: Collins, 1962), p. 159.
23. *Ibid.,* pp. 239-243.
24. M. Rostovtzeff, **The Social and Economic History of the Roman Empire.** Second ed. revised by P. M. Fraser. (Oxford: Clarendon Press, 1957), vol. I, p. 398.
25. *Ibid.,* p. 409.
26. *Ibid.,* p. 408.
27. Gipson, **The British Empire Before the American Revolution,** vol. XI, **The Triumphant Empire, The Rumbling of the Coming Storm, 1766-1770,** pp. 54-55.
28. *Ibid.,* p. 521.
29. Joanne Grant, ed., **Black Protest: History, Documents, and Analyses 1619 to the Present** (Greenwich, Conn.: Fawcett, 1968), pp. 29-30.
30. Hugh Seton-Watson, **The Decline of Imperial Russia, 1855-1914,** p. 165.
31. A. Fenner Brockway, **Non-co-operation in Other Lands** (Madras: Tagore & Co., 1921), pp. 29-30.
32. Stefan Brant, **The East German Rising** (New York: Frederick A. Praeger, 1957, and London: Thames & Hudson, 1955), pp. 161-162.
33. For the "Document" in full and the story of its significance, see Tamas Aczell and Tibor Meray, **The Revolt of the Mind: A Case History of Intellectual Resistance Behind the Iron Curtain** (New York: Frederick A. Praeger, 1969, and London: Thames & Hudson, 1960), pp. 345-368.
34. Ber Mark, "The Herbert Baum Group: German Resistance in Germany in the Years 1937-1942," in Suhl, **They Fought Back,** p. 62.
35. Personal observations.
36. Jacques Delarue, **The Gestapo: A History of Horror** (New York: William Morrow, 1964), p. 317.
37. Jan Karski, **Story of a Secret State** (Boston: Houghton Mifflin Co., 1944), p. 301.
38. Littell, ed., **The Czech Black Book,** p. 184.
39. Inez Haynes Irwin, **The Story of the Woman's Party** (New York: Harcourt,

Brace and Co., 1921), p. 181. I am grateful to George Lakey for this reference.

40. Sharp, Gandhi Wields the Weapon of Moral Power, p. 114.

41. Sternstein, "The *Ruhrkampf* of 1923," in Roberts, ed., Civilian Resistance as a National Defense, p. 118; Br. ed., The Strategy of Civilian Defence, p. 118.

42. Hilberg, The Destruction of the European Jews, p. 374.

43. Report of the Advisory Commission on the Review of the Constitution of Rhodesia and Nyasaland, Cmnd. 1148 (London: H. M. Stationery Office, 1960), p. 8.

44. Littell, ed., The Czech Black Book, p. 144.

45. *Ibid.,* p. 116.

46. *Ibid.,* pp. 184 and 188.

47. George Lakey, "Cultural Aspects of the American Movement for Woman Suffrage, Militant Phase," unpublished mss., Philadelphia, 1968, p. 8.

48. Karski, Story of a Secret State, pp. 302-303. For another leaflet, see *ibid.,* pp. 127-128.

49. Wyller, Nyordning og Motstand, pp. 27, 29, 36 and 45.

50. Ber Mark, "The Herbert Baum Group," in Suhl, They Fought Back, p. 61.

51. A personal account by the sister of the executed Hans and Sophie Schol, together with the text of leaflets, is contained in Inge Schol, Six Against Tyranny, trans. by Cyrus Brooks (London: John Murray, 1955). The leaflets sometimes advocated "passive resistance" as the means of struggle, in one case listing specific recommended activities. An American edition of Six Against Tyranny was published in German by Houghton Mifflin of Boston in 1955.

52. *Peace News* (London), 1 May 1959.

53. Littell, ed., The Czech Black Book, pp. 50-51.

54. *Ibid.,* p. 51.

55. *Ibid.,* pp. 138, 146-147, 172-173, and 185.

56. Franco Venturi, Roots of Revolution: A History of the Populist and Socialist Movements in Nineteenth Century Russia (New York: Alfred A. Knopf, 1960 and London: Weidenfeld and Nicolson, 1960), pp. 178-179 and 748-749, n. 134.

57. See *ibid.;* Hugh Seton-Watson, The Decline of Imperial Russia, 1855-1914; and Leonard Schapiro, The Communist Party of the Soviet Union.

58. Skodvin, "Norwegian Nonviolent Resistance During the German Occupation," pp. 143-144, and Hans Luihn, De Illegale Avisene.

59. Hans Kirchoff, Henrik S. Nissen and Henning Poulsen, Besaettelsestidens Historie (Copenhagen: Forlaget Fremad, Danmarks Radios Grundbøger, 1964), pp. 113 ff., and their reference to Leo Buschardt, Albert Frabritius and Helge Tønnesen, *Besaettelsestidens illegale blade og bøger,* 1954 and supplement 1960.

60. Warmbrunn, The Dutch . . . , pp. 221-258.

61. Karski, Story of a Secret State, pp. 236 and 264-274.

62. New York: M. Whitmark and Sons, 1965. This discussion is stimulated by an unpublished paper, "Music and Nonviolent Action: A Means of Nonviolent Protest," by Kenneth King, a student of mine in 1969 at the University of Massachusetts at Boston.

63. Littell, ed., The Czech Black Book, pp. 80-81.

64. See Littell, ed., The Czech Black Book, and Royal D. Hutchinson, The Radio

and the Resistance: A Case Study from Czechoslovakia (Hellerup, Denmark: Institute for Peace and Conflict Research, 1970).

65. This category and description are based on papers by Michael Schulter, then a student of mine at Tufts University, prepared in 1969 and 1970.
66. Personal observation.
67. *Life,* 3 July 1964. A large photograph is published with the story.
68. Hsiao Kung-ch,un, **Rural China: Imperial Control in the Nineteenth Century** (Seattle: University of Washington Press, 1960), p. 123.
69. Eino Jutikkala, with Kauko Pirinen, **A History of Finland.** Trans. by Paul Sjoblom. (New York: Frederick A. Praeger, 1962, and London: Thames and Hudson, 1962), pp. 230-232.
70. *Peace News,* 24 October 1958 and 7 November 1958.
71. Ruth Daniloff in *Peace News,* 3 January 1964.
72. Littell, ed., **The Czech Black Book,** pp. 134-135.
73. This section is based on a suggestion and draft by Michael Schulter.
74. *Boston Herald Traveler,* 26 November 1969, p. 3.
75. *War/Peace Report,* April 1966, p. 18.
76. *Peace News,* 26 February 1965.
77. Lloyd G. Reynolds, **Labor Economics and Labor Relations** (Englewood Cliffs, N.J.: Prentice-Hall, 1959), pp. 288 and 290. See also on picketing in connection with strikes: John Stueben, **Strike Strategy** (New York: Gaer Associates, Inc., 1950), pp. 289-294; John A. Fitch, "Strikes and Lockouts," **Encyclopedia of the Social Sciences** (New York: Macmillan, 1935), vol. XIV, p. 422; Florence Peterson, **American Labor Unions: What They Are and How They Work** (New York: Harper and Bros., 1945), p. 264; and James Myers and Harry W. Laidler, **What Do You Know About Labor?** (New York: John Day Co., 1956), pp. 74-75.
78. Sharp, **Gandhi Wields . . . ,** pp. 37-226. On the role of picketing in satyagraha, see Diwakar, **Satyagraha,** p. 48; Shridharani, **War Without Violence,** U.S. ed. pp. 18-19, Br. ed., pp. 39-40; and Gandhi, **Non-violent Resistance,** pp. 333-341; Indian ed.: Gandhi, **Satyagraha,** pp. 333-341.
79. Lakey, "Cultural Aspects of the American Movement for Woman Suffrage, Militant Phase," p. 12.
80. *Peace News,* 31 October 1958.
81. Arthur I. Waskow, **From Race Riot to Sit-In: 1919 and the 1960's** (Garden City, N.Y.: Doubleday, 1966), p. 280.
82. Julian Symons, **The General Strike, A Historical Portrait** (London: The Cresset Press, 1957), p. 226.
83. James Farmer, **Freedom — When?** (New York: Random House, 1965), p. 185.
84. Waskow, **From Race Riot to Sit-In,** p. 264.
85. Farmer, **Freedom — When?,** p. 187.
86. Arthur Griffith, **The Resurrection of Hungary: A Parallel for Ireland** (Dublin: Wheland & Son, 1918, Third ed., pp. 39-40.
87. Sharp, **Gandhi Wields . . . ,** p. 38.
88. *The Times* (London), 7 January 1957.
89. *Ibid.,* 28 January 1957.
90. Sharp, **Gandhi Wields . . . ,** pp. 54-55.
91. Rainer Hildebrandt, **2 x 2 = 8: The Story of a Group of Young Men in the**

Soviet Zone of Germany (Bonn & Berlin: Federal Ministry for All-German Affairs, 1961), p. 45.

92. Adam Roberts, "The Buddhist Revolt: The Anti-Diem Campaign in South Vietnam in 1963" (London: The Author, duplicated, 1964), p. 32. Sources for the event cited are the *New York Times* and *The Guardian* (Manchester and London), 10 September 1963.

93. Littell, ed., **The Czech Black Book,** pp. 35, 37, 39 and 50.

94. *New York Times,* 20 January 1969, p. 1.

95. George Lefebre, **The French Revolution from its Origins to 1793** (New York: Columbia University Press, 1962 and London: Routledge & Kegan Paul, 1962), p. 230.

96. Bennett, "The Resistance Against the German Occupation of Denmark 1940-1945," p. 159.

97. Skodvin, "Norwegian Nonviolent Resistance During the German Occupation," p. 141.

98. Reitlinger, **The Final Solution,** pp. 90 and 313-314.

99. Hilberg, **The Destruction of the European Jews,** p. 374.

100. Sharp, **Tyranny Could Not Quell Them.**

101. Littell, ed., **The Czech Black Book,** pp. 111 and 188.

102. Thich Nhat Hanh, **Love in Action: The Nonviolent Struggle for Peace in Vietnam** (pamphlet, mimeo; Paris [?] : Overseas Vietnamese Buddhists Association, 1967 or later), p. 13.

103. Gaetano Salvemini, **The French Revolution, 1788-1792,** p. 122.

104. Schlesinger, **The Colonial Merchants . . . ,** p. 363.

105. Karski, **The Story of a Secret State,** pp. 301-302.

106. Kuper, **Passive Resistance in South Africa** (New Haven: Yale University Press, 1957, and London: Jonathan Cape, 1956), p. 131.

107. Luthuli, **Let My People Go,** p. 196.

108. *Peace News,* 17 November 1961.

109. *Ibid.,* 31 August 1962.

110. Miller, **Nonviolence,** p. 334.

111. Adam Roberts, "Buddhism and Politics in South Vietnam," in *The World Today* (London), vol. 21, no. 6 (June 1965), p. 246.

112. *New York Times,* 10, 11, 14 and 23 June 1966.

113. Hanh, **Love in Action,** p. 13.

114. *Ibid.,* pp. 10-11.

115. *Washington Post,* 1 July 1966.

116. Harcave, **First Blood,** pp. 184-185.

117. Saul Alinsky, a conversation with Marion K. Sanders, "The Professional Radical, 1970," *Harpers Magazine,* January 1970, p. 38.

118. *Peace News,* 3 November 1961.

119. James Farmer, **Freedom — When?,** p. 40.

120. Harvey Seifert, **Conquest by Suffering: The Process and Prospects of Nonviolent Resistance** (Philadelphia: Westminster Press, 1965), p. 142.

121. *New York Times,* 11 March 1962, 8 May 1962, 24 June 1962. Disrobing as a method of political protest was also used on at least one occasion by African women in Northern Rhodesia (now Zambia) prior to independence, but I have not been able to trace the precise reference for this.

122. *The Times* (London), 29 May 1962.

123. *New York Times,* 19 February 1969 and *Esquire,* January 1970.

124. Schlesinger, **The Colonial Merchants . . . ,** p. 227.

125. *Ibid.*

126. *Ibid.,* p. 525.

127. *Ibid.,* p. 486.

128. Sir George Otto Trevelyan, **The American Revolution** (New York, London and Bombay: Longmans, Green & Co., 1908), vol. I, p. 282.

129. *New York Times,* 11 March and 9, 11, 18 and 24 June 1962.

130. Lakey, "Cultural Aspects of the American Movement for Woman Suffrage," p. 14, and Doris Stevens, **Jailed for Freedom** (New York: Boni and Liverwright, 1920), p. 277.

131. Sharp, **Gandhi Wields . . . ,** p. 41 and *passim.*

132. George Mikes, **The Hungarian Revolution** (London: Andre Deutsch, 1957), p. 82.

133. Luthuli, **Let My People Go,** p. 223.

134. *New York Times,* 16 October 1965, p. 1.

135. *Ibid.,* 17 Oct. 1967.

136. Leo Kuper, **Passive Resistance in South Africa,** p. 145.

137. *New York Times,* 20 January 1969, pp. 1 and 11.

138. Sharp, **Gandhi Wields . . . ,** p. 180.

139. Littell, ed., **The Czech Black Book,** p. 111.

140. Brant, **The East German Rising,** p. 129.

141. Miller, **Nonviolence,** p. 353.

142. Karski, **The Story of a Secret State,** p. 301.

143. *Ibid.,* p. 259.

144. Richard M. Watt, **Dare Call It Treason** (New York: Simon and Schuster, 1963), p. 194.

145. Littell, ed., **The Czech Black Book,** pp. 196 and 192.

146. *Peace News,* 26 October 1962.

147. *Sunday Times* (London), 19 March 1967.

148. Bondurant, **Conquest of Violence,** p. 57 and Mahadev Desai, **The Story of Bardoli** (Ahmedabad, India: Navajivan Publishing House, 1929), pp. 188-189.

149. Graham Peck, **Two Kinds of Time** (Boston: Houghton Mifflin, 1950), pp. 394-395.

150. On the possible use of fraternization in resistance, see Ligt, **The Conquest of Violence,** p. 217.

151. *The Times,* 14 December 1956; *Observer* (London), 16 December 1956; M. Fejto in *France Observateur* (Paris), 15 November 1956; and **Report of the Special Committee on the Problem of Hungary,** pp. 25 and 82-83. See also Miller, **Nonviolence,** pp. 357-358.

152. Littell, ed., **The Czech Black Book,** pp. 63-64. This book contains other references to attempts to influence Russian troops. Not all reports suggest that the soldiers were easily influenced.

153. *Ibid.,* pp. 134 and 212.

154. *Suffragist,* 1917 (organ of the Women's Party, Washington, D.C.). I am grateful to George Lakey for this reference.

155. Bondurant, **Conquest of Violence,** pp. 48-49, and Diwaker, **Satyagraha,** pp. 115-117.

156. *Time,* vol. 66, 26 September 1955, p. 31, and vol. 67, 27 February 1956, pp. 35-36, and *Manchester Guardian,* 20 February 1956.

157. *Peace News,* 4 July-22 August 1958.

158. *Peace News,* 9 October 1959, and 1 January and 29 July 1960, and Jeanne Bagby, "Witness Against Germ Warfare," *Christian Century,* vol. 76, 23 September 1959.

159. *Peace News,* 13, 20 and 27 July 1962.

160. Hildebrandt, **2 x 2 = 8,** pp. 39-45.

161. Sternstein, "The *Ruhrkampf* of 1923," p. 113.

162. Hans Jørgen Hurum, **Musikken Under Okkupasjonen,** 1940-1945 (Oslo: H. Aschehoug, 1946), p. 176.

163. Jutikkala, **A History of Finland,** pp. 232-235.

164. Bennett, "The Resistance Against the German Occupation of Denmark 1940-5," p. 159.

165. Alexander Pechersky, "Revolt in Sobibor," in Suhl, ed., **They Fought Back,** pp. 13-14 (italics added). See also *Ibid.,* pp. 27-28, for instance.

166. Luthuli, **Let My People Go,** p. 167.

167. Miller, **Nonviolence,** p. 336.

168. Littell, ed., **The Czech Black Book,** pp. 34 and 38.

169. Hanh, **Love in Action,** p. 11.

170. Alejandro Planchart, **The Ars Nova,** commentary to the phonograph recording of the same title (New York: *Experiences Anonymes,* 1966), p. 1. I am grateful to Michael Schulter for this example and reference.

171. Translation of the motet, "Super Cathedram/Presidentes/Ruina" which appears in **Le Roman de Fauvel,** quoted in *ibid.,* p. 2, from Leo Schrade, **Polyphonic Music of the Fourteenth Century** (Monaco: 1956-68), vol. I.

172. Gipson, **The British Empire Before the American Revolution,** vol. X, **The Triumphant Empire: Thunderclouds Gather in the West,** 1763-1766, p. 279.

173. Harcave, **First Blood,** p. 184.

174. *Ibid.,* pp. 195-196 and 200.

175. Carlton W. Kendall, **The Truth About Korea** (San Francisco: Korea National Association, 1919), p. 29.

176. Sharp, **Gandhi Wields . . . ,** pp. 70-86.

177. *Peace News,* 20 October 1961, pp. 5-12.

178. Matei Yulzari, "The Bulgarian Jews in the Resistance Movement," in Suhl, **They Fought Back,** pp. 277-278.

179. Robert Taber, **M-26: Biography of a Revolution** (New York: Lyle Stuart, 1961), pp. 86-87. I am grateful to William Hamilton for this example.

180. Carrie Champman Catt and Nettie Rogers Shuller, **Woman Suffrage and Politics: The Inner Study of the Suffrage Movement** (New York: Charles Scribner's Sons, 1923), pp. 242-243. I am grateful to George Lakey for this example.

181. *New York Times,* 4 June 1930.

182. *Peace News,* 9 November 1956.

183. *The Times,* 25 August 1958.

184. *Manchester Guardian,* 8 June 1957.

185. Schlesinger, **The Colonial Merchants . . .** , p. 197.

186. Michiya Shimbori, "Zengakuren: A Japanese Case Study of a Student Political Movement," Sociology of Education, vol. 37, no. 3 (Spring 1964), p. 247.

187. Chang Chung-li, **The Chinese Gentry: Studies in Their Role in Nineteenth-Century Chinese Society** (Seattle: University of Washington Press, 1955), p. 55.

188. Harcave, **First Blood,** p. 89.

189. *Ibid.,* p. 93.

190. Pyarelal (Nayar), **Mahatma Gandhi: The Last Phase** (Ahmedabad, India: Navajivan, 1956), vol. I, pp. 353-529.

191. Christian Science Monitor, 11 November 1959.

192. Lawrence Henry Gipson, **The Coming of the Revolution, 1763-1775** (New York and Evanston: Harper & Row, 1962), p. 102.

193. *Ibid.,* p. 103, and Morgan and Morgan, **The Stamp Act Crisis,** p. 173.

194. Miller, **Nonviolence,** p. 235.

195. Karski, **The Story of a Secret State,** p. 52.

196. R. H. Post (then second secretary of the U.S. Embassy in Buenos Aries), "Mourning Becomes Patriotic," in *Win* (New York), vol. 3, no. 13, July 1967, p. 23.

197. Luthuli, **Let My People Go,** p. 222.

198. *Ibid.,* p. 224.

199. *Newsweek,* 27 May 1963, cited in Roberts, "The Buddhist Revolt." p. 8.

200. Morgan and Morgan, **The Stamp Act Crisis**, pp. 247-248.

201. *Ibid.,* pp. 257-258, and Gipson, **The British Empire Before the American Revolution,** vol. X, p. 317.

202. *Peace News,* 17 November 1961.

203. *Dagbladet* (Oslo), 31 March 1965 (a U.P.I. dispatch).

204. The term "demonstrative funeral" is used by J. H. L. Keep, **The Rise of Social Democracy in Russia** (Oxford: Clarendon Press, 1963), p. 237.

205. Schlesinger, **The Colonial Merchants . . .** , p. 180.

206. Harcave, **First Blood,** pp. 117-179.

207. *Ibid.,* p. 200.

208. Edgar Holt, **Protest in Arms** (London: Putnam & Co. Ltd., 1960), pp. 145-147. I am grateful to William Hamilton for this example.

209. Sternstein, "The *Ruhrkampf* of 1923," p. 120.

210. Mark, "The Herbert Baum Group," in Suhl, ed., **They Fought Back,** pp. 60-61.

211. Shimbori, "Zengakuren," p. 247.

212. *Peace News,* 31 May and 7 June 1963.

213. Brant, **The East German Rising,** p. 108. Other examples are described by Venturi, **Roots of Revolution,** pp. 568-569, and *Peace News,* 30 July 1965.

214. Littell, ed., **The Czech Black Book,** p. 194.

215. *Sunday Times* (London), 26 January 1969, p. 1; see also, *Observer* (London), 26 January 1969, and *The Times* (London), 24, 25, and 27 January 1969.

216. Venturi, **Roots of Revolution,** pp. 229-230.

217. Avrahm Yarmolinsky, **Road to Revolution: A Century of Russian Radicalism** (New York: Macmillan Co., 1959, and London: Cassell, 1957), p. 330. See also Venturi, **Roots of Revolution,** *passim.*

218. Personal letter from Josef Korbel (during World War II with the Czechoslovak Government-in-exile in London), 22 December 1966.

219. Edward Crankshaw, **Gsetapo: Instrument of Tyranny** (London: Putman & Co., 1956), p. 213.

220. *New York Times*, 5 December 1956 (cited by Bondurant, **Conquest of Violence**, pp. 226-227), and *The Times* (London), 5 December 1956.

221. **Report of the Special Committee on the Problem of Hungary**, p. 80.

222. Venturi, **Roots of Revolution**, p. 227.

223. Griffith, **The Resurrection of Hungary**, pp. 30-31.

224. Sternstein, "The *Ruhrkampf* of 1923," p. 114.

225. Sharp, **Tyranny Could Not Quell Them.**

226. See the description by Heinz Ullstein above in Chapter Two.

227. Lochner, ed., **The Goebbels Diaries**, p. 276.

228. Luthuli, **Let My People Go**, p. 192.

229. *Guardian* (London and Manchester) 1 September 1962.

230. Gipson, **The British Empire Before the American Revolution**, vol. XI, p. 153.

231. Schlesinger, **The Colonial Merchants . . .** , pp. 279-293.

232. *Ibid.*, pp. 292-293.

233. *Ibid.*, p. 290.

234. Harcave, **First Blood,** p. 176.

235. *Ibid.*, p. 183.

236. Watt, **Dare Call It Treason,** 189-190.

237. Daniel Thompson, **The Negro Leadership Class** (Englewood Cliffs, New Jersey: Prentice Hall, 1963), p. 99.

238. Luthuli, **Let My People Go**, pp. 115-116.

239. Kuper, **Passive Resistance in South Africa,** pp. 10-17.

240. Robert Loh (as told to Humphrey Evans), **Escape from Red China** (New York: Coward-McCann, 1962), p. 299. I am grateful to Margaret Jackson Rothwell for this example.

241. *Peace News,* 16 November 1962,

242. *Ibid.*, 3 November 1961.

243. *Ibid.*, 2 March 1962.

244. John Plamenatz, **The Revolutionary Movement in France, 1815-1871** (London: Longmans, Green & Co., 1952), pp. 61 and 67.

245. Schwartz, **The Russian Revolution of 1905**, p. 33.

246. Harcave, **First Blood,** p. 59.

247. See *ibid.*, pp. 57, 59, 62 and 117, and Schwartz, **The Russian Revolution of 1905,** pp. 33-35.

248. See Louis Menashe and Ronald Radosh, eds., **Teach-ins: U.S.A.: Reports, Opinions, Documents** (New York: Frederick A Praeger, 1967).

249. *Peace News,* 21 and 28 May 1965.

250. *Ibid.*, 21 May 1965.

251. *Ibid.*, 4 June 1965.

252. *Ibid.*, 25 June 1965.

253. Leonard Schapiro, **The Origin of the Communist Autocracy: Political Opposition in the Soviet State, First Phase 1917-1922** (Cambridge, Mass.: Harvard

University Press, 1955, and London: G. Bell & Sons, The London School of Economics and Political Science, 1956), p. 275.

254. Walter Gorlitz, ed., The Memoirs of Field-Marshal Keitel (trans. by David Irving; New York: Stein and Day, 1966), pp. 105-106.

255. *Ibid.,* p. 123.

256. Eyck, **A History of the Weimar Republic,** vol. I, p. 151.

257. William L. Shirer, **Berlin Diary: The Journal of a Foreign Correspondent, 1934-1941** (New York: Alfred A. Knopf, 1941), pp. 142-143. See also other references in John W. Wheeler-Bennett, **The Nemesis of Power: The German Army in Politics 1918-1945** (New York: St. Martin's Press, 1953, and London: Macmillan, 1953), p. 421, n. 2.

258. Brant, **The East German Rising,** p. 63.

259. *Ibid.,* p. 162.

260. Miller, **Nonviolence,** p. 356.

261. *New York Times,* 7 December 1956.

262. *Peace News,* 11 April 1958.

263. *The Times,* 16 and 17 May 1962.

264. Abraham Katz (formerly with the U.S. Embassy, Moscow), talk at the Center for International Affairs, Harvard University, 20 October 1966.

265. "The Berkeley Free Speech Controversy," prepared by "A Fact-Finding Committee of Graduate Political Scientists," the authors, mimeo., 1964, supplemented by information from Dr. Robert Jervis, one of the authors of that report.

266. *The Times* (London) 25 January 1961, p. 1.

267. *Observer* (London), 26 January 1969, p. 1.

268. Case, **Non-violent Coercion,** p. 386.

269. For Tagore's statement on this, see *ibid.,* pp. 384-385.

270. *Ibid.,* p. 293.

271. *Peace News,* 17 January 1964.

272. Philip Davidson, **Propaganda and the American Revolution** (Chapel Hill: University of North Carolina Press, 1941). I am grateful to William Hamilton for this example.

273. Brant, **The East German Rising,** p. 109.

4

The Methods
of Social Noncooperation

INTRODUCTION

Overwhelmingly, the methods of nonviolent action involve noncooperation with the opponent. That is, the actionists deliberately withdraw the usual forms and degree of their cooperation with the person, activity, institution, or regime with which they have become engaged in conflict. People may, for example, totally ignore members of the opposition group, looking through them as though they did not exist. They may refuse to buy certain products, or they may stop work. They may disobey laws they regard as immoral, sit down in the streets, or refuse to pay taxes. The actionists conduct their struggle by reducing or ceasing their usual cooperation, or by withholding new forms of assistance, or both; this produces a slowing or halting of normal operations. In other words, noncooperation involves the deliberate discontinuance, withholding, or defiance of certain existing relationships—social, economic or political.

The action may be spontaneous or planned in advance, and it may be legal or illegal.

The methods of noncooperation are divided below into three main classes: 1) methods of *social noncooperation* (which include social boycotts); 2) methods of *economic noncooperation* (which are subdivided into economic boycotts and strikes); and 3) methods of *political noncooperation* (which might also be called the methods of the political boycott).

This chapter deals with the first of these classes, the methods of social noncooperation. These involve a refusal to carry on normal social relations, either particular or general, with persons or groups regarded as having perpetrated some wrong or injustice, or to comply with certain behavior patterns or social practices. In addition to the methods of social noncooperation listed here, others are likely to emerge from reflection, research and invention. The fifteen specific methods included here in this, at present the smallest, class of nonviolent action methods, are grouped in three subclasses: ostracism of persons, noncooperation with social events, customs and institutions, and withdrawal from the social system as a means of expressing opposition.

OSTRACISM OF PERSONS

55. Social boycott

The most common method in this class, the social boycott, is characterized by a refusal to continue usual social relations with a person or group of persons. Such refusal is also called ostracism. This term derives from the ancient Athenian practice in which citizens voted to send into exile (for ten years, and in a later period only five years) those persons who had become too powerful or popular. The citizens voted by writing the person's name on tiles or on potsherds, called *ostrakon;* to banish by this practice was called *ostrakizein.*

In modern England the social boycott is called being "sent to Coventry" and has been used especially by trade unionists against workers who have refused to take part in strikes and other such activities. The social boycott has also been frequently associated with religious groups. The extent to which this ostracism is carried, and the spirit in which it is practiced, vary considerably. For example, at times it has been accompanied by hatred and vindictiveness; occasionally the boycotters may avow love of the rejected persons who, they hope, will alter their behavior to one acceptable to the boycotting group. The effectiveness of the social boycott seems to depend in large part on how vital or important the social relations in question are to the persons or groups being ostracized. In the context of a political struggle, the social boycott is usually a temporary practice, rarely lasting more than some months or occasionally years. However, in certain social or religious systems, a particular group such as the untouchables in India may be subjected to social boycott for centuries. This should remind us that social boycott—like other methods of nonviolent action—may be used for ignoble causes. For example, in early 1904 a brief social boycott took place against Jews in Limerick, Ireland; it was denounced by the Irish nationalist, Michael Davitt.[1]

Among the various uses to which social boycotts have been put, three stand out as especially significant within the context of resistance movements. This method has been used: 1) to induce large sections of a population to join in resistance activities; 2) to induce particular persons and groups to refrain from, or cease, some special collaboration with or service to the opponent group; and 3) to apply pressure on—and also often to communicate intense rejection or hatred to—the opponent's representatives or especially his police or troops. Let us now explore some examples of each of the uses.

Among the cases where social boycotts have been applied to induce resistance from reluctant sections of one's own population, the American colonies, Finland and India provide good examples. American colonials used social boycotts widely in their struggles with the Mother Country, both to encourage participation in noncooperation campaigns and to punish those who were judged too pro-British. These boycotts took many forms and were frequently combined with economic boycotts. The term social boycott did not come into use until over a century after these events; instead, the term frequently used at this time was "discountenancing," which indicated showing disfavor, putting to shame, showing disapprobation, and withdrawing one's good will and moral support.

During the Stamp Act campaign, for example, "The maids of Providence and Bristol [Rhode Island] displayed the extent of their resolution by bravely agreeing to admit the addresses of no man who favored the Stamp Act."[2] Later, social boycotts—discountenancing—were used to unify colonial nonviolent resistance against the Townshend Acts.

The town meeting in Providence on December 2, 1769, determined to enforce its strong nonimportation, nonconsumption and austerity plan with a discountenancing—"in the most effectual but decent and lawful Manner"—of anyone who refused to sign or obey the new regulations for the campaign.[3] And the previous March Philadelphians had pledged not only to buy no goods imported in violation of the agreement, but also to discountenance "by all lawful and prudent measures" anyone who violated it.[4] Publication of names of violators during this period was also a common form of expressing disapproval and of communicating the names of persons to be socially boycotted. In Boston in July 1769, for example, it was resolved to print the names of violators of the economic boycott agreement.[5]

Social boycotts were again used during 1774–75 to gain compliance with the program of economic and political noncooperation known as the Continental Association, adopted in October 1774 by the First Continental Congress. For example, the Maryland convention in December 1774, in seeking means to enforce the nonimportation, nonconsumption and nonexportation policy of the Continental Association, resolved that lawyers should not prosecute suits for persons who violated this policy and should not seek to recover debts for stores where such violators served as managers.[6] Similar action in support of the Continental Association campaign was also reported from Pennsylvania, New York, Massachusetts Bay, New Hampshire and Maryland.[7] In Massachusetts Bay, persons who had in violation of the colonists' policy of political noncooperation accepted Crown appointments as members of the Council were branded as "infamous Betrayers of their Country" whose names should be published "as Rebels against the States," in order that they might be "handed down to Posterity with the Infamy they deserve . . . ."[8]

Following Tsar Nicholas II's autocratic abolition of the Finnish constitution by the February Manifesto of 1901, the Finns split into two groups: the "Compliants," who approved of submission to the change, and the "Constitutionalists," who favored uncompromising rejection of the new system and refusal to obey laws or decrees issued under it. During the disobedience campaign which followed, the underground leadership group, known as *Kagal,* called for social boycott of the "Compliants":

> According to the "Citizen's Catechism" published by the *Kagal,* those who advocated compliance should be treated in daily life like carriers of the plague or violent criminals. Contacts between relatives and friends were broken off if they happened to take opposite sides in the conflict; they did their shopping in different stores and deposited their savings in different banks; and, in one town, a new secondary school was founded because families belonging to opposite political camps did not want their children to attend the same institution.[9]

The social boycott was also used by Indian nationalists against Indians who refused to join the noncooperation movement during the nonviolent struggles for independence. In this case the avowed aim was not to penalize the dissenter but to remind him constantly of his antisocial attitude and behavior, which put him beyond the pale of social intercourse. No physical harm was done to him or his relatives; in fact, the *satyagrahis* usually saw to it that all his primary needs, such as food, shelter, clothing, and water, were filled. The boycotted person had a standing invitation to see his error, correct it, and "rejoin" the community. (Gandhi strongly reproved the occasionally overzealous enforcers of the social boycott during the 1930-31 campaign, especially when the boycotted persons were denied food.)

After Gandhi's imprisonment early in that struggle, V.J. Patel, a prominent Indian nationalist, urged the social boycott of all government employees for the duration of Gandhi's imprisonment. On June 27, 1930, the All-India Working Committee of the Congress called upon the people ". . . to organize and enforce a strict social boycott of all Government officials and others known to have participated directly in the atrocities committed upon the people to stifle the national movement." [10] In Gandhi's view the social boycott could be permissible or not, depending upon the spirit and manner in which it was carried out. Boycotted persons, for example, should be supplied with food, water and medical care, and the boycotters should not feel hatred or vindictiveness against those boycotted; instead, the attitude should be sorrow, concern and hope that they would rejoin the community by stopping their help to the British government. When Gandhi returned from the Round Table Conference in 1931, the All-India Working Committee modified its earlier instructions by reminding the people that: "Social boycott with the intention of inflicting injury on Government officers, police or anti-nationalists should not be undertaken and is wholly inconsistent with the spirit of nonviolence." [11]

Now we turn to the second use of social boycotts in resistance movements. Individual members of one's own group who have served the opponent in particular ways seen to be traitorous (as political police or puppet officials) or who have clearly defied instructions for a specific noncooperation campaign (as strikebreakers) have often been subjected to social boycott. For example, early twentieth-century American trade unionists often refused to work with nonunionists and practiced social boycott against strikebreakers ("scabs") by avoiding their boarding-houses and restaurants. The local unions circulated lists of strikebreakers to others of the same trade in different cities, thus preventing their admittance to membership. [12]

There are also Irish, Polish, and Czech examples. In the struggle against British rule of Ireland, the social boycott was directed against members of the Royal Irish Constabulary and their families in 1919. Unlike the British police, the R.I.C. carried guns, and many of the members were quartered in barracks throughout Ireland. Charles L. Mowat reports: "A policy of ostracism, including the refusal to sell food to members, demoralized the force far more than a few murders or the threat of more; the men were mostly Irish and resigned in large numbers, and no new recruits came forward." This was described by Mowat as "the most successful weapon in 1919 . . ." [13] The social boycott was similarly used in Poland during the Nazi occupation. There, the underground government's Directorate of Civilian Resistance, which was charged with keeping Poland clear of traitors and collaborators during the German occupation, used the sentence of "infamy" as an alternative to a death sentence:

> A Pole was sentenced to "infamy" who did not follow the prescribed "stiff attitude toward the occupant" and was unable to justify his conduct when asked to do so by us. It meant social ostracism, and was also the basis for criminal proceedings to be held after the war. [14]

As an example, one might cite the sentence of "infamy" which was imposed on a Polish actress who kept a theater open in violation of the underground's specific orders. Her name was published in all the underground papers. [15]

In late August 1968, after the Russian invasion, social boycott and the public "naming" of Czech collaborators or potential collaborators were important means in helping to prevent the early establishment of a pro-Russian puppet government. The Czech Union of Journalists urged in a printed leaflet, probably on August 24: "Help each other and stand together. Ostracize the traitors, ostracize their families. Do not help them." [16] Posters in Prague streets named persons believed to be collaborators; as a result, one of these persons, Karel Mestek, sent a letter to the National Assembly dissociating himself from the occupiers. [17]

Officials, police and troops of a foreign regime are often subjected to social boycott—the third use we are exploring. This is sometimes applied to members of visiting delegations or commissions. For example, in Northern Rhodesia and Nyasaland noncooperation with the 1960 visiting Monckton Commission from London was frequently extended beyond political noncooperation to refusal to have any social relationship with its members. [18] Then there is the case of the policemen who were stationed in the town of Kilmallock, Ireland, during a rent strike in June 1881. The British had not provided them with means of travel and the villagers would have nothing to do with them, with the following results:

> These men had much difficulty in providing themselves even with food, being "boycotted." The licensed publicans refused them the use of any public conveyance, which rendered the men almost powerless to act on an emergency outside the town. [19]

During the 1923 *Ruhrkampf,* members of the French and Belgian occupation forces in the Ruhr were boycotted socially by Germans; when the soldiers entered a tavern for a drink, the German guests would promptly leave. [20] Similar treatment was also accorded German troops in Denmark during the Nazi occupation. Throughout the four years of occupation, some soldiers were never spoken to by civilians in Denmark; the Danes would walk away without replying when spoken to by Germans, and shoppers would either remain silent or leave when Germans entered a store. [21] In Norway the social boycott was sometimes carried to such an extreme that Norwegians would look right through German soldiers as though they did not even exist and would never speak. Refusal to sit beside German soldiers on streetcars was widespread, and it was finally made an offense to stand when there was an empty seat. [22] In addition, social boycott was also at times used against Norwegians who either collaborated with the opponent or refused to join resistance activities. [23]

In 1959 Breton peasants in France used various types of social boycott. Under syndicalist leadership, the artichoke growers attempted to raise prices of that vegetable by reducing the supply of artichoke buds to growers elsewhere. The Artichoke Committee proposed forms of the social boycott as means of enforcing this ban, Suzanne Berger reports. In a circular to district leaders, the Artichoke Committee recommended that a peasant who violated the ban should first be visited by a few of his neighbors. If he persisted in selling the buds for growing artichoke plants, the entire neighborhood was to visit him. That failing, he should be removed as a member of all agricultural organizations, ostracized, refused all neighborly help, and publicly shamed. (Provision was also made for final resort to certain minor acts of damage to property, such as deflating tires or putting sugar in gasoline, if the social boycott provisions failed.) [24]

After a short period during which the Czechs and Slovaks engaged in extensive arguments with Russian soldiers in Prague in late August 1968, a period of deliberate ostracism of Soviet soldiers followed. This was urged on Czechs and Slovaks by the resistance radio and leaflets. By August 23 (troops invaded the night of August 20) it was already reported that "nobody talks to the Soviet soldiers any more. The people are passing by and pay no attention to them. But you can see everywhere written in large letters in the Russian alphabet: 'Go HOME!' 'DON'T SHOOT AT US!' "[25]

56. Selective social boycott

Instead of a social boycott being total or near-total, it may be restricted to one or more particular types of relationship. These particular relationships may have been chosen as a result of a tactical decision, or they may simply happen to be the main points of contact between the particular resisters and the opponent. Thus, shopkeepers or traders may be willing to speak to occupation troops but refuse to sell them anything. This type of social noncooperation differs from a "traders' boycott," which is an economic boycott, because here it is not a refusal to sell the *item* in question, but to sell it to the *particular person*. Hence the act is not economic but social noncooperation. During the *Ruhrkampf,* for example, shopkeepers refused to serve French and Belgian soldiers.[26] And in 1956 during the British and French occupation of Port Said at the time of the Suez invasion, Egyptian street peddlers observed a complete boycott of British and French forces, and Egyptian merchants in the European quarter of the city closed down their shops.[27]

A selective social boycott may, of course, take quite different forms having nothing to do with trading. Following the shooting of peaceful demonstrators in St. Petersburg on "Bloody Sunday," January 9, 1905, for example, the Merchants Club barred its doors to Guards officers because of their participation in the firings.[28] In January 1917 a sharp exchange took place at the Winter Palace between the President of the *Duma,* M.V. Rodzyanko, and the Minister of the Interior, A.D. Protopopov (who was regarded as Enemy Number One of the "progressive forces"). Later, while waiting for the Tsar, Protopopov approached Rodzyanko, obviously intending to shake hands. An eyewitness reported the following scene:

> In one of these groups I saw the heavy figure of Rodzyanko. Protopopov approached him, and wishing him a happy New Year, proffered his hand. The impolite Rodzyanko, without even turning, pronounced in a resounding voice: "Go away! Do not touch me."

. . . . The incident at once became known all over the palace, and by that evening was the talk of all Petrograd.

George Katkov describes this refusal to shake hands as "a calculated discourtesy with political significance." [29]

On March 7, 1917, five days after the abdication of Tsar Nicholas II, a special commission from the *Duma* arrived at Mogilev, where Nicholas then was, with the news that the Provisional Government had decided to put him under arrest. The delegation and the ex-Tsar, accompanied by ten soldiers, then traveled by train from Mogilev to the palace at Tsarskoe Selo. There Nicholas invited the *Duma* Commissars to dinner. The invitation was refused. [30]

57. Lysistratic nonaction

The prescription for stopping war contained in Aristophanes' play *Lysistrata*—that wives should refuse sexual relations with their bellicose husbands—is so special a form of selective social boycott that it merits individual classification. This method has been applied on at least two known occasions. Stan Steiner reports that at the beginning of the seventeenth century the women of the Iroquois Indian nation conducted the "first feminist rebellion in the U.S.":

> The year was 1600, or thereabouts, when these tribal feminists decided that they had had enough of unregulated warfare by their men. Lysistratas among the Indian women proclaimed a boycott on love-making and childbearing. Until the men conceded to them the power to decide upon war and peace, there would be no more warriors. Since the Iroquois men believed that women alone knew the secret of birth, the feminist rebellion was instantly successful. [31]

In late December 1963 the African women in the Mpopoma township in Bulawayo, Southern Rhodesia, sought the wider agreement of wives to deny their husbands all marital rights until an outbreak of bombings and explosions had ceased. [32]

58. Excommunication [33]

One of the forms of social and religious sanctions which churches may apply is excommunication, that is, excluding an individual or group from membership and the associated privileges and participation. This form of social noncooperation is initiated by the leadership of the church, rather than individual members. While such action may at times be prompted by purely personal factors (i.e., excommunication of an individual for conduct considered morally objectionable), in other instances these forms of social noncooperation have been used in political and social struggles.

Excommunication and interdict (discussed below) were both politically crucial sanctions in Europe during the medieval period, when the Church had a great share in temporal power and final political as well as religious allegiance belonged to the Pope. Thus excommunication of a secular ruler might lead to a popular withdrawal of authority and revolution.

During the late eleventh century there was a struggle between Pope Gregory VII and Emperor Henry IV of the Holy Roman Empire (an area now centering upon present-day Germany and Austria). After Henry had associated with excommunicates (a form of social disobedience), he drove an invested archbishop from Milan; in 1076, at a council at Worms, he referred to the Pope as a false monk. At this point:

> Gregory answered by excommunicating and deposing Henry himself —and the news made all men tremble. Henry's rebellious subjects in Saxony made it so clear that they would throw off the yoke of an excommunicate prince, that Henry was driven to circumvent them by submitting. Making a hasty winter journey into Lombardy, and finding Gregory at Canossa, one of the Alpine strongholds of the countess Matilda of Tuscany, he waited three days in the snow of the courtyard as a penitent, imploring release from excommunication. He had appealed from the statesman in Gregory to the priest, and on the fourth day, against the interests of the statesman, Gregory absolved him.[34]

Nevertheless, certain of the Saxon rebels elected a rival emperor in 1077. After a civil war in which neither side accepted the intervention of the Pope, Gregory again excommunicated Henry in 1080, and Henry reacted by designating a rival pope and establishing him in Rome. The struggle was never finally decided.[35]

Excommunication was also used in the United States as a weapon of antislavery forces during the struggle over abolition in the mid-nineteenth century. Often slaveholders were either excommunicated or prevented from joining churches on account of their practice.[36]

59. Interdict

The interdict is the suspension of religious services and other religious activities in a given district or country for a specific period, by the decision of the leadership of the church.

An interdict, although it may be partially punitive in nature, usually has as its primary goal the coercion of a government or population to rectify specific grievances, which may be either strictly religious or (more often) partially political. The pressure is imposed by depriving the district of religious services, sacraments, or canonical burial, or a combination of these. A canon of Pope Innocent II described the interdict as *cessatio a divinorum celebratione*.[37] Edward B. Krehbiel, an authority on the interdict, has written that

> . . . the purpose of the interdict is to secure compliance with demands made by the church on some offender against the welfare of society, church, or priesthood, or against the laws of faith and morals. It is compulsion by a form of passive resistance. It is not an aggressive act and not a punishment; it is a defensive act by which the church withdraws from public service until society "plays fair."[38]

Thus Innocent III placed under interdict London and the land under the barons who opposed King John after he repudiated the Magna Charta; the Lombard cities were disciplined for reforming their league with the intention of resisting Frederick II; and as early as 1031 the Council of Limoges threatened interdiction for the robber barons who fought in violation of the Peace of God.[39]

NONCOOPERATION WITH SOCIAL EVENTS, CUSTOMS AND INSTITUTIONS

60. Suspension of social and sports activities

Social noncooperation may take the form of cancellation of, or refusal to arrange, social and sports activities. This type of social noncooperation may be intended either as a protest by renunciation (hence related to the methods of nonviolent protest and persuasion), or as an attempt to counter efforts (usually by the government) to initiate new controls over the society (hence related to political noncooperation). This method is classed here because it is social in form, although it may be political in intent or result.

During the 1940–45 occupation Norwegians continually refused in one way or another to cooperate in sports activities, both with the Germans and with the Norwegian fascist party, the *Nasjonal Samling*.[40] As early as the summer of 1940 German officers sought to have German-Norwegian football matches. Only a few were played before they were halted, in accordance with a policy adopted in 1939 by both national Norwegian sports organizations prohibiting matches with foreign teams, in support of strict Norwegian neutrality. The prohibition provided a good basis for declining German overtures.

Germans then tried to join Norwegian sports clubs, and officers especially sought out tennis clubs. Everywhere the Norwegians succeeded in declining such an influx of unwanted members. Where German pressure was most persistent, it was settled that the Germans might requisition or rent the tennis courts one or two days a week, but club members stayed away on those days, thwarting Nazi attempts to build friendships with their "Germanic brothers in the North."

Various Norwegian fascist and German attempts were made in September 1940 to establish controls over sports organizations. On October 1 the new Minister of Labor Services and Sports, Axel Stang, ordered the prohibition against international sports contests lifted. Sports organizations' officials, however, insisted on continued freedom and self-determination of sports organizations, without party agitation or interference. On November 4 the annual meetings of sports organizations were banned by the Department for Labor Services and Sports. The steering committee of Norway's Sports Association sent a circular letter to their branches concerning the fascist efforts to establish party control over the sports organizations, and announced that the committee felt unable to continue its activities. No instructions or recommendations for action were given to members. On November 22, Stang announced State control of Norway's Sports Association, with prohibition of dissolution of the constituent organizations; there would be no more elected officials and "Leaders" would be named for each sports organization. A protest letter was drafted by sports officials and sent to Stang; this was later distributed in circulars and illegal papers throughout the country. These officials withdrew, stating that all responsibility now lay with the State Minister.

The members of sports clubs throughout the country now took the initiative—action occurred almost immediately. Plans for wrestling matches between Norway and Denmark had already begun. When the *Nasjonal Samling* (N.S.) official arrived in Tønsberg, where the matches were to be held, he was told that the sixty-four scheduled Norwegian wrestlers had all stayed away. "And thereby the sports front was really created," wrote Olaf Helset, who had been the Chairman of Norway's Sports Association before N.S. control. "Now it was clear that the active sports youths would have nothing to do with the 'New Order.' Now it was necessary to hold the front." [41] With few exceptions, all the activities of the fascist-controlled sports organizations were boycotted, including participation in and attendance at official sports events and contests. The sports strike was not simply conducted on the basis of orders from above, but arose from the rank-and-file members in the sports clubs throughout the country. Illegal and unofficial sports contests in track, skiing, football and tennis were held, however, with high attendance, while official matches attracted almost no spectators.

Helset, later a Major General in the Norwegian Army, described the sports strike as: ". . . the unconditional *no* to every demand for participation in sports contests in which Germans were present, and to the edict to be part of the sports movement for the 'New Order' . . ." Furthermore, he added, "its moral significance for the whole resistance movement lay both in that it was the first organized rally against the German administrative attack and in that it continued under all pressures as long as the war lasted." [42] Thomas Wyller, a Norwegian political scientist analyzing the occupation resistance, points out that the action of the sportsmen "became an example which showed the way when other organizations later were confronted with the choice between existing in a new form or laying down their activities." The sports strike conveyed throughout the whole country the eye-opening message that the Norwegian people were still involved in struggle. [43]

One of the most prominent historians of this period, Magne Skodvin, writes:

The sports strike extended over the whole country and gathered the greater part of the youth. When the sports people disappeared from the sports grounds—and from the newspaper columns, when they stopped appearing officially completely, then one had either to be very stupid, or very much like a hermit, not to notice it. The Germans and N.S. suffered a serious defeat when the sportsmen refused to play, and no tolerably awake Norwegian could be blind to the pattern which was thereby given. [44]

The sports strike was not officially broken until June 3, 1945, when parades of thousands of sportsmen and crowds of people all over Norway celebrated the end of the struggle and the initiation of new uninhibited sports activities. (Parts of this example are also associated with political noncooperation.)

This method took a somewhat different form in Portugal where in the spring of 1962 students in Coimbra suspended their social and sports activities as a protest against the government; this was intended as a protest by renunciation rather than as an attempt to counter governmental efforts to initiate new controls.[45]

61. Boycott of social affairs

A spirit of resistance may also be expressed by a corporate refusal to attend certain social affairs, such as receptions, banquets, parties, concerts and the like. During the Nazi occupation, for example, the Danes refused to attend concerts of German military music.[46] In late 1940 and early 1941 a wave of "cinema strikes" occurred in Norway in which patrons boycotted the cinemas. These began in Stavanger, where the local cinema board was dismissed for refusing to allow members of Quisling's elite organization (the *Hird*) to enter free. Cinema-going was then suspended elsewhere, culminating in the Oslo cinema strike in February.[47] (This example is also related to the economic boycott.) In Poland during the same period the underground forbade Poles to patronize cinemas and theaters which had been started by the Germans. In 1942 the underground determined that Polish theaters as well as German-operated theaters should be boycotted, and that no Pole should operate such a theater. Jan Karski reports that the predominant reason was that "no Pole could be allowed to forget, even for two hours, what was happening in his country, or to amuse himself. It was forbidden to interrupt the fight and insurrection in permanence against the invader."[48]

62. Student strike

Students and pupils of all types of schools, from elementary schools to universities, may as a means of protest or resistance temporarily refuse to attend classes. Or they may refuse to cooperate in a related way—by boycotting only some, not all, lectures, for example;[49] or students may attend classes but refuse to pay attention, as was done at the University of Madrid in 1965 as part of the campaign for an independent student union.[50] Possible variations are legion. It is more usual, however, for all classes to be boycotted. (Student strikes are also called school boycotts or class boycotts.)

The student strike has long been widely used in China, Latin America, and to a lesser degree Africa;[51] in 1970 following the United States' invasion of Cambodia it became a prominent part of university life in the United States. The student strike is not a modern invention, as the Chinese examples show. Student strikes in China have sometimes taken the form of refusal to take the examinations, sometimes in protest against the lack of impartiality by the examiners. In an edict of 1673, for example, the K'ang-hsi emperor noted that "young scholars in the provinces often went on strike in the local examinations, as a result of their quarrel with local functionaries." The Yung-cheng emperor also noted the same type of action in 1734. This type of student strike was also reported from districts of Kwangtung in 1851, this time in protest against action of the magistrates on taxes and money matters.[52]

Other examples include the strike in May 1935 of students at the Belleville Township High School, near St. Louis, in the United States, in protest against the firing for political reasons of teachers with seniority;[53] the 1960 walkout of half the students at the Jesuit secondary school at Chikuni, Northern Rhodesia, in protest against the expulsion of fourteen boys who, in connection with political agitation, had refused to obey orders;[54] and the sit-down strike by pupils at the Fort Jameson Secondary and Grades Schools, Northern Rhodesia (now Zambia), in March 1960, for the purpose of asking that "political" visits to the schools, such as by the visiting Monckton Commission, be stopped.[55]

In 1899 there was a student strike in all universities of the Russian Empire, in protest against the flogging of some students by the police in St. Petersburg.[56] During the 1905 Revolution the student strike which had begun in February was called off in the autumn in order to open the lecture halls to the public for revolutionary talks and discussions in the evenings.[57] During the Egyptian noncooperation movement of 1919, strikes of schoolboys and students became so frequent that the government had to issue a special order to counter them.[58] The noncooperation movement which toppled Guatemalan strongman Jorge Ubico in June 1944 began with a strike of students at the National University.[59] In the Netherlands in the winter of 1940–41 students at Delft and Leiden went on strike in protest against the dismissal of Jewish professors.[60] Early in 1955 students at the East German University of Greifswald went on strike against a government decree transforming the medical faculty into a military school of medicine directed by the "People's Police."[61]

Student strikes may also be directed against certain grievances directly associated with the schools. This was the case in Glasgow in the autumn of 1963 when parents refused to send their children to school because of school arrangements requiring children to cross a dangerous unfenced canal. Instead, the parents organized their own classes.[62] Similar student strikes have been held in the United States to protest *de facto* racial segregation and bad conditions in schools; this happened in New York City on January 3, 1964, when nearly a half million pupils stayed at home[63] and on February 3, 1964, when forty-four percent of the city's total school population was absent. In the latter case substitute private "freedom schools" were held for the children.[64] In neither case were the teachers on strike. In Chicago on October 22, 1963, 224,000, or ninety percent, of the Negro children stayed away as a protest, and on February 25, 1964, also in Chicago, 172,000 Negro pupils were absent.[65] New York City whites have also applied short-term school boycotts in protest against steps to desegregate neighborhood schools.[66]

Following the United States invasion of Cambodia in May 1970, American colleges and universities, and even some high schools, experienced a wave of student strikes without precedent in United States history. According to the *Newsletter* of the National Strike Information Center at Brandeis University, as of May 10 there were 142 high schools on strike or scheduled to strike, and on May 9, 431 colleges and universities were reported on strike.[67]

63. Social disobedience[68]

This is the disobedience of social customs or the rules, regulations, or practices of a nongovernmental social institution (a religious body, club, economic organization, or the like).[69] Such social disobedience may take many forms—for example, breaking factory regulations (short of striking) or disobeying ecclesiastical orders or violating standard forms of speech, dress and behavior. In other cases, persons who disapprove of a social boycott against certain people may fraternize with them, thereby practicing social disobedience. Persons in India who reject untouchability have often deliberately fraternized with untouchables, defying both the religious taboo and social customs. Although social disobedience may not challenge the government at all, or do so only indirectly, there may nevertheless be a counteraction from those offended by the disobedience. Such retaliation may or may not involve action by police. Violation by U.S. civil rights workers of social taboos against social equality between Negroes and "whites" has sometimes aroused extreme violent responses from archsegregationists. The murder in Mississippi, during the 1964 campaign for Negro voter registration, of James Chaney, Andrew Goodman and Michael Schwerner, one Mississippi Negro and two New York "whites," is one example.[70]

64. Withdrawal from social institutions

During conflicts members of various types of social organizations and institutions may, as a means of expressing their views, either resign membership or withhold participation in the body without actually canceling membership. The examples here refer to religious groups, but this method may be applied to other institutions.

In the 1830s, after the failure of attempts to persuade the churches in the United States to take a stronger stand against slavery, many Garrisonian abolitionists took the radical step of withdrawing membership from their traditional denominations: thus in 1840 an abolitionist editor named Rogers withdrew from the Congregational Church of Plymouth, New Hampshire, after having urged it to no avail to denounce all slaveholding congregations and ministers, and fellowship with them. General Agent Wright of the Nonresistance Society (a group actually dedicated to moral nonviolent resistance) excommunicated his church in the same year before it had a chance to excommunicate him; and Congregational deacon Amos Wood, also a member of the Nonresistance Society in Concord, New Hampshire, had withdrawn from his church and was attending "a little meeting of anti-slavery worshippers." [71] (Where members withdraw because a political party or the State has taken control over their organization, this is classed as boycott of government-supported organizations, a method of political noncooperation.)

WITHDRAWAL FROM THE SOCIAL SYSTEM

65. Stay-at-home

The stay-at-home is often applied in close association with forms of the strike or the *hartal,* although it may be practiced entirely after working hours. In this form of noncooperation the population as a whole remains at home for a set period, usually for a political motive. Normally, the stay-at-home will last a short period, such as one or two days. It is usually organized, although it may be spontaneous. In addition to reducing the chances of "incidents," it may serve to demonstrate to the opponent the degree of unity and self-discipline among the population.

This method has been used in South Africa on several occasions. A one-day stay-at-home was held in that country on June 26, 1950, for example, to protest against the Group Areas Bill and the Suppression of

Communism Bill, and also to mourn the dead of the liberation struggle. It was especially effective in Johannesburg, Port Elizabeth and Durban.[72] Another was held following the shootings in Sharpeville, in March 1960.[73] After the Hungarian Revolution of 1956 was crushed and it was announced that former Premier Imre Nagy and others had been executed, people in Budapest conducted a stay-at-home in the evenings, leaving the streets and places of entertainment deserted.[74]

66. Total personal noncooperation

Very rarely, there have been cases in which a prisoner has literally refused to do almost everything except breathe because he believed his arrest to be unjust for moral or political reasons. The best known case is that of Corbett Bishop, an American religious conscientious objector during World War II. Bishop had initially cooperated with the alternative service program provided for conscientious objectors—Civilian Public Service—but over a period of time he concluded that his beliefs required him to discontinue cooperation in *any* form. Refusing to continue C.P.S. work, Bishop was arrested on September 9, 1944; he announced that his spirit was free and that if the arresting officers wanted his body, they would have to take it without any help from him. In the federal prison at Milan, Michigan, he refused to eat, stand up or dress himself. He was force-fed by tube. After eighty-six days he was brought to trial for walking out of C.P.S. camp, but the judge released him without bond until a decision could be made. Bishop refused to return to court and was rearrested in Philadelphia on February 20, 1945. Bishop then went limp and remained limp during his later hearings. He told the U.S. Commissioner: "I am not going to cooperate in any way, shape or form. I was carried in here. If you hold me, you'll have to carry me out. War is wrong, I don't want any part of it." His limp body was carried into the court in Philadelphia on February 26. Shortly afterward, he was returned to Grand Rapids, where he was fined and sentenced to four years in prison. Bishop continued his complete personal noncooperation and finally, after 144 days, he was paroled without signing any papers or making any promises, under the Special Parole Plan of Executive Order 8641. He was, however, expected to work on a cooperative farm in Georgia, and when he refused to do so he was again arrested, on September 1 in Berea, Ohio, this time as a parole violator. Bishop again went limp, resumed his full noncooperation, and was returned to the Milan prison to finish his uncompleted sentence. After continued refusal by Bishop to do *anything,* and considerable newspaper publicity, the Department of Justice on March 12, 1946, released him on parole, with no conditions and without his signing anything; he returned to his home in Hamilton, Alabama, thus ending 193 days of continuous and total personal noncooperation. [75]

67. "Flight" of workers

This precursor of the strike involved both a cessation of work by the peasants or workers and their leaving their homes and fleeing elsewhere, without demands or conditions being stated for their return. In the Egyptian cases described below the withdrawal seems usually to have been intended to be temporary, though not necessarily short, while in the Russian cases the "flight" seems to have been intended to be permanent, as was usually the case with African slaves in America.

When peasant conditions were intolerable in ancient Egypt the peasants resorted to "flights to the temples to seek the protection of gods or to the swamps and the desert . . ." [76] These cases have important features in common with the next method in this class, "sanctuary." This was a "characteristic feature of Egyptian life" and continued at least into the second century A.D. [77] M. Rostovtzeff writes:

> When the demands [of the State] became intolerable and made life a heavy burden for any group of natives, they resorted to passive resistance, to strikes. A strike was a resolve to submit the case to the judgement of the god, and was effected by leaving their usual place of residence and taking refuge in a temple. Here the strikers remained in idle resignation until the wrong was redressed or compulsion was used to make them resume work. In Greek terminology these strikes were called "secessions" . . . [78]

Under the severe conditions prevailing in the Roman Empire during the first and second centuries, ". . . we hear repeatedly of villages refusing to pay taxes or to perform compulsory work and resorting to the ancient Egyptian practice of striking, that is to say, leaving the villages and taking refuge in the swamps of the Delta." [79] During the reign of Emperor Commodus (176-192 A.D.), "The numbers of those who fled from the villages of Egypt to the swamps of the Delta to escape the burden of levies, compulsory work, and taxes became so large that the fugitives . . . , under the leadership of a priest, could challenge the imperial government." [80]

"Flight" as a type of strike in the Roman Empire was not limited to Egypt, however, for one petition to Emperor Commodus from tenants-peasants on an imperial estate elsewhere in North Africa warned that if their grievances were not righted, "we will flee to some place where we may live as free men." [81]

In the 1860s and 1870s Russian workers of peasant origin sometimes rebelled against extremely severe working conditions by collectively leaving their jobs and returning to peasant life. In 1860 and 1861, for example, mine workers and those engaged in constructing roads and new railway lines refused to continue to work under existing conditions:

> The most serious cases involved not so much abstention from work as "flight"—desertion, intended to be irrevocable, by those who had some hope or possibility of obtaining a piece of land and so resuming their normal lives as peasants. Movements of this kind occurred, for instance, among the men digging the New Canal at Ladoga and other similar undertakings. In one case, in 1861, at least fifty workers were flogged for leaving their work. [82]

Venturi reports that "a few concessions" quickly ended most of these protests. This particular method .continued to be used for some years. It clearly was not regarded as a means by which individuals changed jobs, but rather as a means for collective resistance. Venturi adds that between 1870 and 1879 in the Russian Empire there were forty-nine cases in which desertion of work was carried out in an "organized way." [83] "'Flight' was still the means of defence to which the workers sometimes resorted to escape from conditions when they became too oppressive." [84] Where the withdrawal is permanent, this method is closely related to the method of protest emigration described below, although a change in political jurisdiction may not be involved.

Temporary or permanent flight was also used by African slaves in the United States. Slaves who were hired out by their owners to other masters sometimes ran away from the new masters, either returning to their owner or remaining in hiding until they decided to return to work. [85] U.B. Phillips also reports this type of resistance by African slaves:

> Occasionally, . . . a squad would strike in a body as a protest against severities. An episode of this sort was recounted in a letter of a Georgia overseer to his absent employer: "Sir: I write you . . . to let you know that six of your hands has left the plantation. . . They

displeased me with their work, and I give some of them a few lashes . . . On Wednesday morning they were missing. I think they are lying out until they can see you or your uncle Jack . . . ."

The slaves could not negotiate directly at such a time, but while they lay in the woods they might make overtures to the overseer through slaves on a neighboring plantation as to terms upon which they would return to work, or they might await their master's post-haste arrival and appeal to him for a redress of grievances. Humble as their demeanor might be, their power of renewing the pressure by repeating their act could not be ignored.[86]

Frederick Olmsted, a traveler through the slave states in the 1850s, reported cases of flights to "the swamp" by slaves in response to excessive work demands or cruel treatment.

The slave, if he is indisposed to work, and especially if he is not treated well, or does not like the master who has hired him, will sham sickness—even make himself sick or lame—that he need not work. But a more serious loss frequently arises, when the slave, thinking he is worked too hard, or being angered by punishment or unkind treatment, "getting the sulks," takes to "the swamp," and comes back when he has a mind to. Often this will not be till the year is up for which he is engaged, when he will return to his owner, who, glad to find his property safe, and that it has not died in the swamp, or gone to Canada, forgets to punish him, and immediately sends him for another year to a new master.[87]

The importance of "flight" in the slave struggle is also emphasized by Herbert Apteker, who points to its role in producing bargaining:

The method most commonly pursued was for the Negroes to flee to outlying swamps or forests, and to send back word that only if their demands—perhaps for better food or clothes, or fewer beatings, shorter hours, or even a new overseer—were met (or, at least, discussed) would they willingly return. It is interesting to observe that during the Civil War the slaves added a new demand, the payment of money wages, and at times won, thus "lifting themselves by their own boot-straps" from chattels to wage workers.[88]

The latter is potentially of extreme significance as it points to the possibility of self-liberation by nonviolent struggle by the slaves themselves.

African slaves in the United States also undertook "flight" as a means of full escape from slavery by leaving slave territory. One of the early places to which they went was Spanish Florida. In the 1730s many slaves escaped into the Spanish territory of Florida, where they had been promised—and received—freedom under Spanish law. A royal decree had been issued in 1733 to the effect that all fugitive slaves reaching Florida would be permitted to live there as freemen.[89]

Later, many slaves, often with the help of abolitionist groups, escaped to Northern states and frequently went on to Canada. The escape network, called the Underground Railroad, enabled many to reach freedom. Their legal status in Northern states, however, varied from state to state and changed with legislation and court decisions; these particular "flights" therefore have characteristics of both "flight" and protest emigrations in varying proportions.

68. Sanctuary[90]

Sanctuary is an unusual method whereby an individual or, more often, a group of people important to the opponent withdraws to a place where they cannot be touched without violation of religious, moral, social or legal prohibitions. Such violation would, in turn, put the opponent in a new and difficult situation. Temples, churches and other holy places have frequently been such places of refuge. When ancient Egyptian peasants took "flight" to temples, as described in the preceding method, they were using a combination of flight and sanctuary; when they went to hide in the swamps they were using only the method of "flight." There are examples within both the Christian and the Islamic traditions.

In medieval Christian Europe even professed murderers and felons, as well as the innocent, could obtain safety within the sanctuary of shrines and sacred places. The present status of sanctuary in Roman Catholic ecclesiastical law is defined in canon 1179 of the still authoritative *Codex juris canonici* promulgated by Pope Benedict XV in 1917, which is based on earlier codes and laws.[91]

During 1968 the idea of sanctuary was revived in the United States within the context of resistance to military conscription. First in churches and later in universities, a kind of symbolic sanctuary was offered to young men wanted for arrest on grounds of disobedience to military conscription orders. The Rev. William Sloane Coffin delivered a sermon which discussed the subject at a "Service of Acceptance" at the Arlington Street Unitarian-Universalist Church in Boston, when three hundred young men turned their draft cards over to clergymen. Coffin said:

Now if in the Middle Ages churches could offer sanctuary to the most common of criminals, could they not today do the same for the most conscientious among us? . . . . should a church declare itself a "sanctuary for conscience" this should be considered less a means to shield a man, more a means to expose a church, an effort to make a church really a church.

For if the state should decide that the arm of the law was long enough to reach inside a church there would be little church members could do to prevent an arrest. But the members could point out what they had already dramatically demonstrated, that the sanctity of conscience was being violated.[92]

On May 20, 1968, that Boston church offered sanctuary to Robert Talmanson and William Chase, both wanted for acts of disobedience to military duty. On May 23 they were arrested. Talmanson, going limp, was carried from the pulpit where he was reading from the writings of Lao-tse. A Roman Catholic priest, Father Anthony Mullaney, told arresting officers as they entered that they were about "to violate a moral sanctuary." He and another priest were among those beaten outside the church and arrested.

Similar cases of sanctuary took place in Providence, Rhode Island, and churches in New York City, Detroit and San Francisco declared themselves open to those seeking sanctuary.[93] After sanctuaries were provided in chapels at the Harvard Divinity School and Boston University, a nonreligious sanctuary was conducted in the Student Center of the Massachusetts Institute of Technology. Other university sanctuaries were held as far apart as the City College of New York and the University of Hawaii. Noting that in the United States there was no legal recognition of the custom of sanctuary, which had once existed both in Europe and in old Hawaii, the University of Hawaii Resistance group stated: "Yet as a symbol of resistance to injustice, sanctuary remains effective today in stirring the conscience of man."[94]

Probably the most politically significant cases of the use of sanctuary occurred in the Persian Revolution in 1905-06,[95] in combination with certain other methods including the closing of bazaars. These Persian examples are sufficiently important to merit fairly detailed descriptions. Such sanctuary was powerful because the Shah's authority was believed to derive from religious sources; hence, when Islamic leaders of Persia went into sanctuary they were in fact withdrawing the religious basis of his right to rule.

There had been various grounds for dissatisfaction with the Shah, Muzaffaru'd-Din: he was disliked for his extravagance, his love of foreign travel, the tariffs imposed by his imported Belgian officials and their arrogance, the exploitation of the country by foreign *concessionnaries,* and the tyranny of his main Minister, Grand Vizier Abdu'l Hamíd, who was known by his title, *'Aynu'd-Dawla.* This powerful nobleman was also believed to be cooperating with the Belgians and Russians against Persian interests.

When the Shah in April 1905 undertook a pilgrimage to Mashhad, he traveled through Russian territory to reach it and was accompanied by a Russian official; there was disapproval in the Persian capital of Tehran. Many merchants therefore retired to Sháh 'Abdu'l-'Azím, a holy shrine near Tehran, and the bazaars were closed for five days.

Later, various new grievances developed. One of those was the government violence at Mashhad under the oppressive rule of *Áṣaf'd-Dawla.* This official had ordered his soldiers to fire on a crowd of people who in protest against his exactions had taken refuge within the holy precincts of the Shrine of Imám Rizá. *Mullás* (Islamic teachers) and businessmen also had been beaten (bastinadoed).

As a result, in December 1905 a large number of merchants took sanctuary in the Royal Mosque, called Masjid-i-Shah. They were shortly joined by many of the chief *mullás.* The *Imám-Jum'a,* or prayer leader of the congregation, himself a wealthy relative of the Shah, was asked by the Grand Vizier to disperse them. After violent eviction by the followers of the *Imám-Jum'a,* the expelled *mullás* and a few others left the city and took refuge in the holy shrine of Sháh 'Abdu'l-Azím. There was a difference in kind between a mosque and a holy shrine, a shrine being far more sacred. They were joined at the shrine by many others, *mullás* and students, including Shaykh Fazlu'lláh, who was to become famous as one of the three founders of the Constitutional Movement. The aim of this action, however, was simply the dismissal of the disliked *'Aynu'd-Dawla,* the Grand Vizier; for this there was wide support.

The taking of sanctuary was known in Persian as *bast,* and those taking sanctuary were called *bastis.* Three prominent persons including the Crown Prince, Mohamed Ali Mirza, contributed large sums of money for food and other supplies for the *bastis.* The Crown Prince is reported also to have urged the *mullás* of Tabriz to support the *bast.* Despite efforts of *'Aynu'd-Dawla* to prevent new volunteers and supplies from reaching the sanctuary, both got through. More *mullás* and theological students, as well as merchants and traders, joined in the *bast.* The Shah's threats and promises failed to induce them to return to the capital of Tehran, and even a personal trip by the Amír Bahadur Jang, an army commander, accompanied by three hundred horsemen, failed to persuade the *bastis* to return from sanctuary.

The historian Edward G. Browne writes of the events of January 1906:

> At length the scandal became so grave and the inconvenience so intolerable that the Sháh sent them a *dast-khaṭṭ,* or autograph letter, promising to dismiss *'Aynu'd-Dawla;* to convene the 'Adálat-khána, or "House of Justice," which they now demanded, and which was to consist of representatives elected by the clergy, merchants and landed proprietors, and presided over by the Shah himself; to abolish favouritism and to make all Persian subjects equal in the eyes of the law. [96]

After photographic copies of this letter had been distributed throughout the country, the *bastis* returned to Tehran with great pomp, the leaders riding in the royal carriages, and were received by the Shah, who verbally renewed his promises. However, soon there were attempts to interpret away certain of these concessions; the "House of Justice" had never been intended to be a Legislative Assembly, it was said, but only a judicial court. As the weeks went on, there were new grounds for dissatisfaction, including currency problems. Toward the end of April 1906 the *mullás* of Tehran presented a petition to the Shah, asking that the promised reforms be implemented and that he use his executive power in accord with the laws. The petition was published in the official *Gazette,* but it had no results. Things steadily got worse. Spies were everywhere. Cossacks and soldiers filled the streets. A curfew was imposed three hours after sunset. There were more protests against the Grand Vizier, *'Aynu'd-Dawla,* and Islamic leaders preached sermons against autocracy and tyranny. A free National Library was set up to educate the people in patriotic ideas, and a secret society was formed.

The Shah suffered a paralytic stroke, and *'Aynu'd-Dawla* decided on repression. Annoyed by the denunciations of himself from the pulpit, the Grand Vizier expelled Ágá Sayyid Jamal, who then retired to the theological center of Qum, built around the shrine of an important female saint. Then *'Aynu'd-Dawla* also decided to expel Shaykh Muhammad, a very effective preacher *(Wá'iz),* who was very popular among the artisans and humble folk of the bazaars. A crowd of people gathered around the preacher and the soldiers and attempted to prevent his removal. After

Shaykh Muhammad had been imprisoned in a guardhouse, a student who was a descendant of Mohammed rushed at the door trying to free him. The soldiers disobeyed orders and refused to fire, but an officer personally killed the young man. The date was June 21, 1906. The body of the dead Sayyid Husayn was then carried through the streets and bazaars; there were rioting and clashes between people and soldiers who had tried to stop the procession. Fifteen people were killed by shootings into the crowd. The soldiers succeeded in clearing the streets and occupied the whole town. But a large number of *mullás, rawza-khwáns* (who recite to the common people narratives about the sufferings of Mohammed's spiritual descendants), students, merchants, tradesmen, artisans and humble people then took sanctuary in the Masjid-i-Jami, the Mosque of Assembly, in the city's center. There they buried the body of the dead student. They were besieged by soldiers for three or four days, after which the Shah granted their request for permission to leave the city and to retire to Qum, ninety miles to the south.

They left for Qum about July 21. Thousands of people joined the clerical leaders in this procession from the capital to Qum; one Persian author said the road between the two places "was like the street of a town." Among Persians this is known as "the Great Exodus" *(Hijrat-i-Kubrá)*. One historian of Persia writes: "This action amounted to a withdrawal of religious sanction for the regime and thus challenged its legitimacy." [97] The Shah's permission for the *bastís* to leave the Masjid-i-Jami to go to Qum had been given on the condition that the *mujtahids* ("supreme religious judges" of the dominant Shia sect of Islam) depart from the mosque alone. On their way to Qum, these *mujtahids* issued a notice threatening to leave Persia completely unless the Shah fulfilled his promises. General Percy Sykes reports: "As their absence would stop all legal transactions, this threat was really a serious one, for it would be equivalent to placing the land under an interdict." [98]

Meanwhile the bazaars and shops had been closed in protest, and *'Aynu'd-Dawla* had ordered them to open, under threat of looting. On July 19 a few bankers and merchants were assured by the British *Chargé d'Affaires* that if they took refuge in the British Legation in the capital, they would be allowed to remain symbolically under British protection. A few of them proceeded at once to the Legation garden and encamped there. By July 23 their numbers had increased to 858; three days later there were five thousand, all in the Legation grounds. These merchants demanded, as the price for their return to their homes and normal activities, the dismissal of Grand Vizier *'Aynu'd-Dawla,* the promulgation of a Code of Laws, and the recall from Qum of the ecclesiastical leaders.

> The Shah, greatly vexed and perplexed, decided on July 30 so far to yield to the popular demands as to dismiss *'Aynu'd-Dawla,* appoint in his place the popular and liberal Mirza Nasru'lláh Khán, *Mushiru'd-Dawla,* and invite the *mullás* to return from Qum to the capital . . .[99]

The people no longer trusted the Shah, however, and demanded a regular constitution, a representative National Assembly, and satisfactory guarantees of the Shah's good faith. By August 1 there were thirteen thousand persons in sanctuary at the British Legation, and the number still grew, reaching at least fourteen thousand (some said sixteen thousand). During the *bast* at the Legation, according to a British eyewitness, there were tents everywhere. People policed themselves "in a most remarkable manner" and gave little trouble; meals were cooked in enormous caldrons; and at night old, old stories were told.[100] For a long time the *bastis* refused direct negotiations with the Government. Finally, through the good offices of the British representative, an acceptable document was drafted. On August 5, his birthday, the Shah, Muzaffaru'd-Din, granted all the demands of the *bastis,* who then left the Legation. The hated Grand Vizier was ordered to proceed to his estate. The document the Shah issued that day has been called "The *Magna Charta* of Persia."[101]

This same eyewitness to the events reports that the 1905 Russian Revolution had had "a most astounding effect here. Events in Russia have been watched with great attention, and a new spirit would seem to have come over the people. They are tired of their rulers, and, taking examples of Russia, have come to think that it is possible to have another and better form of government."[102] The writer also added, evaluating the whole moment, that after the riots, which followed the killing of the student, Sayyid:

> Finding that they were unable to oppose armed resistance to the Government, the people decided to take *bast* in the British Legation, and this proved a very successful method of obtaining their ends. . . . the exiled *mullás* have asked to return, and will be brought back in triumph, and the Courts of Justice are to be established.[103]

In short, writes General Sykes, "without bloodshed or civil war, the Persians had gained on paper everything demanded by their leaders."[104]

Shortly after the Shah yielded, the religious leaders from Qum returned to the capital escorted by *'Aṣudu'l-Mulk* (who later became Regent) and Hájji Niẓamu'd-Dawla. It was a day of great rejoicing over the "National Victory" *(Fath-i-Milli)*. On August 19 the new House of Parliament was opened by the ailing Shah, in the presence of high ecclesiastical authorities who were the Shah's guests for three days. A few days earlier, a proclamation had been issued announcing the establishment as well of a National Consultative Assembly.

About September 8, 1906, fresh friction arose when the *mullás* refused to accept the ordinances drafted by the Prime Minister, and the Shah refused to allow the changes they demanded. Again *bastis* took sanctuary in the British Legation, and the bazaars were closed. The Shah gave way to the demands concerning electoral districts, membership in the *Majlis* (parliament), and qualifications for election. On September 17, the Shah accepted the proposed ordinance concerning the constitution of the *Majlis,* setting up a parliament of 156 members elected every two years (directly in the capital and by colleges of electors in the provinces), and providing that the deputies were to be inviolable. "Thus," writes Richard Cottam, "by utilizing the time-honored, almost sacrosanct, institution of *bast* the merchants and clergy were able to force their demands for a constitution upon the government." [105] Many problems still remained, but parliamentary constitutional government was thereby established.

69. Collective disappearance

At times the population of a small area, such as a village, may choose to cut off any social contact with the opponent by disappearing and abandoning their homes and village. As one example, the peasants of Kanara in South India used this method in 1799 and 1800 in opposing British attempts to establish rule over them. The British officer in charge, Sir Thomas Munro, wrote that ". . . whenever I approached a village, the inhabitants went to another, so that I was sometimes several weeks in a district without seeing one of them . . ." [106]

E.C. Barber, a nineteenth century English writer, reported an incident of collective disappearance which took place in central China in 1883:

"In very early times," it was said, the magistrate of a *hsien* in central China was directed by the governor "to institute a census of the population." Being dissatisfied with the returns sent in by his subordinates the magistrate undertook to count the inhabitants himself.

The population "alarmed at the pertinacity of the [official] and apprehensive that he was coming to levy some oppressive tax, fled from the city and hid themselves in the fields." The official was thus frustrated in his efforts, and hanged himself to escape the expected punishment. He left the following note:

"Men .... none
Women.. none
Children under 14 years of age, of both sexes .... none

Total .... none" [107]

George Taylor, in describing North China during the Japanese occupation in 1939, also cited similar instances:

So well organized are the villages now that when the Japanese approach, the people evacuate the village completely, bury their food, remove all animals and utensils, and retire into the hills. The Japanese must, therefore, bring with them everything they need. [108]

70. Protest emigration *(hijrat)*

Protest emigration, called *hijrat* in India, is a deliberate emigration from the jurisdiction of the State responsible for certain injustices or oppression in the eyes of the resisters with the objective of expressing their disapproval and protest by this complete severance of all forms of social cooperation. Hence, only certain special cases of emigration are included here. It is sometimes intended to be permanent and at other times is intended to be temporary, especially where the opponent needs cooperation of some type from the emigrants. Joan Bondurant calls this method "voluntary exile." [109] Arabic in origin, the term *hijrat* (also spelled *hizrat)* derives from *hejira,* the flight of Mohammed from Mecca to Medina, which he chose instead of submission to the tyranny in Mecca. [110]

Hijrat (also called in India *deshatyaga*—giving up the country) [111] was extensively used in India during the various campaigns against specific injustices and for independence during British rule. There it was a spontaneous, though peculiar, offshoot of the various "no-tax" campaigns. In terms of Gandhi's teachings, the bravest course was for the *satyagrahis* cheerfully to suffer the worst repression which might be meted out to them, in the belief that this would have the greatest effect in achieving their goals and in melting the hearts of the opponent. However, if the resisters and population felt oppressed and unable to have self-respect while living under such circumstances and if they lacked the strength to bear such repression—strength which came either from a deep inner conviction in *ahimsa* (nonviolence) or from the capacity (though not the willingness) to defend themselves violently—then Gandhi felt there was nothing immoral, dishonorable, or cowardly about self-imposed exile. *Hijrat* was a physical withdrawal from the territory controlled by the State, at the sacrifice of all interests which the emigrants had there. It provided a nonviolent way out of an unbearable situation.[112] This method has been interpreted as a final effort of noncooperation. Clearly, where large portions of the population are involved, this method becomes a form of political noncooperation and not simply an instance of nonviolent protest.

Hijrat was used by the peasants of Gujarat who migrated to Baroda (where the British had no jurisdiction) during the repression following their refusal to pay taxes during the 1930-31 campaign.[113] Similarly, it was used during the 1928 Bardoli tax-refusal campaign, when peasants from Bardoli district also emigrated temporarily to Baroda.[114]

Other examples of protest emigrations range from that of the plebians in 494 B.C. to secure reforms from the patricians of the Roman Republic,[115] described in Chapter Two, to those of various persecuted religious and political groups from Europe to America,[116] and the mass emigrations from Hungary during the 1956 Revolution.[117] It is also reported by Clarence Marsh Case that similar methods were considered in China for combatting foreign control of pockets along the Chinese coast in the days when the Western powers had gained territorial enclaves in China; it was proposed to organize the population of these areas to participate in a "wholesale exodus from foreign concessions" as a drastic means of protest.[118]

Japanese peasants, especially around the middle of the nineteenth century, during the Tokugawa Period, resorted to this type of method to deal with oppressive feudal barons and corrupt officials. The peasants migrated out of the jurisdiction of their opponents and into a neighboring fief or province. These actions were called "desertions," or *chōsan*.[119] Hugh Borton writes:

> Originally, individuals would secretly desert into a neighbouring village or fief to avoid some specific grievance or hardship, but gradually the habit developed into an organized group of one or more villages leaving en masse. If the villagers crossed into the neighbouring fief or province, they would petition the lord of that fief that they

either be allowed to remain within his domain, or that he intervene on their behalf.[120]

Chōsan was most prevalent in the early part of the Tokugawa Period (1603–1867)[121]; the largest such case of the Period occurred in 1853, when some peasants in the north of the Nambu fief at Morioka, angry at the general corruption among the fief officials and their monopoly of all transactions, deserted to Sendai, a neighboring fief, asking to be allowed to live there and finally presenting their complaints to the Sendai officials.[122] It is reported that *chōsan* were illegal and that the feudal barons would send officials out to bring back the peasants who had fled into another fief, but it is not clear whether the permission of the neighboring baron was required for such recapture. The whole feudal structure depended on the ability of the peasant to produce, and hence officials were reluctant to punish the returned peasants whose rice-producing capacity was much needed.[123] One estimate is that *chōsan* constituted 9.2 percent of the peasant uprisings of the Tokugawa Period.[124]

In addition to the large-scale general migration from the German Democratic Republic (East Germany) prior to the building of the Berlin Wall, protest emigration from East Germany also occurred because of specific measures. For example, East German farmers in 1952 expressed their opposition to the introduction of Soviet-like cooperative farms by emigration to the West; between January and April 22, 852 farmers left.[125]

Protest emigrations in large numbers may, as the above Chinese plan suggests, take on the character of political noncooperation. For example, when Frederick William of Prussia threatened them with compulsory military service in 1723, Mennonites living in East Prussia emigrated to Pennsylvania in such large numbers that the project was abandoned. New regulations of 1787 and 1801 which were intended to check the growth of the Mennonites led to a new emigration, this time to Russia, so the government again made concessions.[126] Action thus intended to enable the believers to maintain their religious principles by a total withdrawal from all relations with the interfering government, nevertheless produced political concessions.

The more usual forms of noncooperation in modern societies, however, are not social but economic, and sometimes political. It is to the two main types of economic noncooperation to which we now turn our attention.

NOTES

1. F. Sheehy-Skiffington, **Michael Davitt: Revolutionary, Agitator and Labor Leader** (London and Leipsic: T. Fisher Unwin, 1908), p. 232.
2. Schlesinger, **The Colonial Merchants and the American Revolution,** p. 77.
3. *Ibid.,* p. 111-112.
4. *Ibid.,* p. 129-130.
5. *Ibid.,* p. 162.
6. *Ibid.,* pp. 504-505.
7. See *ibid.,* pp. 292, 301, 316, 319, 324 and 352, and Gipson, **The British Empire Before the American Revolution,** vol. XII, **The Triumphant Empire, Britain Sails into the Storm, 1770-1776,** pp. 162, 170 and 196.
8. Gipson, **The British Empire . . . vol.** XII, p. 162.
9. Jutikkala, **A History of Finland,** pp. 233-234.
10. B. Pattabhi Sitamarayya, **The History of the Indian National Congress, 1885-1935** (Madras: Working Committee of the Congress, 1935), vol. I, p. 684.
11. *Ibid.,* p. 869.
12. Reynolds, **Labor Economics and Labor Relations,** p. 33.
13. Charles Loch Mowat, **Britain Between the Wars, 1918-1940** (London: Methuen & Co. Ltd., 1955), p. 64. I am grateful to William Hamilton for this reference.
14. Karski, **The Story of a Secret State,** p. 235.
15. *Ibid.,* pp. 260-261.
16. Littell, ed., **The Czech Black Book,** p. 151.
17. *Ibid.,* p. 145.
18. **Report of the Advisory Commission on the Review of the Constitution of Rhodesia and Nyasaland,** Cmnd. 1148 (London: H.M. Stationery Office, 1960), pp. 8 and 17.
19. Clifford Lloyd, **Ireland Under the Land League: A Narrative of Personal Experiences** (Edinburgh and London: William Blackwood & Sons, 1892), p. 78.
20. Sternstein, "The *Ruhrkampf* of 1923," p. 116.
21. Conversation with Hagbard Jonassen, Virum, Denmark, March 1957 and Bennett, "The Resistance Against the German Occupation of Denmark 1940-5," p. 159.
22. Conversation with Haakon and Lotta Holmboe, Asker, Norway, 1957, and various later conversations with others.
23. Wyller, **Nyordning og Motstand,** p. 63.
24. Suzanne Berger, **Peasants Against Politics: Rural Organization in Brittany, 1911-1967** (Cambridge, Mass.: Harvard University Press, 1972), p. 204.
25. Littell, ed., **The Czech Black Book,** p. 111. See also pp. 75 and 114.
26. Sternstein, "The *Ruhrkampf* of 1923," p. 116.

27. *New York Times,* 6 December 1956.

28. Harcave, **First Blood,** p. 101.

29. George Katkov, **Russia 1917: The February Revolution** (New York: Harper & Row, 1967), pp. 211, 211 n. 1, and 218.

30. *Ibid.,* p. 351.

31. Stan Steiner, **The New Indians** (New York: Harper & Row, 1968), p. 220. My attention was called to this by Margaret DeMarco, "The Use of Non-violent Direct Action Tactics and Strategy by American Indians," unpublished research paper, Upland School of Social Change, Upland, Pa., July 1968).

32. *Guardian* (Manchester and London), 31 December 1963, and *Peace News,* 10 January 1964.

33. This section and the next on interdict are based on a draft by Michael Schulter.

34. Margaret Deanesly, **A History of the Medieval Church, 590-1500** (London: Methuen and Co. Ltd., 1965), pp. 102-103.

35. *Ibid.,* p. 103.

36. Carleton Mabee, **Black Freedom: The Nonviolent Abolitionists from 1830 Through the Civil War** (New York: Macmillan Co., 1970), pp. 217-221.

37. Edward B. Krehbiel, **The Interdict, Its History and Its Operation** (Washington: American Historical Association, 1909), pp. 13 and 9.

38. *Ibid.,* pp. 11-12.

39. *Ibid.,* pp. 26-27.

40. This description is largely based upon Major General Olaf Helset, "Idretts-fronten," in Steen, gen. ed., **Norges Krig,** vol. III, pp. 7-34.

41. *Ibid.,* p. 25.

42. *Ibid.,* p. 8.

43. Wyller, **Nyordning og Motstand,** p. 11.

44. Magne Skodvin, "Det Store Fremstot," in Steen, gen. ed., **Norges Krig,** vol. II, pp. 640-641.

45. *Peace News,* 18 May 1962.

46. Bennett, "The Resistance Against the German Occupation of Denmark 1940-5," p. 159.

47. Magne Skodvin, "Det Store Fremstot," p. 624.

48. Karski, **The Story of a Secret State,** p. 260.

49. Michael Prawdin, **The Unmentionable Nechaev,** p. 21.

50. *Peace News,* 5 March 1965.

51. Case, **Non-violent Coercion,** p. 333, and L. L. Bernard, **Social Control in its Sociological Aspects** (New York: Macmillan, 1939), pp. 387-388.

52. Hsiao, **Rural China,** pp. 246-247.

53. Bernard, **Social Control in its Sociological Aspects,** p. 388.

54. *The Observer* (London), 20 March 1960.

55. *Ibid.,* 13 March 1960.

56. Seton-Watson, **The Decline of Imperial Russia,** p. 145, and Keep, **The Rise of Social Democracy in Russia,** p. 70.

57. Keep, **The Rise of Social Democracy in Russia,** pp. 217-218.

58. Brockway, **Non-co-operation in Other Lands,** p. 35.

59. *New York Times,* 24 and 27 June 1944.

60. Warmbrunn, **The Dutch Under German Occupation,** p. 105.

61. Brant, **The East German Rising**, p. 181.

62. *Peace News,* 29 November 1963.

63. *Ibid.,* 14 February 1964.

64. *Ibid.,* 21 February 1964.

65. *Ibid.,* 6 March 1964.

66. Waskow, **From Race Riot to Sit-In,** p. 280.

67. National Strike Information Center (Brandeis University, Waltham, Mass.), *Newsletter,* no. 8, 12 May 1970, p. 9 and dittoed 6 pp. memo "Colleges on Strike — State by State Breakdown," 9 May 1970.

68. This description is based upon a draft prepared by Michael Schulter.

69. This is a more narrow usage than suggested by Seifert, **Conquest by Suffering,** pp. 17-18.

70. *Newsweek,* 17 August 1964, p. 28.

71. Mabee, **Black Freedom,** pp. 221-243. I am grateful to Michael Schulter for these examples.

72. Luthuli, **Let My People Go,** pp. 108-110. See also pp. 170 and 182.

73. *The Times,* 29 and 30 March 1960.

74. Lajos Lederer, *The Observer,* 22 June 1958.

75. Mulford Q. Sibley and Philip E. Jacob, **Conscription of Conscience: The American State and the Conscientious Objector, 1940-1947** (Ithaca, N.Y.: Cornell University Press, 1952), pp. 401-409.

76. Rostovtzeff, **The Social and Economic History of the Roman Empire,** vol. I, p. 179. I am grateful to Margaret Jackson Rothwell for these references.

77. *Ibid.,* vol. II, p. 677, n. 52.

78. *Ibid.,* vol. I, p. 274.

79. *Ibid.,* p. 348.

80. *Ibid.,* p. 374.

81. *Ibid.,* 398.

82. Venturi, **Roots of Revolution,** p. 507.

83. *Ibid.,* p. 509.

84. *Ibid.,* p. 510.

85. Raymond A. and Alice H. Bauer, "Day to Day Resistance to Slavery," **Journal of Negro History,** vol. XXVII, no. 4 (Oct. 1942), pp. 400-401.

86. Ulrich Bonnell Phillips, **American Negro Slavery: A Survey of the Supply, Employment and Control of Negro Labor as Determined by the Plantation Regime** (New York: Peter Smith, 1952 [orig. 1918], pp. 303-304.

87. Frederick Law Olmsted, **A Journey in the Seaboard Slave States, with Remarks on Their Economy** (New York: Dix and Edwards, 1856, and London: Sampson Low, Son & Co., 1856), p. 100. I am grateful to Ron McCarthy for this illustration.

88. Herbert Apteker, **American Negro Slave Revolts** (New York: International Publishers, 1964), p. 142. I am grateful to Marilyn Saunders for this citation.

89. Apteker, **American Negro Slave Revolts,** p. 174.

90. This section is based on a suggestion by James Prior, who has also provided the cited references, and clarified certain matters related to Persian terms and religious customs.

91. George Huntston Williams, "The Ministry and the Draft in Historical Perspective," in Donald Cutler, ed., **The Religious Situation – 1969** (Boston: Beacon Press, 1969), pp. 464-512.

92. Quoted in J. Dennis Willigan, S. J., "Sanctuary: A Communitarian Form of Counter-Culture," *Union Seminary Quarterly Review,* vol. XXV, no. 4 (Summer, 1970), p. 532. See esp. his discussion on pp. 531-539. For further discussion and case material, see Cutler, ed., **The Religious Situation – 1969,** pp. 513-537.

93. *Ibid.,* p. 534.

94. *Ibid.,* p. 539.

95. This account is based upon the following sources: Edward G. Browne, **The Persian Revolution of 1905-1909** (Cambridge, England: University Press, 1910), pp. 111-124; Brigadier-General Sir Percy Sykes, **A History of Persia** (London: Macmillan & Co. Ltd., 1963), vol. II, pp. 394-405; and Richard W. Cottam, **Nationalism in Iran** (Pittsburgh: University of Pittsburgh Press, 1964), pp. 139-141.

96. Browne, **The Persian Revolution of 1905-1909,** p. 114.

97. Cottam, **Nationalism in Iran,** p. 141.

98. Sykes, **A History of Persia,** p. 402.

99. Browne, **The Persian Revolution of 1905-1909,** p. 119.

100. *Ibid.,* p. 120.

101. Sykes, **A History of Persia,** p. 403. The full text of that document is published on pp. 403-404.

102. Browne, **The Persian Revolution of 1905-1909,** p. 120.

103. *Ibid.,* p. 121.

104. Sykes, **A History of Persia,** p. 404.

105. Cottam, **Nationalism in Iran,** p. 141.

106. Quoted by Diwaker, **Satyagraha,** p. 147.

107. E. C. Baber, "China in Some of Its Physical and Social Aspects," **Proceedings of the Royal Geographical Society,** N. S., V, (1883), pp. 442-43. Quoted in Hsiao, **Rural China,** p. 582, n. 143. Hsiao comments that although "this story may not literally be true, . . . the situation which it illustrates is authentic."

108. George R. Taylor, **The Struggle for North China,** p. 171. New York: Institute of Pacific Relations, 1940.

109. Bondurant, **Conquest of Violence,** p. 41.

110. On the origin of the term *hijrat* see Shridharani, **War Without Violence,** U.S. ed., p. 28; Br. ed., p. 47.

111. Bondurant, **Conquest of Violence,** p. 119.

112. For Gandhi's views on *hijrat,* see for example Gandhi, **Non-violent Resistance** pp. 212 and 289; Ind. ed.: **Satyagraha,** pp. 212 and 289.

113. Sharp, **Gandhi Wields . . . ,** pp. 188, 190 and 197-198.

114. Shridharani, **War Without Violence,** U. S. ed., pp. 97-98; Br. ed., p. 101.

115. Cowell, **The Revolutions of Ancient Rome,** pp. 41-43.

116. Allan Nevins and Henry Steele Commander, **America: The Story of a Free People** (Boston: Little, Brown and Co., 1943), pp. 12-13 and 29.

117. George Mikes, **The Hungarian Revolution,** pp. 172-173.

118. Case, **Non-violent Coercion**, pp. 345-346. For another example, see Pieter Geyl, **The Revolt of the Netherlands, 1555-1609** (New York: Barnes and Noble, 1958, and London: Ernest Benn, 1962), p. 201.

119. Hugh Borton, **Peasant Uprisings in Japan of the Tokugawa Period** (Second ed.; New York: Paragon Book Reprint Corp, 1968 [First published in **The Transactions of the Asiastic Society of Japan** (Second Ser.), vol. XVI, 1938.]) Preface [p. iii]. I am grateful to Carl Horne for calling my attention to this reference.

120. *Ibid.*, pp. 30-31.

121. *Ibid.*, Preface, [p. iii].

122. *Ibid.*, p. 31.

123. *Ibid.*, Preface [pp. iii-iv].

124. *Ibid.*, p. 31, n. 53. For other details, see also pp. 65-66 and 144 ff.

125. Brant, **The East German Rising**, p. 37.

126. Margaret E. Hirst, **The Quakers in Peace and War** (New York: George H. Doranco, 1923, and London: Swarthmore Press, 1923), p. 32.

5

The Methods
of Economic
Noncooperation:
(1) Economic Boycotts

INTRODUCTION

Economic forms of noncooperation are much more numerous than
the forms of social noncooperation, identified above. Economic noncooperation consists of a suspension of or refusal to continue specific
economic relationships. The first subclass within the broad class of economic noncooperation is that of economic boycotts—the refusal to continue or to undertake certain economic relationships, especially the buying, selling, or handling of goods and services. The second subclass consists of various forms of the strike, which involves the restriction or
suspension of labor. The next chapter is devoted to the strike, while
our focus here is on economic boycotts.

Economic boycotts may be spontaneous, or they may be deliberately
initiated by a particular group. In either case, they usually become organized efforts to withdraw, and to induce others to withdraw, economic
cooperation in ways which restrict the buying or selling market of an

individual or group.[1] Although the word boycott did not come into use until 1880, when it originated with the name of a Captain Boycott against whom the peasants of Mayo County, Ireland, were protesting,[2] examples of this method of noncooperation go back much earlier. The boycott has been practiced on local, regional, national and international levels both by persons directly involved in the grievance and by sympathetic third parties. Motivations and objectives have varied from economic and political to social and cultural.

Economic boycotts have been practiced mainly in labor struggles and national liberation movements, although their use in other situations is not unknown. The economic boycott in industrial disputes had its origin in the American trade union movement,[3] where it emerged in 1880 "almost without warning . . . to become for the next ten or fifteen years the most effective weapon of unionism. There was no object so mean and no person so exalted as to escape its power."[4]

Economic boycotts for nationalist objectives against foreign powers appear to have been most frequently used in China; those cases seem to have drawn upon earlier Chinese experience in economic noncooperation, as Professor John K. Fairbank suggests. He writes that "in Chinese life the boycott had been a widely used form of passive resistance, or non-violent coercion, by which organized groups such as merchant guilds could exert their influence upon officialdom. In the twentieth century they began to be used as expressions of anti-foreignism." As examples he cites the boycott of American products sponsored in 1905 by the merchant guilds of Canton in protest against the exclusion of Chinese from the United States, the boycotts of Japanese goods in 1908 and 1915 in protest against that country's policies, and the prolonged boycott and strike against the British which began in Hong Kong in 1925.[5]

One way of viewing economic boycotts is to divide them into primary and secondary boycotts. The primary boycott is the direct suspension of dealings with the opponent or a refusal to buy, use, or handle his goods or services (sometimes accompanied by efforts to persuade others to do likewise). The secondary boycott is the economic boycott of third parties in an effort to induce them to join in the primary boycott against the opponent. It occurs "where those who fail to support the original movement are themselves boycotted."[6] Leo Wolman defines a secondary boycott as "a combination to withdraw patronage from a person in order to force that person in turn to withdraw his patronage from that individual or firm with whom the union is primarily at odds."[7]

A secondary boycott took place in the United States in 1921 when the International Association of Machinists boycotted not only the Duplex Printing Co., with which it was involved in a conflict, but also all those firms which continued to use the products made by that company.[8] Another American example of a secondary boycott occurred in period preceding the War of Independence, when merchants and other persons were themselves boycotted economically if they did not observe the boycott of English commodities which was part of the resistance to the Stamp Act and the Townshend Acts. Such action sometimes also affected economic relations between the colonies. In 1766, for example, a group in Charleston, South Carolina, agreed that no provisions should be shipped "to that infamous Colony Georgia in particular nor any other that make use of Stamp Paper."[9] When the Boston town meeting heard in May 1770 that traders in Newport, Rhode Island, were importing goods from both England and the East Indies, it voted to sever all commercial relations with that town.[10]

The remainder of this chapter will not distinguish between primary and secondary economic boycotts because different criteria are used to distinguish the specific methods of economic boycotts. Frequently one method of economic boycott may be applied either as a primary or as a secondary boycott.

Since the term economic boycott covers a considerable variety of specific acts, it is desirable to subdivide the classification; this can most usefully be done in terms of the nature of the group responsible (at least primarily so) for conducting the boycott. This classification should not be regarded as rigid, however, for one type often blends into another, and frequently several methods, or action by several groups, may be combined. Economic boycotts may also be combined with a great variety of other methods of nonviolent action.

ACTION BY CONSUMERS

71. Consumers' boycott

The consumers' boycott involves a refusal by consumers to purchase certain goods or services. There may be many reasons for such a boycott: 1) the price may be regarded as too high; 2) the item may not be available to all persons and groups on equal terms; 3) the boycotted item may furnish a convenient symbolic point for expressing a wider grievance or a general discontent with the status quo; 4) the particular boycotted item may be regarded as having certain "immoral" qualities; 5) there may be objection to the conditions, especially of labor, under which the item has been produced; 6) there may be objection to the use to which the profits from such sales will be put; and 7) there may be other less noble motives, including prejudices and political differences. The motives for economic boycotts may, therefore, vary considerably in their origin, which may be economic, political, social, or cultural, or a combination of these.

Examples of consumers' boycotts, taken almost at random, include the New York housewives' boycott of meat in protest against high prices in 1936;[11] the 1907 boycott initiated by U.S. trade unionists against the products of Buck's Stove and Range Co.;[12] the six-year boycott initiated in 1893 by the Knights of Labor against the products of 'the Liggett & Myers Tobacco Co.;[13] the Socialists' boycott in the late nineteenth century of German inns which refused to let rooms for meetings of the Social Democratic Party;[14] the Berlin workers' boycott, in 1894, of beer produced by members of the Brewers' Employers' Association (this was so effective, Leo Wolman reports, that the secretary of the Association stated that the emergence of the boycott added a new and extraordinarily effective weapon to the methods of social and industrial warfare).[15]

Other examples are the 1934 boycott of "immoral" films, organized in the United States by Protestants and the Roman Catholic Legion of Decency;[16] the fifteen-day bus boycott in Barcelona, Spain, in January 1957, to express dissatisfaction with the regime;[17] the famous bus boycott in Montgomery, Alabama, by the city's Afro-Americans, which lasted 381 days (from 1955 to 1957);[18] the boycott in 1959 by Africans in Buganda of all Asian shopkeepers and a few non-African goods;[19] and the June–July 1959 boycott by British businessmen of a grill in Singapore whose name had been changed from "Elizabethan Grill" to "Epicurean" and from which the portrait of the Queen had been removed.[20]

Numerous examples can be drawn from Nazi-occupied Europe, also. Patriotic citizens of Prague, for example, refused to buy German-controlled newspapers during the week of September 14-21, 1941. The call for this boycott (planned for several weeks by a patriotic organization in the city) was broadcast by the Czechoslovak government from London. "It proved to be a tremendous success," reports Josef Korbel, who was then working with the Czech government-in-exile.[21] From time to time during the German occupation the streetcars in Prague were boycotted to such an extent that they traveled completely empty.[22] As a means of testing the discipline of the Poles during the Nazi occupation, during certain periods the underground forbade them to read on Fridays the German newspapers printed in Polish. This order was highly effective all over Poland. (It was often enforced, however, by hostile or even violent action. Sometimes abusive signs were placed on the purchaser's back or home; or after he left the newsstand a brick might be thrown at him.)[23]

Various types of consumers' boycotts have also been used in South Africa by black Africans. Objecting to a slight increase in bus fares, Africans of the township of Alexandra outside Johannesburg on January 7, 1957, launched a total boycott of the bus line, choosing instead to cycle, accept rides with sympathetic motorists, or, most usually, walk (often eighteen miles a day). Despite severe police harassment and some fourteen thousand arrests, the boycott spread elsewhere, including to Pretoria, and eventually involved sixty thousand Africans. The boycott ended after twelve weeks when the Chamber of Commerce negotiated with the Joint Boycott Committee for a working compromise pending an investigation. Full victory for the boycotters came later with the passage in Parliament of an Act which doubled the employers' levy to subsidize African transport, so that fares were kept at the previous rate.[24] Encouraged, the African National Congress (which had not been involved in launching the bus boycott) called for a wide economic boycott of Nationalist-controlled firms and their products.[25] Also, Africans carried out a three-month boycott of their staple food, potatoes, which were largely grown in the Eastern Transvaal and elsewhere by the labor of African prisoners, many of them jailed for violations of the pass laws. The market was glutted with potatoes. Efforts to break the boycott were unsuccessful, and it continued until called off by Albert Luthuli.[26]

Other examples which indicate the widespread use of this method are numerous. Peasant serfs in tsarist Russia in 1859 sought to express in economic ways their hatred for serfdom by "starting a temperance movement so as to deprive the State of its revenues from the vodka monopoly."[27] The German population in the Ruhr refused during the 1923 struggle to ride on the few trains that the occupation authorities managed to get rolling despite the workers' resistance.[28] In 1938, as part of a jobs-for-Negroes movement led by the Rev. Adam Clayton Powell, A. Philip Randolph, and the Rev. William Lloyd Imes, Negroes in Harlem, New York City, conducted a "blackout boycott" every Tuesday night by turning off electricity and lighting candles to induce Consolidated Edison Co. to hire Negroes in jobs above the unskilled level.[29] In Nashville, Tennessee, shortly before Easter 1960, Negroes supporting a student sit-in to integrate lunch counters decided not to buy new Easter clothes as a means of influencing Nashville merchants. On May 10 the lunch counters of the six downtown stores were integrated.[30] During the summer of 1960 about 250,000 people in the Philadelphia area carried out a "selective patronage program" against the Tasty Baking Co. of Philadelphia, in order to obtain equal job opportunities for Negroes.[31] Faced with further boycotts, the Pepsi-Cola Company and Gulf Oil in Philadelphia then quickly capitulated and hired Negroes for positions from which they had previously been excluded.[32]

Consumers' boycotts may sometimes involve the publication of "unfair," "black," "closed," "we don't patronize," and "fair" lists or the use of a union label as a means of guiding purchasing power.[33] "Selective buying campaigns" encouraging patronage of named firms with nondiscriminatory hiring practices—as distinct from listing firms *not* to be patronized—have sometimes been used as means of sidestepping laws against boycotts in some American states.[34]

72. Nonconsumption of boycotted goods

Rejection of boycotted products may be extended to the point of not using them even though they are already in one's possession, when their use would therefore not involve any further purchase. Nonconsumption of boycotted goods cannot exist without a consumer's boycott, but the latter can exist without the former. The nonconsumption method facilitates social pressure against purchase of the goods, for no one can excuse himself by saying he already had the items. Although it is rare and is largely auxiliary to a consumers' boycott, this method has been regarded as a distinctive type of action—for example during the American colonial noncooperation struggles. Nonconsumption was then listed with the nonimportation of British products and the various other "non's" in the program. For example, one of the clauses of the Continental Association, the plan of resistance adopted by the First Continental Congress at Philadelphia in September 1774, declared:

> As a non-consumption agreement, strictly adhered to, will be an effectual security for the observation of the non-importation, we, as above, solemnly agree and associate, that, from this day, we will not purchase or use any tea, imported on account of the East-India company, or any on which a duty hath been or shall be paid; and from and after the first day of March next, we will not purchase or use any East-India tea whatever; nor will we, nor shall any person for

or under us, purchase or use any of those goods, wares, or merchandise, we have agreed not to import, which we shall know, or have cause to suspect, were imported after the first day of December, . . . [except for goods imported between December 1 and February 1 and sold at the direction of the local committee, with profits going to the relief of the poor suffering from the closure of the port of Boston].[35]

73. Policy of austerity

The voluntary giving up of luxuries as part of a nonviolent action struggle contains elements of both symbolic nonviolent protest and of economic boycott. Such austerity may have one or more consequences. It may demonstrate to the opponent and to vacillating potential resisters the depth of the actionists' feelings. Austerities may also have certain psychological influences on the people practicing them, such as increasing the intensity of their commitment to the struggle. Very frequently too— and this is the reason for classifying this method among economic boycotts—giving up the use and purchase of luxuries may have a detrimental economic effect on the opponent.

One of the most important instances of the use of this method was by American colonists. Austerities were then very closely associated with various types of economic boycotts, especially the nonimportation of British goods. One prominent form which the policy of austerity took during the struggle against the Stamp Act in 1765-66 was the extreme simplification of the mourning practices, which at the time were very elaborate and involved expensive imported English goods. Costly mourning clothes for the widow or widower were abandoned, for example, as was the practice of handing out fancy gloves and scarves to other mourners. An agreement to practice this type of austerity, along with others, was signed by fifty Boston merchants in 1764 in anticipation of the enactment of the Stamp Act. Once this austerity was in operation, expensive mourning was soon abandoned in New Hampshire, Rhode Island, New Jersey, New York and Philadelphia. Such renunciation was estimated at the time to have saved more than ten thousand pounds sterling a year.[36] Imported laces and ruffles were also discarded, and expensive lamb was given up in order to make mutton more plentiful. Native substitutes for tea were encouraged, and local manufactures, including American linen, were encouraged.[37]

The use of American products and the adoption of austerities were recommended in another nonviolent campaign several years later: the Continental Association, adopted by the First Continental Congress. The

Continental Association document included a long paragraph on a policy of austerity:

> We will, in our several stations, encourage frugality, economy, and industry, and promote agriculture, arts, and the manufacturers of this country, especially that of wool; and will discountenance and discourage every species of extravagance and dissipation, especially all horse-racing, and all kinds of gaming, cock-fighting, exhibitions of shews, plays, and other expensive diversions and entertainments; and on the death of any relation or friend, none of us, or any of our families, will go into any further mourning-dress, than a black crape or ribbon on the arm or hat, for gentlemen, and a black ribbon and necklace for ladies, and we will discontinue the giving of scarves at funerals.[38]

Such recommendations were widely applied throughout the colonies, taking such forms as abandoning public college commencements, closing at least one puppet show, discouraging public dancing and feasting, refusing to use foreign liquors and imported beers, canceling public balls and fairs, discouraging gambling and horse racing, and encouraging considerable efforts to promote American manufactures.[39]

74. Rent withholding

The withholding of rent is a form of economic boycott practiced by persons renting land or property who feel they have a just grievance against the landlord. Individually or collectively they may withhold payment of further rent until a satisfactory agreement has been reached. This is sometimes also called "rent refusal" or "rent strike." The withholding may be for only a short period, after which the back rent is paid up in full—in which case the withholding becomes a token demonstration. If the rent refusers intend to press the issue, however, they must be willing to face eviction and prosecution. In some states of the United States rent withholding has in recent years been legalized under some conditions to enforce housing codes and so on.

Withholding rent has been widely practiced: in colonial New York, Russia, Ireland, Wales, and modern New York City. In June 1766 between four and five hundred farmers from Dutchess County, Province of New York, and others from Albany and Westchester counties, resolved to refuse to pay rent. They went further and decided also to rescue the men already imprisoned for nonpayment of rent and threatened to march on New York City.[40] When the Tsar decreed the emancipation of the serfs in 1861, many of them were highly disappointed at the decree's failure to acknowledge that the land belonged to them, as they believed, even though they had themselves been owned by the nobility. Many of them expected that a new, more liberal decree including this point would be forthcoming, and therefore refused to comply with certain new regulations imposed on them. This refusal included nonpayment of money due to their former masters in exchange for the land which the ex-serfs still used, as well as refusal to render further services to them or to sign agreements with them.[41]

Refusal by Irish peasants to pay "unjust rents" was one of the main methods of resistance adopted by the National Land League, founded in Dublin in October 1879, under the leadership of Charles S. Parnell, M.P., for the purpose of achieving "a reduction of rack-rents" and "to facilitate the obtaining of the ownership of the soil by the occupiers of the soil."[42] A leaflet of the Land League addressed "To the people of Ireland" read, in part:

> The Government of England has declared war against the Irish people. The organization that protected them against the ravages of landlordism has been declared "unlawfully criminal." A reign of terror has commenced. Meet the action of the English Government with a determined passive resistance. The No Rent Banner has been raised, and it remains with the people now to prove themselves dastards or men,
>
> PAY NO RENT.
AVOID THE LAND COURT.[43]

Speaking widely throughout Ireland, Parnell stressed the self-reliance of the Irish and the need for persistence if victory was to be won:

> Depend upon it that the measure of the Land Bill of next session will be the measure of your activity and energy this winter—it will be the measure of your determination not to pay unjust rents. . . . If you refuse to pay unjust rents, if you refuse to take farms from which others have been evicted, the land question must be settled, and settled in a way that will be satisfying to you. It depends therefore, upon yourselves, and not upon any Commission or any Government.[44]

In early 1965 the owners of 234 house trailers renting sites from St. Donats Holiday Estates, in Nash, Monmouthshire, Wales, refused to pay their rents in protest against a rent increase, as well as deteriorating conditions and facilities.[45]

The final example of rent refusal offered here began in 1963 in Harlem, New York City, as a protest against extreme slum conditions and the failure of landlords to make repairs; the rent strike was led by Mr. Jesse Gray. On November 1 the tenants of sixteen buildings were taking part, but by mid-January 1964, five thousand families in three hundred buildings were reported to be refusing to pay their rent. Furthermore, the strike was reported to have spread to the Lower East Side, Brooklyn and the Bronx. Early that month a New York City civil court judge ordered the tenants to continue withholding rent from landlords and to pay them to the court, which would in turn release the money to landlords only for the purpose of making repairs. Mayor Robert Wagner proposed legislation which would in effect make rent strikes legal in cases of substandard conditions if the money was paid into a special fund to be used for repairs and services—for which the landlord would be charged.[46]

75. Refusal to rent

In contrast to refusal to pay rent for an existing tenancy, refusal to rent involves the refusal of the prospective tenant to rent a residence or land as part of a collective action of noncooperation. In the late 1870s, for example, in pressing for an improvement in their status, Russian peasants "collectively refused to rent even the most indispensable fields when offered at ruinous prices."[47] The Irish no-rent campaign, described in the previous method, included a refusal to rent land from which others had been evicted.

76. National consumers' boycott

The national consumers' boycott involves a refusal by a major part of the consumers of a single country to buy products or use services from another country with which they are in conflict. Such a boycott may be practiced by the people of an independent country, a colony, or an otherwise subjected country seeking to regain its independence.

Motivation for such a boycott may be 1) to weaken or refuse to strengthen the opponent economically; 2) to strengthen the home economy by increased use of home-produced products; 3) to seek self-purification for past preference for foreign goods which may have contributed to the loss of economic independence and hence of political independence; 4) to symbolize revolt against political suppression or injustices; 5) to supplement a broader noncooperation movement against the foreign power, aimed at a restoration of political independence; 6) to force the opponent to right specific wrongs and to desist from such wrongs in the future; or 7) a combination of these. The general motivation is thus national—to weaken the opponent country and to strengthen one's own country in order to achieve some national goal. The national boycott may be against specific goods or services, against all the goods and services of the offending country, or against foreign products in general. Several of the methods of the economic boycott described in this chapter may be used simultaneously.

As already noted, China is often regarded as the classic home of the national consumers' boycott. The Chinese boycotts against Japan in 1908, 1915 and 1919 are examples.[48] However, the Americans were doing very well at this type of boycott in the late eighteenth century. They quite effectively used the national economic boycott (along with nonimportation, nonexportation and nonconsumption of boycotted products) on a wide scale in several campaigns—achieving thereby the repeal of the Stamp Act and the Townshend Acts taxes (except on tea). A still more comprehensive plan for national economic boycott was contained in the Continental Association, adopted by the First Continental Congress in October 1774. This included refusal by the American colonials to import from Britain, export to Britain, or use British and certain other imported products. The Continental Congress declared that this program constituted "the most speedy, effectual and peaceable measures" for righting the colonists' grievances.[49] (The various measures were to be put into effect in stages, with the nonexportation provisions not becoming operative until September 10, 1775—by which time there had been a major shift toward violent rebellion, so that the plan was not fully implemented.)

The spirit behind national consumers' boycotts may vary considerably. This is clear from the cases mentioned and also is reflected in Gandhi's thinking about such boycotts during the Indian struggles. The Indian noncooperation movement of 1920 included a call for merchants and traders to sever foreign trade relations by boycotting foreign goods and actively encouraging home industries.[50] In the 1930-31 campaign Gandhi backed an immediate and complete boycott of all foreign cloth. However, Gandhi then still regarded an extensive economic boycott of the opponent as coercive and hence not permissible under his code of nonviolence. With Gandhi in prison in 1930, however, the nationalist movement turned to a wider boycott of British goods and services than Gandhi would have sanctioned at the time. This included a boycott of almost all British goods, State-owned post offices, and British-owned or -operated telegraph systems, shipping lines, streetcars, and banking and insurance institutions.[51] In January 1932, after Gandhi had returned from the second Round Table Conference, the All-India Working Committee of the Indian National Congress once more sanctioned the extension and renewal of the extensive boycott of goods and services. Its resolution stated:

> Even in nonviolent war, boycott of goods manufactured by the oppressors is perfectly lawful, inasmuch as it is never the duty of the victim to promote or retain commercial relations with the oppressor. Therefore, boycott of British goods and concerns should be resumed and vigorously prosecuted.[52]

Gandhi gradually became more sympathetic to an extensive economic boycott of the opponent and eventually favored an economic boycott of an aggressor nation.

77. International consumers' boycott

A consumers' boycott operating in several countries against the products of a particular country because of a given grievance may be called an international consumers' boycott. In contrast to the above method, not only are consumers in several countries involved, but the issue itself is normally a broader humanitarian one of international concern. It is distinguished from government embargoes, which are discussed later in this chapter. Examples of the international consumers' boycott include the boycott of Spanish goods in 1909 in protest against the execution of Francisco Ferrer,[53] the boycott of Hungarian goods in 1920 in protest against the Hungarian government's repression of labor,[54] and the boycotts of South African goods from 1960 on.[55]

ACTION BY WORKERS AND PRODUCERS

78. Workmen's boycott

This involves a refusal by workers to work with supplies or tools "which have been manufactured under conditions objectionable to organized labor and whose continued manufacture is interpreted by such labor as constituting a menace to its welfare."[56] This type of boycott has been used against foreign products, prison-made goods and materials, goods made by new machinery regarded as a threat to jobs, goods produced by nonunion men, and inferior goods produced under bad working conditions.[57] In 1830, for example, the journeymen stone cutters of New York imposed a boycott on convict-cut stone and also made ef-

forts to get others to refuse to work stone from the state's prisons.[58]
In 1885 members of the Knights of Labor on the Union Pacific Railroad, its branches, and Jay Gould's Southwestern system refused to handle or repair the rolling stock of the Wabash Railroad Co. because of that company's hostility to the Knights of Labor.[59] About 1900 the U.S. Journeymen Stone Cutters Association required its members not to finish or set machine-cut stone, which was seen as contributing to the loss of jobs for the stone cutters.[60] From 1896 to about 1910 the United Brotherhood of Carpenters and Joiners refused to install building trim manufactured in nonunion mills which employed women and children.[61]

79. Producers' boycott

The producers' boycott, or "selling strike," [62] involves a refusal by producers to sell or otherwise deliver their products. It may even involve a refusal to produce the product, so that delivery becomes impossible. This form of noncooperation may be practiced by any type of producer, from farmers to manufacturers. The reasons may vary. In one case the motive may be a desire to boost prices by reducing available goods on the market. In another it may be a means of supporting boycotted fellow producers. At other times the producers' boycott may be part of a wider noncooperation movement directed against a hostile or occupying regime.

The examples offered here range from the days of the Roman Empire to Nazi-occupied Netherlands and Japanese-occupied China. Toward the end of the second century A.D., at Ephesus in Asia Minor, the shop managers of bakeries (most of whom were also owners) held meetings which were apparently concerned with common grievances, and collectively stopped making bread. These activities were the subject of an edict of the Roman Proconsul of Asia: he forbade them to hold meetings, demanded that they obey the regulations, and ordered them "to supply the city unfailingly with the labour essential for bread-making." [63]

Norwegian peasants in the eleventh century refused to deliver to the king either men or provisions for his military expeditions against Denmark, Sweden and England. As a consequence, the wars were brought to a complete halt.[64] In the American colonies a few American newspapers suspended publication after November 1, 1765, when the Stamp Act went into effect, in order to avoid the legal requirement to use such tax stamps on each newspaper.[65]

In 1886 in the United States the Brewers' Association attempted to counter union-initiated consumer boycotts of particular breweries by ruling that no member of the association could sell "beer, porter or ale" to any retail customers of another brewery in the association which was involved in a boycott; the aim was thus to force retailers to buy the boycotted beer by cutting off other supplies.[66] In 1932 there was widespread refusal by farmers in the United States to sell milk and livestock until prices had improved.[67]

This type of economic boycott occurred also in Nazi-occupied Europe. In the Netherlands in late April 1943, in solidarity with striking anti-Nazi urban workers Dutch farmers refused to deliver milk to dairy factories.[68] And in Poland during at least the early years of the German occupation, despite many pressures, "the peasants developed many ways of outwitting them [the Nazis], managing by shrewd devices to save food for themselves and either to turn over to the Germans the most inferior produce or to destroy what they could not salvage."[69] In occupied North China it had proved impossible for the "Border Government"—which was a kind of resistance organization-*cum*-parallel government—to prevent the sale of the 1937 cotton crop to the Japanese. Therefore, it instructed peasants to reduce cotton production by about seventy percent and to use the land so released to produce food, which the peasants did—and hence there was less cotton for the Japanese.[70]

ACTION BY MIDDLEMEN

80. Suppliers' and handlers' boycott

A suppliers' and handlers' boycott involves a refusal by workers or middlemen (wholesalers, jobbers and distributors) to handle or supply certain goods. The reasons for this refusal may include: 1) objection to the use to which the goods are to be put, such as by struck firms or in wars or by antipathetic regimes; 2) objection to the intrinsic nature of the goods; and 3) objection to the conditions under which the goods have been produced (slavery, *Apartheid* or oppression, or milder conditions deemed unfair to organized labor, such as sweatshops or employment of strikebreakers).

There are many examples of this form of boycott in support of strikes. In 1912 in Italy, for instance, a boycott was called in support of a marble quarry strike. By refusing to load sand destined for the boycotted quarry the workmen in neighboring towns made it impossible to cut marble, even had the firm successfully obtained strikebreakers.[71] Also, trade unions have often made efforts to convince producers and suppliers to refuse supplies to firms against which they were conducting a consumers' boycott.[72]

K.G.J.C. Knowles regards such a refusal to handle goods as a form of the sympathetic strike,[73] and there are situations in which the suppliers' and handlers' boycott and the sympathetic strike merge, primarily if the former is carried out on a large scale. In the summer of 1894, for example, the American Railway Union headed by Eugene V. Debs ordered its members to refuse to work on any train to which a Pullman car was attached, thus indicating their support for the striking employees of the Pullman Palace Car Co. This soon developed into a major sympathetic strike, as nearly all trains to Chicago included Pullman cars.[74]

A handlers' boycott was imposed on coal in Britain in 1925. The owners of the coal mines had given a one-month notice of the termination of the National Wages Agreement of 1924—the end of which would have cut earned wages between ten and twenty-five percent. Unionists responded with a ban on the movement of coal after July 31, when the notice went into effect, imposed by the General Council of the Trades Union Congress.[75]

In 1942 on the island of Lewis, also in Britain, dockworkers belonging to the same union as the island's spinners refused to handle not only imported weaving yarn sold at prices which threatened the economic welfare of the spinners, but also the finished cloth made from this cheap yarn.[76] British dockworkers in 1920 refused to load arms destined for use against Russian revolutionaries; in 1937-38 dockers at Liverpool, Glasgow and Southampton refused to load arms to be used by Japan against China; and in 1946 New Zealand and Australian trade unionists refused to load arms for use against the Indonesians.[77] In 1943 Portuguese cinema owners refused to show German films; ultimately Goebbels concluded that Germany would have to buy its own motion picture theatres in Portugal.[78] This method has also been given atypical expression on two occasions, when American brokerage firms refused to sell bonds from Southern states involved in brutal actions against civil rights workers. After June 1964—the time of the civil rights murders in Philadelphia, Mississippi—Baxter & Co. of New York and Cleveland refused to handle bonds from Mississippi and Alabama; and in the spring of 1965—after Governor Wallace had announced that the state did not have enough money to protect civil rights marchers from Selma to Montgomery—Childs Security Corporation informed the governor that it would not deal in the state's bonds since his statement had made clear that it was a poor financial risk.[79]

A very different case of handler's boycott by paper mill workers, combined with a selective strike by linotypists, was applied by Communist-controlled trade unions in Czechoslovakia in the period before the

Communist *coup*. "Several times, as the result of an article critical of the Soviet Union or the policy of the Communist Party, workers in paper mills refused to deliver paper to democratic newspapers in Prague and Bratislava or to load or unload it, and linotypists refused to set up the paper." [80] In February 1948—still in the pre-*coup* period—similar action was taken again. "In Bratislava, the capital of Slovakia, printers refused to run the Democratic Party presses. In Bohemia, workers in several paper mills refused to produce paper for National Socialist and Catholic newspapers; railwaymen refused to load and unload it." [81]

During the 1951-53 conflict which followed Iran's nationalization of the Anglo-Iranian Oil Co., the international oil cartel gave notice that shipping firms which allowed their tankers to transport oil from Iran's newly-nationalized oil company would receive no more shipping business from companies affiliated with the cartel. As a consequence, no more than forty tankers dared to transport Iranian oil overseas during the whole period of Mossadegh's government (April 1951-August 1953). [82]

ACTION BY OWNERS AND MANAGEMENT

81. Traders' boycott

The traders' boycott involves a refusal by retailers to buy or sell certain goods. Just as producers and suppliers may refuse to sell their products to particular firms in furtherance of their economic interests, so retailers may elect to make their purchases from particular producers and wholesalers for similar reasons. [83] Political motives or national grievances may also furnish reasons for such actions.

The traders' boycott may in addition involve a refusal to sell certain products even though they may already be in his possession. Such refusal may be carried out, for example, in support of widespread consumers' boycotts of foreign goods during wider national struggles. In 1930, in addition to canceling foreign orders, Indian cloth merchants sometimes refused to sell foreign cloth already on their shelves because of the extensive consumers' boycott of such cloth during the campaign for independence. [84] During the Chinese boycott of Japanese goods in 1919, Chinese merchants also refused to buy or sell Japanese goods, even when they had them in stock. [85]

The American colonists' Continental Association of 1774 pledged that from December 1 of that year traders would ". . . wholly discontinue the slave trade, and will neither be concerned in it ourselves, nor will we hire our vessels, nor sell our commodities or manufactures to those who are concerned in it." [86]

82. Refusal to let or sell property

Owners of houses or other buildings or property may refuse to offer them for rent or sale to certain persons or groups for a variety of reasons. This method, which has been widely applied in the United States against Negroes and other groups, was also widely used in nineteenth century China against Christian missionaries—for Westerners were regarded as "barbarians" and "foreign devils." A missionary reported that in August 1868 efforts to rent some thirty different houses in Yang-chou, Kiangsu province, had failed before one was found which the owner would rent to the missionary; the house was later attacked by a mob.[87]

83. Lockout

In a lockout the employer—not the workers—initiates the work stoppage when he temporarily closes down the operation of a particular firm or other economic unit as a means of forcing employees into line.[88] The shutting down of operations of this type is clearly within nonviolent action. However, the use of public or private armed police or troops in behalf of the management would introduce violence into the lockout, just as violence by workers or employers would bring violence into strike situations. In strikes, of course, it is the workers who bring the operations to a halt by withdrawal of their labor, as described in detail in the next chapter. In a particular industrial conflict it is sometimes difficult to determine whether the stoppage began as a strike or a lockout.

A lockout may be applied by a single firm. It has also been applied simultaneously by a large number of employers in an area or industry, using a kind of sympathetic lockout in an effort to deal with workers. For example, in England in the 1860s employers' associations instituted a general lockout of *all* men in a particular industry in order to bring under control dissident employees in one or two firms. This was particularly widespread in 1865 when Staffordshire ironworkers and shipbuilding operatives on the Clyde in Scotland were locked out.[89]

The lockout is usually applied in industry but not always. In England when farm laborers attempted to form unions in 1833-34 the employers' response was frequently a lockout, such as one near the village of Chipping Norton in Oxfordshire. Similarly, in 1874, when the agricultural unions sought payment of thirteen to fourteen shillings for a fifty-four-hour week, there was an immediate widespread lockout in the Eastern and Midland counties, with over ten thousand union members put out of work.[90] These examples make clear that a lockout occurs when the employer suspends his activities as employer, not simply when certain doors are physically locked against the employees.

Lockouts were used in the United States against the Knights of Labor, especially in 1886. In New York State in that year fifteen thousand laundry workers were put out of work by lockouts in Troy, and twenty thousand knitters at Cohoes and Amsterdam, while in Chicago twenty thousand packinghouse workers were locked out.[91] In Russia, as the tide of the 1905 Revolution ebbed, industrialists formed organizations to resist trade union advance by means of common action which included lockouts.[92]

84. Refusal of industrial assistance

Economic or political opposition may under special circumstances be expressed by the refusal to provide desired economic and technical assistance and advice. For example, in 1936, in an effort to counter the demand by steel industrialists for a significant price rise, Göring sought to establish a new government steel plant, the Hermann-Göring-Works. The majority of steel producers in Germany, however, tried to defeat Göring's new project by proposing that "none of the private steel firms should lend any assistance" to the new government steel plant. (Krupp and Röchling, however, fully cooperated with the Göring-Works).[93]

85. Merchants' "general strike"

Whereas a general strike involves a withdrawal of labor by workers, a paralysis of the economy of a city or region may also be caused by the simultaneous closing of stores and businesses by the merchants. Such action would not only affect small shops and stores run by a single person or family, but would also close larger businesses without the initiative of the employees. For example, in 1742 a general strike of merchants *(pa-shih)* took place in several districts of northern Kiangsu, China, in disapproval of the way the local official had conducted relief work following a flood.[94] When a merchants' "general strike" is combined with a general strike of workers, the result is an "economic shutdown," which is described in the following chapter on strikes.

ACTION BY HOLDERS OF FINANCIAL RESOURCES

86. Withdrawal of bank deposits

Money deposited in private or government banks or government savings systems may be withdrawn either as an expression of protest against the government or as a means of noncooperation intended to help overthrow an unsteady government. For example, the withdrawal of bank deposits was called for at least twice during the 1905 Revolution in Russia—first by the All-Russian Peasant Union at its founding conference in midsummer 1905, in case the government should seek to repress the Union,[95] and second, by the St. Petersburg Soviet on December 2, 1905. This was designed to weaken foreign confidence in the Russian economy and government and thus prevent the government from obtaining a foreign loan to be used to combat the revolution. To the embarrassment of the government, there were extensive withdrawals of funds from banks in the following weeks, apparently as a result of the call.[96]

In a very different context, in December 1966 a moderately successful appeal was made to depositors of the First National City Bank and the Chase Manhattan Bank, urging them to withdraw their deposits from those banks and to place them elsewhere, because of the banks' financial involvement in the South African economy.[97]

87. Refusal to pay fees, dues and assessments

Individuals, groups, or governments may on occasion deliberately refuse to pay fees, dues, or assessments to a private organization, public institution, government, or international body. Norwegian teachers in 1942 refused to make voluntary payments to a new fascist-controlled teachers' organization.[98] Japanese students in 1947 used the refusal to pay university fees as a means of demonstration.[99] Probably the best-known example is the refusal of Soviet bloc countries, France, Belgium and Portugal to pay their share of the costs of the United Nations forces in the Congo, on the ground that *ad hoc* expenses of that special operation could not legally be regarded as "expenses of the organization" under the terms of the Charter, payment of which was obligatory for members.[100]

88. Refusal to pay debts or interest

Nonpayment of debts (or, rarely, refusal to pay only the interest due) has also been used as a method of economic boycott. This primarily occurs when the debts are owed to an opponent or to persons or firms in a country whose government is the opponent. Sometimes an attempt has been made to apply this method to government debts; people have been urged not to pay taxes for government debts, or foreign creditors have been warned that if they loan money to a tottering regime, the debt will not be honored when the government falls. This was attempted in the Financial Manifesto of the St. Petersburg Soviet in December 1905 [101] and in the Vyborg Manifesto, signed by about two-thirds of the members of the *Duma* after the Tsar and dissolved it on July 21, 1906:

> Therefore, now that the Government has dissolved the Duma, you [the people] are justified in giving neither money nor soldiers. If the Government contracts loans to procure funds, these loans are invalid without the consent of the people's representatives. The Russian people will never recognise them and will not feel itself called upon to repay them. [102]

Nonpayment of debts has been most demonstrably effective, however, where it was applied to private debts to private persons or firms in the course of a political struggle with a government, that is, in the American colonists' struggles against British rule from London. This method was used especially in 1765 and 1766, in the struggle against the Stamp Act. Most of the trade between Britain and British North America was on credit, with the latter a heavy borrower. Clearly, stopping trade would have had severe economic repercussions in England; but stopping payment of debts resulted in a more severe and a more rapid economic squeeze. Payment of debts was halted well before the Act went into effect, for by August 1765 a Bristol merchant already reported: "We have no Remittances, and are at our Witts End for Want of Money to fulfill our Engagement with our Tradesmen." [103]

One of the reasons that English merchants were later unable to use the courts to collect debts, as usual, was that frequently the courts themselves closed rather than use the tax stamps on legal documents or operate without them in defiance of the law. Sometimes the decision to close the courts had been taken to prevent their being used to collect debts to English merchants. George Washington clearly suggested this tactic on September 20, 1765, several weeks before the Stamp Act went into effect:

> Our Courts of Judicature must inevitably be shut up; for it is impossible . . . under our present Circymstances that the Act of Parliament can be complied with . . . and if a stop be put to our judicial proceedings I fancy the Merchants of G. Britain trading to the Colonies will not be among the last to wish for a Repeal of it. [104]

Horace Walpole later described the situation which resulted:

> But the weapon with which the Colonies armed themselves to most advantage, was the refusal of paying the debts they owed to our merchants at home, for goods and wares exported to the American provinces. These debts involved the merchants of London, Liverpool, Man-

chester, and other great trading towns, in a common cause with the Americans, who forswore all traffic with us, unless the obnoxious Stamp Act was repealed. [105]

Gipson reports that the debts amounted to some four million pounds sterling and that these "were now wielded as a club with telling force." [106] In the summer of 1774, prior to the First Continental Congress, there was discussion in the newspapers of New York and Philadelphia as whether once again to use this method in the then current conflict. [107] Some local bodies had already begun to refuse to pay debts or to allow use of the courts for collecting them. For example, on May 25 of that year, following the British closure of the port of Boston, a meeting of inhabitants of Annapolis resolved that, in addition to a nonimportation and nonexportation agreement, no suit in law be brought "for the recovery of any debt due from any inhabitant of this province to any inhabitant of Great-Britain, until the said act be repealed." [108] One of the resolves passed by Westmoreland County, Virginia, under the leadership of men like Richard Henry Lee, the county's representative in the House of Burgesses, was that for the duration of the planned nonexportation agreement, the lawyers of the county should not "bring any writ for the Recovery of Debt, or push to a Conclusion any such Suit already brought." [109]

An instance of refusal to pay interest on loans, while continuing to repay the principle of the loan, took place in Germany shortly before the Nazi rise to power, when the "Nazified leaders" of middle-class organizations organized not only campaigns against the foreclosure of farms, but also collective refusal by the farmers to pay interest on their bank loans. [110]

89. Severance of funds and credit

Economic pressures can also be exerted by cutting off the opponent's sources of money, such as salaries, appropriations, loans and investments. This may be done by individuals, firms, or governments. In certain American colonies, the assemblies withheld appropriations for the salaries of governors and judges as a means of keeping them from acting too much out of line with the assemblies' political wishes. [111]

Segregationist whites in the southern United States have cut off bank credit as well as other types of credit to individual Negroes who have been active in abolishing segregation. [112] Also, when school officials in Prince Edward County, Virginia, were ordered in May 1955 to integrate the school system, in which fifty-three percent of the pupils were Negro, the officials immediately and unanimously cut off all funds for the operation of public schools in that county. Without public schools, there could be no integration in public schools.[113] When the Virginia legislature met in August 1956 to consider thirteen antiintegration bills, House Bill No. 1 proposed by Governor Thomas Stanley was to cut off state school funds from any school district which integrated. State money amounted to forty-two percent of operating costs. The bill passed both houses, though only narrowly in the Senate.[114] Later, Prince Edward County officials resumed appropriation of funds to operate the schools, but not on the usual annual basis. Instead, appropriations were made on a monthly basis, "with a publicly declared intention of discontinuing that appropriation if schools in the county are mixed racially at this time," reported Federal Judge Sterling Hutcheson in a decision on January 23, 1957.[115] Opposition to the abandonment of public education developed, however, and that form of resistance was discontinued.

Federal funds and contracts have been withheld or withdrawn from various types of activities—such as welfare and education—which did not conform to established federal standards or practices, especially where there was racial discrimination. James Farmer has described "the withdrawal of financial support from any discriminatory activity" as the "most powerful weapon" available to the federal government. "If the threat of economic withdrawal were made palpable, an army of Southern bigots would alter their ways."[116] There have also been various calls for the withdrawal of foreign investments from South Africa as a means of abolishing *Apartheid.*[117]

90. Revenue refusal

This method involves a refusal by the resisters to provide the government with revenue voluntarily. Since such revenue is owed to a government, or an agency of it, and is required by statute or regulation, this method may also be classed as political noncooperation. Where this action is more than symbolic its most important characteristic usually is the withholding of financial resources from the government; where the political disobedience element is dominant, however, this method would fall primarily within political noncooperation. But it is both economic and political in form.

This method involves the refusal to pay various types of taxes—including income taxes, property taxes (rates), sales or purchase taxes—or the refusal to purchase certain required licenses (dog, car, radio, television, and the like) either as a protest against a particular injustice directly related to the license in question or as a symbol of a wider protest against the government. Revenue refusal might also involve the boycott of goods on whose sale there is a sales or purchase tax. Where land or property rent is paid to the government, these may also be refused. A related way of denying funds to the government (though not technically revenue) is to refuse to purchase government loans and bonds, national savings accounts, and so on, and the withdrawal of such existing loans and deposits.

In advanced stages of a struggle, the resister may sell taxed items but refuse to collect or pay the tax. Whereas the refusal to purchase loans or to use national savings accounts as a means of providing revenue to the government is usually legal, the refusal to pay taxes or rents to the government is illegal—this is a direct refusal of supplies to the government. The refusal of revenue is usually regarded as a very strong expression of disapproval of the government. Where it is undertaken in large numbers it may become a severe threat to the existence of the government, either because of the threat to the State's treasury or because of the extent and depth of the population's refusal to submit to the regime, as indicated by the extremity of their resistance. Collective refusal of taxes is probably an ancient method, as reports from Egypt are frequent as early as the second century, for example. [118]

Norwegian peasants rebelled against greatly increased taxes demanded by the Danish King Christian II to support his war against Sweden from 1515. The peasants refused to pay taxes and killed tax collectors; in turn, they were severely repressed. [119] Widespread peasant tax refusal, especially along the Norwegian coast around the 1630s, led to both repression and tax reform. [120] Another major tax rebellion occurred in Norway in 1764 and 1765 in protest against high taxes, presumed corruption of the tax collectors, and such practices as government seizure for tax payments of the farmers' and fishermen's indispensable tools. In Romsdal "the peasants absolutely refused to pay and drove the tax-collectors away. In 1764 there was unrest along the whole coast, and everywhere less and less of the tax went in," although the 1762 and 1763 taxes had been fully paid. There was a massive demonstration in Bergen and intimidation of officials. Even in the period after repression less than half the assessed taxes were collected in most places. [121]

Refusal to pay certain taxes by boycotting the taxed goods, especially during the Stamp Act struggle, was one of the methods of resistance used prior to the American War of Independence, as has been mentioned repeatedly in examples of other methods. During the French Revolution of 1789 refusal to pay taxes and feudal dues was very widespread. [122] When the Third Estate, joined by some clergy, constituted itself as the National Assembly on June 17, 1789, it attempted to protect itself from counterattack by the King by authorizing refusal to pay taxes; only future taxes approved by the National Assembly were legal, and existing taxes were payable only while it continued in session.[123] By the end of 1789 "everyone refused to pay former taxes and fees."[124]

Both Hsiao Kung-ch,üan and Chang Chung-li report in their studies of their studies of nineteenth-century Chinese society that several cases of organized tax refusal occurred in China around 1860.[125] In Hungary in 1861 there was massive resistance to the collection of taxes under Austrian laws, the tax collectors being politely told that they were "illegal persons."[126] During the first two and a half years of the 1902 and 1914 tax refusal campaign in England that was directed against tax aid for parochial schools, 70,000 summonses were issued, and there were 254 imprisonments.[127]

During the 1905 Russian Revolution payment of taxes was often refused by the populace seeking the overthrow of the tsarist regime. In Georgia, for example, neither taxes nor dues were paid.[128] On two occasions the revolutionaries offically launched refusal of taxes as a major part of a resistance program to topple the regime. The first was urged by the St. Petersburg Soviet on November 23 and December 2, 1905 (the Financial Manifesto), and was stimulated by Parvus' study of the regime's economic problems.[129] The second was the famous Vyborg Manifesto signed by about two-thirds of the members of the dissolved *Duma* on July 23, 1906. Since consent of the people's representatives gave government its right to tax and to conscript soldiers ". . . now that the Government has dissolved the *Duma,* you are justified in giving neither money nor soldiers . . . . Be firm in your refusal . . ."[130]

Tax refusal was also an important form of resistance during the Indian independence struggles, in both local and national campaigns.[131] In Germany, prior to the Nazi rise to power, the pro-Nazi leaders of certain middle-class organizations used tax strikes (among other means) to oppose "unfair" competition, foreclosure of farms, and the like.[132] Nonpayment of taxes was part of the nonviolent resistance program adopted in April 1953 by the Nyasaland African Congress to defeat the imposition of the Central African Federation despite united black African opposition.[133] In 1956 ten Welshmen were prosecuted for having refused to pay for their radio licenses because the British Broadcasting Corporation maintained the Welsh Service on a wavelength which was subject to serious evening interference from an East German station.[134] Africans were being arrested in Northern Rhodesia in September 1962 for refusing to pay the poll tax and for not having identity certificates, which they had burned in 1961 as a sign of defiance against the government.[135]

A case of tax refusal in 1966 has been reported from Eastern Angola, where it took place at a time when guerrilla warfare was the major means of African resistance to the Portuguese. This account, from the American peace worker James Bristol, is based on his conversations with an Angolan nationalist leader in Lusaka, Zambia:

> Recently, he told me, they had been able to organize a tax refusal movement in a group of villages. Apparently, the system has called for the chiefs to collect taxes from the people and then turn the money over to the Portugese. Twelve chiefs refused to demand the taxes from the people; they stated that there was unemployment on a large scale, and that as long as this unemployment continued and they could see no tangible benefits from the taxes they paid, they would refuse to give orders to their people to pay taxes. The 12 chiefs were arrested, and taken away by plane to another part of Angola. As they were in the plane, the Portugese pointed out to them how powerful they, the Portugese, were; they had weapons, they had these big planes; the Angolans had nothing. The chiefs replied that the Portugese still could not force the people to do what they had decided not to do. They were put in jail; they were questioned; they were threatened, but still they refused to give the order for the people to pay the taxes. Finally, the Portugese said that they would release them and take them back to their villages, on condition that the chiefs engage in no further subversive action. The chiefs replied that they *would continue to oppose* the payment of unjust taxes and other injustices imposed by the Portugese. But after a time the Portugese released them anyhow, and returned them to their villages. [The Angolan leader] . . . said that the Portugese know how to handle the guerrillas, but not how to deal with this sort of united resistance by the villagers themselves.[136]

Refusal of revenue can also take the form of refusing to pay fines and court costs. For example, in Americus, Georgia, in the fall of 1963, the local Sumter County civil rights movement announced: "Don't forget that our fines and court costs every morning are helping to pay for new police cars and extra policemen who are just here to intimidate Negroes." In consequence, for weeks the income from payment of fines, court costs, and bail bonds averaged only five hundred dollars weekly instead of the normal two to three thousand dollars.[137]

91. Refusal of a government's money

This method is the refusal, as a political act, to accept a government's printed money, either completely or in all but minor transactions. In other situations the motives could be partly economic (in case of high inflation). Alternatives to the printed money might be gold, silver, barter, and the like. This method appears to have been deliberately used with the intent of undermining a regime only rarely. The Financial Manifesto of the St. Petersburg Soviet, referred to in the discussion of the preceding method, not only asked that gold be demanded when deposits were withdrawn from banks, but also urged people to demand gold in payment for wages and in all major financial transactions. [138]

ACTION BY GOVERNMENTS

92. Domestic embargo

A domestic embargo may be briefly defined as an economic boycott initiated by the government to operate within its own country. This method of noncooperation was applied, for example, in Nazi Germany between 1933 and 1935 as part of the Nazi cartel program. In July 1933 two cartel laws were issued, one of which authorized the State to form compulsory cartels and to regulate investments, while the other authorized the Minister of Economics to supervise cartel prices and to deal with firms which were not cartel members. One way this supervision operated was to limit the firms allowed to trade in coal, both as wholesalers and retailers. No firm not a cartel member could expect delivery of coal. Dealers not on the approved list because they were deemed unsuitable or unnecessary were driven out of business, both by a boycott (apparently a consumers' boycott) and by the delivery embargoes imposed by the cartel court in accordance with the above laws, or, after a decree from the Minister of Economics, simply by the court's chairman. As a result of these and other government measures, approximately 2,000 of 54,000 coal dealers were put out of business in two years. Similar action occurred in the radio industry; in one year during this time the number of radio retailers was reduced from 60,000 to 37,000, and of radio wholesalers, from 1,500 to 750. [139]

93. Blacklisting of traders [140]

During wartime or during a policy of embargo, one government may seek to block indirect transfer of embargoed goods through firms or individuals in a neutral country by prohibiting trade with them as well as with the enemy country itself. A blacklist of such traders is normally published, and transactions with them prohibited. At times, however, the blacklist remains unpublished, becoming a "graylist" which may cause a listed firm to "lose time waiting for a deal to go through before it realizes that it has been listed and seeks other arrangements," as Professor Thomas C. Schelling has written. These were standard United States practices during World War II.

94. International sellers' embargo

An international sellers' embargo is a refusal by government decision to sell certain or all products to another country. The action may be taken by one or several governments; it is normally national and the effect international. The motives may vary from objections to the existence of the regime itself (arising from its political orientation or from the means it used to come to power or to maintain itself) to objections to a particular policy or action of the country. In some cases, however, the international seller's embargo may be an attempt to halt or prevent a war or, under the guise of that objective, to assist one side by preventing sales of arms to the weaker side.

When the British King on October 17, 1807, proclaimed the right of impressment of neutral merchant vessels, measures stronger than the recent ban on importation of various articles of British manufacture were deemed to be necessary in the United States. In accordance with "Jefferson's doctrine, that foreign nations could be coerced by peaceable means into respect for neutral rights . . . ," the President obtained from Congress the permanent Embargo Act, which was intended to coerce Europe by stopping supplies to West Indian colonies and by halting the export of cotton and corn to Europe. This was to be done by placing an embargo on all shipping owned by United States citizens to prevent them from transporting such supplies for sale. Jefferson was successful in getting the country to adopt "the experiment in peaceable coercion." (Various Republicans had argued that a standing army would be dangerous to popular liberties.) "In the scheme of President Jefferson's statesmanship, non-intercourse was the substitute for war—the weapon of defense and coercion which saved the cost and danger of supporting an army or navy and spared America the brutalities of the Old World." The embargo encountered widespread economic problems, and evasion and violation by Americans; the army and navy had to be used to enforce it at home. Jefferson and his policy became highly unpopular, and after the election of

Madison as President the embargo laws were repealed [141] but replaced with a similar nonintercourse policy.

The embargo on arms during the Chaco War of 1933–36 between Bolivia and Paraguay is another example of this method. [142] Attempts to apply economic sanctions against Italy during its attack on Ethiopia in 1935–36 constitute a further example. [143] In 1950 the United States government imposed an embargo on Communist China, prohibiting ships registered in the United States from calling at Chinese ports and banning United States exports to Communist China. [144] This remained in force without major relaxation for about twenty years.

95. International buyers' embargo

The international buyer's embargo involves the prohibition of general or particular purchases from a specific country. Again, the motives vary: the intent may be to produce a change in a particular policy, to force a broader modification in the regime, or to contribute to the downfall of the regime. Examples of an international buyer's embargo include the Non-Importation Act of April 18, 1806 (before the Embargo Act), which prohibited the import of various articles of British manufacture and made their possession illegal. As the historian Henry Adams put it:

> The measure was in its. nature coercive. The debates in Congress showed that no other object than that of coercion was in the mind of the American government; the history of the Republican Party and the consistent language of Jefferson, Madison, and the Virginian school proclaimed that the policy was their substitute for war. England was to be punished, by an annual fine of several million dollars, for interference with American trade to the continent of Europe. [145]

Stronger measures were required, however, before this Act could really take effect, and the Embargo Act was pushed through Congress. It was repealed on March 1, 1809, by the Non-Intercourse Act, which also contained provisions to exclude all British and French vessels from United States waters and forbade the import of British and French goods. [146]

96. International trade embargo

An international trade embargo is a combination of the international seller's embargo and the international buyer's embargo. It involves a total prohibition of trade with the opponent country, or a near-total ban, exempting perhaps medicines and the like. For example, after the news of the armed engagements at Lexington and Concord, the British government passed the Prohibitory Bill, which barred all trade and commerce with the rebellious colonies, under the threat of the seizure of all ships and cargoes. [147] (Where this ban was effective because of voluntary acceptance or possible economic sanctions against British violators, it falls within this technique; however, the use of naval power to enforce the ban combines the economic sanction with military action.)

International economic sanctions have been seen by various American political leaders as alternatives to military action. Sometimes their recommendations have clearly referred to a complete cessation of all trade: at other times the extent and types of the embargoes recommended have been left more flexible. Halt to international trade of all types by government initiative was seen by Thomas Jefferson as an alternative to war sometime before the particular measures cited under the two methods above. As early as March 1793, in a letter to James Madison, Jefferson contemplated what action should be taken if the naval powers blockaded France, at the time of the French Revolution, stopping imports of supplies and provisions. Jefferson wrote:

> Should this be formally notified I should suppose Congress would be called, because it is a justifiable cause of war, & as the Executive cannot decide the question of war on the affirmative side, neither ought it to do so on the negative side, by preventing the competent body from deliberating on the question. But I should hope that war would not be their choice. I think it will furnish us a happy opportunity of setting another precious example to the world, by showing that nations may be brought to do justice by appeals to their interests as well as by appeals to arms. I should hope that Congress instead of a denunciation of war, would instantly exclude from our ports all the manufactures, produce, vessels & subjects of the nations committing this aggression, during the continuance of the aggression & till full satisfaction made for it. This would work well in many ways, safely in all, & introduces between nations another umpire than arms. It would relieve us too from the risks & horrors of cutting throats. [149]

Referring to the means of enforcing the antiwar provisions of the League of Nations Covenant, President Woodrow Wilson said in the autumn of 1919:

> If any member of the League breaks or ignores these promises with regard to arbitration and discussion, what happens? War? No, not war but something . . . more tremendous than war . . . .
>
> Apply this economic, peaceful, silent, deadly remedy and there will be no need for force . . . .

The boycott is what is substituted for war. [149]

In 1932 John Foster Dulles, who later became Secretary of State, wrote:

> The great advantage of economic sanctions is that on the one hand they can be very potent, while on the other hand, they do not involve that resort to force which is repugnant to our objective of peace.
>
> If any machinery can be set up to ensure that nations comply with their covenant to renounce war, such machinery must be sought primarily in the economic sphere. [150]

On February 3, 1962, the United States government applied an international trade embargo against Cuba. Under the Department of State declaration of October 1960, American exports to Cuba had already been prohibited. The Presidential proclamation of February 3, 1962, however, extended its scope by placing an embargo on *all* trade with Cuba. [151]

International embargoes of all three types have not produced many notable successes. Peter Wallensteen points to the small proportion of successes they had between 1933 and 1967. [152] How much of this lack of success is a result of intrinsic limitations of these methods and how much is a consequence of insufficient care in their application and an unwillingness to apply them seriously remain to be investigated. [153]

Wallenstein cites two successful cases during this period. British economic sanctions against the Soviet Union in 1933 ended with a negotiated agreement between the governments, removal of the sanctions, and release of arrested British subjects. [154] The other case involved the Dominican Republic in 1960–62, with economic action being imposed by the United States and the Organization of American States in condemnation of Dominican participation in an attempt to assassinate President Betancourt of Venezuela. The real objective, however, was condemnation of the Trujillo dictatorship in the Dominican Republic itself. In May 1961 Trujillo was assassinated, but apparently this was unconnected with the economic sanctions, which were continued for six more months, until all members of the Trujillo family had left the country to ensure a real change in the regime. [155]

A very large number of the methods of economic noncooperation involve the withdrawal of labor, and we now turn to the various methods of the strike.

NOTES

1. This definition is adapted from those offered by Harry Laidler, "Boycott," **Encyclopedia of the Social Sciences** (New York: Macmillan, 1935, vol. II, pp. 662-66; Laidler, **Boycotts and the Labor Struggle, Economic and Legal Aspects** (New York: John Lane Co., 1913), pp.27 and 55; Leo Wolman, **The Boycott in American Trade Unions**, Johns Hopkins University Studies in Historical and Political Science, Series XXXIV, No. 1 (Baltimore: Johns Hopkins Press, 1916), pp. 11-12; and Clarence Marsh Case, **Non-violent Coercion: A Study in Methods of Social Pressure** (New York: Century Co., 1923), pp. 320-24.

2. See Case, **Non-violent Coercion**, p. 305.

3. *Ibid.*, pp. 314-15; Wolman, **The Boycott in American Trade Unions**, p. 41.

4. Wolman, **The Boycott in American Trade Unions**, p. 24; see also Laidler, "Boycott," pp. 663-664; and Philip Taft, **The A.F. of L. in the Time of Gompers** (New York, Harper and Bros., 1957) pp. 264-266.

5. John King Fairbank, **The United States and China** (Cambridge, Mass.: Harvard University Press, 1958) pp. 167-168. I am grateful to Carl Horne for this reference.

6. Case, **Non-violent Coercion**, p. 316.

7. Wolman, **The Boycott . . .** , p. 14; see also Reynolds, **Labor Economics and Labor Relations**, p. 134.

8. Laidler, "Boycott," p. 665.

9. Schlesinger, **The Colonial Merchants and the American Revolution**, p. 82.

10. Gipson, **The Coming of the Revolution, 1763-1775**, p. 204.

11. L. L. Bernard, **Social Control in Its Sociological Aspects·** (New York, Macmillan Co., 1939), p. 386.

12. Case, **Non-violent Coercion**, pp. 332-340; Taft, **The A. F. of L. in the Time of Gompers**, pp. 268-271; and Wolman, **The Boycott . . .** , pp. 80-82.

13. Wolman, **The Boycott . . .** , p. 28.

14. *Ibid.*, p. 41.

15. *Ibid.*

16. Bernard, **Social Control . . .** , pp. 393-395.

17. *The Times* (London), 31 January 1957.

18. Martin Luther King, Jr., **Stride Towards Freedom.** The boycott is reported to have cost the bus company between $3,000 and $3,500 a day, in addition to major financial losses to the white-owned businesses in the center of Montgomery. (William Peters, **The Southern Temper**, [Garden City, N.Y.; Doubleday & Co., 1959] , p. 232.)

19. *Observer,* (London) 23 August 1959.

20. *The Times,* 6 July 1959.

21. Josef Korbel, **The Communist Subversion of Czechoslovakia 1938-1948: The**

Failure of Coexistence (Princeton, N.J.: Princeton University Press, 1959), p. 57. Also a personal letter dated 22 December 1966.

22. Josef Korbel, personal letter dated 22 December 1966.

23. Karski, **The Story of a Secret State**, p. 259.

24. Miller, **Nonviolence**, pp. 273-275, and Luthuli, **Let My People Go**, pp. 174-178.

25. Miller, **Nonviolence**, p. 275.

26. *Ibid.*, and Luthuli, **Let My People Go**, pp. 217-219.

27. Venturi, **Roots of Revolution**, p. 191.

28. Sternstein, "The *Ruhrkampf* of 1923", p. 116.

29. Arna Botemps, **100 Years of Negro Freedom**, (New York: Dodd, Mead & Co., 1962) p. 254.

30. Louis E. Lomax, **The Negro Revolt** (New York: New American Library, Signet Book, 1963), p. 143.

31. *Peace News*, 26 August 1960.

32. Hannah Lees, "The Not-Buying Power of Philadelphia's Negroes," **The Reporter**, vol. 24, no. 10 (11 May 1961), pp. 33-35.

33. Wolman, **The Boycott . . .** , pp. 33, 34 and 42; and Laidler, **Boycotts and the Labor Struggle**, pp. 60-63.

34. Waskow, **From Race Riot to Sit-in**, p. 239.

35. Text quoted from Schlesinger, **The Colonial Merchants . . .** , p. 609.

36. Morgan and Morgan, **The Stamp Act Crisis**, p. 50. See also Schlesinger, **The Colonial Merchants . . .** , p. 77.

37. Schlesinger, **The Colonial Merchants . . .** , pp. 73-74, 76-77.

38. *Ibid.*, p. 610.

39 *Ibid.*, pp. 483, 486, 492, 500-503, 508-509, 518-519, and 528.

40. Gipson, **The British Empire Before the American Revolution**, vol. XI, **The Triumphant Empire: The Rumbling of the Coming Storm, 1766-1770**, p. 49.

41. Venturi, **Roots of Revolution**, p. 101.

42. G. Locker-Lampson, **A Consideration of the State of Ireland in the Nineteenth Century** (New York: E. P. Dutton & Co., 1907, and London: Archibald Constable & Co., Ltd., 1907), p. 372.

43. H. O. Arnold Forster, **The Truth About the Land League, Leaders and its Teaching** (pamphlet - London: National Press Agency, Ltd., published for the Property Defence Association, 1883), p. 57.

44. From a speech at Ennis on September 19, 1880. Quoted in Patrick Sarsfield O'Hegarty, **A History of Ireland Under the Union, 1880-1922** (with an Epilogue carrying the story down to the acceptance in 1927 by the De Valera of the Anglo-Irish Treaty of 1921) (London: Methuen Press, 1952) p. 491.

45. *Peace News*, 5 February 1965.

46. Nat Hentoff, **The New Equality** (New Edition; (New York: Viking Press, 1965) pp. 201-202. See also **New York Times**, 7 January 1964.

47. Venturi, **Roots of Revolution**, p. 576.

48. Case, **Non-violent Coercion**, pp. 330-342.

49. Schlesinger, **The Colonial Merchants . . .** , p. 608. These boycott campaigns are highly significant, in terms not only of early American history, but of the history of nonviolent action generally and the potentialities of economic boycotts. For details of these campaigns, see the following studies, all of which

contain references to original sources: Schlesinger, **The Colonial Merchants . . . ,** esp. pp. 78, 97, 104-121, 157, 179, 185, 194, 215-219, 300-301, 312-315, 324, 339-340, 344, 351-353, 356-357, 360-363, 366, 369, 398-399, 402, 414-419, 427 and 608-609. Gipson, **The Coming of the American Revolution,** esp. 104, 106-107, 114-115, 187-188, 196-198, 203-205, 208-209, and 230. Gipson, **The British Empire ....** Vol. XI esp. pp. 84, 143, 145, 181-190, 242, 254, and 256n. *Ibid.,* vol. XII, **The Triumphant Empire, Britain Sails Into the Storm, 1770-1776,** esp., pp. 152-153, 207, 217, 251, and 254.

50. Case, **Non-violent Coercion,** p. 383.

51. Sharp, **Gandhi Wields the Weapon of Moral Power,** pp. 125-127.

52. Pattabhi Sitamarayya, **The History of the Indian National Congress, 1885-1935,** vol. I, p. 870.

53. Laidler, "Boycott," p. 666.

54. *Ibid.*

55. See William A. Hance, "Efforts to Alter the Future Economic Action" for a good discussion of international economic boycott and other economic sanctions in relation to South Africa, in Amelia C. Leiss, editor, **Apartheid and United Nations Collective Measures,** (New York: Carnegie Endowment for International Peace, 1965) pp. 95-130.

56. Wolman, **The Boycott . . . ,** p. 43.

57. *Ibid.,* pp. 44-49.

58 *Ibid.,* p. 23.

59. *Ibid.,* p. 59.

60. *Ibid.,* p. 45.

61. *Ibid.,* pp. 49-52.

62. Bernard, **Social Control . . . ,** p. 385.

63. W. H. Buckler, "Labour Disputes in the Province of Asia Minor", in W. H . Buckler and W. M. Culder, eds., **Anatolian Studies Presented to Sir William Mitchell Ramsay** (Manchester, England: The University Press, 1923), p. 31. See also, Rostovtzeff, **The Social and Economic History of the Roman Empire,** vol. II, p. 621, no. 45.

63. Andreas Holmsen, *Norges Historie Fra de Eldste Tider til 1660,*(Third Edition: Oslo and Bergen: *Universitetsforlaget,* 1964), p. 179. Professor Holmsen has written to me about this case: "What is maintained on p. 179 in my book about the farmers' opposition against Harald Hardràde's frequent raids against Denmark around 1050, is only a reasonable conclusion based on the fact that gradually the raids had to be abandoned. There are no sources specifically saying that this was caused by the farmers' opposition."

64. Morgan and Morgan, **The Stamp Act Crisis,** p. 241.

66. Wolman, **The Boycott . . . ,** p. 39.

67. Bernard, **Social Control . . . ,** p. 385.

68. L. de Jong, "Anti-Nazi Resistance in the Netherlands," in **European Resistance Movements 1939-1945. First International Conference on the History of the Resistance Movements held at Liege-Brusseles-Breendonk, 14-17 September 1958** (Oxford: Pergamon Press, 1960), p. 141.

69. Karski, **The Story of a Secret State,** p. 255.

70. Taylor, **The Struggle for North China,** pp. 114-115. I am grateful to Abraham Halperin for this reference and certain others on China.

71. Wolman, **The Boycott . . . ,** p. 42.

72. Laidler, **Boycotts and the Labor Struggle**, pp. 64-65.

73. K.G.J.C. Knowles, **Strikes – A Study in Industrial Conflict with Special Reference to British Experience Between 1911 and 1945** (New York: Philosophical Library, 1952; Oxford: Basil Blackwell, 1954), p. 17.

74. Case, **Non-violent Coercion,** p. 315, and Wolman, **The Boycott in American Trade Unions,** p. 32, and Almont Lindsey, **The Pullman Strike: The Story of a Unique Experiment and of a Great Labor Upheaval** (Chicago and London: University of Chicago Press, Phoenix Books, 1964 [orig. 1942]).

75. Symons, **The General Strike,** pp. 13-15.

76. Knowles, **Strikes,** p. 17.

77. *Ibid.*

78. Lochner, ed., **The Goebbels Diaries,** pp. 508-509.

79. James Farmer, **Freedom – When?,** p. 117.

80. Korbel, **The Communist Subversion of Czechoslovakia,** p. 144.

81. *Ibid.,* p. 227.

82. Bahman Nirumand, **Iran: The New Imperialism in Action** (New York and London: Modern Reader Paperback, 1969), p. 70. I am grateful to James Prior for this reference.

83. Laidler, **Boycotts and the Labor Struggle,** p. 49.

84. Sharp, **Gandhi Wields . . . ,** p. 166.

85. Case, **Non-violent Coercion,** pp. 337-339.

86. Schlesinger, **The Colonial Merchants . . . ,** pp. 608-609.

87. Hsiao, **Rural China,** pp. 488 and 496.

88. Fitch, "Strikes and Lockouts."

89. Sidney and Beatrice Webb, **The History of Trade Unionism. Revised Edition to 1920** (New York: Longmans, Green & Co., 1920), pp. 255-256.

90. *Ibid.,* pp. 332-334.

91. Joseph G. Rayback, **A History of American Labor,** (New York: Macmillan, 1964), p. 174.

92. Seton-Watson, **The Decline of Imperial Russia,** p. 228.

93. Arthur Schweitzer, **Big Business in the Third Reich** (Bloomington; Indiana University Press, 1964; London: Eyre & Spottiswoode, 1964), p. 539.

94. Hsiao, **Rural China,** p. 247.

95. Seton-Watson, **The Decline of Imperial Russia,** p. 230.

96. Richard Charques, **The Twilight of Imperial Russia** (London: Phoenix House, 1958), p. 135, and Harcave, **First Blood,** p. 232.

97. "An Appeal" (leaflet), issued in New York City by the Committee of Conscience Against Apartheid and a list of sponsors.

98. Sharp, **Tyranny Could Not Quell Them.**

99. Shimbori, *"Zengakuren,"* p. 247. Shimbori does not supply any details.

100. King Gordon, **U. N. in the Congo: A Quest for Peace** (New York: Carnegie Endowment for International Peace, 1962), p. 150, and Catherine Hoskyns, **The Congo Since Independence: January 1960-December 1961** (London: Oxford University Press, 1965), pp. 295 and 467.

101. Harcave, **First Blood,** p. 232.

102. This is quoted from the text of the Manifesto, from R. W. Postgate, **Revolution**

from 1789 to 1906 (New York, Harper Torchbooks, Harper & Brothers, 1962), p. 391.

103. Gipson, The Coming of the Revolution, p. 106.

104. Quoted by Gipson, The British Empire Before the American Revolution, vol. X, The Triumphant Empire: Thunder-Clouds Gather in the West, 1763-1766, p. 360.

105. Quoted by Ibid., pp. 106-107.

106. Ibid., p. 107.

107. Schlesinger, The Colonial Merchants . . . , pp. 404-405.

108. Quoted by Gipson, The British Empire . . . , vol. XII, p. 194.

109. Ibid., p. 202.

110. Arthur Schweitzer, Big Business in the Third Reich (Bloomington, Ind.: Indiana University Press, 1964 and London: Eyre and Spottiswood, 1964) p. 88.

111. Gipson, The Coming of the American Revolution, p. 175.

112. Waskow, From Race Riot to Sit-in, p. 279.

113. Benjamin Muse, Virginia's Massive Resistance (Bloomington: Indiana University Press, 1961), p. 13.

114. Ibid., pp. 29-30.

115. Quoted by Ibid., pp. 59-60.

116. Farmer, Freedom — When?, p. 178.

117. Luthuli, Let My People Go, p. 210.

118. Rostovtzeff, The Social and Economic History of the Roman Empire, vol. I, p. 348.

119. Holmsen, Norges Historie Fra de Eldste Tider til 1660, pp. 386-387. See pp. 413-414 for a fairly localized case of tax refusal by Norwegian peasants in Gauldai, Trøndelag, from 1573.

120. Ibid., p. 451.

121. Magnus Jensen, Norges Historie Under Eneveldet 1660-1814 (Third Ed.; Oslo and Bergen: Universitetsforlaget, 1963) , pp. 83-84.

122. Lefebvre, The French Revolution from its Origins to 1793, pp. 120, 127, 157-158 and 184, and Salvemini, The French Revolution, 1788-1792, pp. 120, 131, 165, 170 and 209.

123. Salvemini, The French Revolution, 1788-1792, p. 124.

124. Lefebvre, The French Revolution from its Origins to 1793, p. 134.

125. Hsiao, Rural China, p. 305, and Chang, The Chinese Gentry, p. 46.

126. Griffith, The Resurrection of Hungary, p. 32.

127. Case, Non-violent Coercion, pp. 230-231.

128. Keep, The Rise of Social Democracy in Russia, p. 160.

129. Ibid., pp. 240-241 and Charques, The Twilight of Imperial Russia, p. 135.

130. The full text appears in R. W. Postgate, Revolution from 1789 to 1906, p. 391.

131. See Desai, The Story of Bardoli, and S. Gopal, The Viceroyalty of Lord Irwin 1926-1931, pp. 19-34. Pattabhi Sitaramayya, The History of the Indian National Congress, 1885-1935, vol. I, p. 605, and, Sharp, Gandhi Wields . . . pp. 106-211 passim.

132. Schweitzer, Big Business in the Third Reich, p. 88.

133. **Report of the Nyasaland Commission of Inquiry** Cmnd. 814 (London: H. M. Stationery Office, 1959), p. 11.
134. **Bulletin of the Non-violence Commission of the Peace Pledge Union** (London), no. I, March 1956.
135. *Guardian,* 5 September, 1962.
136. Letter from James Bristol dated 8 October 1966, from Lusaka, Zambia, to Stewart Meacham.
137. Nat Hentoff, **The New Equality**, p. 55.
138. Harcave, **First Blood**, p. 232.
139. Schweitzer, **Big Business in the Third Reich**, pp. 269-287.
140. This section is based upon discussion by Thomas G. Schelling, **International Economics** (Boston: Allyn and Bacon, 1958), pp. 488-489.
141. Henry Adams, **History of the United States During the Second Administration of Thomas Jefferson** (New York: Charles Scribners' Sons, 1890), vol. II, pp. 166-177, and Adams, **The Formative Years** (Cond. and ed. by Herbert Agar; London: Collins, 1948), vol. I, pp. 458-466, and vol. II, 487-542. The quotations are respectively from **The Formative Years**, vol. I, p. 461; **History . . .** , vol. II, p. 176; **The Formative Years**, vol. II, p. 495.
142. The Royal Institute of International Affairs, **International Sanctions** (London: Oxford University Press, 1938), pp. 27-30, and F. P. Walters, **A History of the League of Nations** (London: Oxford University Press, 1960), pp. 131, 393-395, 525-536, and 787.
143. Walters, **A History of the League of Nations**, pp. 623-691; Royal Institute of International Affairs, **Sanctions** (Second Edition; London: R.I.I.A., 1935), and R.I.I.A., **International Sanctions**; and G. W. Baer, **The Coming of the Italian-Ethiopian War** (Cambridge, Mass.: Harvard University Press, 1967), see esp. Chapt. 12.
144. See **American Foreign Policy, 1950-1955: Basic Documents** (Washington: Department of State, 1957), vol. II, p. 2595, and **American Foreign Policy: Current Documents, 1956** (Washington: Department of State, 1959), pp. 1085-1095.
145. Adams, **History of the United States During the Second Administration of Thomas Jefferson**, vol. II, pp. 165-166.
146. Adams, **The Formative Years**, vol. II, pp. 540-542.
147. Gipson, **The British Empire . . .** , vol. XII, pp. 346-349.
148. H. A. Washington, ed., **The Writings of Thomas Jefferson** (Washington, D. C.: Taylor and Maury, 1853), vol. III, p. 519. I am grateful to Michael Schulter and Ron McCarthy for this information.
149. Hamilton Foley, **Woodrow Wilson's Case for the League of Nations** (Princeton: Princeton University Press, 1933, and London: Humphrey Milford, Oxford University Press, 1933), pp. 67, 71 and 72.
150. John Foster Dulles, "Practicable Sanctions," in Evans Clark, ed., **Boycotts and Peace** (New York and London: Harper & Bros., 1932), p. 21.
151. See **American Foreign Policy: Current Documents, 1960** (Washington, D.C.: Department of State, 1964), pp. 240-241, and Department of State **Bulletin**, vol. XLVI, pp. 283-284.
152. Peter Wallensteen, "Characteristics of Economic Sanctions," **Journal of Peace Research** (Oslo), 1968, no. 3, pp. 250-51.

153. The reader is referred to other literature specifically dealing with international economic sanctions, including the following: Baer, **The Coming of the Italian-Ethiopian War**, especially Chapter 12; Clark, ed., **Boycotts and Peace** (this report contains a bibliography); Johan Galtung, "On the Effects of International Economic Sanctions, with Examples from the Case of Rhodesia," **World Politics**, vol. XIX, no. 3 (April 1967), pp. 378-416; Frederik Hoffmann, "The Functions of Economic Sanctions, A Comparative Analysis," in **Journal of Peace Research**, 1967, no. 2, pp. 140-60; Amy Leiss, ed., **Apartheid and the United Nations: Collective Measures** (New York: Carnegie Endowment for International Peace, 1965); Ronald Segal, ed., **Sanctions Against South Africa** (Baltimore: Penguin Books, 1964); Rita Falk Taubenfeld and Howard J. Taubenfeld, "The 'Economic Weapon': The League and the United Nations," **Proceedings of the American Society of International Law**, 1964, pp. 184-205 (this article is largely based on the cases of Italy, Cuba, Dominican Republic, China, and South Africa); Wallensteen, "Characteristics of Economic Sanctions," pp. 248-67; Walters, **A History of the League of Nations**.

154. Wallensteen, "Characteristics of Economic Sanctions," p. 251.

155. *Ibid.*

PART TWO: METHODS

6

The Methods of Economic Noncooperation: (2) The Strike

INTRODUCTION

The second general subclass of methods of economic noncooperation is the strike. The strike[1] involves a refusal to continue economic cooperation through work. It is a collective, deliberate and normally temporary suspension of labor designed to exert pressure on others within the same economic, political and, sometimes, social or cultural unit. That is to say, though the issues are normally economic, they are not necessarily so, even though the means of action are economic. The aim of a strike is to produce by this leverage some change in the relationships of the conflicting groups. Usually this takes the form of granting of certain demands made by the strikers as a precondition for their resumption of work. It is the collective nature of the strike which gives this type of noncooperation its characteristics and power. Strikes are largely associated with modern industrial organizations; they also occur, however, in agricultural conflicts and within various institutions. Strikes are possible wherever people work for someone else.

Strikes are almost always specific, in the sense of being *for* or *against* something which is important to the strikers. In theory any number of workers might act together to produce a strike, but in practice the number of strikers must be sufficiently large to disrupt seriously or to make impossible continued operations of at least that economic unit. As with violence and other more powerful forms of nonviolent action, the mere *threat* of a serious strike may be sufficient to induce concessions from the opponent group; some examples of such threats are included in this chapter. Strikes may be spontaneous or planned, "official" (authorized by the unions) or "wildcat" (not authorized by the unions).

The motives for strikes vary considerably. Economic motives, which include wages, working conditions, union recognition, and hours, have been predominant. Even these types of strikes may be directed against a government agency, though an employer is usually the target. Political and social aims may accompany economic objectives or may be independent of them. Those wider issues may take many forms.

Now to the classification of the forms of the strike. The broad categories which must be used in classifying the many methods of nonviolent action are too rigid to suit the reality, as we noted at the beginning of Part Two. Consequently, in every general class and subclass—such as the strike—there are some methods which also have one or more characteristics of another class (or do so under certain conditions) or which differ in at least one respect from the general characteristics of its class. This is especially true in the case of the strike. Normally, the strike is a temporary withdrawal of labor, but there are methods in which the withdrawal is, or at least is intended to be, permanent. Also, some methods are combinations of economic boycotts and strikes. Other methods operate by withdrawing labor but do so only symbolically, so that they might also be included within the class of nonviolent protest and persuasion. One solution might be to develop a much more complicated classification system than that offered in this book; that indeed needs to be done, for there are many methods which should have at least dual classifications. Also, the effects and leverages of particular methods differ with the situation in which they are applied and the manner in which they are conducted. For our purposes here, however, several methods which fall on a borderline between classes or which have mixed characteristics are grouped within the strike, coming closer to belonging here than in any other class or subclass of the methods. This is instructive and humbling, for the reality of social dynamics is always more complex and flexible than the intellectual tools which we use in efforts to understand it. Three of the groupings of methods of the strike which follow consist of such borderline forms or are offspring of mixed parentage. These are often some of the fresher, more imaginative ones; because they are less usual or because they combine more than one type of leverage or population group, they may also make a disproportionate impact.

SYMBOLIC STRIKES

97. Protest strike

In a protest strike,[2] also called token strike[3] and demonstration strike,[4] work is stopped for a preannounced short period—a minute, an hour, a day, or even a week—in order to make clear the feelings of the workers on a particular issue: economic, political, or other.[5] No set demands are made. The aim is to demonstrate that the workers feel deeply about a certain matter and that they possess strength to strike more effectively if necessary, thus warning the officials that they had best take the workers' feelings into consideration. An additional aim may be to catch the imagination of workers and the public. This method may also be used in the early stages of a protracted struggle to accustom the workers to the idea of striking on the issue involved; in instances in which the unions are not prepared for a longer strike; where longer strikes would incur more severe retaliation than the workers are, at that particular point, prepared to suffer; or where serious damage to the economy is not desired. The token strike may be varied by combining it with periods of silence, "stay-at-home" days, or other methods. There may be protest general strikes, protest industry strikes, protest sympathy strikes and the like.

On January 15, 1923, four days after the Franco-Belgian invasion of the Ruhr, the population of the Ruhr area and the occupied Rhineland held a thirty-minute protest strike to express their will to resist.[6] A one-day strike to protest the ill-treatment of the Jews was called in Amsterdam on February 25-26, 1941.[7] Other examples include a one-hour strike on April 10, 1959, by about five hundred building workers in a factory making rockets in Stevenage, Hertfordshire, England, in support of the unilateral renunciation of nuclear weapons;[8] the ten- to fifteen-minute work stoppage by nine million people in Belgium (half the population), as a demonstration against nuclear weapons, which occurred at 11 A.M. on May 8, 1962;[9] the one-day strike (except on ships at sea, troop carriers, and relief ships) by various U.S. maritime unions in protest against delays in bringing servicemen home after World War II.[10]

Protest strikes were frequent during the Russian 1905 Revolution. In February, for example, streetcar workers in Astrakhan held a one-day strike,[11] and in October the printers in St. Petersburg held a three-day strike to show sympathy for the striking printers of Moscow.[12] A conservative bureaucrat described the November strike movement in the capital: "One day the barbers would strike; another day it would be the restaurant and hotel employees. No sooner would these strikes end than the newsboys would strike; then it would be the salesmen in stores."[13]

A twenty-four-hour protest general strike was held in Ireland on April 23, 1918, and was solidly observed throughout the country, except in Belfast. "Factories stood idle, shops and bars were closed, transport was stopped," writes Edgar Holt. "It was now clear that Southern Ireland had no intention of standing patiently by in the remote hope that conscription, when the Government chose to impose it, would be accompanied by Home Rule."[14]

Several short protest strikes were conducted in Czechoslovakia the week after the Russian invasion in August 1968. On August 21 at 12 noon, only hours after the invasion, in response to a call for a two-minute protest strike issued by representatives of the creative artists' unions and broadcast on television and radio, all movement on the streets of Prague came to a halt.[15] A broadcast plea from the North Bohemian region brought about a one-hour general strike starting at noon the following day.[16] The Declaration of the Extraordinary Fourteenth Party Congress of the Communist Party of Czechoslovakia on August 22 contained a call for a one-hour protest strike at noon on Friday, August 23. Appeals were posted that morning that everyone leave the streets of Prague during that hour. "Prague is to become a dead city." The Communist Party newspaper *Rude Pravo* reported that strike as seen in the center of Prague:

> From the National Museum, a line of young people marches down Wenceslas Square. They are holding hands and shouting: "Evacuate the streets!" Behind them there is only the empty, wide space of the Square. The sirens begin to wail; car horns join them. The soldiers in tanks look around. They don't know what is going on. They are scanning buildings on either side, watching the windows. Some of the tanks are closing their hatches. The machine guns and cannon are turning around, looking for targets. But there is no one to shoot at; nobody is provoking them. The people have begun a general strike, as proclaimed by our Communist Party.
>
> All of a sudden Wenceslas Square is empty; only dust, papers,

posters rise up in the wind. All that is left are tanks and soldiers. Nobody around them, none of our people. [17]

98. Quickie walkout (lightning strike)

Short, spontaneous protest strikes undertaken without deliberation to "let off steam" or to protest over relatively minor issues have come to be known as quickie walkouts in the United States[18] and lightning strikes in England;[19] they rarely last more than a few hours or involve more than a few workers in a plant. This is one of the form which wildcat strikes may take. They were fairly common in the United States during World War II in situations where major strikes were banned. Jack Barbash cites an example of such a walkout by department store workers because of inconveniences in a new pay system and the company's misrepresentation of the union's attitude toward the employment of a handicapped worker.[20] In the summer of 1963 a lightning strike occurred on the Paris *Métro*. (The government in turn sought legislation to require at least five days' strike notice.)[21]

AGRICULTURAL STRIKES

99. Peasant strike

Under feudal and semifeudal conditions peasants have collectively refused to continue to work on the properties of their landlords. The examples here are Russian. In 1861 peasants in the department of Kazan were influenced by Anton Petrov, a peasant political prophet, to begin a series of actions in which they would rely on themselves alone to improve their living conditions. These included peasant strikes. "The peasant communities met together in assemblies and began by deciding on collective abstention from all work on the landlords' properties."[22] During the 1905 Revolution, the second congress of the Peasants' Union resolved upon the "refusal of conscript military service and peasant strikes on the large landed estates"[23] as methods for advancing their demands for a change in the system of land ownership and for an early constituent assembly. In the autumn of 1905, strikes by agricultural laborers were reported from the provinces of Kiev, Volhynia, Podolia, Kharkov, Poltava, Chernigov, Saratov, Samara, Orlov, Kursk, Tambov, Moscow, Nizhny Novgorod, and Penza, and also from the Don Cossack region. At the time there was still relatively little looting and burning of estates.[24]

Peasant strikes are among the means of protest and resistance frequently used in Latin America, Solon Barraclough has written.[25] For example, in July and August 1952 Indian *campesinos* (farm workers) in Bolivia refused to work and applied other methods of nonviolent action: organizers from the Ministry of Rural Affairs and various political parties had been active among the peasants.[26] Peasant unions in Northeast Brazil in 1962 conducted a strike of over 200,000 peasants. Landlords made many concessions, and various national and regional proposals for agrarian reforms were stimulated. It has also been claimed that this strike was one factor in the military *coup* two years later; the new military regime is reported to have backed the organizations of the large farmers and to have suppressed peasant union activity. Peasant leaders were jailed, exiled, or murdered.[27]

In Peru during 1960-63, peasant strikes were conducted in the valley of La Convención. Led by Hugo Blanco, permanent laborers on the large plantations of the valley simply withdrew the labor they had provided to landlords for almost no wages. Some of the peasants were able to work instead on the plots assigned for their own use, and thereby even increased their incomes while on strike. Leaders were jailed and military force was used to crush the movement. However, a special decree was issued breaking up the large holdings in that area and selling them to peasants, and a first attempt at agrarian reform legislation for all Peru passed the legislature.[28]

100. Farm workers' strike

Farm workers hired for wages may, like any other group, withdraw their labor by striking with the aim of achieving certain objectives. The years 1929 to 1935 witnessed in California "a series of spectacular strikes" stimulated by the wage cuts of the Depression and expectations aroused by policies of the new Roosevelt administration. Carey McWilliams writes: "Beyond question, the strikes of these years are without precedent in the history of labor in the United States. Never before had farm laborers organized on any such scale and never before had they conducted strikes of such magnitude and such far-reaching social significance."[29] Migrant farm laborers expressed their unrest in spontaneous strikes, as well as organized ones.

These strikes were frequently failures and usually resulted in severe repression by both local government and unofficial groups. In January and February, 1930, for example, in the Imperial Valley two spontaneous strike movements occurred among Mexican and Filipino field workers and American workers in the packing sheds: the issues were wage reductions and demands for wage increases and improved conditions. Trade union organizers became active during the strikes and were arrested on suspicion and watched. After the strikes failed, the union called for a conference of agricultural workers for April 20, but six days before that there were raids on residences and public meeting places. Over a hundred workers were arrested and kept on forty thousand dollars bond; eight of them were convicted under the Criminal Syndicalism Act. The union was crippled.[30]

In November 1932 Communist Party organizers of the Cannery and Agricultural Workers' Industrial Union led fruit workers at Vacaville in a strike, which was met with "formidable intimidation, beatings and prosecution." Six strike leaders were kidnapped, were flogged with tug straps, had their heads clipped with sheep clippers, and had red enamel poured over them. Communists arriving in the area found 180 deputized armed vigilantes and also strikebreakers carrying gas pipes and pruning shears. After this strike was broken, other strikes occurred during 1933. Three thousand pea pickers striking in April also met wholesale arrests, floggings and general intimidation, but nevertheless they forced payment for a "hamper" (about thirty pounds) of peas up from ten cents to seventeen and twenty cents. One man was dead, however, and many injured.[31]

Repression against other farm workers' strikes included severe beatings, broken bones, shootings (resulting in injuries and death), arrests, acquittal of identified murderers of strikers, excessive bail for strikers, misuse of various laws and regulations to harass and prosecute strikers, tear gas, raiding parties, jailing of strikers in a stockade, forcible eviction from a strike camp, and burning of strikers' shacks. Agricultural workers involved in strikes during this period included pickers of various tree fruits as well as pickers of grapes, cotton and vegetables. During 1933 about fifty thousand strikers were involved; of the thirty-seven recorded strikes (there were many more), gains for strikers resulted in twenty-nine cases; in the union-led strikes the wage rates were increased from fifteen cents an hour to an average of twenty-five cents.[32]

The most famous agricultural strike in the United States in recent years has been that of the grape workers of Delano, California, under the leadership of Cesar Chavez. The strike began in September 1965, and it was not until the summer of 1970 that growers of table grapes in large numbers signed union contracts. Leading the National Farm Workers' Association, and later the United Farm Workers' Organizing Committee,

A.F.L.-C.I.O., Chavez repeatedly insisted on adherence to nonviolent discipline. The strike was supplemented by a nationwide consumers' boycott—first of all California grapes, then, after the first union contracts, of non-union grapes. In March 1966 the strikers conducted a 250 mile pilgrimage from Delano to the state capital at Sacramento to protest the spraying of pickets with insecticides and fertilizer and to publicize the boycott. Evening rallies were held along the way. At each rally the union plan was read:

> We are suffering. . . We shall unite. . . We shall strike. . . . We shall overcome . . . Our pilgrimage is the match that will light our cause for all farm workers to see what is happening here, so that they may do as we have done.[33]

STRIKES BY SPECIAL GROUPS

101. Refusal of impressed labor

Demands that certain people perform impressed labor for others have on occasion been met with a refusal to do such work. Refusal has usually been aimed at the abolition of impressed labor, rather than merely at improved conditions. In 1921, for example, in the district of Kotgiri (or Kotgarh) in India, an organized, disciplined campaign of nonviolent refusal was conducted against the very old system of *begar,* or forced labor. This system had allowed Europeans to demand at will that poor cultivators perform hard labor at extremely low wages, despite the consequent detrimental effect on the agriculture of the hill tribes. The cultivators' demands were met; a strict limitation was placed on the types of service that Europeans could demand, and reasonable rates of pay were fixed for any work performed.[34]

During the American War of Independence, the British sought to revive the former French system of *corvée* (compulsory unpaid labor) in the province of Quebec. For two years, from 1776 to 1778, Quebec farmers and villagers, such as those in Chambly, often simply refused to work on the roads or to carry out any other military transport duties. Then the British withdrew the law and abolished *corvée,* providing payment for those already "hired."[35] In 1781 in Yang-ku, Shantung, China, a scholar *(sheng-yüan)* incited villagers to refuse to do river-dredging work. (The villagers, however, also took out their anger on government property—they attacked the prison and destroyed the tax collector's office.)[36]

102. Prisoners' strike

Prisoners have also at times refused to do work required of them by prison officials; the refusal may have various motives: an objection to being incarcerated at all, an effort to improve specific conditions in the prison, or other motives. During World War II a number of strikes by conscientious objectors took place in U.S. prisons. One of these, by nineteen prisoners, began at the Federal Correctional Institution at Danbury, Connecticut, on August 11, 1943, in protest against the official policy of racial segregation at meals. After 133 days of restriction to their cells, with only limited exercise, a monotonous diet, and restrictions on visits, the prisoners noted the gradual introduction of a cafeteria system, which the strikers expected would permanently eliminate the policy of segregation.[37] During the summer of 1953 coal-mining prisoners at the huge camp at Vorkuta, U.S.S.R., conducted a strike for improved conditions,[38] as described briefly in Chapter Two. Because the area industry (coal) was involved and this was a one-industry complex, this case had additional characteristics of both the industry strike and the general strike.

103. Craft strike

"A craft strike is a suspension by the workers of a single craft in one or in many shops of a local, regional, national, or international area. The variations in geographic scope may be indicated as shop craft strike, local craft strike, regional craft strike, etc."[39] The craft strike almost always takes place where the union is a craft union rather than an industrial union which includes all the workers in a plant or industry.[40] Examples of the craft strike include the following: In 1741 the New York City master bakers struck against municipal regulation of the price of bread (the first American strike);[41] Boston journeymen carpenters struck in 1825 for a ten-hour day;[42] in January 1890 over three thousand New York cloak makers struck against sweatshop conditions;[43] and fifteen thousand shirtwaist and dress makers in New York struck from November 1909 to February 1910 for improved wages and conditions.[44]

104. Professional strike

Groups of salaried persons or self-employed persons in a particular profession may go on strike for economic, political, or other reasons. Where the motive is political, the professional strike usually takes place within the context of a wider struggle involving other sections of the population and other methods of nonviolent action, which may precede, accompany, or follow the professional strike.

An early example of a professional strike took place in Oxyrhynchus, Egypt, in A.D. 260. M. Rostovtzeff writes:

> . . . the tremendous depreciation of the currency led to a formal strike of the managers of the banks of exchange. . . They closed their doors and refused to accept and to exchange the imperial currency. . . The administration resorted to compulsion and threats. The *strategus* issued an order to the bankers and to other money-changers "to open their banks and to accept and exchange all coin except the absolutely spurious and counterfeit." The trouble was not new, for the *strategus* refers to "penalties already ordained from them in the past by his Highness the Prefect." [45]

About 200 A.D. shipmasters who took cargoes of grain from Asia Minor to Rome apparently threatened a professional strike if certain demands were not met. The Minister of Food *(praefectus annonae)* wrote to a provincial subordinate that the seafaring shipmasters of the five unions of Arles were "virtually giving notice that their service will shortly be suspended if the grievance continues." [46]

The suspension of practice by lawyers as part of a political struggle has occurred on several occasions. For example, when the courts in the American colonies were required under the Stamp Act to use tax stamps —which the colonists refused to do—lawyers frequently responded by suspending practice and seeking closure of the courts. [47] Lawyers in St. Petersburg, Russia, reacted to "Bloody Sunday" in January 1905 by refusing to appear in court and by issuing a formal protest against the "pitiless hand of the government." [48] The following October various government employees went on strike in the city: printers for the navy, actors, port and customs staff, and the State Bank's local staff. [49]

Other groups which have used the professional strike are teachers, doctors and civil servants. The teachers in Mayfield Borough, Pennsylvania, struck in January and April 1934, after working six and a half months without receiving salaries. [50] In December 1956 the general strike and economic shutdown directed against the attempt of Haitian strongman General Paul E. Magliore to stay in power despite constitutional restrictions included strikes by civil servants and bank and school employees, as well as the refusal of lawyers to accept court cases. [51]

ORDINARY INDUSTRIAL STRIKES

105. Establishment strike

An establishment strike "involves all the crafts in one or more plants under one management irrespective of their spatial distribution." [52] Examples of the establishment strike include: the strike, in February and March 1936, of Goodyear rubber workers in Akron, Ohio, for union recognition; [53] and the strike of five hundred Scandinavian Airlines System workers in Norway in March and April 1954, on the issue of wage increases. [54]

106. Industry strike

An industry strike is "a suspension of all the establishments of an industry (e.g., mining, printing, etc.) of a local or other area." [55] Local and regional industry strikes have occurred frequently. Examples include: the strike in 1902 of the United Mine Workers against the operators of the "anthracite monopoly" in eastern Pennsylvania; [56] the strike in 1912 of textile workers employed by several companies in Lawrence, Massachusetts, led by the Industrial Workers of the World; [57] the dockworkers' strike in June-July 1959, led by several unions, in Colombo, Ceylon; [58] and the July–August 1953 strike of the Cannery Workers Union (A.F.L. Teamsters), which closed sixty-eight canneries affiliated with the Canners Association in Northern California. [59] Other examples include: politically motivated strikes in the coal mines during the *Ruhrkampf*; [60] the Dutch shipyard workers' strike on February 17 and 18, 1941, which "forced local German authorities to abandon the plan of deporting workers to Germany against their will;" [61] the strike of Dutch railway workers which, beginning in September 1944 and continuing into 1945, was called for by the Dutch government-in-exile to aid the Allied armies; [62] and the Spanish strike movement in the Asturian mines in April–May 1962. [63]

107. Sympathetic strike

In a sympathetic strike workers withdraw their labor, not to help themselves, but to support the demands of fellow workers by bringing additional pressure to bear upon the employer. The two groups of workers may or may not have a common employer; the sympathetic strikers may simply believe that their participation may force other employers, the public, or the government to bring sufficient pressure to bear on the employer directly involved so that he will grant the desired concessions.[64] The sympathetic strike is reported to have originated about 1875, although the present name for it was not adopted until 1886.[65] Sympathetic strikes were illegal in Britain between 1927 and 1946.[66]

Fred Hall elaborates on motivations for the sympathetic strike:

> A sympathetic strike receives its name not so much because its motive is sympathy only . . . but because its motive is not selfish only . . . The ordinary striker protests against an injury which affects, or definitely threatens to affect, some fellow workmen, but which, he believes, will affect himself at some more or less definite time in the future. . . . Sympathetic strikers object, not to their employer's attitudes to *them,* but to his attitude toward *certain other parties*—an attitude which is hostile to labor.[67]

Examples of the sympathetic strike include: the railroad system strike in 1886, which originated on the Texas and Pacific Railroad and soon extended sympathetically to cover the entire Missouri Pacific Railroad as well;[68] and the 1924 Norwegian paper mill workers' strike in sympathy with locked-out transport workers.[69] In Imperial Russia in July 1903, sympathetic strikes were declared in Odessa, Kiev, Nikolaev and Ekaterinoslav, in support of strikes for increased wages and shorter hours in Baku, Tiflis and Batum.[70] In an unusual case, Guatemalan railroad workers in late June 1944 went on sympathy strike in support of the student strike at the National University. The ostensible purpose of this student strike was to oust the university rector, but the basic aim was to oust President Jorge Ubico, who had suspended five constitutional articles concerned with political freedoms,[71] with the consequences described in Chapter Two.

RESTRICTED STRIKES

108. Detailed strike

In the detailed strike, as originally understood, the workers one by one stop work or take up other jobs, until the employer is compelled to inquire about their grievance and is informed of their demands. This type of detailed strike was practiced by English craft unions in the middle of the nineteenth century—for example, in the case of the Flint glass makers in the years following 1854. Their magazine described the effect of this form of strike: "As man after man leaves . . . then it is that the proud and haughty spirit of the oppressor is brought down and he feels the power he cannot see." [72]

According to E.T. Hiller, the term detailed strike has come to include any piecemeal stoppage by persons engaged in a dispute. Where a strike is to cover a number of factories in a single industry (or, conceivably, in a number of industries), it may be organized in such a way that the workers in one factory or industry after another stop work on succeeding days or weeks, progressively increasing the strike. Allowance is made, however, for the possibility of a settlement before the full working force is withdrawn. Another variation of this method would be the withdrawal, each day, of a certain number of workers from a plant, the number being gradually extended accumulatively to include all the workers.

This method enables the unions to concentrate their forces on particular points, plants, or firms, while other workers either remain at work or are made jobless by a strike in which they are technically not participating—and hence, in some countries, they are eligible for unemployment benefits.

Examples of the detailed strike include: the strike of United Auto Workers at the General Motors plant in Flint, Michigan, in the summer of 1938, in which only the skilled tool-and-die workers struck; under the existing regulations the other then-unemployed "nonstriking" production workers could draw unemployment insurance;[73] the detailed strike by American cigar makers union in 1886;[74] and finally a New York clothing strike (1914?) in which the pants-makers struck one day, the vestmakers the next, and finally the coat-makers, as a means of demonstrating the workers' power and obtaining optimum impact.[75]

109. Bumper strike

A type of strike closely related to the detailed strike is the bumper strike, in which the union strikes only one firm in an industry at a time; by dealing with the firms individually, the union exposes each struck firm to the competition of rivals during the strike.[76] The bumper strike was used in the British radio industry in 1946.[77]

110. Slowdown strike

In the slowdown strike (also known as the go–slow and in Britain and elsewhere by the Welsh word *ca'canny*[78] instead of leaving their jobs or stopping work entirely, the workers deliberately slow down the pace of their work until the efficiency is drastically reduced.[79] In an industrial plant this slowdown has its effects on profits; in governmental offices it would, if continued, reduce the regime's capacity to rule.

Slowdowns in work by African slaves in the United States are reported in statements by ex-slaves and others. Raymond and Alice Bauer summarize these:

> The amount of slowing up of labor by the slaves must, in the aggregate, have caused a tremendous financial loss to plantation owners. The only way we have of estimating it quantitatively is through comparison of the work done on different plantations and under different systems of labor. The statement is frequently made that production on a plantation varied more than 100 percent from time to time. Comparison in the output of slaves in different parts of the South also showed variations of over 100 percent.[80]

Russian serfs in 1859 showed their opposition to their serfdom by doing less work,[81] and two years later in the early weeks of 1861, following an explicit promise of emancipation, the peasants conducted go-slows on the *corvées.*

> The peasants carried out these duties, from which they thought they would soon be exempted, more and more slowly and more and more reluctantly. A sort of spontaneous strike, aimed at loosening the bonds of serfdom, and making submission to the local administrative authorities less specific, accompanied, and often partly replaced an open but sporadic refusal to yield to the landlord's will.[82]

Franz Neumann describes the *ca'canny* or the slowdown as "one of the decisive methods of syndicalist warfare" and claims that its first large-scale use—he presumably means in industrial conflicts—was by Italian railway workers in 1895.[83] It had, however, previously been used by Glasgow dockers after an unsuccessful strike in 1889.[84]

During the Nazi occupation, "Dutch factory workers went slow, particularly when they were forced to work in Germany . . ."[85] In 1942 Sir Stafford Cripps broadcast an appeal to workers in Nazi-occupied Europe to "go slow" in their work. Goebbels thought silence the best means of fighting the appeal, since he wrote, "the slogan of 'go slow' is always much more effective than that of 'work fast.'"[86] German workers themselves appear to have used slowdown strikes very effectively in 1938 and 1939. Go-slows by the coal miners during that period led to a significant drop in production, which in turn prodded the government to launch efforts to raise production and to grant significant wage increases.[87] The wage freeze of September 1939, other worsening labor conditions, and the "clear . . . intention of the regime at the outbreak of the war . . . to abolish all social gains made in decades of social struggle" led to similar more widespread action by German workers. Neumann writes:

> . . . it is at this point that passive resistance[88] seems to have begun on a large scale. The regime had to give way and to capitulate on almost every front. On 16 November 1939, it reintroduced the additional payments for holiday, Sunday, night, and overtime work. On 17 November 1939, it reintroduced paid holidays and even compensation to the workers for previous losses. On 12 December 1939, the regime had finally to enact new labor-time legislation, and strengthen the protection of women, juveniles, and workers as a whole.[89]

In Nazi-occupied Czechoslovakia, "there was of course also in general the go-slow campaign when workers would either absent themselves from work or reduce the tempo of their work."[90]

111. Working-to-rule strike

The working-to-rule strike is "the literal carrying out of orders in a way calculated to retard production and reduce the employer's profit margin."[91] The workers remain at their jobs but meticulously observe all the rules and regulations of the union, employer, and the contract concerning how the work should be done, safety regulations, and so on, with the result that only a fraction of the normal output is produced. It is thus a variation of the slow-down strike under the technical excuse of doing the job extremely well. Neumann (who lumps the work-to-rule together with the broader slowdown strike) states that this kind of strike was applied successfully by the Austrian railway workers in 1905, 1906 and 1907 in the form of "scrupulous compliance" with all traffic and security regulations[92] It was also used in a series of local railway disputes in Britain preceding the General Strike in 1926, and during the 1949 British railway wage dispute.[93]

112. Reporting "sick" (sick-in)

Where strikes are prohibited by law, decree, or contract, or are not feasible for other reasons, workers may achieve anything from a slowdown of production to the equivalent of a full strike by falsely claiming to be sick. This is an especially useful method when sick leave has been granted in the contract or law but strikes have been prohibited.

A great deal of feigned illness was reported among African slaves in the southern United States, sufficient to have had considerable economic impact. Sometimes the illness ratio was nearly one sick to seven well. Slaves were frequently sick on Saturday but rarely on Sunday, which was not a normal workday; more sickness often occurred when the most work was required. Although there was a great deal of genuine illness among the slave population, it is also clear that much of it was feigned in order to get out of work, to avoid being sold to an undesirable master, or to get revenge on a master (by feigning a disability while on the auction block and hence fetch a lower price). Women pretending pregnancy received lighter work and increased food. The Bauers write:

> Of the extent to which illness was feigned there can . . . be little doubt. Some of the feigning was quite obvious, and one might wonder why such flagrant abuses were tolerated. The important thing to remember is that a slave was an important economic investment. Most slave owners sooner or later found out that it was more profitable to give the slave the benefit of the doubt. A sick slave driven to work might very well die.[94]

Another example is reported from China in late 1952. In this instance the workers, although lacking an independent union, by the very strength of their numbers maintained a capacity to act.

> Gradually the workers learned to offer passive resistance, which, although never on a planned or organized basis, nevertheless became a serious problem for the regime. Basically the passive resistance was expressed in a kind of slowdown. Outwardly, the workers seemed animated with the zeal demanded by the authorities but both the quantity and the quality of production fell noticeably.
>
> The most noticeable aspect of the resistance was absenteeism. Taking advantage of the stipulation in the Labor Insurance Regulations that only a small reduction in pay would result from medically approved sick leave, the workers now formed long queues outside the clinics. Most of the "patients" had undiagnosable symptoms which the doctors dealt with by authorizing a few days' leave.[95]

Caught between the pressure of officials and legal responsibility if a genuinely ill patient had an accident after having been refused sick leave, the doctors tended to grant leave. In many factories absenteeism ran as high as twenty percent. After the Health Committee of the Trade Unions organized "Comfort Missions" to visit every sick worker to determine whether he was really ill, absenteeism in one group of flour mills dropped from sixteen to five percent; but in a few weeks it returned to the original rate, after families learned to keep a lookout for the visit of the "Comfort Mission." "Thus by the time we arrived," said one such visitor, "the patient is always having a severe attack of pain." [96]

113. Strike by resignation

Another means of bypassing contractual or legal prohibitions against strikes (it may be used also on other occasions), is the strike by resignation. In this method a significant proportion of the personnel involved formally submit individual resignations. These may be timed so that the dates on which the resignations are submitted or go into effect are phased, so that the total number of resigned personnel steadily increases. Alternately, the whole group may resign simultaneously. At the end of August 1967 in Haverhill, Massachusetts, 85 nurses out of a nursing staff of 175 at Hale Hospital submitted resignations after the failure of negotiations over wages and working conditions. Fifty-eight of the resignations went into effect immediately, while the remainder were postponed for a few weeks. This was believed to be the first case of mass resignation by nurses during wage negotiations in the state. Haverhill City Manager J.P. Ginty called the nurses' action "tantamount to a strike." [97]

114. Limited strike

In the limited strike, which has also been called a "running-sore strike," the workers continue to perform most of their normal duties in an efficient way, but refuse to perform certain marginal work (either within or beyond their required working hours) or refuse to work on certain days. Such a strike may involve, for example, a refusal to work overtime or to work longer than is deemed reasonable. Transport workers have on occasion refused to operate the last scheduled bus, either for a predetermined period or until a settlement was reached. [98]

In 1870 miners in Fifeshire, Scotland, refused to work longer than eight hours a day. [99] Workers in St. Petersburg in October and November 1905 introduced the eight-hour day by "the simple expedient of ceasing work eight hours after they had reported for duty." [100] Strikes limited by refusal to work certain whole days are illustrated by the "Sundays only" strikes by British railway workers in 1945 and 1949, [101] and the alternative days" strike of Argentine railway workers in November 1947.[102] In 1942 Dutch mine workers in the strongly Catholic province of Limburg refused to work on Sundays, not primarily for religious reasons but because of opposition to the Nazi occupation.[103]

When German officials in Denmark in World War II met increased public opposition and sabotage with executions, prohibitions of all meetings and groups of more than five in the streets, and a curfew of 8 P.M. to 5 A.M., workers at Burmeister and Wain in Copenhagen, Denmark's largest shipyard, retaliated with a type of limited strike. On June 26, 1944, they left their places of work and sent a message to *Dagmarhus,* the Nazi headquarters, saying that since the Germans could not guarentee enough food, the workers had to tend their garden plots—and therefore had to leave work early. They were not striking, they said; but the potatoes and vegetables from their gardens were more important to them than the German war industry. These became known as the "go-home-early-strikes."[104]

115. Selective strike

In a selective strike workers refuse only to do certain *types* of work, often because of some political objection. The objection is to the tasks themselves, not hours, conditions, or the like. The intent is thus both to prevent the work itself from being carried out and to induce the employer in the future not to request the workers to do that type of work.

The first example here, from the American colonies, occurred in the interim between the appointment of delegates to the First Continental Congress (elections began in June 1774) and its adjournment on October 26. In the commercial provinces, Arthur M. Schlesinger writes, "the most striking development was the combination of workingmen of two of the chief cities to withhold their labor from the British authorities at Boston. Early in September 1774, Governor Gage sought to hire Boston workingmen for fortifying Boston Neck, but was met with refusals wherever he turned." New York workers were persuaded not to go to Boston to work on the fortifications. General Gage's brief success in getting a few days' work done on barracks by Boston carpenters and masons was shortlived; the workmen left the jobs, and a meeting of committees of thirteen towns adopted a labor boycott program. Under this program they resolved that should anyone from Massachusetts or any other province supply the troops at Boston with labor or materials which would enable them "to annoy or in any way distress" the citizens, such persons would be deemed "most inveterate enemies" and should be "prevented and defeated." The leading towns at the meeting appointed Committees of Observation and Prevention for enforcement, and the resolves were sent to all towns in the province. As a result, "the labor boycott was made effective," and the barracks were not completed until November—and then only because workers had been brought from Nova Scotia, and a few from New Hampshire. [105]

In other examples, German rail workers refused to take coal trains to France during the *Ruhrkampf,* and the personnel of the coal-shipping companies joined them in that refusal. When occupation officials imposed a Franco-Belgian administration to run the railroads in the Ruhr, in March 1923, only 400 of the 170,000 preinvasion rail employess were willing to work for it. [106] In August 1943 Danish dockworkers at Odense refused to repair German ships. [107] At Gothenburg, Sweden, in the summer of 1963, dockers refused to unload 180 tons of South African canned fruit after dockers at Copenhagen and Aarhus, Denmark, had similarly refused. [108]

MULTI-INDUSTRY STRIKES

116. Generalized strike

When several industries are struck simultaneously as part of a general grievance but the strikers constitute less than a majority of the workers in the important industries of the area, the strike may be termed a generalized strike. [109] For example, because of common involvement in government wage regulations and procedures, several industries may be struck simultaneously, as happened in the metal, textile, shoe, mining and building industries in Norway in 1926 and again in 1927, in protest against wage reductions; the Norwegian strikes in 1931 again involved several industries, including newspapers, breweries and the tobacco industry. [110]

117. General strike

The general strike is widespread stoppage of labor by workers in an attempt to bring the economic life of a given area to a more or less complete standstill in order to achieve certain desired objectives. [111] The method may be used on a local, regional, national, or international level. Wilfred Harris Crook defined the general strike as "the strike of a majority of the workers in the more important industries of any one locality or region." [112] When confined to a city it may be called a localized general strike, such as occurred in Seattle, Washington, and Winnipeg, Canada, in 1919 and Vienna in 1927. [113] While a general strike is usually intended to be total, certain vital services may be allowed to operate, especially those necessary for health, such as provision of milk, water, and food; sewage disposal; and hospital services. Crook distinguishes three broad types of the general strike—political, economic, and revolutionary:

> There is the *political* general strike, with the aim of exacting some definite political concession from the existing government, as the demand for universal suffrage in the Belgian General Strikes, or, more rarely, for the purpose of upholding the existing government against a would-be usurper, as the German strike against the *Kapp-Putsch* in 1920. The *economic* type is perhaps the most common form, at least at the beginning of the strike, and is exemplified by the Swedish strike of 1909. The *revolutionary* general strike, aiming at the definite overthrow of the existing government or industrial system, may be revolutionary in its purpose from the very start, or it may develop its revolutionary purpose as it proceeds. It is more likely to be found in countries where labor has not been long or extensively organized, or where the influential leaders of labor are largely syndicalist or anarchist in viewpoint, as Russia in 1905, Spain or Italy. [114]

The general strike has been widely advocated in radical socialist, syndicalist and anarchist thought; it has been practiced by English, Russian and Scandinavian socialists, and French, Italian, Spanish and South American anarchists and syndicalists. [115]

There are a large number of examples of general strikes, with considerable geographical and political variations. The Belgian general strikes of 1893, 1902 and 1913 supported demands for political reforms, including universal manhood suffrage. [116] Early general strikes in Imperial Russia were held at Rostov-on-Don in 1902 and Odessa in 1903, [117] and general strikes were widely used during the 1905 Russian Revolution. Perhaps the largest and most important of these was the Great October Strike of 1905, involving most of the cities of Imperial Russia that had any degree of industrial life. [118] The situation in Moscow is illustrative:

> Within a week, Moscow was virtually isolated, and most of her important public activities were at a standstill. All train connections were severed. All telegraphic connections along the lines emanating from the city were silent. Only the central General Telegraph Office remained in operation in the city to provide communication with the outside and the railroadmen were planning to close it. [119]

The general strike was also used against the Kapp *Putsch* in Weimar Germany in 1920, as we saw in Chapter Two.

> By the late afternoon of March 14, 1920, the greatest strike the world had ever seen was a reality. The economic life of the country came to a standstill. . . Kapp attempted to break the strike . . . [and] made picketing a capital offense. But his efforts proved totally ineffectual. [120]

The general strike in Norway in 1921 was against wage reductions, [121] and the Chinese general strike of 1925 was over economic and nationalist grievances. [122] The British General Strike of May 3-12, 1926, was the outgrowth of unsatisfied claims of the coal miners, and developed into a major test of power between workers and the government, complicated by the capitulation by the trade union leaders. [123]

In Amsterdam a general strike was held on Febrary 25 and 26, 1941, to protest maltreatment of the city's Jews. [124] The 1943 Dutch general strike, or wave of strikes, from April 29 to as late as May 8 in some places, involved a majority of industrial workers, who opposed the planned internment of Dutch army veterans in Germany. [125] In Copenhagen, too, the general strike was applied during the Nazi occupation, from June 30 to about July 4, 1944, with the aim of forcing the Germans to withdraw the state of martial law and to remove the hated Danish fascist *Schalburgkorps* from the country. Negotiations led to German concessions, though not to the granting of the full demands. [126]

General strikes played a very important role in many cities and towns during the East German Rising of June 1953. [127] A general strike in Haiti in February 1957 ousted the temporary president, Pierre Louis. [128]

COMBINATION OF STRIKES AND ECONOMIC CLOSURES

118. The hartal

The *hartal* is an Indian method of nonviolent action in which the economic life of an area is temporarily suspended on a voluntary basis in order to demonstrate extreme dissatisfaction with some event, policy, or condition. It is used not to wield economic influence, but to communicate sorrow, determination, revulsion, or moral or religious feelings about the matter in question. Although the form of this method is largely economic, the effect is one of symbolic protest. The *hartal* is usually limited to a duration of twenty-four hours; it may rarely be extended to forty-eight hours or even longer in an extremely serious case. The *hartal* is usually city-wide or village-wide, although it may occur over a more extended area, including the whole nation. Generally speaking, there is greater emphasis in the *hartal* than in the general strike on its voluntary nature, even to the point of the laborers abstaining from work only after obtaining permission from their employers. Also, shop owners and businessmen fully participate by closing their establishments and factories.

This is one of the forms of nonviolent action known to ancient India, where it was used against the prince or king to make him aware of the unpopularity of a certain edict or other government measure.[129] The *hartal* is also used at a time of national mourning. Gandhi employed this ancient method in resistance movements he led. He often used the *hartal* at the beginning of a struggle with the intent of purifying participants in the struggle, of testing their feelings on the issue, and arousing the imagination of the people and the opponent. It was used, for example, at the beginning of the nationwide *satyagraha* campaign in India against the Rowlatt Bills in 1919,[130] and at the beginning of and during the 1930–31 *satyagraha* campaign for independence, especially to protest the arrest of important leaders.[131]

119. Economic shutdown

An economic shutdown occurs, producing economic paralysis, when the workers strike while management, businessmen, commercial institutions, and small shopkeepers simultaneously halt their economic activities ; this method thus includes characteristics of both strikes and economic boycotts. Tendencies in this direction may occur in general strikes for widely supported political objectives. Economic shutdowns vary in the extent to which the different types of economic activities are shut down and the extent to which businessmen, management, and so on, participate, just as participation in the general strike ranges widely.

In late 1905 a national economic shutdown was a factor in the restoration of Finnish autonomy within Imperial Russia; Finnish employers expressed their solidarity by paying their employees wages for the duration of the strike.[132] J. Hampden Jackson writes:

> Trains stopped, telegraphs went dead, factories stood empty. This lead was followed spontaneously by the whole nation: shops, offices, schools, restaurants were shut. The police went on strike and . . . university students formed a corps to maintain order . . . . There was no bloodshed; it was merely passive resistance with a whole nation behind it.[133]

After six days constitutional government with free elections was granted, although several years later the Tsar's regime once more attempted Russification. [134]

In Esbjerg, Denmark, an economic shutdown broke out on July 11, 1943, "where not only the workers, but also the functionaries went home, and the traders closed the stores." [135] In Port-au-Prince, Haiti, in December 1956, General Paul Magliore, strongman since 1946, was confronted with an economic shutdown to protest his modified martial law; this involved a general strike of workers and closure of businesses by owners or managers. Almost all concerns shut down, including gasoline and oil works, docks, most of the public market, downtown shops, schools and banks; civil servants were on strike and lawyers refused to take court cases; there were even strikes in some hospitals. "The resistance was completely passive. Haitians simply stayed away from their jobs." After Magliore's resignation from the presidency on December 12, the shutdown continued with the demand that he also resign from the army, which he did after additional support for the resignation demand came from the army itself and the Papal Nuncio. On December 14 it was reported that Magliore had left for exile in Jamaica. [136]

During the Buddhist struggle against the Diem regime in 1963, the majority of shops in Hué closed down on at least two occasions in support of the opposition movement, although it is not clear to what degree this was or was not accompanied by the shutdown of other sections of the city's economic life. [137]

Certain examples of strikes show that they have been used for political objectives, and in some cases (as when civil servants have gone on strike) the events themselves have become mixed with aspects of political noncooperation. Where certain methods of the strike have been illegal or have continued despite government edicts to the contrary (say, in a case of an economic shutdown intended to destroy a government), there has also been a mixture of economic and political forms of noncooperation. Let us now turn to methods of political noncooperation and examine them in detail.

NOTES

1. This general definition of the strike is based upon the following studies: Fitch, "Strikes and Lockouts," pp. 419-426; Jack Barbash, **Labor Unions in Action: A Study of the Mainsprings of Unionism,** (New York, Harper and Bros., 1948) pp. 124-141; Florence Peterson, **Survey of the Labor Economics,** rev. ed. (New York, Harper and Bros., 1951), pp. 565-572; E. T. Hiller, **The Strike: A Study in Collective Action** (Chicago: University of Chicago Press, 1928), esp. pp. 12-24 and 278; Steuben, **Strike Strategy;** and Reynolds, **Labor Economics and Labor Relations,** pp. 284-286.
2. The term is used by Warmbrunn, **The Dutch Under German Occupation,** p. 108.
3. Knowles, **Strikes,** p. 11.
4. Barbash, **Labor Unions in Action,** p. 129.
5. This inclusion of political issues as possible motivations in the protest strike diverges from Barbash, **Labor Unions in Action,** p. 131. Here the form of the strike rather than its motivation is regarded more significant in developing a classification.
6. Sternstein, "The *Ruhrkampf* of 1923", p. 111.
7. Warmbrunn, **The Dutch . . . ,** p. 110.
8. *Peace News,* April 10 and 17 April 1959.
9. *Ibid.,* 18 May 1962.
10. Barbash, **Labor Unions in Action,** p. 130.
11. Harcave, **First Blood,** p. 134.
12. *Ibid.,* p. 178.
13. Vladimir Gurko, quoted in Harcave, **First Blood,** p. 198.
14. Edgar Holt, **Protest in Arms,** p. 157. I am grateful to William Hamilton for this reference.
15. Littell, ed., **The Czech Black Book,** pp. 41 and 45-46.
16. *Ibid.,* pp. 76 and 85.
17. *Ibid.,* p. 115. On the announcements, see also pp. 81 and 112.
18. Barbash, **Labor Unions in Action,** pp. 126-127.
19. Knowles, **Strikes,** p. 11.
20. Barbash, **Labor Unions in Action,** pp. 126-127.
21. *Peace News,* 19 July 1963.
22. Venturi, **Roots of Revolution,** pp. 214-215.
23. Charques, **The Twilight of Imperial Russia,** p. 138.
24. Harcave, **First Blood,** pp. 170-171.
25. Solon L. Barraclough, "Agricultural Policy and Land Reform" (mimeo), (Conference on Key Problems of Economic Policy in Latin America, University of Chicago, November 6-9, 1966), p. 45. I am grateful to Jeffrey B. Peters for this and the following references.

26. Dwight B. Heath, Charles J. Erasmus and Hans C. Buechler, **Land Reform and Social Revolution in Bolivia** (New York: Frederick A. Praeger, 1969), pp. 42-44.

27. Barraclough, "Agricultural Policy and Land Reform," pp. 45-46; and Barraclough, "Farmers' Organizations in Planning and Implementing Rural Programs" (unpublished paper, n.d., prepared for a reader on rural development being edited by Professor Raanan Weitz) pp. 11-12.

28. Barraclough, "Farmers' Organizations in Planning and Implementing Rural Programs," pp. 11-12.

29. Carey McWilliams, **Factories in the Field: The Story of Migratory Farm Labor in California** (Boston: Little, Brown & Co., 1939), p. 211.

30. *Ibid.*, pp. 213-14.

31. *Ibid.*, pp. 215-16.

32. *Ibid.*, pp. 210-229.

33. John Gregory Dunne, **Delano: The Story of the California Grape Strike** (New York: Farrar, Straus & Giroux, 1967), p. 133. Also on the grape strike, see Peter Matthiessen, **Sal Si Puedes: Cesar Chavez and the New American Revolution** (New York: Random House, 1969).

34. Diwakar, *Satyagraha*, pp. 124-126.

35. Dan Daniels, "Nonviolent Actions in Canada," in **Our Generation Against Nuclear War** (Montreal), vol. 3, no. 1 (June 1964), p. 70.

36. Hsiao, **Rural China,** pp. 247-248.

37. Mulford C. Sibley and Asa Wardlaw, "Conscientious Objectors in Prison," in Staughton Lynd, ed., **Nonviolence in America: A Documentary History,** (Indianapolis, etc.: Bobbs-Merrill Co., 1966), pp. 301-302. See also James Peck, **Freedom Ride** (New York: Simon and Schuster, 1962), pp. 39-41.

38. Brigitte Gerland, "How the Great Vorkuta Strike Was Prepared" and "The Great Labor Camp Strike at Vorkuta," *The Militant* (New York), 28 February and 7 March 1955.

39. Steuben, **Strike Strategy,** p. 278.

40. On craft unions and industrial unions, see Peterson, **American Labor Unions,** pp. 71-75.

41. Selig Perlman, **A History of Trade Unionism in the United States** (New York: Macmillan Co., 1923), p. 3.

42. *Ibid.*, p. 8.

43. Benjamin Stalberg, **Tailor's Progress: The Story of A Famous Union and the Men Who Made It** (New York: Doubleday, Doran and Co., 1944), p. 38.

44. *Ibid.*, pp. 59-64.

45. Rostovtzeff, **The Social and Economic History of the Roman Empire,** vol. I, p. 472.

46. Buckler, "Labour Disputes in the Province of Asia Minor," p. 29.

47. Morgan and Morgan, **The Stamp Act Crisis,** pp. 223-224.

48. Harcave, **First Blood,** p. 101.

49. *Ibid.*, p. 183.

50. David Ziskind, **One Thousand Strikes of Government Employees** (New York: Columbia University Press, 1940), pp. 75-76.

51. *New York Times,* 12, 13 and 14 December 1956.

52. Hiller, **The Strike,** p. 278.

53. McAlister Coleman, **Men and Coal** (New York: Farrar and Rienhart, 1943), pp. 164-166.

54. Harriet Holter, "Disputes and Tensions in Industry" (reprint from **Scandinavian Democracy** [Copenhagen], 1958, pp. 3 4.

55. Hiller, **The Strike,** p. 278.

56. Herbert Harris, **American Labor** (New Haven: Yale University Press, 1938), pp. 120-129.

57. Foster Rhea Dulles, **Labor in America: A History** (New York: Thomas Y. Crowell, Co., 1949), pp. 215-219.

58. *The Observer* (London), 5 July 1959.

59. *Militant,* 10 and 17 August 1953.

60. Sternstein, "The *Ruhrkampf* of 1932," pp. 118-119.

61. Warmbrunn, **The Dutch . . . ,** p. 108.

62. Jong, "Anti-Nazi Resistance in the Netherlands," in **European Resistance Movements 1939-1945,** pp. 141-142. The failure of Field-Marshal Montgomery's military plan and German counter measures to the strike led to over 15,000 deaths from starvation, de Jong reports. Warmbrunn **(The Dutch . . . ,** pp. 141-146) offers a more detailed account and evaluation.

63. *The Times,* 3, 7, 8, 10, 14, 16, 17, 21, 22, 23, 24, 26, 28 and 29 May 1962.

64. Peterson, **American Labor Unions,** p. 270, and **Survey of Labor Economics,** pp. 568-569.

65. Fred S. Hall, **Sympathetic Strikes and Sympathetic Lockouts** (New York: Published Ph.D. dissertation in Political Science, Columbia University, 1898), pp. 11-12.

66. Symons, **The General Strike,** p. 226.

67. Hall, **Sympathetic Strikes and Sympathetic Lockouts,** pp. 14-15.

68. *Ibid.,* pp. 82-84.

69. Walter Galenson, **Labor in Norway** (Cambridge, Mass.: Harvard University Press, 1949), p. 165.

70. Seton-Watson, **The Decline of Imperial Russia,** p. 130.

71. *New York Times,* 23, 24 and 27 June 1944.

72. *Flint Glass Makers' Magazine,* July 1850, quoted by Hiller, **The Strike,** p. 136.

73. Irving Howe and B. J. Widick, **The U.A.W. and Walter Reuther** (New York: Random House, 1949), pp. 78-79.

74. Hiller, **The Strike,** p. 137.

75. *Ibid.*

76. Knowles, **Strikes,** pp. 12-13.

77. *Ibid.*

78. Knowles, **Strikes,** pp. 18-19.

79. Peterson, **American Labor Unions,** p. 268.

80. Raymond A. Bauer and Alice H. Bauer, "Day to Day Resistance to Slavery," **The Journal of Negro History,** vol. XXVII, no. 4 (Oct. 1942), p. 397.

81. Venturi, **Roots of Revolution,** p. 191.

82. *Ibid.,* pp. 207-208.

83. Franz Neumann, **Behemoth: The Structure and Practice of National Socialism 1933-1944** (New York: Octagon Books, 1963), p. 344.

84. Knowles, **Strikes,** p. 19.

85. Jong, "Anti-Nazi Resistance in the Netherlands," in **European Resistance Movements 1939-1945** p. 144. On slow-downs by Dutch miners, see Warmbrunn, **The Dutch . . .** , p. 138.

86. Lochner, ed., **The Goebbels Diaries,** p. 107. Diary entry by Goebbels for 1 March 1942.

87. Neumann, **Behemoth,** pp. 344-345.

88. Neumann uses this term as identical with the *ca'canny* and the slow-down.

89. *Ibid.,* p. 347. Neumann (p. 348) offers reasons for believing that the concessions followed from the workers' action, while he acknowledges a possible primary role for reduced demands resulting from the "phoney" war of 1939.

90. Personal letter from Josef Korbel, 22 December 1966.

91. Knowles, **Strikes,** p. 18.

92. Neumann, **Behemoth,** p. 344.

93. Knowles, **Strikes,** p. 18.

94. Bauer and Bauer, "Day to Day Resistance to Slavery," p. 408.

95. Loh, **Escape from Red China,** pp. 109-111. I am grateful to Margaret Jackson Rothwell for this reference.

96. *Ibid.*

97. *Boston Globe,* 27 and 29 August 1967.

98. Knowles, **Strikes,** pp. 11-12.

99. *Ibid.,* p. 12.

100. Keep, **The Rise of Social Democracy in Russia,** p. 237, and Harcave, **First Blood,** p. 224.

101. Knowles, **Strikes,** p. 12.

102. *Ibid.*

103. Warmbrunn, **The Dutch . . .** , p. 138.

104. Kirchhoff, et al., *Besættelsestidens Historie,* p. 204.

105. Schlesinger, **The Colonial Merchants and the American Revolution,** pp. 386-388.

106. Sternstein, "The *Ruhrkampf* of 1923," p. 115.

107. Reitlinger, **The Final Solution,** p. 346.

108. *Peace News,* 19 July 1963.

109. Hiller, **The Strike,** pp. 139, 243-244 and 278.

110. Galenson, **Labor in Norway,** pp. 166-168.

111. For more detailed discussion of the general strike, see esp. Wilfred H. Crook, "General Strike," **Encyclopedia of the Social Sciences,** vol. VI, pp. 607-612; Crook, **The General Strike;** and Crook, **Communism and the General Strike** (Hamden, Connecticut: The Shoe String Press, 1960).

112. Crook, **The General Strike,** p. vii.

113. *Ibid.*

114. *Ibid.,* pp. vii-viii.

115. Ligt, **The Conquest of Violence,** pp. 110-111 and Peterson, **American Labor Unions,** p. 257, for example.

116. Crook, **The General Strike,** pp. 54-103.

117. Seton-Watson, **The Decline of Imperial Russia,** pp. 128 and 130.

118. See Harcave, **First Blood,** pp. 180-186.
119. *Ibid.,* p. 181.
120. Halperin, **Germany Tried Democracy,** pp. 179-180.
121. Galenson, **Labor in Norway,** p. 162.
122. Crook, "General Strike," p. 610.
123. Symons, **The General Strike,** and Crook, **The General Strike,** pp. 367-445.
124. Jong, "Anti-Nazi Resistance in the Netherlands," p. 140, and Warmbrunn, **The Dutch . . . ,** pp. 106-111.
125. Warmbrunn, **The Dutch . . . ,** pp. 113-118. Jong, "Anti-Nazi Resistance in the Netherlands," p. 141 and personal letter confirming the participation of a majority of industrial workers from Dr. L. de Jong, 7 July 1966.
126. Kirchhoff, **et al.,** *Besættelsestidens Historie,* pp. 206-209.
127. Brant, **The East German Rising,** pp. 69-136 *passim.*
128. *Time,* 18 February 1957, p. 23.
129. Bondurant, **Conquest of Violence,** pp. 118-119.
130. *Ibid.,* p. 79.
131. *Ibid.,* p. 94 and Sharp, **Gandhi Wields . . . ,** pp. 91, 104, 109, 121 and 132.
132. Eino Jutikkala, **A History of Finland,** pp. 240-242.
133. J. Hampden Jackson, **Finland** (New York: Macmillan, 1940), pp. 74-75.
134. Miller, **Nonviolence,** p. 248.
135. Kirchhoff, **et al.,** *Besaettelsestidens Historie,* pp. 168-169.
136. *New York Times,* 7-14 December 1956.
137. Adam Roberts, "Buddhism and Politics in South Vietnam," in **The World Today** (London), vol. 21, no. 6 (June 1965), p. 246.

7

The Methods
of Political
Noncooperation

INTRODUCTION

Political noncooperation is the third subclass of methods of noncooperation; these methods involve refusals to continue the usual forms of political participation under existing conditions. Sometimes they are known as political boycotts. Individuals and small groups may practice methods of this class. Normally, however, political noncooperation involves larger numbers of people in corporate, concerted, usually temporary suspension of normal political obedience, cooperation and behavior. Political noncooperation may also be undertaken by government personnel and even by governments themselves. The purpose of suspension of political cooperation may simply be protest, or it may be personal dissociation from something seen as morally or politically objectionable, without much consideration as to consequences. More frequently, however, an act of political noncooperation is designed to exert pressure on the government, on an illegitimate group attempting to seize control of the government apparatus, or sometimes on another government. The aim of the political noncooperation may be to achieve a particular limited objective or a change in broader government policies. Or it may be to change the nature or composition of that government, or even to produce its disintegration. Where political noncooperation is practiced against usurpers, its aim may be to defend and to restore the legitimate government.

The political significance of these methods increases in proportion to the numbers participating and to the need for their cooperation for the operation of the political system. In actual struggles this class of methods is frequently combined with other forms of nonviolent action.

Political noncooperation may take an almost infinite variety of expressions, depending upon the particular situation. Basically they all stem from a desire not to assist the opponent by performance of certain types of political behavior. The thirty-eight methods included here are grouped into six subclasses: rejection of authority, citizens' noncooperation with government, citizens' alternatives to obedience, action by government personnel, domestic governmental action, and international governmental action. Many other possible forms have not been included here. For example, among the forms not specifically listed in this chapter which have to do with only one particular area of behavior—responses to arrest, fines, court orders, and the like—are refusal to accept bail, refusal to pay securities, suspension of publication of newspapers when faced with restrictions, refusal to make parole rounds, defiance of restraining and prohibition orders, and refusal to buy confiscated property. There is room for much more research.

REJECTION OF AUTHORITY

120. Withholding or withdrawal of allegiance

This form of political noncooperation involves a refusal to recognize a particular regime as legally or morally deserving of allegiance. A clear illustration is to be found in Hungarian resistance to Austrian rule in the nineteenth century. For instance, Emperor Franz Josef was not accepted as King of Hungary as long as he was unwilling to abide by the Hungarian constitution and had not been crowned King of Hungary.[1] Therefore, the members of the Hungarian parliament refused to recognize the legality of its dissolution by Franz Josef. When the Pesth County Council protested the dissolution of the parliament, it was itself dissolved, though it refused to recognize this dissolution and continued to meet.[2] When the County

Councils, which had refused to carry out ordinances issued by the Austrians,[3] were generally dissolved, their members refused to transfer their services to the Austrians.[4]

The conscious withdrawal by the people of authority from their rulers was also seen during the struggle of the Netherlands against Spanish rule in the sixteenth century. In 1565, for example, "lampoons were circulated, branding Philip as a perjurer who violated the privileges, and to whom, following the old law of the 'Joyous Entry,' no further allegiance was due."[5] In the summer of 1581 the States General meeting in The Hague passed a resolution

> whereby Philip, on account of his tyrannical rule and his trampling underfoot of the privileges of the country, was deposed from domination over his Netherland provinces. Following this resolution all authorities, officials, military commanders, and the like, were required to take a new oath, in the absence of Anjou, to the United Provinces . . . . The "Placard of Dismissal" . . . was a brilliant, though late, expression of the sturdy medieval tradition of freedom . . . [6]

The American colonists' rejection of the British government's authority over them was also a crucial point in the establishment of American independence. Thomas Jefferson wrote in 1774: "The true ground on which we declare their [Parliament's] acts void is, that the British parliament has no right to exercise authority over us."[7] This denial of authority to the British government, and its bestowal elsewhere, seem to have been highly important supportive factors in John Adams' later declaration that "the revolution was complete in the minds of the people, and the Union of the colonies, before the war commenced in the skirmishes of Concord and Lexington on the 19th April, 1775."[8]

Sometimes the withdrawal of allegiance may be expressed by a symbolic act, as on November 13, 1905, when the Russian cruiser *Ochakov* "raised the red flag in a dramatic gesture of 'non-recognition' of the government . . ."[9] The same month "in Vilna the two thousand delegates to the Lithuanian nationalist congress declared that they did not recognize the legitimacy of the Russian government under which they were living."[10]

During the *Ruhrkampf* Germans withheld allegiance from the French and Belgian occupation regime, denying the legality and therefore the validity of occupation decrees and orders. On January 19, 1923, the German government declared that "all state, provincial and local authorities were forbidden to obey any orders issued by the occupation authorities, and were told to confine themselves strictly to directions given by the appropriate German authorities.'' As one expression of this refusal of allegiance, German policemen refused to salute foreign officers.[11]

American Indians have frequently and in a variety of ways rejected the authority of the United States and Canadian governments over them. A number of these cases have been collected by Margaret DeMarco,[12] who writes that in 1921 Canadian Iroquois of the Six Nations Confederacy refused to become Canadian citizens and, asserting their sovereignty, brought a petition against the Dominion Government to the League of Nations.[13] Again, in the 1940s and 1950s American as well as Canadian members of the Confederacy sought both hearings before and membership in the United Nations. A band of Chippewas seeking a hearing in a treaty rights case appealed to the U.N. in 1946,[14] and another band of the same tribe requested a U.N. seat in 1960.[15]

In the early days after the August 1968 Russian invasion of Czechoslovakia, citizens and officials of that country refused to acknowledge that the Russians had any authority over political activities in that country. For example, on August 24 the lord mayor of Prague simply refused to see the occupation forces sent to negotiate with him.[16] Two days later, Communists working for State security asserted that they accepted the authority only of their own, not the Russian, officials:

> The All-Unit Committee of the Communist Party in the main administration of State Security in Sadova Street [Prague] declares again that it stands fully behind the legitimate Czechoslovak constitutional and Party organs and that it is guided in its work solely by the orders of Minister of Interior Josef Pavel.[17]

121. Refusal of public support

There are political circumstances in which failure to express openly support for the existing regime and its policies becomes an act of political noncooperation. Under political conditions of organized unanimity and coerced enthusiasm, silence may often be dangerously noticeable. Even where the regime is not fully totalitarian, some individuals may be expected or ordered to express their public support for the regime; their refusal to do so may be regarded as an act of opposition. During the 1963 Buddhist struggle against the Diem regime in South Vietnam, for example, government-staged demonstrations of support for the regime failed, and at least once a general did not appear at an announced press conference at which he was to declare his support for government raids on Buddhist pagodas.[18] It was clear that his ''support'' was not very enthusiastic.

Following the defeat of the 1956 Hungarian revolution, the country's writers publicly demonstrated their lack of support for the imposed regime by maintaining a "writers' silence" and submitting nothing for publication. In the circumstances, the publication of articles, stories, or books with their names listed as authors would have implied that the writers were passively accepting, or positively endorsing, the new regime. Conversely, their silence made it clear that they were refusing to give it their support. In late January 1957 François Fejto wrote: "One seeks in vain the signature of any reputed writer in all the official newspapers and periodicals. The voluminous Christmas issue of *Nepszabadsag* was published without a single article or poem by any known living writer." [19]

During the spring of 1968, when Russian broadcasts aimed at Czechoslovakia had been stepped up, it was reported that Czechoslovak employees working for the Soviet Union in Moscow as broadcasters refused to broadcast polemics critical of the liberalization taking place at home. Soviet spokesmen later denied the report. News accounts also indicated that Czechoslovak Radio had sent a legal adviser to Moscow to assist those employees concerning their legal status with the Soviet radio. [20]

122. Literature and speeches advocating resistance

In many situations, the making of speeches and the publication and distribution of literature which call on people to undertake some form of nonviolent noncooperation or nonviolent intervention themselves become acts of defiance and resistance. This is especially so in those countries where any call for resistance, especially for illegal acts of resistance, is itself illegal or seditious.

In England, for example, six members of the Direct Action Committee Against Nuclear War were imprisoned in December 1959 for distributing leaflets calling upon people illegally to enter a rocket base site at Harrington. [21] In Madrid fourteen men from Murcia province were charged with incitement to military rebellion and sentenced to imprisonment for terms of from six months to six years for distributing leaflets calling for a nationwide general strike on June 18, 1959. [22]

CITIZENS' NONCOOPERATION WITH GOVERNMENT

123. Boycott of legislative bodies

In undemocratic systems, legislative bodies may be used to bolster the regime's prestige and influence and to offer the appearance of democracy.

A resistance movement may then decide on a permanent or temporary boycott of participation in such bodies. Nonparticipation would be designed to: 1) remove the facade of democracy; 2) increase the degree of noncooperation with the opponent regime; 3) obtain the active participation in the resistance movement of those politicians who would otherwise spend time attending legislative sessions which produce no changes; and 4) offer by withdrawal a symbolic or newsworthy protest in cases where defeat of the dissident minority in the legislature seems certain. Frequently, of course, withdrawal from the legislature simply means that the opponent group can proceed without legislative opposition.

A national minority may similarly boycott participation in a multinational or imperial parliament of an "oppressor" State. This form of boycott may be undertaken by the nationalists on grounds of principle—a refusal to recognize or accept the political integration of their country with the "oppressor." Or, the boycott may be based on strategy, as an action intended to protest or achieve a particular point, or as part of a program of noncooperation intended to make the foreign rule unworkable. In 1861, for example, the elected Hungarian representatives refused to attend the Imperial Parliament in Vienna and insisted on sitting as the parliament of Hungary alone.[23] In Serbia, the Radicals precipitated a crisis in early 1882 by leaving the parliament after their demand for an investigation of a railroad scandal had been rejected[24] Prior to the *Duma*'s voting of war credits to the Russian Tsar's regime in mid-1914, the Social Democratic deputies walked out of the chamber.[25]

During the 1930-31 campaign in India there was strong effort to get members of the provincial Legislative Councils and the national Legislative Council to refuse to attend further sessions and to resign their seats.[26] On March 18, 1967, when the new parliament was opened by President S. Radhakrishnan in New Delhi, over one hundred opposition members boycotted the session in protest against the way Prime Minister Indira Gandhi's government had prevented a non-Congress party ministry from being formed in the state of Rajasthan. This was the first legislative boycott since the Indian constitution had been established seventeen years previously.[27]

Anthony de Crespigny reports two additional European cases of boycott of particular sessions of legislatures. In December 1961, in Greece, over one hundred newly elected opposition deputies boycotted the opening of parliament by King Paul as a means of calling attention to their challenge to the validity of the elections. In May 1962 various legislators withdrew from a plenary session of the West German *Bundestag,* preventing a quorum and thus blocking approval of the Cabinet's decision to cut tariffs on foreign cars.[28]

124. Boycott of elections

Where there is reason to believe that an election will not be conducted fairly or where there is refusal to recognize the authority of the regime conducting the election, an opposition movement may refuse to put up candidates and may urge people to refuse to vote. The aim of such a boycott is usually to protest the use of the election to deceive people as to the degree of democracy present; or it may be an attempt to prevent the "real" issue or issues, as seen by the resistance group, from being overshadowed by "lesser" issues. Sometimes election boycotts have also been attempted by minority groups seeking to deprive the elected government of legitimacy and thereby making it more vulnerable to later attack by various means, including guerrilla warfare.

When the Jacobins sought in 1793 to calm political discontent by submitting to a plebiscite a constitution which declared that after the emergency Frenchmen could once again choose their form of government, three out of four citizens abstained from voting.[29] Later the electors acted similarly: "The result of the illegalities of *fructidor* made the election of 1798 almost farcical. Practically all the moderates abstained from voting. What was the use of voting if the Directors refused to accept the results of the elections?"[30]

Following the Russian Tsar's manifesto of 1905, which contained very limited steps toward greater local autonomy for Finland, the Finnish Social Democrats returned to their earlier minimum demand for a Constituent Assembly and boycotted the elections to the new Diet.[31] Socialist Revolutionaries meeting in Russia in January 1906 told their followers to boycott the elections to the *Duma,* though most of them voted anyway.[32]

Another example is that of the Puerto Rican Nationalists, who for many years boycotted elections because they refuse to recognize the United States government's right to control the island and to operate the election machinery.[33]

Crespigny reports three cases from the years 1961 and 1962.[34] In November 1961 the opposition in Portugal withdrew from the coming parliamentary elections and urged citizens not to vote, in order to avoid the false appearance of a fair election.[35] In Uganda, in April 1962, the rulers of Ankole, Bunyoro, Toro and Busoga threatened election boycotts in an effort to gain full federal status for their territories.[36] That same month all major opposition parties boycotted the federal elections of the Central African Federation (also called the Federation of Rhodesia and Nyasaland), as part of their eventually successful campaign for the federation's breakup. [37] Also in April 1962 the opposition party in El Salvador refused to take part in the presidential election, declaring that the election of 1961 had been fraudulent: the government's candidates had won all seats. [38]

Militant Vietnamese Buddhist leaders in mid-August 1966 called on their followers not to vote in the election of a constitutional assembly on September 11, charging that the Ky government was trying to exploit the election in order "to form a dictatorial regime to serve foreign interests." [39]

A variation on this approach was the "Voters' Veto" campaign in Britain during the 1959 General Election, in which there was no opposition to candidates being nominated or to the holding of the election, but there was a refusal to support any candidates, of whatever party, who did not clearly state their willingness to vote in Parliament for unconditional unilaternal nuclear disarmament. In practice this meant a boycott of all candidates in most constituencies. [40]

125. Boycott of government employment and positions

This type of political noncooperation occurs when people refuse to assist the government by serving it in some job or post. They may either resign from current positions or refuse to accept new ones—either all posts (as in a dictatorial or foreign regime) or only particular ones associated with an objectionable policy. In either case, the objections to government service are normally more serious than the usual run of strike demands. The posts boycotted may range widely, from government ministries to quite menial jobs.

This method produces in varying degrees a withdrawal of labor, skills and other support by individuals; at times such resignations or withholding of aid may cumulatively involve a large number of people, or they may be the result of a corporate resistance strategy. But this is not a form of strike, which is normally a short-term (or relatively so) withdrawal of labor to achieve certain demands, rather than a voluntary quitting of the opponent's employ. The boycott of government employment and positions is *not* a conditional and temporary suspension of activities while in government employ, but a resignation from, or refusal to accept, government employment. The noncooperation is long-term: it may be permanent; it may last for the duration of the regime or policy; on occasion it may last only for some months during a particular campaign of resistance.

This method may be applied by individuals with or without regard to political consequences, simply to dissociate themselves from something they regard as immoral. When used as a method of corporate resistance, however, the aim of this type of political boycott is to reduce the number of officials and employees willing to carry out the policy or assist a regime regarded as oppressive. Effectiveness will therefore depend largely on the numbers involved and their particular talents, skills, positions, or influence.

Examples of this method range fairly widely. When the Austrians in 1861 seized goods to pay the taxes refused by the Hungarians, they found that Hungarian auctioneers refused to work for the Austrian government in selling the confiscated goods.[41] In the Soviet Union on December 9, 1920, dissident Communist representatives of water transport workers opposed centralized government control by resigning from *Tsektran* (the Joint Central Transport Committee).[42]

From Nazi Germany there are a series of individual resignations, as well as threats to resign and unsuccessful attempts to resign, both by prominent officials and by subordinate aides who found themselves opposed to one or another of Hitler's policies or actions, or who simply could not continue to carry out particularly distasteful duties.[43] There was also a plan to use this method on a large scale in an African colonial situation. On August 31, 1962, as part of a "master plan" to dismantle the Central African Federation (of Northern and Southern Rhodesia and Nyasaland, under white rule), Kenneth Kaunda, then President of the United National Independence Party (later to become President of Zambia), announced that he intended to call upon Northern Rhodesia's 11,000 civil servants employed by the Federal government to resign.[44] It did not, however, prove necessary to carry out this master plan.

Resignations for political reasons have also occurred among staffs of government-sponsored universities, especially in protest against government interference in the university. In 1911, for example, about a hundred members of the faculty of Moscow University resigned in protest against political suppression by the Minister of Education and the forced resignations of the rector and vice-rector.[45] During the Buddhist struggle in Vietnam against the Diem regime in 1963, forty-seven faculty members of Hué University resigned in protest against the dismissal of Father Cao Van Luan, the Catholic rector of the University who had supported the Buddhist struggle.[46]

Sometimes the members of a government agency or institution may resign *en masse* because of opposition to acts and policies of the regime. For example, when Louis XV of France forbade the thirteen *parlements* (roughly, courts of justice) to regard themselves as representatives of the nation and to supervise the work of other branches of the government, the members of the *parlement* of Paris resigned in a body in 1770. When they and members of other *parlements* persisted in their noncooperation, these institutions were suppressed.[47] During the Nazi occupation, between February and April 1942, Norwegian bishops, deans and pastors resigned as employees of the State church in protest against violations of Norwegian constitutional priciples and government interference with the church. However, they continued to hold their spiritual positions and to carry out their pastoral duties—in effect disestablishing the church and making it for the time an independent body.[48]

High ranking officials and ministers may resign their posts and new candidates may refuse to accept appointment to such posts because of opposition to government policies. Modern examples have a forerunner in the Netherlands' struggle against Spanish rule in the 1560's: on two occasions the Prince of Orange, the Count of Egmont, and the Count of Hoorn withdrew from the Council of State in order to press King Philip II of Spain to correct various grievances.[49] On August 9, 1943, Danish Premier Scavenius threatened to resign if the Germans required Danish courts to try the men arrested after a wave of anti-German strikes and riots; on August 28 he and his government did resign, in the political context of increased repression and resistance.[50] African Members of the Legislative Council in preindependence Kenya refused to accept ministerial posts, especially in March 1960, because of their opposition to the British-imposed Lennox-Boyd constitution.[51] In the summer of 1963 the Vietnamese Foreign Minister and the Ambassador to the United States both resigned in support of the Buddhist struggle against the Diem regime.[52]

There are relatively few examples of attempts to destroy a regime by corporate withholding or withdrawal of assistance by current or potential employees and officials. During the Indian nonviolent campaigns, however, there were frequent efforts to induce government employees to resign their positions, whether they were village headmen or top departmental officers in New Delhi. These efforts were particularly strong during the 1930–31 campaign.[53]

A case in which there was a stillborn attempt to overthrow a regime by widespread resignations suggests a possible alternative to both the *coup d'état* and regicide, and therefore merits mention in discussion of this particular method even though it was not actually carried out. In 1938 the Chief of the German General Staff, Colonel-General Ludwig Beck, opposed the impending Nazi attack on Czechoslovakia, fearing an unwanted general European war. Beck not only decided to resign himself; he also sought to obtain the resignation and support of Commander-in-Chief Walter von Brauchitsch. With his full support (seen as crucial) Beck planned to provoke a mass resignation of Germany's senior commanding generals and the conservative members of the coalition government—that is, Minister of Economics Schacht, Foreign Minister Neurath, Finance Minister Krosigk, and Minister of Justice Gürtner. Beck resigned, but Brauchitsch refused either to resign or to play the role Beck had intended for him, that he appeal for support for the plan to the full conference of the High Command of the Army, and that he then lead the officers to a direct personal confrontation with Hitler.[54]

126. Boycott of government departments, agencies and other bodies

In refusing to recognize the authority of the government or to support one of its particular policies, the resisters may refuse to cooperate with all government departments or only with the governmental bodies responsible for the particular objectionable policy. Such noncooperation may sometimes be conducted even at the financial expense of the noncooperators. This type of boycott may involve either withholding new forms of cooperation or severing existing forms of cooperation. Many types of departments, agencies and bureaus may be boycotted. This method may also involve a refusal to accept government loans, grants-in-aid, and the like.[55]

It is frequently applied in colonial conflicts, as our examples from Egypt, India and Central Africa show. Lord Milner's mission to Egypt in 1919 to prepare a constitution for the then-British protectorate met with such complete boycott that after three months it had to return to Britain without having consulted a single representative Egyptian.[56] Similarly, in 1928 the Indian nationalists carried out a complete boycott of the Simon Commission which had been instructed to make recommendations concerning the future status of India, but had no Indian members. There were refusals to give evidence. "Go back, Simon," was a popular slogan.[57] During noncooperation campaigns the Indian nationalists promoted a boycott of the British law courts by lawyers, solicitors and litigants and encouraged the alternative of settling civil disputes by private arbitration, including by the *panchayat* (the village-five advisory council.)[58]

The Central African Federation (or the Federation of Rhodesia and Nyasaland) has already been referred to in this chapter. From the time that this Eupropean-dominated Federation was first proposed at the beginning of the 1950's, African nationalists from the constituent territories undertook a policy of noncooperation. Although this did not prevent its establishment, their refusal to accept and cooperate with the new federal government ultimately led to its dissolution. This African noncooperation provides three examples of the use of this particular method. Africans from Northern Rhodesia and Nyasaland refused to participate in the April-May meetings in London which were to draft the Federal Scheme. They similarly refused to attend the meeting in London in January 1953 which prepared the final Scheme for the Federation. When the Monckton Commission visited the Federation in 1960 to gather information needed to make recommendations concerning the review of the federal constitution, African political organizations in Northern Rhodesia and Nyasaland maintained an effective boycott of the Commission and refused to give evidence before it. [59]

This method has also been used in other types of situations, including cases of political revolution, resistance to foreign occupation, guerrilla struggle, and resistance to government control over business. During the Russian 1905 Revolution, the Mensheviks organized in Georgia, and especially in Kutais province, a successful boycott of the Russian administration, courts and schools. It was the summer of 1906 before Russian authority and control were reestablished. [60] During the *Ruhrkampf*, despite an acute food shortage Germans refused to use the soup kitchens and shops set up by the occupation authorities. [61] In Quang Nang province, Vietnam, in September–November 1964, Buddhists repeatedly refused to cooperate with the National Liberation Front administration and were finally left alone. [62]

Another example of this form of boycott comes from Nazi Germany in 1935 and derives from an attempt by the Nazi Party's Labor Front to establish party control over both large and small business organizations. To this end, a decree issued on June 13 by Dr. Robert Ley, head of the Labor Front, formed the National Chamber of Labor and eighteen regional chambers, an act which was intended to give the party's Labor Front a counterpart to the Chambers of Industry. Ley ordered employers to become individual members, and the Minister of War was invited to delegate officers to attend the meetings of the regional chambers. These new chambers were intended to be used to control private business. The business groups, however, boycotted the Chambers of Labor, and the Minister of War authorized only civilian officials to attend. The boycott was effective, and this attempt at establishing effective control over private business failed. [63]

When the U.S. House of Representatives Committee on Internal Security in July 1970 requested 177 colleges and universities to supply it with the names of radical speakers, their sponsors, fees and sources of the funds, they were met with sharp noncooperation from Tufts University, in Medford, Massachusetts, and milder lack of help from Harvard University. Tufts Vice-President John W. Scheetz declared:

> We feel the request immediately suggests grave and ominous implications involving constitutionally guaranteed rights of free speech and other freedoms which the university has traditionally enjoyed and protected. . . . To avoid possible infringement on these freedoms of such deep concern to us all, Tufts University chooses not to respond to the committee's request.

The Harvard reply, from Charles P. Whitlock, simply stated that the university had no information on the speakers invited to the campus by student organizations. The *Boston Globe* editorially called these acts of noncooperation "new blows for political as well as academic freedom." [64]

This type of political boycott has sometimes also been practiced within various nongovernmental international organizations. For example, a brief boycott of a session in Geneva of the International Labor Organization took place on June 22, 1966, when African delegates, followed by delegates from many other countries, walked out during a discussion of a committee report on the ways member governments abide by I.L.O. obligations. These Africans and other delegates were protesting Portugal's denial of independence to African colonies; charges of forced labor were especially prominent. [65] The same day it was announced that the delegation to the I.L.O. from the American Federation of Labor and Congress of Industrial Organizations would end its boycott of the I.L.O. and would attend that agency's executive board meeting on June 23. Mr Faupl of the A.F.L.-C.I.O. had boycotted the three-week conference in protest against the election at the I.O.L.'s annual session of a representative from Poland, the first to be elected from a Communist delegation. [66]

127. Withdrawal from government educational institutions

The permanent or indefinite withdrawal of children and youths from schools owned or controlled by the government during a major campaign of resistance to that government is also a method of political noncooperation. This was done, for example, during the Indian independence struggle.[67] Such withdrawal may have the fourfold effect of: 1) contributing to the establishment and growth of "national" schools and colleges independent of the established authority; 2) checking the influence of the authorities and those in educational circles still loyal to the old order, who might use their positions to seek to instill loyalty to the established regime in their pupils and students; 3) providing the resistance movement with youthful recruits who would otherwise have been occupied with studies; and 4) contributing to the general disruption of the *status quo* and increasing the totality of noncooperation with the government. The National Conference of the African National Congress in 1954 called for a boycott of educational institutions as long as the South African government's Bantu Education policy remained in force—which meant indefinitely.[68]

128. Boycott of government-supported organizations

This type of political noncooperation expresses itself in a refusal to join, or decision to resign from, organizations which are regarded as instruments of the government or political movement which is being opposed. One example is the refusal of the Norwegian teachers in 1942 to join the Quisling government's new teachers' organization, which was to be used as the cornerstone of the Corporative State and as a wedge for indoctrinating the children.[69] As the Quisling government, still pursuing the plan for the Corporative State, sought to take control of various existing Norwegian organizations, the great bulk of members resigned: estimates for the summer of 1941 range from seventy to ninety percent of the total membership of individual organizations.[70] Following the crushing of the June 1953 Rising, East German workers practiced a related type of resistance; as a body they refused to pay membership dues to government-controlled trade unions.[71]

129. Refusal of assistance to enforcement agents

It is fairly common for the general population, in areas where there is either sympathy with criminal elements or fear of them, to refuse to provide information to the police or to disclose the whereabouts of wanted persons. Similarly, the general population living under foreign occupation or a domestic dictatorship may refuse to supply the police with information on political and patriotic resisters. This constitutes an act of political noncooperation.

American colonists repeatedly refused to inform against persons wanted for committing various acts of destruction against British property or resistance to political control. This was illustrated on two prominent occasions. When, in late 1771, a group of disguised men captured a boat and its contents which had been seized in the lower Delaware by a revenue vessel, even the offer of a reward of two hundred pounds sterling by Pennsylvania's Lieutenant Governor Richard Penn for information leading to their arrest failed to bring forward any informers. In Rhode Island waters, when the revenue vessel *Gaspée* ran aground on June 8, 1772, a group of undisguised and prominent citizens of Providence boarded it (after having openly organized the action), injured the commander, overpowered the crew, and burned the vessel; despite a royal proclamation offering a large reward and setting up a royal commission to investigate the incident, the guilty parties "were so well shielded both by their fellow citizens and by the government of the colony that no evidence could be obtained against them." [72]

This method may also involve the refusal of other types of assistance. For example, during the 1928 Bardoli revenue-refusal campaign in India, Joan V. Bondurant reports:

> Peasants met revenue collectors with closed doors, or receiving them, read extracts aloud from Patel's speeches and tried by argument to persuade them that they could not collect the revenue. When police reenforcements broke down doors and carried away equipment, peasants began to dismantle carts and other equipment, hiding the parts in different places. [73]

In the summer of 1881 Irish tenants took various actions in order not to assist the seizure of property for back rent, which was being refused. An eyewitness reports one such case:

> After the men's dinners, the sheriff again started, protected by a considerable force, for the farm of one Murnane, where a seizure was also to be made for rent due. When we arrived at the farm, which seemed to be one of some value, it was found that there was not a single head of cattle upon it . . . in fact, everything movable had been taken away.

The sheriff and his men had to leave empty-handed, but when they returned unexpectedly a few days later, they were able to seize the cattle which had been removed for the previous visit. [74]

Irish gypsies, camping with their horses and caravans on the outskirts of Dublin in January and February 1964, resisted eviction from certain sites by refusing to harness their horses to the caravans, so that each had to be pulled away from the sites by hand.[75]

Sometimes the refusal to assist enforcement agents has been applied by the persons being arrested themselves, in "going limp" when arrested. Martin Oppenheimer and George Lakey offer the following definition of this type of action:

> "Going limp" is just what the phrase implies. It is a relaxation of all the body in a kind of physical non-cooperation with the situation, so that the non-cooperator has to be dragged or carried to wherever authorities want him moved. It can be modified by putting hands in pockets, or in situations of violence by folding up (as in football) and covering up the head and other sensitive areas with your arms.[76]

130. Removal of own signs and placemarks[77]

The removal, alteration, or replacement of house numbers, street signs, placemarks, railway station signs, highway direction and distance signs, and the like may temporarily misdirect, impede, or delay the movement of foreign troops and police. Such efforts, which seem to have only a stalling potential, are most likely to be effective where the troops or police are quite unfamiliar with the territory, where the country or layout of streets is especially bewildering or complicated, and where the population is unwilling to provide accurate directions. One of the potential uses of this method is to delay the political police until wanted persons have had time to escape, or until resistance headquarters or equipment can be relocated. The time thus gained may be minimal in some cases, although a psychological impact on both occupation forces and the resisting population may remain a significant factor.

The clearest example of the use of such methods was in Prague the first week of the Russian occupation in August 1968. (Troops entered late on August 20.) Czechoslovak Radio reported on Friday, August 23, at 5:25 p.m., that arrests were expected during the night. An appeal was made to paint over or remove street signs and number plates on homes and to make name plates on apartments illegible. Highway direction signs throughout the country were to be repainted. Such action had already started, however. On Thursday night many street signs were already painted over, as were direction signs on the main highways. After noon on Friday Prague had been flooded with leaflets urging the removal or painting over of street signs and signs on important offices and plants. The newspaper *Prace* reported: "There was a lightning reaction to this appeal. Prague streets have lost their names!" [78] The paper *Lidova Demokracie* reported that hundreds of thousands of people had participated in such action:

> Prague names and numbers have died out. For the uninvited guests, Prague has become a dead city. Anyone who was not born here, who has not lived here, will find a city of anonymity among a million inhabitants. . . . let us follow the slogan: The mailman will find you, but evil-doers won't! Bravo Prague and other cities that followed and follow its example! [79]

The Communist Party paper *Rude Pravo* reported that many young boys had participated in the removal of signs or painting over them, "to see to it that the only people who find their way around the city are those who are supposed to." [80]

The Czech film *Closely Watched Trains,* made long before the Russian invasion, illustrated well the disruptive effects during the Nazi occupation of altering the names of railroad stations, when this is combined with disruptive assistance from railroad workers determined to see that a particular train does not reach its destination until hours or days later than scheduled.

131. Refusal to accept appointed officials

The political unit over which an official has been appointed to serve may on occasion refuse to accept the appointee. In the example to follow the appointee was persuaded to depart promptly, but in cases where this does not happen, this method would involve refusal to recognize the appointee in his official role and noncooperation with him if he attempts to carry out his duties. This example, which occurred in Ping-fang, Hupeh, China, in the 1840's, was reported by a Western missionary. Opposition to the appointment of a certain mandarin to the post of governor (magistrate) of the town was based upon his previous administration in another district, which had been corrupt, arbitrary and tyrannical. When a deputation to the Viceroy (governor-general) of the province failed to win cancellation of the appointment,

> The principle people assembled, and held a grand council. . . . It was decided that the new governor should not be permitted to install himself, and that he should be civilly ejected from the town. . . .
> Scarcely had he entered the tribunal, [when] . . . it was an-

nounced to him that the chief citizens of the town requested an audience. . . . The deputation prostrated themselves . . . before their new
Prefect [magistrate]; then, one of them stepping forward, announced to him, with exquisite politeness and infinite grace, that they
came in the name of the town, to request that he would set off directly to return whence he came, for they would have none of him.

The Prefect . . . endeavored first to soothe, and then to intimidate,
the rebellious citizens, but all in vain. . . . The spokesman very calmly
told him that they had not come there to discuss the matter; that the
thing was settled, and they had made up their minds that he should
not sleep in the town . . . the town would pay his traveling expenses,
beside providing a brilliant escort to conduct him safely to the capital
of the province.

Encouraged by a noisy crowd outside, the appointee yielded and left, escorted by the chief men of the town. They went directly to the Viceroy.
After reading a petition signed by all the most important people of Ping-
fang, the Viceroy told the delegation that their arguments were reasonable
and should be attended to.[81]

132. Refusal to dissolve existing institutions

When governments seek to abolish independent institutions in order to
control the population better, to abolish a particular opposition movement,
or to restructure the society on the basis of some ideological preconception,
political, educational, labor, cultural and many other types of organizations may refuse voluntarily to accept such dissolution. They may then
continue to operate either openly or secretly and keep up as many of their
normal activities as they can, resisting collectively the governmental measures intended to destroy them. The widespread preservation of domestic
institutions is a key objective in resisting foreign occupations seeking to re-
mold the society. Refusal to disband such institutions may be combined
with the boycott of government-supported institutions described above.
Both methods may thus be used when nonviolent action is employed to
defend a legitimate government and the society's institutions against illegitimate attack.

German Chancellor Prince Otto von Bismarck wrongly linked two
assassination attempts against Emperor Wilhelm II to the Social Democrats and with this excuse induced the new parliament in 1878 to pass
the Socialist Law. This enabled the government within eight months to
dissolve many workingmen's unions and associations, suppress a multi-

tude of publications, dissolve *bona fide* cooperative societies, prohibit political meetings of Social Democrats, imprison and expel Socialists, destroy the entire Social Democratic Party organization, and launch many forms of police harassment of people connected with the Social Democratic Party. After three years, however, the Socialists, refusing to accept the dissolution of their party, began meeting again secretly; they circulated literature smuggled from Switzerland and organized and nominated candidates for elections. At each election after 1881 there was a significant increase in the votes recorded, reports J. Ellis Barker, a historian of this period, "notwithstanding, or rather because of, all the measures taken against it by the Government." By 1890, when Bismarck was dismissed by the Emperor and the Socialist Law withdrawn, the Social Democratic vote had risen from 437,158 in 1878 to the new high of 1,427,298. Barker writes: "The effect of the Socialist Law, with all its prosecution, was the reverse of what Bismarck had expected for it had made that party great." [83]

CITIZENS' ALTERNATIVES TO OBEDIENCE

133. Reluctant and slow compliance

Where opponents of regimes or policies do not feel able to resist unconditionally, they may at certain points postpone compliance as long as possible, finally complying with a marked lack of enthusiasm and thoroughness. Thus, while not entirely blocked, the ability of the regime to carry out its will may be slowed and somewhat limited. In East Germany, for example, when so-called voluntary plans for the collectivization of agriculture were announced by Walter Ulbricht in July 1952, opposition by farmers was expressed not only by thousands of emigrations to the West, but also by a widespread disinclination to join the new cooperatives. "Party speakers organized 'foundation meetings' in every village. Generally these functions were ignored or sparsely attended; often the speakers were shouted down; sometimes they were forced to withdraw in haste." In at least one case even the local mayor and Party secretary ignored invitations to attend. Although at the end of four months two thousand cooperative farms had been established, and six months later five thousand, the government plan had obviously been stalled. [84]

This type of behavior has often been applied to tax collection, although the motives in such cases are frequently less clearly political than economic. In both seventeenth and nineteenth century China, members of the gentry often deliberately postponed payment of their land tax or grain tribute to the government in hopes that they might eventually evade payment.[85] During the nineteenth century payment of the rice tribute was often made very reluctantly and in unhelpful ways. Not only were payments often late, but wet and impure rice was often substituted for dry, clean rice, less than the quantity required was often delivered, and sometimes even that was simply dumped outside the granaries. Occasionally a mild inquiry from the official or clerk at the granary would provoke a refusal to deliver the rice at all or formal charges against the clerk and complaints to a superior official.[86]

In a very different situation during World War II, on the evening of the violent revolt and escape by Jewish prisoners from the Sobibor extermination camp in Poland on October 14, 1943, German officials sent an urgent message by railway-telegraph: "SEND MILITARY REINFORCEMENTS AT ONCE TO PURSUE REBELS." A young woman telegrapher who received it at the nearby Chelm station withheld the telegram from the German contact for over four hours, even though she was risking her life.[87]

134. Nonobedience in absence of direct supervision

Another type of political noncooperation involves the population's ignoring and noncompliance with laws, edicts and regulations in all situations where there is no immediate, direct supervision or enforcement. When soldiers are around to see that a particular order is carried out, for example, the population obeys; but when the soldiers leave, the people resume their noncompliance. This is a method that has often been used in China against unpopular regimes and foreign invaders. But this type of behavior is very difficult to document.[88]

135. Popular nonobedience

There are a large number of instances in which the general population, or part of it, has consciously disregarded and violated laws or regulations, but in ways which do not amount to civil disobedience. One or more characteristics of either of the types of civil disobedience may be absent—for example, the disobeyed law may not be seen as illegitimate. Primarily, however, this method involves ignoring or disregarding the law or regulations more than blatant defiance, the resisters choosing not to flaunt their noncompliance. The acts may be open and unhidden but not advertised, the resisters preferring to remain, as far as possible, personally unknown and unpunished and to continue to be part of a larger opposition group. This method frequently takes the form of unobtrusively ignoring the law or regulation in question, often by large numbers of people, as though it did not exist.

Efforts in 1686 by King Christian V of Norway-Denmark to build Christiansand into a major city, as planned by Christian IV, were partially frustrated by the refusal of the inhabitants of Risør, Arendal, Mandal and Flekkefjord to comply with a clear order, backed by threats of severe punishments, to move to Christiansand within six months. "Not once did this help. The inhabitants continued living quietly, and the coastal towns thrived and bloomed."[89] During the French Revolution, in the late autumn of 1789, a decree reestablished freedom of the grain trade, but "no one obeyed it."[90] And on June 20, 1792, in defiance of a prohibition of a demonstration, people marched in front of the Assembly to celebrate the anniversary of the Tennis Court Oath and then invaded the Tuileries and sought out the King, whom they cursed and threatened.[91]

When the French government abolished the national workshops in June 1848, and then sought to avoid trouble and revolution by sending some of the workmen back into the country, "They refused to leave. On the 22nd of June, they marched through Paris in troops, singing in cadence, in a monotonous chant, 'We won't be sent away, we won't be sent away . . .'" Within days there was bloodshed.[92] During the 1905 Revolution in Imperial Russia, *de facto* freedom of the press was temporarily established late in the year by direct action in the form of popular nonobedience. All the censorship regulations were simply ignored and newspapers published what they liked. Without the required permission, new newspapers with strong political views sprang up.[93] Trade unions similarly ignored the law and operated openly.[94]

Acts of popular nonobedience also occurred during World War II. In the Netherlands, for example, German orders that the population turn in metal coins were generally disregarded, and private and illegal listening to broadcasts from Britain was regarded as an act of opposition to the German occupation.[95] In several sections of Copenhagen during the June 1944 strike and resulting German emergency measures, the populace simply ignored the curfew.[96] Among Jews deported from Belgium in November 1942 were some who had removed the required yellow star from their clothes[97] and in June 1942 there were various types of noncompliance with the decree requiring the wearing of the yellow star in occupied France:

Some of the Jews decided not to wear the star. Others wore it in the wrong way. Still others wore several stars instead of one. Some Jews provided their star with additional inscriptions. And, finally, a number of non-Jews took to wearing the star or something that looked like it. Angrily, the Germans arrested some of the Jewish offenders and their French supporters to intern them in one of the camps.[98]

One reason for the inefficiency of regulations aimed at preventing the rural people of China from migrating to urban areas between 1950 and 1958 reportedly was that frequently the regulations were "ignored altogether by those wishing to leave."[99]

136. Disguised disobedience

Disobedience of laws, regulations, or orders may be carried out in ways which give the disobedience the thinly disguised appearance of compliance. During the noncooperation campaign which achieved the nullification of the Stamp Act, the undisguised refusal of merchants, shippers and the like to use the required stamps on shipping documents generally brought the trading ports to a standstill when the law went into effect on November 1, 1765. But in Philadelphia a form of disguised disobedience was used which kept ships moving for some weeks—and without the hated stamps:

> In Philadelphia, by an ingenious device not apparently thought of elsewhere, trade had been kept moving throughout November. In all colonial ports merchants had cleared out every ship they could load before November first, but in Philadelphia they cleared ships which were only partially loaded. Although clearances were not supposed to be granted until the entire cargo was declared, all the ships in Philadelphia which had any part of their cargoes aboard obtained clearance papers in the last days of October. When the cargoes had been completed, the owners went to the custom-house and had undated additions entered on their papers . . . . Since it normally took three to four weeks for a ship to complete her cargo, there was relatively little pressure in Philadelphia until the end of November.[100]

One way banned newspapers may practice disguised disobedience is by quickly reappearing with new names. This happened during the *Ruhrkampf*, when banned newspapers even sometimes adopted the names of other newspapers which had not been banned.[101] This also happened in Russia in 1905,[102] and in late spring of 1929 British suppression of *Forward*, a newspaper in Calcutta, was followed by the appearance of *New Forward*; upon its being banned, *Liberty* was issued.[103]

With jazz having been banned by the Nazis during World War II and defiant jazz musicians being hunted by the Gestapo, German jazz enthusiasts changed the names of American jazz numbers to innocent-sounding German titles, Richard W. Fogg reports. "Organ Grinder Swing" became *"Hofkonzert im Hinterhaus"* (Court Concert in the

Back Yard), "Tiger Rag" became *"Schwartzer Panther"* (Black Panther). "Black Bottom" became *"Schwartze Erde"* (Black Earth), and "Lady, Be Good" became *"Frau, Sei Gut."* One of these German jazz enthusiasts, Jutta Hipp, recalled: "We played American tunes, but we had to give the Nazis a list, so we translated the titles into German. . . . We translated them in the most stupid way, because we thought the whole idea of requiring a list and banning American music was stupid. Nobody found out, either. The Nazis listened and applauded it, and we laughed inside." One such number was even played by the official *Wehrmacht* (German army) band! [104]

Young men in Nazi Germany who did not wish to be conscripted into the army, but who also wanted to avoid outright resistance, claimed exemption on medical grounds as a "standard technique." They would obtain a certificate of ill-health from a *"Guten-Tag* doctor"—a doctor who greeted a new patient with *"Guten Tag"* rather than *"Heil Hitler."* One such young man, Horst Lippmann, who was also a jazz enthusiast, successfully used this technique for a year; he had to try to look sick when the inspector called at the house and (since unfit young men were not issued passes) had to stay off the streets. When he was later arrested for jazz activities, Lippmann's father got doctors to testify to the Gestapo that young Lippmann's health was too delicate for him to withstand a jail sentence. Young Horst was released. [105]

The remaining examples are Chinese. Indirect evidence is sometimes the only documentation available for such behavior. One such bit of evidence is found in the Chinese emperor's edicts issued in 1814. These stated that it had been the practice of provincial and local officials (especially those who registered the inhabitants) to present "a good appearance for the moment" but be negligent in carrying out their official duties. The emperor spoke of "officials [who] obey ostensibly and actually disregard Our wishes, i.e., . . . respond to a standing requirement with empty gestures." [106]

Another example of disguised disobedience is drawn from the late 1930s, after the Japanese had established the Hopei-Chahar Political Council in North China, a council which they hoped would be a willing political instrument in Japanese plans for economic development. The Chinese government, however, regarded the council as a buffer between it and the Japanese. Faced with Japanese economic demands, therefore, instead of simply rejecting them the Chinese adopted the device of stretching out the negotiations and stalling for time:

> When pressed with demands General Sung Cheh-yuan, Chairman of the Political Council, in order to evade the issue, retired to his native village "to sweep the graves of his ancestors." Such tactics inevitably exasperated the Japanese who spoke of "Chinese insincerity." They

soon came to realize that as a political instrument the Political Council would not serve the ends for which it was set up. [107]

In 1942 in Chungking the government closed ice cream and coffee parlors and prohibited the sale of coffee and soda pop; once more the response was a type of disguised disobedience:

> The very fancy "Sing Sing Café" reopened as the "Sing Sing Kitchen" and would serve ice cream only after plates and butter plates, water glasses, knives, forks and spoons had been set on the table to give it the look of a dessert after a full meal. Soda pop was served in soup plates and had to be eaten with soup spoons. [108]

Chinese soldiers, too, had learned comparable responses to orders, as Graham Peck observed in Chungking in December 1940:

> After a while a line of shabby soldiers in gray cotton uniforms and straw sandals came slogging up the hill, technically in double-time, but really mocking the quick step. For all their jogging up and down, they moved forward less rapidly than the burdened housewives. Like soldiers all over China, they were chanting numbers to keep in pace: "One, two, three . . . (step, step, step) . . . FOUR!" When their officer screamed at them to hurry it up, they began chanting faster and faster, out of time, while their feet pounded the road as slowly as ever. They all wore that smile. [109]

137. Refusal of an assemblage or meeting to disperse

A formal meeting or an informal gathering of some type may express opposition by refusing official or unofficial demands that it disperse. This method may at times be closely related to popular nonobedience or to civil disobedience of "illegitimate" laws, but this is not always the case.

On several occasions during the American colonists' struggles, town meetings, public assemblies and conventions formally defied specific orders to disperse, given by the governor or some other official. In one such case Lieutenant Governor Hutchinson, long disturbed at the activities of the city's merchants and the Boston town meeting, in January 1770 sent the sheriff to Faneuil Hall, where the merchants were meeting, with a message denouncing the gathering as unjustifiable "by any authority or colour of law," and condemning their house-to-house marchings as dangerous and conducive to terror. As representative of the Crown Hutchinson ordered them to disperse and "to forbear all such unlawful assemblies for the future . . ." The merchants paused in their meeting only long enough to vote unanimously that in their opinion the meeting was lawful; then they resumed their transactions. [110]

On June 23, 1789, in an atmosphere of popular rebellion against the powers of the French king and the nobility, Louis XVI gave a speech to the representatives of the three estates outlining their roles, and then he ordered the deputies to adjourn and to meet the next day in separate chambers. "When the King withdrew, the nobles and most of the clergy followed him, while the commons remained silently in their seats." Their spokesman told the King's representative that they had decided not to adjourn without a debate and that ". . . no one can give orders to the assembled nation." [111]

In a very different situation, on May 15, 1848, the Assembly in Paris was invaded by a crowd which sought to force the Assembly to "pronounce forthwith in favour of Poland." For hours there were no troops to evict the crowd, and while the Assembly refused to comply with the demand, it neither adjourned nor sought to evict the rebels. "During all this disorder in its midst, the Assembly sat passive and motionless on its benches, neither resisting nor giving way, silent and firm," reports Alexis de Tocqueville, an eyewitness. A vote for the motion would have dishonored the Assembly and shown it to be powerless; one against it would have risked cut throats among the members. "This passive resistance irritated and incensed the people; it was like a cold, even surface upon which its fury glided without knowing what to catch hold of . . ." The crowd finally shouted: "We can't make them vote!" After some chaos and the expectation that troops were coming, a member of the crowd declared the Assembly to be adjourned—without, however, the crowd's having achieved its objective. [112]

During the Hungarian Protestants' struggle against restrictive Austrian religious laws and efforts to subordinate them to imperial control, the Calvinists of the Trans-Tisza Church District played a prominent role. Defying a government order, their council met as scheduled in Debrecen on January 11, 1860, with five hundred church officials and thousands of laymen attending. William Robert Miller quotes a description of the occasion by Imre Révész, a church historian:

> Immediately after the opening prayer, the Austrian Imperial Government representative . . . stood up and called upon the meeting to disperse. The chairman [Deputy Bishop Peter Balogh] then asked those present whether they wished to disperse or not, whereupon the huge crowd roared in reply: "We shall hold the meeting; we will not disperse." Then as the meeting proceeded, fear began to show on the face of the Imperial representative, as he saw thousands of angry eyes turned in scorn upon him. Finally, he could bear the situation no longer, and got up and left; and no one did him harm. [113]

The gathering refusing to disperse, however, need not be an official assembly; it may simply be a public meeting or an improvised protest gathering. On February 17, 1959, for example, a crowd of from 150 to 200 Africans in the Kota Kota district of Nyasaland went to the police station to protest ten arrests for illegal acts which had taken place the previous day and to demand that they be arrested also; rejecting the District Commissioner's explanation for the arrests and his offer to receive a delegation, they refused orders to disperse. "The police then used tear smoke and made a baton charge." [114]

A variation on this refusal to disperse was applied by the Czechoslovak delegation which negotiated in Moscow following the 1968 invasion. At Moscow Airport they discovered that one of their members, Frantisek Kriegel, was missing. Kriegel was a liberal member of the Presidium of the Czechoslovak Communist Party and a Jew to whom the Soviet officials particularly objected. The remaining delegates refused to depart without Kriegel, and it was not until Soviet officials produced him that the delegation flew back to Prague. [115]

138. Sitdown

The sitdown is an act of noncooperation in which the participants actually sit down on the street, road, ground, or floor and refuse to leave voluntarily, for either a limited or an indefinite period of time. The sitdown may be a spontaneous act, or a reaction decided on in advance, as a response to orders for a march or other demonstration to disperse. Or it may be combined with civil disobedience to some regulatory law as a serious type of symbolic resistance. The sitdown may also be used to halt ordinary traffic or tanks, or to prevent workers or officials from carrying out their work. In these cases it becomes a method of nonviolent intervention (either nonviolent interjection or nonviolent obstruction, which are described in the next chapter). In recent years the sitdown appears to have been more widely used than previously.

Toward the end of April 1960, during the Algerian War, over five hundred demonstrators protested the internment of six thousand North Africans in France, without trial or hearing, by marching to the Centre de Tri de Vincennes (one of the French reception centers for Arabs) and sitting down in front of it. New waves of demonstrators came when the first persons were arrested and driven away in vehicles. [116] Demonstrators protesting the same policy held a sitdown near the Champs Elysées in Paris in late May, after the police had stopped their march toward the Ministry of the Interior. [117]

In the autumn of 1961 three hundred Norwegians opposing nuclear tests held a sitdown outside the Soviet Embassy in Oslo after the Soviet announcement of its intention to explode a fifty-megaton nuclear bomb.[118] In May 1962 about one thousand Lisbon University students staged a sit-down in protest against a decision by the Portuguese Minister of Education to ban their student-day celebrations.[119]

On June 19, 1964, about five hundred young Russian art fans attended the opening (delayed until 5 P.M.) at the Manege Gallery in Moscow of works by the controversial painter, Ilya Glazunov. When the Soviet Ministry of Culture announced that the scheduled public debate on the exhibited works had been postponed, the young people refused to leave, saying they would have their own discussion. When officials turned out the lights, the people sat down on the floor, first clapping in unison and then airing opinions of every kind. The militia finally induced them to leave three hours after the opening.[120] Students at Madrid University, campaigning for an independent student union, on February 24, 1965, first conducted a silent march and then sat down at the police barrier which blocked their way.[121]

A variation on the usual patterns occurred on at least two occasions during the Indian struggle in 1930–31 when the police who halted a march or parade of nonviolent actionists also staged a sitdown in the street or road to block their passage. On May 15, 1930, during the Dharasana salt raids, a group of *satyagrahis* headed for the salt depot under the leadership of the poet Sarojini Naidu was halted by a police superintendent who said to her: "We are going to stay here and offer Satyagraha . . . ourselves as long as you do." But after twenty-eight hours of a dual sitting confrontation, police patience wore out and they returned to more violent methods.[122] Some weeks later armed police in Bombay stopped a procession of about thirty thousand men, women and children who then sat down in the streets, whereupon the police also sat down, and they confronted each other for hours. When sympathizers brought food, water and blankets during the night's rain, the *satyagrahis* passed these on to the obstructing police as a token of good will. Finally the police gave in and the procession ended in a triumphant midnight march.[123]

139. Noncooperation with conscription and deportation

Opposition to various types of government conscription and deportation may be expressed by a refusal either to register as ordered, or to report for duty or participate in deportation. (The motives of the opponent in initiating deportation may vary: the opponent may want to de-populate the area, remove political dissidents, produce forced labor, or exterminate an unwanted group.) Such noncooperation may also be a form of civil disobedience or popular nonobedience. It is classified separately here because it is not the disobedience itself which is important but the refusal to cooperate with a program of conscription or deportation. This kind of noncooperation may include several specific types of acts, not simply disobedience.

Noncooperation with military conscription has been practiced on a number of occasions. For example, in Hungary from 1820 to 1825 there was a mass refusal to comply with a levy of troops imposed on the country by Austria,[124] and this happened again beginning in 1861.[125] In their struggle for autonomy from Imperial Russia, the Finns similarly refused military conscription. When the Russian conscription system was imposed on Finland by imperial decree in 1901, "The pastors refused to proclaim the law in the villages, the judges and lawyers to apply it, the conscripts to execute it."[126] To make the conscription less obnoxious, the Tsar decreed that with each conscription only one percent of the recruits (to be chosen by drawing lots) were to be taken into the army. Eino Jutikkala writes:

> Nevertheless, [during the conscription of 1902] three-fifths of the youths of conscription age—the proportion among the university students was as high as five-sixths—refused to report for the draft. . . .
>
> In the following two conscriptions, the resistance was less successful but still strong enough to cause the Russians to abandon their campaign in this field. . . . the Finns were released from personal military service, and Finland was obliged to pay a small annual tax to the imperial treasury as compensation.[127]

Finnish soldiers were consequently not available for the Russo-Japanese War or for service to the Tsar during the 1905 Revolution.

In New Zealand there was widespread refusal to be conscripted for military training in 1913, with many being sentenced to detention camps, and in 1930 some fifty thousand young men from fourteen to eighteen refused to take military instruction.[128]

This method of noncooperation has also been practiced against conscription and deportation for forced labor and against deportation for extermination. There were some cases (apparently only a minority) of Jews under Nazi rule refusing to register or report as ordered. Although there probably were 85,000 Jews in Belgium in May 1939, only about 42,000 registered with the police when ordered to do so in October 1940; Gerard Reitlinger attributes the bulk of this difference to a refusal to register.[129] In Athens in December 1943 only 1,200 Jews registered with the

Judenrat (Jewish Council) when ordered to do so, although eight thousand Jews were believed to be in the city.[130] For a period in August 1944 Jews in the Lodz ghetto in Poland noncooperated with German evacuation orders, refusing, for example, to collect their rations (i.e., report) at the local railroad station or the Central Prison.[131] When all surviving Jews in Bratislava, Czechoslovakia, were ordered on November 16, 1944, to report to the Bratislava *Rathaus* (town hall) for transfer to Sered camp, only fifty obeyed, while at least six thousand remained hidden in bunkers.[132] This method was also used by non-Jews against the Nazis. In the Netherlands only a few thousand of the ex-soldiers reported, as ordered, for deportation and internment in Germany, and about seventy percent of the students refused to report for work in Germany. It appears that the Germans did not make any special effort to arrest these students.[133]

140. Hiding, escape and false identities

Hiding, escape and false identities are not usually a part of nonviolent action. Normally they are not protest or resistance as such, and they commonly reflect fear which, as will be discussed in Chapter Nine, disrupts the effective operation of the technique. However, there are certain circumstances under which they may constitute a method of nonviolent action. These are largely political circumstances in which the regime seeks the arrest, internment and perhaps extermination of particular groups of people for ideological reasons or as part of a massive wave of repression. It could also apply to groups wanted as hostages or for reprisals, forced labor, or military duty. And of course escape by slaves is resistance to the institution of slavery. In certain circumstances members of the resistance movement might also seek to disappear.

In the United States before the Civil War escapes and assistance to escaped slaves from the South were reasonably effective methods of opposition to the institution of slavery. As many as 100,000 slaves are estimated to have successfully escaped in the generation before the Civil War, and despite the federal Fugitive Slave Law requiring the return of escapees, more slaves escaped in the 1850s than ever before, Carleton Mabee reports.[134]

As an act of political noncooperation this method was very widely practiced in the Netherlands during World War II. According to Dr. L. de Jong this method was practiced not only by members of the resistance groups who needed false identities, but also by large sections of the population who were wanted by Germans for one reason or another. Approximately 25,000 Dutch Jews went into hiding; those who "submerged" later included much larger groups in the population who were to be deported to Germany, such as members of the Dutch armed forces, students who had refused to declare loyalty to the new regime, and workers needed to boost German production. By the summer of 1944 there were more than 300,000 "underdivers" who had to be provided with shelter, false identity papers, food and usually ration cards.[135]

Some Dutchmen also used escape to counter Nazi measures, especially those Dutch students who—in contrast with those cited in the previous section—registered for work in Germany. Conditions for them in the camps in Germany were extremely bad. Some died. An escape route from Germany back to their own country was arranged, and before the end of the war most—one writer even says "by far the greater number"—had escaped and returned to the Netherlands.[136]

This method was one common means by which Jews in other parts of Europe also sought to counter Nazi measures.[137] When German forces invaded Belgium in May 1940, about one-third of the Jews in that country fled to France, and of the 52,000 remaining toward the end of 1940, German agencies managed to deport only 25,000. An important reason for German difficulties was, as a Foreign Office representative, Bargen, reported in September 1942, the large-scale evasions, including Jews hiding with Belgian families, the use of Belgian identification cards, and flights to occupied and unoccupied France.[138] Of the 8,000 Jews in Athens in December 1943, about 6,800 remained hidden when ordered to register on December 18; only a few hundred of these were later discovered.[139] For some months in 1941-42 the main activity of the Baum Group of young Jewish resisters in Berlin was the raising of money to obtain Aryan documents and foreign passports, largely forged, which enabled Jews to escape, or even to live on the outskirts of Berlin.[140] It is estimated that in Warsaw, 25,000 Jews posed as Aryans, using forged papers. Yuri Suhl describes how Simcha Poliakiewicz, who escaped from the Treblinka extermination camp, was provided with false papers by friendly Poles; these showed him to be Stanislaw Frubel, a Pole of German descent.[141] Several hundred Jews are estimated to have lived through those years in Slovakia either in hiding or by using false documents.[142]

In Canada during World War I, French Canadians resisted military conscription by sending their youths into hiding and refusing to disclose their whereabouts. Over forty percent of the registered draftees were never found and still others were never registered.[143]

141. Civil disobedience of "illegitimate" laws

Civil disobedience is a deliberate, open and peaceful violation of particular laws, decrees, regulations, ordinances, military or police instructions, and the like which are believed to be illegitimate for some reason. One of the most drastic forms of political noncooperation, civil disobedience is an expression of the doctrine that there are times when men have a moral responsibility to disobey "man-made" laws in obedience to "higher" laws. At least since Socrates,[144] members of religious and political groups have often experienced a conflict of loyalties in which they had to choose between obeying the laws of the established government, thus violating their own beliefs, and disobeying such laws, thus remaining true to their deeper convictions.

Sometimes civil disobedience is seen to be called for because of a belief that a certain law is illegitimate, the body or person which instituted the law having had no authority to do so. For example, in February 1766, Edmund Pendleton, one of Virginia's most notable lawyers (he was also a magistrate and a member of the House of Burgesses), wrote to James Madison, Sr., telling him his views on the current debate over whether the courts should noncooperate with the Stamp Act by open disobedience to it, or noncooperate without such disobedience. The courts could suspend activities, and hence not use the required tax stamps on certain documents, or they could operate normally but, in defiance of the law, refuse to use the tax stamps. Pendleton's view was that "he had taken an oath to determine cases according to the law, and since he believed that Parliament had had no authority to pass the Stamp Act, he could not regard that Act as a law and felt that it would be a violation of his oath if he refused to proceed because of it."[145]

In more modern times the theory of civil disobedience was refined and popularized through the action of Henry David Thoreau and a famous essay by him.[146] It was Gandhi, however, who made the greatest single contribution to developing civil disobedience as a means of social and political action on a mass scale. Gandhi wrote: "Disobedience to be civil has to be open and non-violent."[147] Civil disobedience is regarded as a synthesis of civility and disobedience, that is, it is disobedience carried out in nonviolent, civil behavior. It is generally used only after other attempts to remove the undesirable situation have failed and there appears to be no alternative, or in situations where the individual or group is placed in a position of deciding where their higher loyalty lies.

Modern justification for civil disobedience of this type is frequently based on a conviction that obedience would make one an accomplice to an immoral or unjust act or one which is seen to be, in the last analysis, itself illegal. A vivid expression of this view was offered by Pawel Herst in Poland in 1954, at the meeting of the Council of Art and Culture which ousted its Secretary-General, Jerzy Putrament, after he had imposed rigid controls on behalf of the Comminist Party. Herst declared: "If Putrament should tell me to jump out of the window, and I jumped, then we would both be guilty, he for giving the order, and I for obeying it." The phrase became widely repeated in Poland. [148]

Civil disobedience of "illegitimate" laws as a method of political noncooperation may be practiced by individuals, groups or masses of people, and by organized bodies, even governmental ones. The disobedience may be undertaken reluctantly by persons who have no real desire to disturb the status quo but desire only to remain true to their deepest beliefs *(purificatory civil disobedience).* Or civil disobedience may be aimed at changing only a particular aspect of the regime's policies or a particular law or regulation regarded as immoral or unjust *(reformatory civil disobedience).* Or it may be used during a major social or political upheaval as a means of undermining, paralyzing and disintegrating a regime which is seen as unjust or oppressive, with the aim of replacing it with a new system *(revolutionary civil disobedience).* Or civil disobedience may be practiced against a new illegitimate regime (of domestic or foreign origin) and in defense of the legitimate regime or order *(defensive civil disobedience).* These classifications may merge into each other.

Gandhi regarded civil disobedience as a potent way of helping to destroy unjust laws; he also felt that it could be applied far more widely than that objective. "Complete civil disobedience is rebellion without the element of violence in it," he said. [149] In his view civil disobedience could be 1) used to redress a local wrong, 2) applied as a means of self-sacrifice to arouse people's awareness and consciences about some particular wrong, or 3) focused on a particular issue as a contribution to a wider political struggle. [150] Gandhi regarded civil disobedience as dangerous to the autocratic State, but harmless in a democracy which is willing to submit to the will of public opinion. Furthermore, he regarded it as an "inherent right of a citizen" and stated that any attempt to put it down was an "attempt to imprison conscience." [151]

There are a multitude of examples of civil disobedience. The practice of publishing accounts of debates in the British Parliament, for example, was established by acts of civil disobedience. Orders by the House of Lords in 1660 and the House of Commons in 1661 had banned publication of reports of parliamentary debates; the Commons had reaffirmed the ban in 1723 and enforced it in 1760.

> Nevertheless [writes Gipson], John Almon in 1768 had begun to give detailed accounts of proceedings in Parliament, and other daily and weekly papers had followed his lead. As a result, eight newspapers were prosecuted by the House of Commons during the early part of 1771. The issue became acute when printers John Wheble of the *Middlesex Journal* and Roger Thompson of the *Gazetteer* openly defied a House order for their arrests . . .

These two cases were dismissed when the men were brought before sympathetic magistrates, one of whom was John Wilkes. However, the Commons then committed two of these magistrates, who also happened to be members of the House, to imprisonment in the Tower of London:

> The issue aroused the populace to such a degree that popular demonstrations were made not only against Lord North but even against the king. But the upshot of the matter was that the offending printers went unpunished and newspapers continued to print parliamentary debates.
>
> Thus, although the old resolutions prohibiting parliamentary reporting were never officially rescinded, Parliament in 1771 permitted a constitutional amendment to come into being by not fully pressing the charges against the printers in the face of popular sentiment.[152]

The refusal of American colonial merchants to use the tax stamps would not have been civil disobedience had they merely refused to cooperate by suspending the various activities for which stamps were required; but when they continued business without using stamped papers and documents, their defiance became civil disobedience.[153]

Governmental bodies, too, may commit civil disobedience. Salem, in the Province of Massachusetts Bay, for example, held an official town meeting on August 20, 1774, in defiance of Governor Gage's orders.[154] As the Massachusetts Bay House of Representatives met to plan for the First Continental Congress, Governor Gage sent the Secretary of the province to the meeting to announce its dissolution. The members of the House, however, refused to unlock the doors, and continued their business until it was completed, with the Governor's messenger reduced to reading the proclamation of dissolution on the wrong side of the door.[155]

In North Carolina, Governor Martin's proclamation forbidding "illegal Meetings" of the towns and counties—and especially a planned meeting of the whole province—"had the same effect as the executive interdicts, in other provinces, of the right of the people to organize and act. The provincial convention of August 25 assembled at Newbern with a representation from thirty-two of the thirty-eight counties and two of the six towns, while the governor and his council sat futilely by." [156]

In Imperial Russia in 1875, the poor peasants in the villages in the Chigirin district near Kiev practiced a form of civil disobedience in the aftermath of the abolition of serfdom. Opposing the attempts of the richer peasants to legalize their possession of the larger holdings (which had been obtained by unfair means at the emancipation), the poorer peasants sought an equable redistribution of the land. Declining to seize the land by violence but firmly believing they were acting "in accordance with the Tsar's will, they refused to put their mark on the official deeds and some would not make the customary payments" despite severe repression, flogging and imprisonment. In the end they lost even their existing allotments. [157]

During the winter of 1914-15 in Sioux City, Iowa, eighty-three members of the Industrial Workers of the World were imprisoned for violating city restrictions on the holding of street meetings; many had come from other parts of the country specifically to break down the ban. [158] During the famous Toledo, Ohio, automobile strike in the 1930s, the strikers ignored an injunction and "quietly and voluntarily submitted to arrest and filled all police wagons and the jails to overflowing." [159]

In the 1930-31 campaign in India, civil disobedience was expressed in a number of ways, which included the making and public sale of salt in violation of the law, the sale and reading in public of prohibited and seditious literature, defiance of bans on parades and meetings, disobedience of ordinances and police orders, and the violation of a number of other selected laws. [160] During the 1952 Defiance Campaign in South Africa, in which over seven thousand persons went to prison for civil disobedience, the main points attacked were the pass law and apartheid regulations, mainly on the railroads. [161] In March 1960 the South African Pan-Africanist Congress called on Africans to leave their passes at home, to surrender themselves at the nearest police station (remaining completely nonviolent), and to repeat the process when released from prison. [162]

In 1965 American Indians, many of whom depended on fishing for their livelihood, conducted civil disobedience against restrictive regulations of the Conservation Department of the state of Washington by committing "fish-ins" in defense of their rights to fish in ancestral fishing areas. These rights had originally been unlimited and had even been acknowledged—by the Treaty of Medicine Creek of 1854 with the United States and later treaties. Planned by youthful college-educated Indians from various tribes, the direct action was also intended to counter the stereotyped image which American society had of the American Indians and which was held by the Indians themselves. One of the leaders, Mel Thom, said: "We decided to take direct action. We decided to show this country, and ourselves, that the Indians had guts." [163] On a cold day in March 1965 Indians set out with boats and forbidden nets, but without fishing licenses, to fish on the Quillayute River. Hundreds of Indians watched from the banks. The game wardens and state police were armed with warrants and guns. "The tribe was small," reports Stan Steiner. "It had never done anything this bold; for fishing off the reservation, without licenses, was an act of civil disobedience to the game laws. . . And the wardens were white with wrath." [164] Other fish-ins continued into 1966.

> And before it ended the hundreds of Indians had swelled to thousands. There were Fish-Ins in half a dozen rivers. There were dozens of arrests, war dances on the steps of the capitol rotunda, an Indian protest meeting of several thousand at the state capitol. There were Treaty Treks on the streets of the cities and Canoe Treks, of sixty miles, through Puget Sound. There was a gathering of more than one thousand Indians from fifty-six tribes throughout the country who came to join their brothers. [165]

Several prominent non-Indians joined them, including film star Marlon Brando, comedian Dick Gregory, and the Rev. John J. Yaryan, Canon of Grace Cathedral of San Francisco.

Occasionally there was scattered minor violence—women and children throwing rocks, for example, and young men of the Yakimas carrying rifles to guard tribal fishermen—but the fish-in campaign was predominantly nonviolent. Mel Thom called it the "first tribal direct action in modern history." [166]

Nearly two-and-a-half years after the first fish-in, the United States Department of Justice appeared before the Supreme Court of Washington State "in behalf of a tribe which had been enjoined from exercising its treaty fishing rights." [167] The case was lost in 1968 in the United States Supreme Court. Stan Steiner quotes Patrick Hamilton, an Indian sociology student at the University of Washington, to show the mood of the Indian youth after the campaign had subsided:

> The past decade has shown us the power of civil disobedience. Wake up! . . . . see what your people have done to us and then decide if breakage of a few fishing laws is justifiable. [168]

ACTION BY GOVERNMENT PERSONNEL

142. Selective refusal of assistance by government aides

Government employees, administrators, officials, agents and officers, individually or collectively, may refuse to carry out particular instructions or orders, and inform their superior officers of their refusal. The refusal is clear and open, at least to the superior officers, which is what distinguishes this method from the more hidden types of evasion and obstruction described below. The selective refusal of assistance may or may not be announced to the public.

The examples offered here are all associated in some way with Nazi Germany.[169] In March 1942, for example, Goebbels complained that whenever he requested the imposition of harsh measures of "justice," Schlegelberger, the undersecretary for such matters in the Ministry of Justice, "always refuses my requests on the grounds that there is no legal basis for action."[170] Later he wrote again of the need for "brutal punishment," but once more complained of the refusal of the Ministry to go along: "Our Ministry of Justice is unable to understand a line of reasoning that is so obvious. It still moves in formal grooves." A change in the law was made to eliminate the legal justification for such refusal of assistance.[171]

In late 1938 the Nazi Party in *Gau* (party district) Franken decided to take advantage of the anticipated expropriation of Jewish property; calling in Jews from the district, it sought to force them to sign documents transferring their property, almost without compensation, to the city of Fürth, the *Gau* or some other body. Some court officers, however, doubted the legality of this procedure and refused to enter the transactions in the real estate book *(Grundbuch)*—thus voiding the transfers.[172]

Hitler was sometimes confronted with the direct rejection of orders by his army officers, even after he had become Commander-in-Chief. In 1941, for example, he visited the headquarters of the Army Group Center at Borisov on the Russian front and was immediately confronted with a sharp difference of opinion concerning strategy and the utilization of available forces—Hitler wished to concentrate on Leningrad and the Ukraine, while his officers intended to concentrate the campaign on Moscow. When the *Führer* ordered the transfer of two Tank Armies, commanded by Hoth and Guderian, he "came up against a blank wall of refusal," backed by claims that the units needed two or three weeks for regrouping and repairs. The two commanders were supported by their colleagues, including the War Office and the Army Group Center, who "put up a united front to their Führer. He was convinced that they did not *want* to do it and had just claimed that they were not *able* to . . ." [173] Hitler seems to have been correct on this point.

The German Army High Command *(O.K.H.-Oberkommando des Herres)* was appalled at the military risk and dangers involved in the invasion of Denmark and Norway proposed by Hitler, and "braving their *Führer*'s wrath, they flatly refused to participate in the preliminary preparations. The Scandinavian operation was subsequently planned entirely by O.K.W. [High Command of the Armed Forces—*Oberkommando der Wehrmacht]* . . ." [174]

The German officials in direct charge of the deportation of Danish Jews, having no forces of their own and unable to count on Danish help, obtained formations of the Order Police from Germany (there were no German police in Denmark), and then sought help from the German occupation army. But General Hermann von Hannecken refused to transfer his men for that task or to issue a decree ordering Jews to report at *Wehrmacht* (German army) offices for "work." This forced the police to undertake a door-to-door search. After Hannecken unsuccessfully sought postponement by intervention in Berlin, he agreed to cooperate only to the extent of providing a mere fifty soldiers to cordon off the harbor area during the loading of Jews on ships, arguing that this was for the maintenance of law and order, and not participation by the army in the "arrests" of Jews. [175]

143. Blocking of lines of command and information

The effective power of a ruler may be limited by his subordinates if they quietly block the relay downwards or execution of orders, or the passage of information from the lower echelons upwards. Members of different levels of the hierarchy may seriously interfere with the regime's capacity to deal with various problems and crises simply by not forwarding to appropriate superiors or departments the information needed to help the regime. Withheld information may concern a variety of matters, such as economic conditions, public opinion, and the state of supplies; it may also include a refusal to report secret resistance organizations, plans and activities.

In Nazi Germany, this blocking of information took an extreme form: presumably loyal officials kept quiet and even shielded men whom they knew to be plotting Hitler's overthrow and assassination, as Wheeler-Bennett describes:

. . . within O.K.W. . . . departmental chiefs—for example, Canaris and Thomas—were frankly disloyal to the regime to the extent of plotting its downfall, and in O.K.H. . . . both the Commander-in-Chief and Chief of the General Staff were cognizant of, if not participant in, subversive conversations and activities, which grew in volume and intent as the war progressed, and never reported them to Security authority. [176]

Even Fritz Fromm, Commander-in-Chief of the Home Army, refrained from reporting the conspiratorial activities of his subordinates Olbrich and Stauffenberg, although Fromm was unwilling to further the conspiracy by direct participation. [177] Field Marshall Keitel reported that officers in the War Office and in military intelligence had known of the July 20, 1944, attempt to assassinate Hitler but had not reported it. [178]

One way to block the chain of command is simply to fail to relay orders to one's subordinates, so that they never reach the men who are to carry them out. For example, the 1939 German generals' plot to prevent the planned offensive against the Western Allies and the invasions of Luxembourg, Belgium and the Netherlands, as a step toward peace, depended to a considerable degree on an act of noncooperation by them. Wheeler-Bennett writes: "On the understanding that they would receive a direct order from the Commander-in-Chief [General Walter von Brauchitsch, himself one of the plotters] they agreed to hamstring the offensive by the simple means of not transmitting to their subordinates the essential order to attack." [179]

As late as 1940 employees of the foreign organization of the Nazi Party had to be reminded to submit documents proving their Aryan ancestry. "Most employees in the office had simply ignored an earlier directive for submission of records, without even giving an excuse or explanation for failure to comply." [180]

The notorious Commissar Decree issued by Hitler in May 1941, which ordered the execution of captured Communist political officials and leaders in the occupied Soviet Union, including military prisoners, was reduced in effectiveness by the refusal of some officers to relay the instructions to their subordinates. Field Marshal Fedor von Bock, Commander-in-Chief of the Army Group Center, refused to issue it, as did others including Field Marshal Wilhelm von Leeb and Colonel-General Erich Hoepner. [181] Walter Görlitz reports that the Commissar Decree was complied with only partially, and then during the first months of the war in the East, but "it was then gradually and quietly dropped, so that by 1942 it was no longer valid. [182]

This method of noncooperation may also take the form of ignoring orders which have actually been received, rather than either obeying or blatantly refusing to obey them. This is neither simple forgetfulness nor accidental inefficiency: such orders are ignored because of lack of sympathy or outright opposition on the part of the person who is refusing to cooperate. One reason for the lax control of funds of various enterprises in Communist China from 1950–63 is reported to have been the tendency of plant managers to ignore most financial regulations; another was a lack of sympathy from even high party officials for tight financial controls. [183]

Reichskommissar Erich Koch of the Ukraine was directed by the East Ministry on September 7, 1942, to seize all Jewish and other abandoned property and to use former Ukrainian officers and civil servants for the job. Koch, however, ignored the order and on March 16, 1943, informed Alfred Rosenberg that the decree was a "political and organizational impossibility." [184] Rosenberg headed the *Ostministerium,* the civilian administration of the occupied East.

144. Stalling and obstruction

Administrative officers and other governmental employees may express political noncooperation by stalling and obstruction carried out under the guise of compliance with a particular order or policy. This method falls within the approach which Sir Basil Liddell Hart defined as "Apparent acquiescence that conceals, and is combined with, a strategy of noncompliance . . ." It may be also described as "Fabian tactics" and "polite procrastination." Liddell Hart argued that this approach can be "maintained more continuously and extensively than others, so as to yield the minimum to the occupying power and create a cumulative sense of frustration." It may be made all the more baffling if practiced "with a cheerful smile and an air of well-meaning mistake, due to incomprehension or clumsiness . . ." [185] The degree of outward appearance of support and compliance may vary.

Again, all the examples offered here except one are from within the Nazi regime itself (especially its bureaucracy) or within puppet or pro-Nazi governments. The final Czech example is very different.

Goebbels repeatedly complained about the lack of leadership and initiative for promoting Nazi measures shown by government ministries and departments, [186] particularly the Ministry of Justice, where, as we have already noted, he encountered problems. Goebbels wrote on March 19, 1942:

> We propose a multitude of reforms, improvements, and drafts of laws, but they don't have the right effect because a sort of quiet sabotage is going on in the central offices. The bourgeois elements dominate there, and as the sky is high and the Fuehrer far away, it is

very difficult indeed to prevail against this tough and solid bureaucracy. [187]

Hitler is reported by Goebbels to have been convinced of the need for drastic measures, not only in the administration of justice but "against certain types of swivel-chair generals and against the whole bureaucracy." [188] Nearly a year later, in March 1943, Goebbels reported that Hitler agreed with most of his proposals for waging "total war" against the Allies, but added: "He [the *Führer*] merely complains of resistance that is always offered to our measures by the bureaucracy. In some cases this resistance is simply intolerable . . ." [189] The specific cases here dealt with treatment of captured Allied fliers, efforts to develop nuclear weapons, and anti-Jewish measures.

Stalling and obstruction thwarted Hitler's two attempts to apply lynch law to the Allied so-called terror fliers. Görlitz describes this as a specific example of a general phenomenon—the blocking of Hitler's more extreme intentions by various uses of prevarication, stalling and postponement:

> . . . often it will be found that the sole purpose of the central figures was to create a paper war around certain questions and prosecute this paper war for as long as was necessary for the whole matter to be dropped and filed, because Hitler had either forgotten all about it or had become interested in new problems. [190]

Hitler's attempt in the summer of 1944 to establish a systematic program of terror against captured Allied "terror fliers" was effectively stalled by the combined efforts of Field Marshal Keitel (Chief of the High Command), Colonel-General Jodl (Chief of Operations Staff O.K.W.), and *Reichsmarschall* Göring (Commander-in-Chief of the Air Force). This was done by pretending to clarify the concept of "terror flier" in international law and by prolonging the debate in memoranda, lengthy discussions and correspondence. In March 1945 Hitler again sought to establish such a policy, and again was thwarted (despite Martin Bormann's assistance) by the obstructive tactics of Jodl's aide, Air Staff Officer Major Herbert Büchs, Field Marshall Keitel, *Reichsmarschall* Göring and General Karl Koller, the Chief of the Air Force Operations Staff. In neither case was the order demanded by Hitler ever issued. [191]

One very important reason that Nazi Germany did not develop atomic weapons was that the nuclear scientists who worked on the task deliberately stalled and obstructed the effort. The German atomic researchers not only refused to push for the development of an atomic bomb but diverted attention from the idea. Their efforts, as described by Robert Jungk, were considered and deliberate. They refrained from passing on preparatory theoretical studies to their superiors, labeled suggestions from others as unrealistic though not impossible in principle, kept memoranda on research locked away, and kept the military departments in the dark about the imminent feasibility of making atomic bombs—all while pretending to cooperate. "It was considered that an open strike of research workers would be dangerous, as it would leave the field open for unscrupulous and ambitious persons. So long as a policy of delay and postponement proved practicable, it was resolved the risk should be taken." [192]

Various of the more extreme Nazi anti-Jewish measures, especially those concerning extermination, met a significant degree of stalling and obstruction. These obviously were not sufficiently widespread and effective to halt the whole effort, and the examples offered here are certainly not cited with any intent of whitewashing any individual or any group. It is, nevertheless, highly significant that these acts of noncooperation occurred and that they did save the lives of many Jews. Such stalling and obstruction occurred within the German bureaucracy, in the Foreign Office, among German occupation officials in the East, and among officials of Nazi-allied Bulgaria, Vichy France, and Mussolini's Italy.

Following the decisive Grosse Wannsee Conference of January 1942, at which Reinhardt Heydrich announced the necessity of "treatment" of those Jews who survived forced labor to prevent them from going free and beginning "a new Jewish development" (that is, he announced the extermination program, the "Final Solution"), "a wave of obstruction began to grow" within the various chancellories and ministries with the very limited aim of obtaining a series of exceptions to the policy which prevented its extension to partners of mixed marriages and their children. [193]

Within the Foreign Office, matters related to Jewish deportations were dealt with by the Department Deutschland, headed by Martin Luther. Nazi deportation policies had specifically excluded Jews of certain nationalities, but Foreign Minister Ribbentrop requested Luther to prepare a report on the possibility of extending the deportations to Jews of *all* nationalities. Baron Ernst von Weizsäcker (head of the Foreign Office under Ribbentrop) then sent Luther's report to Emil Albrecht, of the office's legal department, "in hope that it might be buried there for some time—a favorite device when dealing with Department Deutschland." [194]

Although by no means wholly innocent concerning the "Final Solution," *Reichskommissar* Heinrich Lohse in *Ostland* (an administrative district of occupied Eastern territories) contributed to the delay and prevented the completion of the Riga massacres. In October 1941 Lohse had been reported to Rosenberg's *Ostministerium* for impeding the massacres in Libau. On November 15 he requested a ruling on whether Jews under his jurisdiction were to be killed regardless of the economic situation; an affirmative reply was not received until over a month later. On November 7 Lohse telegraphed *Stadtkommissar* Hingst in Vilna calling attention to the protests of General Braemer; the latter on December 1 urged the civil commissars to stop the execution of irreplaceable Jews, and two days later Lohse distributed Braemer's manifesto.[195]

Various types of administrative and diplomatic stalling and obstruction were also used elsewhere—in Bulgaria (an Axis partner),[196] Vichy France, and Mussolini's Italy—to thwart Nazi extermination efforts. Italian occupation forces in France, for example, proved very obstructive in the face of German orders for the expulsion of Jews. Italian military officers reinterpreted German orders of December 1942 that they expel *all* Jews from French frontier and coastal areas to mean only *French* Jews. The Italian Fourth Army stopped the Prefect of Lyons from arresting from two thousand to three thousand Polish Jews in the Grenoble district and prevented their dispatch to Auschwitz. When German Foreign Minister Joachim von Ribbentrop objected about this to Mussolini himself, Mussolini replied that he sympathized with Ribbentrop's request; but he nevertheless refused to interfere with his generals, who continued to free the arrested Jews. The Italian military officers, Mussolini said, had a "different intellectual formation." When the Italian police did expel Jews from the coastal area, they placed them safely in hotels well within their zone.[197] There was similar Italian obstruction in the Italian Zone of Greece[198] and the Italian Military Zone II in Croatia.[199]

While sharing responsibility for the fate of many Jews who lived in France, the Vichy government nevertheless undoubtedly saved a great number by administrative and diplomatic stalling and obstruction; Pétain and Laval, as well as subordinate officials and police, contributed to these tactics. "The *Commissariat aux Questions Juives* was never sure of the support of the Vichy Government, and its police obtained less and less cooperation from the regular *gendarmerie.*"[200] Xavier Vallat, appointed by Vichy as its first Commissary for Jewish Affairs, early opposed any deportations of French (as distinct from foreign) Jews and the imposition of the Jewish badge—the wearing of which could not be enforced in Vichy territory even after full German occupation.[201] French police in Bordeaux arrested only stateless Jews for deportation (and then only 150 of them) so that Lieutenant-Colonel Karl Adolph Eichmann—who was in charge of the whole deportation system for exterminations—wondered whether he might have to give up France completely as a source of deportations.[202] Laval stalled on German demands for a decree to revoke post-1933 naturalized citizenship of Jews (such a revocation would have made them eligible for deportation). Finally, Laval informed the Germans that Pétain—whose approval was necessary—was disgusted with a decree to take French citizenship obtained by naturalization from women and children and told them that Laval himself had lost his copy of the draft decree. This meant that a three months' waiting period for Jewish objections would be necessary before a new draft could be submitted to the *Conseil de Ministres*. Italian approval would also be needed. During that period the French police could not help in roundups of Jews, he said. Gerald Reitlinger, in his study *The Final Solution,* says that the Gestapo suddenly appeared "singularly powerless" and were supported neither by the High Command nor the Foreign Office. Hitler must have lost interest in the extermination of French Jews, he writes. "This man, who cared nothing for the opinion of the world and who was unamenable to reason, could be undermined completely by slow obstruction." [203] No large-scale roundups were possible without the cooperation of the French police, and even after Italian protection of French Jews collapsed on September 8, 1943, only three transports left the departure station Dracy for Auschwitz. [204]

In the first days of the Russian occupation of Czechoslovakia, the hidden radio transmitters were extremely important in continuing support for the legitimate government and Communist Party, and in arousing nonviolent resistance against the occupation and any possible puppet regime. In order to counter this radio attack, the Russians sought to bring in by railroad jamming equipment (some reports said tracking equipment) to destroy the resistance broadcasts. An account of how its trip was "assisted" was published in Prague in *Politika* on August 27, 1968. It was written by a Czechoslovak rail worker who took part in the action:

I tell you frankly, that train should have been stopped at Cierna [near the border]. But there was nothing peculiar about it—except that it was so short, eight cars only. At first we wanted to throw it off the track, but that could have had terrible consequences. Near Olomouc, it got ahead of a long freight train. Then it accidentally broke up into three sections, and it took four hours to fix. Exactly according to all regulations. Then I collapsed. Another maintenance worker needed another four hours to fix it. Then it moved on to Trebova and, with repair work going on all the time, as far as Chocen. From there, we wanted to steer them on to Poland, but by that time they had maps.

Suddenly they were in a great hurry because they had eaten up everything they had in their two parlor cars. Before Moravany, we threw the trolley wires down, and the train got all tangled up in them. That took two maintenance squads, and they were unable to put it together. The Russians were quite nervous. They wanted the machine to run on batteries, and they could not understand why it should not be possible when all the various pieces of equipment seemed to be functioning all right. In Pardubice, they wanted steam, but we told them that that was an electrified line. In Prelouc, a piece of the track was dismantled, then a trolley thrown off, and they decided that they would go on by way of Hradec. In Steblova, again a thrown-off trolley; it's a single-track stretch so there was nothing to be done. Not too quickly, anyway. Six Soviet helicopters picked up our dispatchers as hostages. We put fifteen freight trains in front of them, and there is no yard in Prague that could take all of that. Our own trains suffered because of it; everything was delayed. I myself got to Kolin with a completely empty passenger train. Now they are somewhere around Lysa on the Elbe. But such a [Good Soldier] Schweik-type operation cannot last indefinitely.[205]

Czechoslovak radio reported on August 25 that the train was halted at Lysa nad Labem and that the jamming equipment was being reloaded into Russian helicopters.[206]

145. General administrative noncooperation

The great majority of a government's administrative personnel may refuse to cooperate with a usurping regime. This may be either an occupation government or a group which has seized control of the State apparatus by *coup d'etat* or other illegal means.

After the Bolsheviks seized power in October 1917 from the post-revolutionary Provisional Government headed by Kerensky, for instance, the new regime was immediately boycotted by the civil servants, who disobeyed the orders of the new occupants of the seats of power. In the Ministry of Public Welfare all but forty of the functionaries went on strike.[207] As has already been pointed out, this kind of noncooperation was instrumental in defeating the Kapp *Putsch* in 1920 against the Weimar Republic.[208]

146. Judicial noncooperation[209]

This method of intragovernmental noncooperation occurs when members of the judicial system—judges, jurors, and the like—refuse to carry out the will of the regime or of some other portion of the judicial system. An example of the latter would be the refusal of a jury to convict a political prisoner despite the wish of the presiding judge that he be convicted. In certain cases determination by a court that a given law or policy is unconstitutional would also be an act of political noncooperation with the regime. Or, a judge could refuse to convict or punish, despite the evidence and pleas of the prosecutor.

Resignation of an entire judicial institution may occur in reaction to interference with the court's independence by a usurper. In December 1940, for example, the Norwegian Supreme Court resigned in protest against the declaration by *Reichskommissar* Terboven that the Court had no right to declare his German occupation "laws" unconstitutional.[210]

Judicial noncooperation may also operate within the judicial system. A noteworthy case of nullification by judicial noncooperation was the abolition of capital punishment for petty theft in England during the early nineteenth century. The law specified a certain minimum value of goods at which the death penalty became applicable. Often the juries would find the value of the stolen goods to be just a penny or a shilling lower than the crucial figure—regardless of the actual value—in order to avoid a hanging. Arthur Koestler writes:

> The deterrent of the gallows affected the jury more than the criminal; the juries went on strike as it were. They made it a rule, when a theft of goods worth forty shillings was a capital offense to assess the value of the goods at thirty-nine shillings; and when, in 1827, the capital offense was raised to five pounds, the juries raised their assessments to four pounds and nineteen shillings.[211]

Some juries refused outright to convict persons for other crimes against property, such as forging banknotes. Merchants and bankers themselves demanded the abolition of capital punishment in order that there be some kind of effective punishment against such crimes. Finally, the legislation on capital punishment was altered, in 1837 and 1861, to abolish hanging for property crimes.

Occasionally, judicial noncooperation may involve open disobedience by a jury of a judge's instructions where they find them unreasonable. In 1670 William Penn and William Mead were arrested for "unlawfully and tumultuously" assembling in a Quaker Meeting, which Penn addressed outdoors after the entrance to the house where the Meeting was to have been held had been barred by soldiers. The trial itself was a remarkable one, and when it came time for a verdict from the members of the jury, they found Mead "not guilty" and Penn simply "guilty of speaking or preaching to an assembly." The latter was not a crime; nor was this a legal verdict. The foreman refused to say whether the assembly to which Penn spoke was itself legal or illegal. After threats of indefinite confinement by the Recorder, one of the two justices in the case, the jury again returned the same verdict. The Recorder then announced:

> Gentlemen, you shall not be dismisst till we have a Verdict, that this Court will accept; and you shall be lock'd up, without Meat, Fire,

Drink, or Tobacco; you shall not think thus to abuse the Court; we shall have a verdict, by God, or you shall starve for it.[212]

After two nights of such detention the jury found Penn "not guilty." Both the defendants and the jury were then fined for contempt of court. A year later a higher court ruled that the jury was correct and that it had been illegally detained.

147. Deliberate inefficiency and selective noncooperation by enforcement agents

Police, soldiers and other enforcement officials may at times deliberately carry out their orders with less than full efficiency, either out of political motivation, sympathy for the resisters, or distaste for the repressive measures. Or, police and others may selectively refuse certain orders on a scale too limited to be described accurately as mutiny. To the degree to which this method of political noncooperation is practiced, the ruler's ability to implement his will is reduced and the effect of repression lessened. Let us first survey some examples of deliberate inefficiency. These come from tsarist Russia, British-occupied India, and German-occupied Norway.

A.T. Vassilyev, the former head of the *Ochrana,* the tsarist secret police, has reported that the law prohibiting Jews from settling in certain provinces of Imperial Russia "was constantly evaded, and that countless Jews, with the consent of the authorities, lived in towns that should have been closed to them. The Police looked upon the fact with benevolence and shut both eyes."[213]

And in India during the 1930 nonviolent raids on the salt depot at Dharasana, Indian police ordered to beat the nonviolent volunteers with *lathis* (heavy bamboo rods, often steel-shod) were not always efficient, as an eyewitness, Webb Miller, reports: "Much of the time the stolid native Surat police seemed reluctant to strike. It was noticeable that when the officers were occupied on other parts of the line the police slackened, only to resume threatening and beating when the officers appeared again."[214]

In 1941, in Hanover, former Gestapo chief Rudolf Diels refused the *Gauleiter*'s orders to arrest Jews, and Graf Faber-Castell refused to shoot five hundred Jews in Poland. Neither was harshly punished.[215] Lieutenant-General Hans Rauter of the S.S. complained in September 1942 that there was almost no cooperation from the Dutch police in the roundup of Jews in the Netherlands.[216]

In occupied Norway both Norwegian police and German soldiers were sometimes deliberately inefficient and either facilitated escapes or did less than was expected of them in making arrests. In one case a Norwegian policeman sent to arrest a Jew who happened to be out left a message that he would return at twelve noon—which gave the hunted man time to gather his belongings and get away. During this early roundup, large numbers of Jews were warned in advance of the arrests.[217] Similar events later took place prior to the arrests of the remaining Jews, including women and children, on November 26, 1942. Norwegian policemen informed resistance people of the impending arrests, and some personally went the night before to warn the Jews.[218] When many students at the University of Oslo were arrested on November 30, 1943, German soldiers sent to private homes often encouraged escapes by taking the word of someone answering the door that the wanted student was not at home and going away, rather than entering and searching the house, as was expected.[219]

In addition to such types of action, a certain amount of open refusal of cooperation and flouting of orders occurred among Norwegian police, although it would not be accurate to say that this was a model of full refusal of cooperation with fascism. These various acts of noncooperation have been reported by Lars L'Abée-Lund, who later became chief of criminal police in Oslo and an appeals court judge.

The very day on which the Germans entered Oslo, April 6, 1940, Vidkun Quisling, leader of the Norwegian fascist party, *Nasjonal Samling,* declared himself to be State Minister, and ordered Kristian Welhaven, the chief of police in Oslo, to meet him in conference. Chief Welhaven did not appear at Quisling's office, however. When Quisling phoned Welhaven the next day enquiring as to why he had not appeared, the police chief replied that he had indeed been at his own office and was at present, if Quisling wished to confer with him. For the moment Quisling had to back off, but in September *Reichskommissar* Terboven permitted Welhaven's dismissal and arrest. He was kept in Grini concentration camp in Norway until 1943, then in Gestapo headquarters in Berlin, and finally in Bavaria until he was released in early 1945 as a result of negotiations led by the Swede Count Folke Bernadotte. Not all Norwegian police officers followed Welhaven's example, however, and within a short time almost all higher police officials were members of the *Nasjonal Samling;* sixty percent of all officers, including assistant chiefs, voluntarily joined Quisling's *N.S.*[220] About forty percent of the other policemen also joined the party. Nevertheless, reports L'Abée-Lund, "the regime could not rely on the police apparatus."[221]

In July 1940 the police were ordered to salute fascist-style with outstretched right hand. "Bitterness among the police was great. In Oslo, the force at headquarters that was ready for duty refused to go out, and in Kristiansand the police chief, one of the few who was not a member of *Nasjonal Samling,* resigned. He was followed by his assistants."[222]

The Kristiansand chief was arrested and, after still refusing to comply, was imprisoned and deported to Germany.

In the autumn of 1941 three assistant chiefs of the Oslo criminal police refused to obey an order to confirm a confiscation of food that the *Hird,* Norwegian storm troops, had seized during the night. These officers were themselves jailed but later released, after which they set up in the district of Østlandet the core of a secret resistance organization of police. From the autumn of 1942 instructions were sent out from resistance leaders for police to boycott *N.S.* propaganda meetings and to refuse to apply for promotions when vacant police positions were listed for applicants.

When the fascists launched their program of labor mobilization of Norwegian citizens—the "National Work Effort"—in 1943, the underground gave instructions in June that every policeman should refrain from actions which would help this conscript labor program. Two months later Gunnar Eilifsen, assistant police chief in Oslo, refused to obey an order to bring in two young girls for the work effort. He was court-martialed and executed on August 16, 1943. The same day all the Oslo police—between six and seven hundred—were called to a meeting with Police Chief Jonas Lie, an *N.S.* member. Lie told them of Eilifsen's execution and demanded that they sign a statement promising to obey orders. *N.S.* members promptly signed, but some others simply marched past the table where they were expected to sign. After both friendly conversations and warnings that if they refused they would be shot the next day, fourteen policemen still refused. They were driven away in German cars but apparently not executed. [223]

In the autumn of 1943 the police set up an illegal police leadership organization, in line with *Milorg* (the military resistance group) and *Sivorg* (the civilian, nonviolent, resistance group). The police organization cooperated with *Milorg,* setting up an information service about coming police raids and arrests against home front personnel and organizations; they also operated to discover and "neutralize" agents who were working for the Nazis. [224]

148. Mutiny

In advanced stages of a noncooperation movement, the opponent's troops, police, or both may mutiny and flatly refuse to carry out orders to repress the resistance movement. In other situations mutiny has itself constituted a major—sometimes the dominant—method of resistance and revolutionary struggle where the army itself is in revolt. Whereas in essentially violent revolutions a mutiny may be followed by the troops joining in the violent struggle on the side of the revolutionaries, in an essentially nonviolent struggle, a mutiny may express itself entirely through the refusal to carry out usual functions of forcing the regime's will on the populace or waging war against a foreign enemy. This refusal may contribute to a paralysis of the regime's ability to rule, by increasing the totality of defiance and noncooperation, paralyzing the regime's organs of enforcement, and destroying its conventional military capacity.

During the Russian 1905 Revolution mutinies were not uncommon. The former head of the *Ochrana* reports an early mutiny in St. Petersburg on February 24, 1905:

> When the attempt was made to relieve the Police by employing detachments of Cossacks, a very serious state of matters was revealed: the Cossacks, who had once been the terror of a riotous crowd, now actually fraternized with the mob and gave not the least sign of taking serious measures against it. [225]

During this revolution (especially from November 1905 to mid-1906) troops returning across the Trans-Siberian Railway from the war with Japan often violated discipline:

> The soldiers disobeyed officers and fraternized with civilian radicals in centers where authority was being broken down—particularly Harbin, Chita, Krasnoyarsk, and Irkutsk. Their contempt for discipline ranged from simple gestures of insubordination to quite serious excesses—such as their retaliation at Chita for a general's insult to some railworkers: they detached his coach and left him there. [226]

The mutiny at Irkutsk in Siberia particularly appears to have displayed the characteristics of this nonviolent method; with virtually everyone opposed to the central government, the Social Democrats obtained official permission to address crowds of soldiers, who then refused to perform their military duties, J.H.L. Keep reports. [227]

During the February 1917 Revolution, mutinies of Russian troops played a very important role. For example, the Volynsky Regiment mutinied on February 27, after having fired, under orders, on nonviolent demonstrators in Znamensky Square, Petrograd, on the previous day and after the shooting of their officer the next morning by an unknown assassin: "The men of the Volynsky Regiment were firing their rifles into the air and proclaiming their support for the people's rising. But they soon lost their cohesion and mingled with the demonstrators to form part of the same motley crowd." [228] The mutiny spread to other units, and as patrols dispersed to their barracks for supper, "On the way they merged with the crowds." [229] The troops generally did not remain in their units and did not oppose the regime by military means:

> The soldiers who came out into the streets preferred the anonymity

of the milling crowd to an identifiable position in their units. They sold their rifles to the highest bidder, adorned their greatcoats with pieces of red ribbon, and joined one or other of the demonstrations, smashing police stations, opening up prisons, setting fire to court buildings, or indulging in other forms of "bloodless" revolutionary activity.[230]

The Army Headquarters no longer knew on which troops they could rely. On February 27 the Minister of War sent telegrams to the Tsar reporting the spreading mutiny, arson and total loss of control by Khabalov (the Commander of the Petrograd Military District), and asking for really reliable troops immediately in considerable numbers.[231] Occasionally, however, rebellious troops violently turned on loyal units, as in the ambush in Luga during this period.[232]

In May and June 1917 large-scale mutinies also took place in the French Army as a sign of general rebellion against the war and the immense casualties which were being suffered in the military stalemate. By official admission mutinies—or "collective indiscipline"—took place in almost exactly half the French fighting forces. "The revolts began as they would continue—spontaneous mutinies without a realizable objective, devoid of organized leadership, and without individual heroes or villains," writes Richard Watt.

The mutinies, which began on a small scale, provoked punishments. But as the numbers of mutineers increased vastly, the disobedient troops sensed that they were too numerous to be punished. The first full-fledged mutiny was that of the Second Battalion of the Eighteenth Infantry Regiment. This battalion had been ordered back into battle on April 29, less than two weeks after about four hundred of its six hundred men had been killed or injured. Even the approximately two hundred remaining alive and physically uninjured were badly shell-shocked. Finally, this battalion was induced to return to the front; later five men of the battalion were condemned to death with little regard as to whether they were in fact leaders of the rebellion. Mutiny, however, spread. "Almost overnight the entire basis of discipline had evaporated. The officers suddenly found that they were not in control of their men but were only scurrying about on the perimeter of what had become a huge, disorderly mob." Watt describes these mutinies as

. . . a kind of "professional strike," a strike stimulated by the fact that they suddenly and completely lost faith in their generals and their generals' strategies and were no longer willing to entrust their lives to a high command which they felt was indifferent and careless of their suffering.

The terrible casualties and the offensive without victory launched by the Commander-in-Chief, General Robert Nivelle, were important in bringing about the mutinies. The French government, appalled by both the mutinies and the failure of the offensive, on May 15, 1917, dismissed General Nivelle and appointed in his place General Henri Pétain.[233]

On April 23, 1930, during the 1930-31 campaign in India, a Garhwali regiment refused to fire on peaceful demonstrators in Peshawar, an act for which its members were prosecuted.[234]

DOMESTIC GOVERNMENT ACTION

149. Quasi-legal evasions and delays

Units of government may not directly defy the laws, court decisions, or the like which require them to carry out some policy or take some measure which they reject, but instead use the reality or appearance of some other law or regulation, or some quite different criteria than those which may be in dispute, in order to evade indefinitely, or at least delay as long as possible, compliance with the requirements of the law, order, or court decision being resisted. These measures are similar to stalling and obstruction, described above, except that these are not the acts of individuals, administrative units, and the like, but are actions by subordinate or constituent units of government as such.

These types of actions have been widely used in the United States South from the end of the post-Civil War Reconstruction period to the present writing. There is, however, nothing intrinsic to the method which limits it to the uses to which it has been put by its Southern segregationist practitioners. Although the Fifteenth Amendment to the United States Constitution denied to the states the authority to refuse Negroes the right to vote, various states pursued alternative means to achieve the same objective. For example, when Oklahoma in 1910 amended its constitution to set up a literacy test as a qualification for voting, the enacted law made a significant exception among the citizens required to take the literacy examination. No one "who was on January 1, 1866, or at any time prior thereto, entitled to vote under any form of government . . . and no *lineal descendant of such person* [was to be] denied the right to register and vote because of his inability to so read and write . . ." (italics added). "In other words," write A.P. Blaustein and C.C. Ferguson, Jr., in their study *Desegregation and the Law,* "the only persons who would be required to pass a difficult literacy test in order to vote were those whose grandfathers had been slaves."[235] This "Grandfather Clause" as a means of disfranchisement was declared unconstitutional by the U.S. Supreme Court. Then Oklahoma passed, in 1916, a statute to the effect that all persons hitherto denied the right to vote must register within a twelve day period. Again, this was intended to apply only to Negroes; various "practical difficulties" would keep many from voting. This was also declared unconstitutional. The U.S. Supreme Court wrote that the Fifteenth Amendment "nullifies sophisticated as well as simpleminded modes of discrimination." [236]

Various other means of a legal or quasi-legal character have been used by Southern states to bar Negroes from voting. The 1961 "Report to the U.S. Commission on Civil Rights" from the North Carolina State Advisory Committee cites sworn written complaints from Negroes in five counties that literacy tests were applied in a discriminatory manner in order to prevent their registration as voters. It has frequently been charged that Southern states enacted such literacy laws precisely to be used to that end. The "Report" states: "It was alleged that the reading and writing tests were applied to the complainants in a manner different from the way in which such tests were applied to white applicants, so as to discriminate against the complainants and deny them the privilege of registering and voting solely because of their race." In 1961 the North Carolina Supreme Court ruled that one of the complainants must be given another opportunity to register and that the examination which she had been given was beyond the intent of the law. [237]

Various states have used several legal and quasi-legal means of avoiding compliance with the United States Supreme Court ruling in 1954 which outlawed racial segregation in public schools. For example, Florida's Pupil Assignment Law allowed the Board of Education to set regulations to establish "uniform tests" for "classifying the pupils according to intellectual ability and scholastic proficiency," so that there would be in each school "an environment of equality among pupils" of similar qualifications. The tests were to take into consideration "sociological, psychological, and like intangible social scientific factors" in order to avoid any "socio-economic class consciousness" among pupils in any given school. Assignments of pupils to a particular school would consider "the psychological, moral, ethical and cultural background" of the pupil as compared with those already assigned to that school. [238]

During this period North Carolina set up a pupil assignment plan, authorizing the school boards to assign each pupil to a particular elementary or high school, subject to a very complicated and time-consuming system of appeal for pupils dissatisfied with their assignment. Blaustein and Ferguson write that this plan was "designed to take advantage of the fact that no proceedings can be begun in the federal courts until a plaintiff has exhausted all the possible remedies which might be available through the action of state courts." [239] When a suit brought under this law, on behalf of all Negro children in one district, finally reached the

North Carolina Supreme Court in May 1956, it was dismissed on the grounds that the given Act required proceedings on an individual basis, and hence such a group suit was outlawed. A separate suit would have to be commenced afresh in behalf of each of the children. [240]

150. Noncooperation by constituent governmental units

Where there is widespread opposition to and noncooperation with the central government, and where local, provincial or state governmental bodies are responsive to public opinion, they may themselves undertake official noncooperation with the central government. Crane Brinton believes that this was an important factor in the American Revolution, during which "town meetings and colonial legislatures were part of the legal government, but were often controlled by men active in the illegal government." [241] Probably the most extreme act of nonviolent government noncooperation during the American colonists' struggle occurred in Rhode Island, where in September 1765 the Assembly instructed the officials of the province to ignore the Stamp Act, resolving

> That all the officers in this colony, appointed by the authority thereof, be, and they are hereby, directed to proceed in the execution of their respective offices in the same manner as usual; and that this Assembly will indemnify and save harmless all the said officers, on account of their conduct, agreeably to this resolution. [242]

Not only did the Stamp Distributor for Rhode Island resign, but the Governor himself refused to take the required oath to help enforce the Stamp Act. [243] The colony's courts accordingly remained open and operated as usual without the use of the stamps (required by the law) on their documents. [244]

The New York General Assembly stalled and procrastinated when requested in 1766 to make provisions for quartering the King's troops, as required by the British Quartering Act; in an address replying to the Secretary of State for the Southern Department in London it pleaded that the expense of such provisions was excessive for the colony and its people, ". . . and therefore we humbly intreat your Excellency to set our Conduct . . . in its true Light, by representing that our Non Compliance on this Occasion proceeds entirely from a just Sense of what our Duty requires." [245]

Following the military occupation of Boston, which began on September 30, 1768,

> Boston, through its constituted authorities, met the invasion with pas-

sive, but most effective and irritating resistance [writes George Tre-velyan]. The Colonels called upon the Council to house and feed their men. They were reminded that under the statute the city was not bound to provide quarters or supplies until the barracks in the Castle were full; and the Council and the Colonels alike knew that the regiments had been sent, not to defend the Castle, (which stood on an island in the Bay,) but to occupy and annoy the city.

When the Commander-in-Chief in America, General Gage, went to Boston and saw his soldiers sleeping in tents on the Common, with winter fast approaching, he found it necessary to hire private houses at exorbitant rates, and the British Treasury had to pay.[246] Until the shift to military struggle in 1775, colonial town meetings and provincial legislatures themselves repeatedly took the initiative in launching and conducting various economic boycotts, which were used as primary weapons in the colonial struggles with the government in London.[247]

One of the early and crucial constitutional problems of the United States government after its establishment was the question of who would determine when a law or action had exceeded or violate the purposes and powers set out by the new Constitution. Although the Supreme Court soon assumed this role, this was not the only possibility. Thomas Jefferson and James Madison developed the doctrine of nullification, which said that the legislature of a given state could decide that an Act passed by Congress violated the Constitution, and hence was null and void within that state. This was the basis for the famous Virginia Resolutions of 1798 and the Kentucky Resolutions of 1798 and 1799.

Aroused by antidemocratic tendencies in the new United States government, of which he saw the Alien and Sedition Acts as only the beginning, Thomas Jefferson concluded that it was necessary to erect a strong barrier against the encroachments of the Federal Government. He privately participated in drafting these resolutions, introduced in both Kentucky and Virginia. (James Madison introduced them in the Virginia Assembly.) One of the 1798 Kentucky Resolutions declared:

> *Resolved,* that the several States composing the United States of America, are not united on the principle of unlimited submission to their general government; but that . . . they constituted a general government for special purposes . . . ; and that whensoever the general government assumes undelegated powers, its acts are unauthoritative, void, and of no force . . .

It further asserted that the constituent states, not the federal government itself, must be able to judge when the Constitution had been exceeded.[248]

One of the Virginia Resolutions of that year also asserted that when the Federal Government had exceeded its constitutionally authorized powers, "the states, who are parties thereto, have the right and are in duty bound to interpose for arresting the progress of the evil, and for maintaining within their respective limits the authorities, rights, and liberties appertaining to them." [249] The 1799 Kentucky Resolutions asserted that extension of the activities of the Federal Government beyond the bounds set by the Constitution would lead to "an annihilation of the state governments . . .", and that the doctrine that the Federal Government alone should judge the extent of its constitutionally delegated powers, not the constituent states, would lead to a process of increasing federal powers which would "stop not short of *despotism* . . ." [250]

This theory was the basis for the nullification doctrine adopted by Vice-President John C. Calhoun in 1828, when he denounced the tariff law of that year. Calhoun claimed the right of a state to declare inoperative within its boundaries any law that it judged to be unconstitutional. [251] He saw this as an alternative to secession and as a defense of the Constitution. This general doctrine was later extended by certain states to actual secession from the Union. By itself secession was not an act of war; it only became so when military clashes occurred between Union troops and secessionist soldiers. (Had slavery—an institution impossible to defend by nonviolent means—not existed in the South and had the South wished to secede on other grounds, it is theoretically possible that it might have done so and applied a widespread program of nonviolent noncooperation which would have been, given a very different type of society in the South, very difficult indeed for Federal forces to crush.)

When the Russian government sought to bring Finland under tighter control in 1910, it tried to avoid clear rejection by the Finnish parliament of the bill to achieve that aim which was then being considered in the Russian capital, St. Peterburg. The Finns were asked to deliver a *report* on the proposed new law which would formalize Finland's subordination to the Russian government—not to *vote* on the bill (that is, accept or reject it). The Finnish parliament, however, refused to draw up such a report on the grounds that it, not the Russians, held full legislative power over such matters. [252]

As described in Chapter Two, the various *Länder* (states) in Germany under the Weimar Republic, at the call of the legal Ebert government, refused to cooperate with the usurping group of putschists headed by Dr. Kapp and General Lüttwitz.

During the 1930-31 struggle for Indian independence the Municipal Board of Ahmedabad informed British officials that they were unable to cooperate with the coming census because the Indian National Congress had decided upon a boycott of it. Insisting that there was widespread and determined opposition to the census, they said they would lack full public cooperation should they take part in it. Furthermore, if the Board was supposed to represent the public, it ought not to take action in conflict with public opinion. [253]

INTERNATIONAL GOVERNMENTAL ACTION

A more thorough classification of the types of noncooperation between governments than that offered here should be undertaken, for a large number of variations appear even at first glance. The illustrative nature of the seven methods described here should be kept in mind. These methods range from relatively mild ones of largely symbolic significance to more extreme measures which may disrupt the normal international activities and functions of the country. The League of Nations Covenant imposed on its members the obligation of a *total* international embargo —diplomatic, political, social and economic, the severance of all intercourse—of any State resorting to war in violation of the Covenant, Crespigny reminds us. [254]

151. 'Changes in diplomatic and other representation

In order to express disapproval of the policies of another country, a government will at times recall its own diplomat or other officials without breaking diplomatic relations, or ask that a foreign diplomat be replaced. Sometimes one government will place at the head of its diplomatic corps in another country an official holding a rank so low as to be an insult to the host country. At other times a country will voluntarily close, or be requested by the host country to close, certain of its offices, such as consulates—again, without breaking diplomatic relations.

Or officials other than members of the diplomatic staff may be withdrawn. As the differences between the Soviet Union and Yugoslavia sharpened in 1948, after the Central Committee of the Yugoslav Communist Party rejected Stalin's demand that Yugoslavia and Bulgaria immediately establish a federation, the Soviet Union replied on March 18 by recalling its military advisers from Belgrade. [255]

The host country may ask for the withdrawal of an ambassador, as Sir Douglas Busk notes, "for political and not personal reasons, i.e., because of displeasure with the policy of his government." [256] Diplomatic matters in the host country are then handled by a subordinate official. On occasion a government's request for withdrawal of a certain ambassador has been rejected by his home government. As a result, writes Charles W. Thayer, "the host government simply ceases to do business with the ambassador and there is nothing much the sending government can do but retaliate by breaking relations." [257] Thus during the 1848 revolution, after the British Ambassador to Spain, Henry Bulwer, somewhat exceeding his instructions, had strongly intervened to halt repression of Spanish liberal politicians, the British government rejected Spain's demand for Bulwer's recall. After various diplomatic exchanges the two governments broke diplomatic relations. [258]

During World War I the German military attaché in Washington, Franz von Papen, was declared *persona non grata* for allegedly engaging in plots to blow up American ammunition plants and was consequently withdrawn by the German government. There are many other examples of requested withdrawal for alleged improper behavior by diplomats. [259]

The closing of consulates is also common. After the sinking by a German submarine of the U.S. merchant ship *Robin Moor* on May 21, 1941, for example, the U.S. government ordered all German and Italian assets in the United States frozen and also ordered the closing of all German and Italian consulates. Germany and Italy retaliated by closing U.S. consulates in their countries. [260]

During the period of United States dissatisfaction with Sweden's policy of opposing U.S. involvement in the war in Vietnam, the U.S. Ambassador, William Heath, was recalled in March 1968 for consultations with President Johnson. [261] Heath did not return, nor was he replaced with a new ambassador. In November 1969 the U.S. Consulate in Göteborg was closed, the official reason being to cut U.S. foreign spending. It was the oldest American consulate, having been established by George Washington in 1797 after Sweden became the first government to recognize the new U.S. government. [262] Then the Nixon administration, which came to office in January 1969, declined to appoint a new ambassador to Sweden for a time. The new Swedish Premier, Olof Palme, thought the U.S. policy rather "impractical": "If Washington really wants to explain where we are wrong, there should be someone here to do the explaining." [263] Finally Dr. Jerome Holland was appointed and took up his post as the new U.S. Ambassador to Sweden in the spring of 1970.

152. Delay and cancellation of diplomatic events

Governments may stall or completely halt certain negotiations, meetings, conferences and the like as a result of displeasure with the actions or policies of another government involved in such events. For example, Gordon A. Craig argues that in the past it has been the practice of the Soviet Union to prolong negotiations for months and even years, sometimes also shifting the level of negotiation (say, from the ambassadorial to the ministerial level, and then to heads of state), with the result that the issues at stake and original points of difference become blurred, with assistance from publicity efforts. Craig cites as examples "the repeated and protracted negotiations in the 1920s over the question of the Russian debts," which resulted in avoidance of payment without penalty, and later various negotiations concerning Berlin and Germany, especially during the time of Premier Khrushchev. [264]

As Stalin began to apply pressure in early 1948 against Yugoslovia, the Soviet Union canceled the planned April meeting at which Soviet-Yugoslav commercial agreements were to be renewed. [265]

The announcement in early May 1960 that a United States U-2 plane photographing the Soviet Union from a great height had been shot down by a Soviet rocket was followed by denunciations of "spy flights" by Premier Khrushchev and demands that those responsible be punished. He said that the summit conference then taking place in Paris between the Soviet Union, the United States, France and Great Britain could not go on unless the U.S. government gave a full apology. So "after a brief meeting on the morning of 16 May the summit conference of 1960 was at an end," Wilfrid Knapp writes. [266]

The North Vietnamese and the National Liberation Front's delegations canceled the sixty-sixth plenary session of the Vietnam peace talks in Paris on May 6, 1970, in protest against five days of renewed United States' bombing of North Vietnam, Nguyen Thanh Le, the North Vietnamese spokesman, described the extraordinary move as "a political decision." The date for the next scheduled session, May 14, was not immediately accepted by the United States and South Vietnamese delegations; the latter indicated that it might make this same type of threat itself. [267]

153. Withholding of diplomatic recognition

The general practice of governments to recognize other governments which are effectively in control of the countries they rule is sometimes replaced by deliberate refusal of diplomatic recognition. This is often because of objection to the way in which that government came to power or to its basic political character. President Woodrow Wilson, for example, refused United States' recognition of the Mexican regime of Victoriano Huerta, harsh spokesman of propertied groups, who had ousted the revolutionary regime of Francisco Madero and had been responsible for his murder in prison. Wilson declared: "My ideal is an orderly and righteous government in Mexico; but my passion is for the submerged eighty-five per cent of the people of that Republic who are now struggling toward liberty." [268]

After Japan seized China's Manchuria and proclaimed the puppet state of Manchukuo in February 1932, the United States pursued the Stimson (or Hoover-Stimson) Doctrine: nonrecognition of international changes produced by means contrary to the provisions of the Kellogg-Briand Pact, which outlawed wars of aggression. Consequently, although rejecting both proposed economic sanctions and military means, the United States refused diplomatic recognition to Manchukuo. The U.S., however, continued trade relations and kept consular officials there, although they remained accredited to the Chinese National government. [269] In March 1932 the Assembly of the League of Nations unanimously adopted a resolution against Japan which followed almost verbatim the Hoover-Stimson Doctrine of Nonrecognition, Thomas Bailey reports. [270] For many years the United States refused to recognize the Communist government of the Soviet Union, on the basis of various grievances and charges, until recognition was agreed to in 1933. [271]

United States' long refusal to grant diplomatic recognition to the Peoples' Republic of China is one of the best-known examples of the use of this method. Diplomatic nonrecognition was in this case intended to contribute to the collapse of the Communist regime, as the State Department statement of August 11, 1958, indicated: "The United States holds the view that communism's rule in China is not permanent and that it one day will pass. By withholding diplomatic recognition from Peiping it seeks to hasten that passing." [272] Secretary of State John Foster Dulles further explained the policy on December 4, 1958: "Such recognition and the seating of the Chinese Communists in the United Nations would so increase their prestige and influence in the Far East, and so dishearten our allies there, that the Communist subversive efforts would almost surely succeed." [273]

Refusal of diplomatic recognition to Israel has been a basic part of Arab policy since the establishment of Israel. In addition, they have used more severe means, such as refusing other direct dealings with the Israeli government, trying to block its membership in international organizations, and imposing economic embargoes. [274]

Following the crushing of the 1956 Hungarian Revolution, various Western governments imposed a diplomatic boycott on the Kadar regime which was not broken until January 1, 1958. Even thereafter, however, the United States maintained only a *chargé d'affaires* in Budapest. Ferenc Váli writes: "The Soviets have considered the refusal by the United States to grant full recognition to the post revolutionary Hungarian government as the greatest stumbling block in the way of eliminating the bitterness caused by its armed intervention." [275]

The threat by one country of permanent nonrecognition of a government has also been used to help defeat a *coup d'etat* in another country. For example, Major-General Sir Neill Malcolm, Head of the British Military Mission in Berlin, told General Lüttwitz on March 16, 1920, that Britain would never recognize the new Kapp regime which Lüttwitz was helping to impose, "and thereby completed its discomfiture," reports Wheeler-Bennett. [276]

One variation of this nonrecognition is to recognize the government in question, but to do so conditionally. Harold Nicolson in his book *Diplomacy* cites the case of the British government's recognizing the Portuguese Republic on the condition that the new regime be confirmed by a general election. [277]

154. Severance of diplomatic relations

Severance of diplomatic relations "normally involves the departure of the entire Missions from both capitals, though sometimes only the Ambassador or High Commissioner and some others are forced to leave," writes Busk. Consular officials may or may not be allowed to remain. If the entire diplomatic staff is withdrawn, another country is asked to represent the country's remaining interests in that land. [278] Nicholson points out that the breaking of diplomatic relations "is by no means always a prelude to war and is often resorted to as a means of expressing profound moral indignation. Thus the British Minister was withdrawn from Belgrade after the [June 1903] assassination of King Alexander and Queen Draga, even as a similar diplomatic rupture occurred when Colonel Plastiras murdered M. Gounaris and his ministers in November 1922." [279] After the German announcement on January 31, 1917, of a submarine campaign to sink *all* ships, including neutrals, in the war zone, in an effort to break the British blockade, President Wilson appeared before the United States Congress to announce the termination of diplomatic relations with Germany. [280]

In a very different case, on April 25, 1943, the Soviet Union broke diplomatic relations with the Polish government-in-exile in London. This followed the discovery by the Germans of the Katyn graves, where ten thousand Polish army officers who had been missing for two years were buried. The Polish government-in-exile was convinced of Russian guilt for the executions, and after the Polish Minister of Defense called for an investigation by "a proper international body, such as the International Red Cross" the Soviet Union broke diplomatic relations. [281]

155. Withdrawal from international organizations

Governments may withdraw from either membership in or the activities of various types of international organizations and conferences. The motive may be to express dissatisfaction with their policies or to give the withdrawing country the freedom to take action which might receive disapproval from those bodies. For example, on October 14, 1933, Hitler announced that because of a denial of equal rights to Germany, that country was withdrawing from the Disarmament Conference and also the League of Nations. He argued that the hoped-for reconciliation with former foes had not been achieved, nor had the restoration of equal rights to the German people; hence Germany could no longer tolerate humiliation. The same day Hitler announced that he would submit withdrawal from the League to a plebiscite on November 12, the day after the anniversary of the Armistice of 1918. [282]

In 1950 the Soviet Union's delegates withdrew from United Nations activities—but not from membership—in protest against the continued seating of Nationalist China's delegates instead of those of the Communist government which controlled mainland China. Knapp reports that after Jacob Malik, the Soviet representative to the U.N. walked out of the Security Council on this issue on January 10, 1950, "Malik announced that he would not participate in the work of the Security Council until the Kuomintang [Nationalist Chinese] delegate had been replaced. The Soviet delegates thereupon withdrew from all United Nations bodies of which China was a member." [283] The absence of the Soviet delegate to the Security Council enabled it to take rapid action against North Korea when the Korean War broke out.

During the Indonesian "confrontation" against Malaysia, Indonesia notified the President of the United Nations General Assembly and the Office of the Secretary-General on December 31, 1964, that it was withdrawing from membership in the U.N. because Malaysia had been elected to the Security Council. Despite various appeals and private talks, in late January 1965 Indonesia confirmed her withdrawal from the U.N. and also some of its specialized agencies. (There is no provision for withdrawal in the U.N. Charter.) [284]

156. Refusal of membership in international bodies

Governments may be refused membership by international institutions because of political rivalries, disapproval of the government in question, and other reasons. The most outstanding example of this was the refusal for more than twenty years by the United Nations to seat delegations from the Communist government of mainland China as the representatives of China, in place of the delegates from the Nationalist government, which controlled only the island of Formosa (Taiwan). By the end of 1949 the Communist government (the People's Republic of China) had gained control of all of mainland China, and the Nationalist government (the Republic of China) had moved to Formosa. Consequently, the delegate of the Soviet Union on the Security Council sought unsuccessfully to exclude the Nationalist delegation.[285] After 1961 the question of Chinese representation was regarded by the U.N. General Assembly as "an important question," thereby requiring a two-thirds majority approval, rather than a simple majority.[286] Under heavy pressure from the United States, United Nations bodies declined to seat representatives of the Chinese Communist government until 1971 when they replaced the Nationalist delegates.

157. Expulsion from international organizations

One sanction sometimes used by international bodies against States violating its policies or constitution is expulsion from membership. The League of Nations Covenant provided that any member which violated "any covenant of the League" might be declared to be no longer a member.[287] This was applied only once—against the Soviet Union following its attack on Finland in 1939. On December 14, 1939, the Assembly of the League, with the Soviet delegate absent, unanimously condemned the invasion and declared that "in virtue of Article 16 paragraph 4 of the Covenant [the Assembly] finds that, by its act, the U.S.S.R. had placed itself outside the League of Nations. It follows that the U.S.S.R. is no longer a member of the League." [288]

The United Nations Charter, Article 6, provides "A Member of the United Nations which has persistently violated the Principles contained in the present Charter may be expelled from the Organization by the General Assembly upon the recommendation of the Security Council." [289] The Soviet Union proposed inclusion of such a provision in the Charter during the Dumbarton Oaks Conference and strongly supported the proposal at the San Francisco founding conference.[290] This article has never yet been applied, although suggestions have been made to expel South Africa and Portugal.[291]

Expulsion of Yugoslavia from the *Cominform* (an international Communist organization) was one of the sanctions applied in 1948 when Tito refused to submit to Stalin.[292]

Political noncooperation has been the last of the three subclasses of methods of nonviolent noncooperation. Our attention now turns to the final class of methods of nonviolent action, those of "nonviolent intervention."

NOTES

1. Griffith, **The Resurrection of Hungary,** esp. pp. 22, 43 and 48.
2. *Ibid.,* p. 30.
3. *Ibid.,* p. xxiv.
4. *Ibid.,* p. 31.
5. Geyl, **The Revolt of the Netherlands, 1555-1609,** p. 84.
6. *Ibid.,* pp. 183-184.
7. Gipson, **The British Empire Before the American Revolution,** vol. XII, **The Triumphant Empire: Britain Sails into the Storm 1770-1776,** p. 243.
8. Gipson, **The Coming of the Revolution,** p. 231.
9. Charques, **The Twilight of Imperial Russia,** p. 135.
10. Harcave, **First Blood,** p. 225.
11. Sternstein, "The *Ruhrkampf* of 1923," pp. 114-115. See also Halperin, **Germany Tried Democracy,** p. 249.
12. Margaret DeMarco, "The Use of Non-violent Direct Action Tactics and Strategy by American Indians."
13. "Iroquois of Canada Refuse to Become Canadian Citizens," *New York Times,* 12 March 1921, p. 6.
14. "Chippewa Indians Seek Help of UN to Restore Sovereign Rights," *Philadelphia Evening Bulletin,* 18 November 1946.
15. "Indian Tribe Asks United Nations Seat," *Philadelphia Evening Bulletin,* 8 July 1960.
16. Littell, ed., **The Czech Black Book,** p. 143.

17. *Ibid.*, p. 191.
18. Adam Roberts, "Buddhism and Politics in South Vietnam," p. 247.
19. *France Observateur* (Paris), 24 January 1957; quoted from Miller, **Nonviolence,** p. 362.
20. *New York Times,* 5 June 1968. I am grateful to Carl Horne for this reference.
21. *Peace News,* 27 November and 18 December 1959.
22. *The Times,* 24 March 1960.
23. Griffith, **The Resurrection of Hungary,** pp. 24-28 and 36.
24. Seton-Watson, **The Decline of Imperial Russia,** p. 170.
25. Katkov, **Russia 1917,** p. 4, n.l.
26. Sharp, **Gandhi Wields the Weapon of Moral Power,** pp. 51-219 *passim,* and Pattabhi Sitaramayya, **The History of the Indian National Congress,** vol. I, p. 605.
27. *Sunday Times,* (London), 19 March 1967.
28. Anthony de Crespigny, "The Nature and Methods of Non-Violent Coercion," **Political Studies** (London), vol. XII, no. 2 (June 1964), pp. 264-65. The respective sources are *The Times* (London), 5 Dec. 1961 and 21 May 1962.
29. E. L. Woodward, **French Revolutions** (London: Oxford University Press [Humphrey Milford], 1939), p. 55.
30. *Ibid.*, p. 74.
31. Seton-Watson, **The Decline of Imperial Russia,** p. 242.
32. *Ibid.*, p. 249. See also Charques, **The Twilight of Imperial Russia,** pp. 145 and 174.
33. Personal conversations with Ruth Reynolds, New York 1954-55.
34. Crespigny, "The Nature and Methods of Nonviolent Coercion," p. 264. The following are sources for the particular cases. ˙
35. *New Statesman* (London), 10 Nov. 1961; *The Times* (London), 14 Nov. 1961.
36. *The Times,* 2 and 3 April 1962.
37. *The Observer* (London), 22 April 1962.
38. *The Times,* 30 April 1962.
39. *Washington Post,* 17 August, 1966.
40. *Peace News,* 11 July 1958 and 23 January, 6 and 27 February 1959.
41. Griffith, **The Resurrection of Hungary,** p. 32.
42. Schapiro, **The Origin of the Communist Autocracy,** p. 280.
43. See Lochner, ed., **The Goebbels Diaries,** p. 396; Reitlinger, **The Final Solution,** pp. 53, 97, 187 and 192; Schweitzer, **Big Business in the Third Reich,** pp. 142 and 183; Walter Gorlitz, ed., **The Memoirs of Field-Marshal Keitel** (New York: Stein & Day, 1966) pp. 100-102, 123, 163-164 and 247; Crankshaw, **Gestapo,** p. 166; Alan Bullock, **Hitler: A Study in Tyranny,** revised edition. (U.S. ed.: New York: Harper and Row, 1962, British ed.: London: Odhams, 1964), p. 300, and Wheeler-Bennett, **The Nemesis of Power,** p. 319.
44. *Guardian,* 1 September 1962.
45. Charques, **The Twilight of Imperial Russia,** p. 207.
46. Roberts, "Buddhism and Politics in South Vietnam," p. 246.
47. Salvemini, **The French Revolution, 1788-1792,** p. 86.
48. Høye and Ager, **The Fight of the Norwegian Church Against Nazism,** pp. 88-104.

49. Geyl, **The Revolt of the Netherlands,** pp. 75 and 78-79.
50. Reitlinger, **The Final Solution,** pp. 346-347.
51. *The Times,* 19 and 23 March 1960.
52. Roberts,"Buddhism and Politics in South Vietnam," p. 247.
53. Sharp, **Gandhi Wields . . . ,** pp. 53-219 *passim.,* and Bondurant, **Conquest of Violence,** pp. 57-58 and 94.
54. Wheeler-Bennett, **The Nemesis of Power,** pp. 398-405.
55. Bernard, **Social Control in its Sociological** Aspects, p. 398.
56. A. Fenner Brockway,**Non-co-operation in Other Lands,** pp. 34-39.
57. Sharp, **Gandhi Wields . . . ,** pp. 37-40 and Pattabhi Sitaramayya, **The History of the Indian National Congress,** vol. I, pp. 534-546.
58. Shridharani, **War Without Violence,** pp. 30, 18, 41, and 161, and Case, **Non-violent Coercion,** p. 383.
59. **Report of the Advisory Commission on the Review of the Constitution of Rhodesia and Nyasaland,** pp. 8, 14 and 16.
60. Seton-Watson, **The Decline of Imperial Russia,** p. 240.
61. Sternstein, "The *Ruhrkampf* of 1923," p. 117.
62. Roberts, "The Buddhists, the War and the Vietcong," pp. 219-220, in *The World Today,* vol 22, no. 5 (May 1966).
63. Schweitzer, **Big Business in the Third Reich,** pp. 147-148.
64. *Boston Globe,* 6 and 8 August 1970.
65. *New York Times,* 23 June 1966.
66. *Ibid.*
67. Case, **Non-violent Coercion,** p. 383, and Shridharani, **War Without Violence,** p. 49.
68. Luthuli, **Let My People Go,** p. 147.
69. Sharp, **Tyranny Could Not Quell Them,** and Amundsen, ed., *et al.,* **Kirkenes Ferda 1942.**
70. Wyller, **Nyordning og Motstand,** pp. 62-63.
71. Brant, **The East German Rising,** p. 161.
72. Gipson, **The British Empire Before the American Revolution,** vol. XII, p. 21, and Gipson, **The Coming of the Revolution,** pp. 208-209. See also Schlesinger, **The Colonial Merchants and the American Revolution,** pp. 252-253.
73. Bondurant, **Conquest of Violence,** p. 57.
74. Lloyd, **Ireland Under the Land League,** pp. 123-126.
75. *Peace News,* 5 June 1964.
76. Martin Oppenheimer and George Lakey, **A Manual for Direct Action** (Chicago: Quadrangle Books, 1965), p. 107n.
77. This section is based on a draft prepared by Michael Schulter.
78. Littell, ed., **The Czech Black Book,** p. 118.
79. *Ibid.,* pp. 118-19.
80. *Ibid.,* p. 185.
81. Quoted in Hsiao, **Rural China,** pp. 449-450.
82. This section is based on a draft prepared by Michael Schulter.
83. J. Ellis Barker, **Modern Germany: Its Rise, Growth, Downfall and Future** (New York: E. P. Dutton & Co.,1919), pp. 293-299.

84. Brant, **The East German Rising,** pp. 34-37.

85. Chang, **The Chinese Gentry,** p. 45.

86. Hsiao, **Rural China,** pp. 134-135.

87. Alexander Pechersky, "Revolt in Sobibor," in Suhl, ed., **They Fought Back,** p. 46.

88. It has not been possible to locate precise documentation or specific cases for this method, although several China authorities have assured me that it has been frequently applied in China. For example, Professor Wolfram Eberhard has written to me in a personal letter, dated 27 April 1966:
"I am acquainted with the kind of 'non-obedience' which you are referring to. In class-room and other discussion I call this 'apathy' and I regard this attitude as a part of the conditions in a traditional society as I have briefly outlined it in the introduction to the second edition of my **Conquerors and Rulers.** The trouble is only, that one cannot expect that Chinese writers (being of the class of scholar/officials) write about this, because they either do not know conditions in villages or would not like to describe these conditions as a description would reflect upon their (non-) efficiency as administrators. The only references which you might be able to find, would be in non-Chinese sources, especially reports by travellers and officials (British) who worked or travelled in China during the 19th Century."
There is evidence that the government during the Ming dynasty and later learned that taxes would not be paid unless a collector or some official was physically present to "prompt" payment. See Hsiao, **Rural China,** pp. 97-99.

89. Magnus Jensen, **Norges Historie: Norge Under Eneveldet 1660-1814,** p. 39.

90. Lefebvre, **The French Revolution from its Origins to 1793,** p. 134.

91. *Ibid.,* p. 234.

92. J. P. Mayer, ed. and trans., **The Recollections of Alexis de Tocqueville,** (New York: Meridian Books, 1959), pp. 151-152.

93. Schapiro, **The Communist Party of the Soviet Union,** p. 68 and Keep, **The Rise of Social Democracy in Russia,** p. 227, and Harcave, **First Blood,** p. 214.

94. Harcave, **First Blood,** p. 174.

95. Warmbrunn, **The Dutch Under German** Occupation, p. 112 and p. 105.

96. Kirchhoff *et al.,* **Besaettelsestidens Historie,** p. 204.

97. Hilberg, **The Destruction of the European Jews,** p. 388.

98. *Ibid.,* p. 405.

99. Dwight H. Perkins, **Market Control and Planning in Communist China** (Cambridge, Mass.: Harvard University Press, 1966), p. 141.

100. Morgan and Morgan, **The Stamp Act Crisis,** pp. 206-207.

101. Sternstein, "The *Ruhrkampf* of 1923," p. 118.

102. Harcave, **First Blood,** p. 215.

103. Sharp, **Gandhi Wields . . . ,** p. 43.

104. Richard W. Fogg, "Jazz Under the Nazis," in *Music 66, Down Beat's* annual, 1966, p. 99.

105. *Ibid.,* p. 98.

106. Hsiao, **Rural China,** p. 52.

107. Taylor, **The Struggle for North China,** p. 120.

108. Peck, **Two Kinds of Time,** p. 414.

109. *Ibid.,* p. 93.

110. Schlesinger, **The Colonial Merchants . . . ,** p. 177. For other examples see also

pp. 286 and 463-464, and Gipson, **The British Empire** . . . , vol. XII, pp. 79-80.

111. Salvemini, **The French Revolution,** p. 125.
112. Mayer, ed., **The Recollections of Alexis de Tocqueville,** pp. 126-132.
113. Miller, Nonviolence, pp. 234-235. The passage is from Imre Révész, History of the Hungarian Reformed Church (Washington, D. C.: Hungarian Reformed Federation of America, 1956), p. 128.
114. **Report of the Nyasaland Commission of Inquiry,** p. 61.
115. Littell, ed., **The Czech Black Book,** p. 223, n. l.
116. *Peace News,* 6 May 1960.
117. *Ibid.,* 3 June 1960.
118. *Ibid.,* 17 November 1961.
119. *Ibid.,* 18 May 1962.
120. Ruth Daniloff, in *ibid.,* 3 July 1964.
121. *Peace News,* 5 March 1965.
122. Sharp, **Gandhi Wields** . . . , pp. 136-137.
123. *Ibid.,* p. 167.
124. Griffith, **The Resurrection of Hungary,** p. xix.
125. *Ibid.,* p. 33.
126. Seton-Watson, **The Decline of Imperial Russia,** p. 165.
127. Jutikkala, **A History of Finland,** p. 237. See also Miller, **Nonviolence,** p. 246.
128. Ligt, **The Conquest of Violence,** p. 144.
129. Reitlinger, **The Final Solution,** p. 342.
130. *Ibid.,* p. 377.
131. *Ibid.,* pp. 302-303.
132. *Ibid.,* p. 394.
133. Warmbrunn, **The Dutch** . . . , pp. 118 and 152.
134. Mabee, **Black Freedom,** p. 314.
135. Jong, "Anti-Nazi Resistance in the Netherlands," in **European Resistance Movements, 1939-1945,** p. 146.
136. Warmbrunn, **The Dutch** . . . , pp. 152-53, and 301 n. 153.
137. Philip Friedman, "Jewish Resistance to Nazism: Its Various Forms and Aspects," in **European Resistance Movements 1939-1945,** p. 204.
138. Hilberg, **The Destruction** . . . , pp. 387-388.
139. Reitlinger, **The Final Solution,** pp. 377-378.
140. Ber Mark, "The Herbert Baum Group," in Suhl, ed., **They Fought Back,** pp. 62-63.
141. Suhl, "The Evidence," pp. 144-46, in Suhl, ed., They Fought Back.
142. Emil F. Knieza, "The Resistance of the Slovak Jews," in Suhl, ed., **They Fought Back,** pp. 177-179.
143. Daniels, "Non-violent Actions in Canada," p. 68.
144. Isidore Abramowitz, ed., **The Great Prisoners: The First Anthology of Literature Written in Prison** (New York: E. P. Dutton and Co., 1946), pp. 2-27.
145. Morgan and Morgan, **The Stamp Act Crisis,** p. 222.
146. Thoreau, "On the Duty of Civil Disobedience," in **Walden and Other Writings of Henry David Thoreau,** pp. 635-663; or Thoreau "On the Duty of Civil Disobedience " (pamphlet).

147. M. K. Gandhi, **Young India** (Triplicane, Madras, India: S. Ganesan, 1922, vol. I, p. 22.

148. Flora Lewis, **The Polish Volcano: A Case History of Hope** (New York: Doubleday & Co., 1958 and London: Secker and Warburg, 1959), pp. 85-86.

149. Gandhi, **Young India,** vol. I, p. 938.

150. M. K. Gandhi, **The Constructive Programme** (pamphlet; Ahmedabad, India: Navajivan, 1941), p. 26

151. Gandhi, **Young India,** vol. I, p. 943.

152. Gipson, **The British Empire Before the American Revolution,** vol. XI, **The Triumphant Empire, The Rumbling of the Coming Storm, 1766-1770,** pp. 219-220.

153. Schlesinger, **The Colonial Merchants . . . ,** p. 70.

154. Gipson, **The British Empire . . . ,** vol. XII, p. 158.

155. *Ibid.,* p. 396, and Schlesinger, **The Colonial Merchants . . . ,** pp. 151-152.

156. Schlesinger, **The Colonial Merchants . . . ,** p. 372.

157. Yarmolinski, **Road to Revolution,** pp. 199-200.

158. Hiller, **The Strike,** pp. 237-238.

159. Myers and Laidler, **What Do You Know About Labor?,** p. 76.

160. Sharp, **Gandhi Wields . . . ,** pp. 51-219, *passim.*

161. Kuper, **Passive Resistance in South Africa,** esp. pp. 17-18, 20-22, 122 and 125-138.

162. *The Times,* 21 March 1960.

163. Steiner, **The New Indians,** p. 55.

164. *Ibid.,* p. 50.

165. *Ibid.*

166. *Ibid.,* p. 53.

167. *Ibid.,* p. 61.

168. *Ibid.,* p. 63.

169. Many other examples are, however, possible. For example, for Finnish examples, see Miller, **Nonviolence,** p. 248 and Jutikkala, **A History of Finland,** p. 238; as civil servants, etc., during the Kapp *Putsch,* see Goodspeed, **The Conspirators,** pp. 129-135; on withholding of *Duma* speeches from the police in 1917, see Katkov, **Russia 1917,** p. 291; and on a large number of acts of noncooperation of officials in the American colonies, see Morgan and Morgan, **The Stamp Act Crisis,** pp. 61, 67, 194, 206, 222 and 228, and Schlesinger, **The Colonial Merchants . . . ,** pp. 253, 305-306, 512 and 522.

170. Lochner, ed., **The Goebbels Diaries,** p. 133.

171. *Ibid.,* p. 229.

172. Hilberg, **The Destruction . . . ,** p. 86.

173. Görlitz, ed., **The Memoirs of Field-Marshal Keitel,** pp. 150-151. See also pp. 166-167 and 247, for other cases.

174. Wheeler-Bennett, **The Nemesis of Power,** p. 494.

175. Hilberg, **The Destruction . . . ,** pp. 360-362.

176. Wheeler-Bennett, **The Nemesis of Power,** p. 457.

177 *Ibid.,* pp. 585 and 625.

178. Görlitz, ed., **The Memoirs of Field-Marshal Keitel,** p. 193.

179. Wheeler-Bennett, **The Nemesis of Power,** p. 470.

180. Hilberg, **The Destruction . . .** , p. 49.
181. Wheeler-Bennett, **The Nemesis of Power,** p. 514, and Alexander Dallin, **German Rule in Russia 1941 and 1945,** p. 32.
182. Görlitz, "The Indictment," in Görlitz, ed., **The Memoirs of Field-Marshal Keitzel,** p. 252. Alexander Dallin even maintains that the order "did not become operative because of the tacit opposition of the generals." (Dallin, **German Rule in Russia 1941-1945,** p. 32.) Görlitz reports that the Commando Order, drafted by Hitler personally (which decreed that all members of Allied commando or sabotage units were to be killed, whether armed or unarmed, even if voluntarily surrendered) was only partially complied with Görlitz, *op. cit.* p. 257.
183. Perkins, **Market Control and Planning in Communist China,** p. 122.
184. Hilberg, **The Destruction . . .** , p. 240.
185. B. H. Liddell Hart, "Lessons from Resistance Movements – Guerilla and Nonviolent," in Roberts, ed., **Civilian Resistance as a National Defense,** p. 207; Br. ed.: **The Strategy of Civilian Defence,** p. 207.
186. Lochner, ed., **The Goebbels Diaries,** pp. 134, 312 and 373.
187. *Ibid.,* p. 128.
188. *Ibid.,* p. 192 (Entry for 27 April 1942).
189. *Ibid.,* p. 314.
190. Görlitz, "The Indictment," p. 261.
191. *Ibid.,* pp. 261-264.
192. Robert Jungk, **Brighter than a Thousand Suns: The Story of the Men who Made the Bomb** (New York: Grove Press Black Cat Edition, n.d.), pp. 88-97.
193. Reitlinger, **The Final Solution,** pp. 97 and 173-79.
194. *Ibid.,* p. 95.
195. *Ibid.,* pp. 218-219.
196. *Ibid.,* p. 380 and Hilberg, **The Destruction . . .** , pp. 478 and 481-484.
197. Reitlinger, **The Final Solution,** pp. 321-324.
198. *Ibid.,* pp. 375-376 n.
199. *Ibid.,* pp. 366-368.
200. *Ibid.,* p. 306.
201. *Ibid.,* pp. 307 and 313.
202. *Ibid.,* p. 320.
203. *Ibid.,* p. 321. See also p. 320, and Hilberg, **The Destruction . . .** , p. 417.
204. Reitlinger, **The Final Solution,** pp. 325-326.
205. Littell, ed., **The Czech Black Book,** pp. 215-16.
206. *Ibid.,* p. 170.
207. Isaac Deutscher, **Stalin: A Political Biography** (New York and London: Oxford University Press, 1961), p. 178.
208. Goodspeed, **The Conspirators,** pp. 130-132.
209. This section is based on a draft by Michael Schulter.
210. Magne Skodvin, "Norwegian Non-violent Resistance During the German Occupation," in Roberts, ed., **Civilian Resistance as a National Defense,** p. 142; Br. ed.: **The Strategy of Civilian Defence,** p. 142.
211. Arthur Koestler, **Reflections on Hanging** (New York: Macmillan, 1967), p. 51. See also pp. 27 and 52.

212. "Afterword," in **Contempt** (no author) (Chicago: Swallow Press, 1970), p. 250. On other details of this case, see pp. 245-254. On Irish juries refusing to bring in convictions, see Locker-Lampson, **A Consideration of the State of Ireland in the Nineteenth Century,** p. 373.

213. A. T. Vassilyev, **The Ochrana: The Russian Secret Police,** ed. by Rene Fülöp-Miller (Philadelphia and London: J. B. Lippincott Co., 1930), p. 100.

214. Sharp, **Gandhi Wields . . . ,** p. 141.

215. Reitlinger, **The Final Solution,** pp. 192-93 n.

216. *Ibid.,* p. 335. Concerning German police in the *Ruhrkampf,* see Halperin, **Germany Tried Democracy,** p. 250; on police etc., during the Kapp *Putsch,* see Goodspeed, **The Conspirators,** pp. 129-135.

217. Interview with Lars Porsholt, Oslo, February 1965.

218. Interview with Inge Ingebretsen (pseud.), Oslo, February 1965.

219. Interview with Professor Arne Næss, Oslo, 1965.

220. Police Inspector Lars L'Abee-Lund, *"Politiet over og Under Jorden,"* in Steen, gen. ed., **Norges Krig,** vol. III, pp. 276-77.

221. *Ibid.,* p. 278.

222. *Ibid.*

223. *Ibid.,* pp. 279-80.

224. *Ibid.,* pp. 281-82.

225. Vassilyev, **The Ochrana,** p. 213.

226. Harcave, **First Blood,** p. 223. On other mutinies, usually more violent, see also pp. 156-158, 190, and 220ff.

227. Keep, **The Rise of Social Democracy in Russia,** p. 263. See also pp. 246-247 and 258, and Charques, **The Twilight of Imperial Russia,** pp. 119 and 135.

228. Katkov, **Russia 1917,** p. 273.

229. *Ibid.,* p. 274.

230. *Ibid.,* p. 276.

231. *Ibid.,* pp. 306-307.

232. *Ibid.,* pp. 314-315. See also pp. 327-328.

233. Watt, **Dare Call It Treason,** pp. 175-211.

234. Sharp, **Gandhi Wields . . . ,** p. 196, and Muhammed Yunus, **Frontier** Speaks (Bombay: Hind Kitabs, 1947), p. 118.

235. Albert P. Blaustein and Clarence Clyde Ferguson, Jr., **Desegregation and the Law: The Meaning and Effect of the School Segregation Cases** (New Brunswick, N. J.: Rutgers University Press, 1957), p. 256.

236. *Ibid.*

237. **The Fifty States Report,** submitted to the Commission on Civil Rights by the State Advisory Committees, 1961 (Washington: U.S. Government Printing Office, 1961), p. 451. See also pp. 460-467.

238. Blaustein and Ferguson, **Desegregation and the Law,** pp. 253-254.

239. *Ibid.,* p. 250.

240. *Ibid.,* p. 251.

241. Crane Brinton, **The Anatomy of Revolution** (New York: Vintage Books, 1962), p. 142.

242. Morgan and Morgan, **The Stamp Act Crisis,** p. 133.

243. *Ibid.,* p. 194.

244. *Ibid.,* pp. 226-227.
245. Gipson, **The British Empire . . .,** vol. xi p. 53. See also pp. 48-63.
246. Trevelyan, **The American Revolution,** p. 88.
247. See Schlesinger, **The Colonial Merchants . . .,** esp. pp. 111-154, 181-182, 256ff, 323, 365-366, and 432-472.
248. Henry Steele Commager, ed., **Documents of American History** (New York and London: Appleton-Century-Crofts, 1948), p. 178.
249. *Ibid.,* p. 182.
250. *Ibid.,* p. 184.
251. *Ibid.,* pp. 250-251.
252. Jutikkala, **A History of Finland,** p. 246.
253. Sharp, **Gandhi Wields . . .,** pp. 195-196.
254. Crespigny, "The Nature and Methods of Non-violent Coercion," p. 261, n. 3.
255. André Fontaine, **History of the Cold War: From the October Revolution to the Korean War 1917-1950** (New York: Pantheon Books, 1968), p. 347.
256. Sir Douglas Busk, **The Craft of Diplomacy: How to Run a Diplomatic Service** (New York: Frederick A. Praeger, 1967), p. 15.
257. Charles W. Thayer, **Diplomat** (New York: Harper & Bros., 1959), p. 217.
258. *Ibid.,* p. 217.
259. *Ibid.,* pp. 217-219.
260. Thomas A. Bailey, **A Diplomatic History of the American People** (sixth ed.; New York: Appleton-Century-Crofts, 1958), pp. 724-725.
261. *Time,* vol. 91, 22 March 1968, p. 33.
262. *New York Times,* 29 Nov. 1969.
263. C. L. Sultzberger, "Foreign Affairs: The Missing Envoy," *New York Times,* 28 Nov. 1969.
264. Gordon A. Craig, "Totalitarian Diplomacy," in Lawrence W. Martin, ed., **Diplomacy in Modern European History** (New York: Macmillan Co. and London: Collier-Macmillan Ltd., 1966), pp. 90-91.
265. Fontaine, **History of the Cold War,** p. 347.
266. Wilfrid F. Knapp, **A History of War and Peace 1939-1965** (London, New York and Toronto: Oxford University Press, 1967), p. 480.
267. *New York Times,* 7 May 1970, pp. 1 and 11.
268. Quoted by Bailey, **A Diplomatic History of the American People,** p. 555.
269. Taylor, **The Struggle for North China,** p. 195.
270. Bailey, **A Diplomatic History of the American People,** pp. 694-699.
271. *Ibid.,* pp. 633-34 and 671-72.
272. Quoted in Robert Blum, **The United States and China in World Affairs** (ed. by A. Doak Barnett; New York: McGraw-Hill [for the Council on Foreign Relations], 1966), p. 121.
273. *Ibid.,* p. 122.
274. Charles D. Cremeans, **The Arabs and the World: Nasser's Arab Nationalist Policy** (New York and London: Fredrick A. Praeger [for the Council on Foreign Relations], 1963), pp. 195-197.
275. Ferenc A. Váli, **Rift and Revolt in Hungary: Nationalism versus Communism** (Cambridge, Mass.: Harvard University Press, 1961, and London: Oxford University Press, 1961), p. 484.

276. Wheeler-Bennett, **The Nemesis of Power,** p. 79. For references to continued efforts by the Kappists to obtain diplomatic recognition, see p. 79, n. 2.
277. Harold Nicholson,**Diplomacy** (sec. ed.; London, New York and Toronto: Oxford University Press, 1960 [orig. 1950]), p. 191.
278. Busk, **The Craft of Diplomacy,** pp. 15-16.
279. Nicholson, **Diplomacy,** p. 192.
280. Bailey, **A Diplomatic History of the American People,** pp. 590-91.
281. Knapp, **A History of War and Peace,** p. 44, n. 16, and Fontaine, **History of the Cold War,** pp. 184-85.
282. Bullock, **Hitler,** pp. 322-324.
283. Knapp, **A History of War and Peace,** pp. 198 and 200-201.
284. Leland M. Goodrich, Edvard Hambro and Anne Patricia Simons, **Charter of the United Nations: Commentary and Documents** (Third and rev. ed.; New York and London: Columbia University Press, 1969), p. 76.
285. *Ibid.,* pp. 77-80, 109-10, 200-201, 251, and 523.
286. U. S. Department of State *Bulletin,* vol. 59 (9 December 1968), p. 613, and Goodrich, Hambro and Simons, **Charter of the United Nations,** pp. 171-175, 174 n. 252.
287. Goodrich, Hambro and Simons, **Charter of the United Nations,** p. 99.
288. Knapp, **A History of War and Peace,** p. 4.
289. Goodrich, Hambro and Simons, **Charter of the United Nations,** p. 98.
290. *Ibid.*
291. *Ibid.,* p. 100 and n. 91.
292. Knapp, **A History of War and Peace,** p. 128.

8

The Methods of Nonviolent Intervention

INTRODUCTION

One final class of the methods of nonviolent action remains, that of nonviolent intervention. The forty-one methods in this class differ from those in the classes of protest and persuasion and of noncooperation in that in some way they *intervene* in the situation. Such methods of intervention operate both negatively and positively: they may disrupt, and even destroy, established behavior patterns, policies, relationships, or institutions which are seen as objectionable; or they may establish new behavior patterns, policies, relationships, or institutions which are preferred. Some of these methods contribute primarily to the first of these results, some to the second.

Compared with the methods of the classes of protest and persuasion and of noncooperation, the methods of nonviolent intervention pose a more direct and immediate challenge. *If successful,* the victory is likely to come quicker by the use of methods of this class than with the use of methods of the previous classes, because the disruptive effects of the intervention are harder to tolerate or withstand for a considerable period of time. For example, intervention by a sit-in at a lunch counter disrupts more immediately and completely than would, say, picketing or a consumers' boycott, though the objective of each of these actions be to end racial discrimination. However, though the challenge of methods of intervention is clearer and more direct, the result is not necessarily more rapid success; precisely because of the character of intervention, speedier and more severe repression may be a first result—which, of course, does not necessarily mean defeat.

In most cases, use of the methods of this class may induce change through the mechanisms of accommodation or of nonviolent coercion, i.e., without the opponent's being convinced that he *ought* to change his policy on the matter in question. However, certain of these methods (especially those classed as psychological intervention) and also the repression which frequently occurs against others (especially those of physical intervention) may contribute to the opponent's conversion, or at least to his becoming less certain of the rightness of his previous views. These mechanisms of conversion, accommodation and nonviolent coercion are discussed in detail in the final Part of this book.

To a greater degree than in the classes discussed earlier, methods of nonviolent intervention are associated with initiative by the nonviolent actionists. The methods of intervention may be used both defensively—to thwart an opponent's attack by maintaining independent initiative, behavior patterns, institutions, or the like—and offensively—to carry the struggle for the actionists' objectives into the opponent's own camp, even without any immediate provocation. These methods, therefore, are not simply defensive responses to the opponent's initiative.

The range of methods within this class is wide. In this chapter they have been classified according to the dominant manner of expression of the intervention itself: psychological, physical, social, economic, or political. This is quite often different from the influences the method may have. For example, an act of social intervention may have strong psychological influence. An act of psychological intervention may have a political impact. An act of physical intervention may have social repercussions, and so on. All the methods of nonviolent action are likely to have some type of psychological influence; as considered here, psychological intervention includes methods in which the psychological element is the dominant form of expression.

Obviously these five subclasses are somewhat arbitrary. Alternative classifications of particular methods are possible, especially in a given conflict situation. Furthermore, not every use of these methods will actually produce intervention. A given act may be too limited, weak, or restricted in time, numbers, or focus to constitute significant intervention, and may instead become primarily an act of nonviolent protest and persuasion. Of the five subclasses of intervention we turn first to psychological intervention.

PSYCHOLOGICAL INTERVENTION

The four methods of psychological intervention described here differ significantly from each other in attitudes toward the person or group to which they are directed, in the intended process of change, and in the actual types of behavior. They have in common only the characteristic that the intervention is predominantly or exclusively on a psychological level.

158. Self-exposure to the elements

Exposure of one's own body to discomfort or suffering from the elements, such as the heat of the sun, is one form which psychological intervention has taken. This method is one of the several forms in which self-retribution may be expressed. Self-retribution involves putting psychological, moral, or emotional pressure on others to induce them to change their attitudes or to take certain action, by voluntarily taking discomfort, humiliation, penalties, or suffering upon oneself. Other ways in which self-retribution is expressed within nonviolent action include protest disrobing, destruction of one's own property (as used by some Doukhobors) both already discussed, and the fast, which follows.

An example of self-exposure to the elements comes from the mid-nineteenth century China and concerns the action of a judge, Lu Chia-shu, who dealt with a "legal fight" between brothers. Ch'ien Yung recorded:

> There were two brothers who fought against one another without stopping (i.e. reconciliation). Mr. Lu told them: "If brothers are not harmonious, this represents a great change in the human relations. I am the father and mother of the people here. So this must be my fault, that I did not teach you well." Then he knelt down in the blazing sun. The fighting (parties) were touched and cried. From then on, they were good to one another. [1]

Professor Wolfram Eberhard, who provided this example, comments:

> The judge Lu, in this case, could have severely beaten both claimants for their violation of the Confucian rules of brotherly love. This would have been the normal action of the judges at the time. No judge would have looked into the case in order to find out who is right and who is wrong. Lu's actions (to take the guilt upon himself) shamed the brothers, corrected their behavior, and did not involve the expected violence. [2]

A related but much milder type of action was used, probably in the 1880s, by temporary farm laborers in the province of Kherson of Imperial Russia, in order to protest the poor diets provided by the landowners. Trotsky records seeing this as a child on his father's farm:

> The laborers would leave the fields and collect in the courtyard. They would lie face downward in the shade of the barns, brandishing their bare, cracked, straw-pricked feet in the air, and wait to see what would happen. Then my father would give them some clabber, or watermelons, or half a sack of dried fish and they would go back to work again, often singing.[3]

In the summer of 1972 some English and American prisoners protested by staying for long periods, and with danger to themselves, on the slanting roofs of prison buildings, or even on top of the prison water-tower (as at the Federal Correctional Institution at Danbury, Connecticut).

159. The fast

The fast is often used as a method of psychological intervention. Abstention from certain or all foods may be undertaken for a number of reasons, including health, religion, penance, self-purification, and desire to achieve social and political objectives. The latter reason is most relevant here, although fasts undertaken for reasons of religion, penance and self-purification may under certain circumstances also constitute intervention. In addition, fasts may serve simply as a form of moral protest. Three types of the fast will be distinguished in this context: the *fast of moral pressure*, the *hunger strike*, and the *satyagrahic fast* as applied on some occasions by Gandhi.

The *fast of moral pressure* has characteristics which fall between the other two types. It is also much more likely not to fulfill completely the requirements of nonviolent intervention, and to become instead a form of nonviolent protest and persuasion (although for simplicity this form of the fast is not listed under both classes). Fasts of moral pressure are usually conscious attempts to exert moral influence on others to achieve an objective, though they lack the openly coercive intent of the hunger strike, and the full "conversion" intent of the satyagrahic fast. Many people have argued that the fast is incomprehensible in the West; however, there are a multitude of Western examples, and in cases where fasts have been initiated where they have been unfamiliar, the response has often been unexpectedly favorable. For example, in 1960 and 1961 exponents of nuclear disarmament and pacifists in England had argued that fasts should not be used in the disarmament campaign since they would be incomprehensible to Englishmen. However, when this method was introduced in 1962 in support of the unilateral nuclear disamament movement and simultaneously to raise money for famine relief, the number of fasts grew rapidly during that year and 1963, and they were received with considerable public understanding and sympathy.[4]

Examples of fasts of moral pressure are varied. St. Patrick once fasted against King Trián of Ulster to compel him to have compassion on his slaves. On another occasion he fasted three days and three nights against the Pelagian heresy in a city to compel the inhabitants to become orthodox.[5]

Fasting was on several occasions also practiced by American colonists. For example, on May 24, 1774, the Virginia House of Burgesses resolved to observe June 1 (the day the Boston Port Act was to go into effect) as a day of "Fasting, Humiliation, and Prayer." The objective was to implore divine interposition to avert the "destruction to our Civil rights, and the Evils of Civil War . . . and that the Minds of his Majesty and his Parliament, may be inspired from above with Wisdom, Moderation, and Justice, to remove from the loyal People of America all cause of danger, from a continued pursuit of Measures, pregnant with their ruin." Two days later, after the Governor had summoned the members of the House to meet with him immediately in the Council chamber, he declared that the resolve was conceived "in such Terms as reflect highly upon his Majesty and the Parliament of Great Britain," and thereupon he dissolved the House,[6] thus preventing its continuing to meet and preventing it from taking other "hostile" actions.

There is an interesting story behind this case which introduced fasting into the American colonists' struggles. Earlier, in response to the action of some Bostonians in dumping tea belonging to the East India Company into Boston harbor, the British government had decided to close the port of Boston on June 1, 1774, and published the Boston Port Act to that end. This news reached Virginia while the House of Burgesses was in session. Thomas Jefferson later wrote that the lead in the House was no longer being left to the older members. A small group of younger members which included Patrick Henry, Richard Henry Lee, Jefferson himself, and four or five others, met to consider what to do. They were determined to take a bold, unequivocal stand in support of Massachusetts. As Jefferson described it, they gathered to

> consult on the proper measures in the council chamber, for the benefit of [i.e. to have the use of] the library in that room. We were under conviction of the necessity of arousing our people from the lethargy into which they had fallen as to passing events; and thought that the appointment of a day of general fasting and prayer would be most likely

to call up & alarm their attention. No example of such a solemnity had existed since the days of our distresses in the war [against the French] of [17]55, since which a new generation had grown up. With the help therefore of Rushmore, whom we rummaged over for the revolutionary precedents & forms of the Puritans of that day, preserved by him, we cooked up a resolution, somewhat modernizing their phrases, for appointing the 1st day of June, on which the Port bill was to commense, for a day of fasting, humiliation & prayer, to implore heaven to avert from us the evils of civil war, to inspire us with firmness in support of our rights, and to turn the hearts of the King & parliament to moderation & justice. [7]

Edmund Randolph credits Jefferson and Charles Lee with originating the "fast to electrify the people from the pulpit." [8] The young men who drafted the resolution "were famed more for skill with the violin and grace in dancing than for piety and prayer." [9] In order, therefore, to avoid ridicule and defeat if they offered so grave a resolution, the next morning they persuaded Robert Carter Nicholas, the pious, elderly chairman of the committee of religion, to move the resolution. Mr. Nicholas did so the same day, and it was passed without opposition. [10] One opponent denounced the fast as "a Schem calculated to *inflame* and excite an *enthusiastic* zeal in the Minds of the People under a Cloak of Religion . . ." [11] After dissolution, the members of the House met elsewhere and agreed to call for a meeting of an American Congress of Deputies for all the colonies; and then they returned to their own districts to arouse the clergymen and people to patriotic feelings. When the first of June came, B.O. Flower writes:

the great fast day led to the crystallizing of the revolutionary sentiment of the colony, just as the leaders had predicted it would. Never before, and rarely since, have the clergy been so brave and outspoken. "The cause of liberty is the cause of God!" exclaimed one minister; and this was the sentiment echoed from ocean to mountain. [12]

Later Jefferson himself wrote: "The people met generally, with anxiety & alarm in their countenances, and the effect of the day thro' the whole colony was like a shock of electricity, arousing every man & placing him erect & solidly on his centre." [13]

In the summer of 1774, "a day of fasting and prayer, on account of the dark aspect of our publick affairs" was proclaimed in Rhode Island. [14] The next spring, on February 16, 1775, the Massachusetts Bay Provincial Congress (the unconstitutional legislature of members of the previous House of Representatives), meeting in Cambridge, set aside a day for fasting and prayer, with a request included for prayers for King George III, pointedly indicating the conflict was not with the King but with the King's government. Boston observed the day with "marked solemnity." However, while a religious service was in progress that day, the King's Own corps played their drums and fifes within ten yards of the church. [15]

There are many more examples of the fast of moral pressure. For example, in April 1962 a number of Frenchmen fasted for peace in Algeria, [16] and a French pacifist, Louis Lecoin, fasted in June of that year to obtain legal recognition of French conscientious objectors. [17]

Danilo Dolci has used both the individual and mass fast in his efforts to relieve poverty in Sicily. When a child died of malnutrition in December 1952, Dolci resolved to fast to draw attention to the misery and unemployment in Trappeto, and to refuse food until a certain amount of money had been received for the relief of the starving. On January 30, 1956, he led about one thousand unemployed fishermen in a twenty-four hour mass fast on the beach to call attention to their plight; the demonstration was broken up by the police. [18] On January 16, 1966, Dolci completed a seven-day fast against the Mafia; and he called for casting off the fear which imposed the *omertà* (the law of silence) and prevented the gathering of evidence on Mafia crimes. Dolci fasted in a traditional Sicilian one-room family habitation in Castellammare del Golfo in Western Sicily—the district whose parliamentary representative was Signor Mattarella, the former Minister for Foreign Trade who had been accused of connections with the Mafia. The fast was reported to have brought about a "revolution" in people's willingness to criticize authority and an increased willingness to defy the Mafia. [19]

Buddhists also used fasting in nonviolent struggles in South Vietnam during the 1960s. Sometimes individuals have fasted alone, sometimes a group, and sometimes thousands of people have taken part in the fast. On occasion only elders of the Buddhist church took part. Trich Nhat Hanh reports that the Venerable Thich Tri Quang fasted for one hundred days at the Duy Tan Clinic in 1966. Hanh continues: "The purpose of fasting is for prayer, for purifying one's heart and consolidating one's will, or for arousing the awareness and compassion latent within the people." [20]

The *hunger strike*, the second type of fast considered here, may be defined as a refusal to eat with the aim of forcing the opponent to grant certain demands but without any serious effort to convert him or to achieve a "change of heart." On this point it differs sharply from the satyagrahic fast, as applied by Gandhi, which is discussed next. The hunger strike may be undertaken for a set period of time, for an indefinite period, or unto death if the demand is not granted. Prisoners who feel they have no other powerful method of protest at their disposal often use the fast. The examples are many and varied.

According to the legal code of ancient Ireland it was the duty of an injured person, when all else had failed, to inflict punishment directly on the wrongdoer. In some cases before a settlement involving reimbursement by seizure of property (such as cattle or other effects),

> . . . the plaintiff *fasted* on the defendant; . . . and this process, called *troscad,* "fasting," was always necessary before distress [removal of goods in compensation] when the defendant was of chieftain grade and the plaintiff of an inferior grade. . . The plaintiff, having served due notice, went to the house of the defendant, and, sitting before the door, remained without food. It may be inferred that the debtor generally yielded before the fast was ended, i.e., either paid the debt or gave a pledge that he would settle the case. If the creditor continued to fast after an offer of payment, he forfeited all the debt due to him . . . .
>
> From some passages it would appear that the debtor was bound to remain fasting as long as the creditor or complainant fasted . . . it was considered disgraceful for a defendant not to submit to it: "He that does not give a pledge to fasting is an evader of all: he who disregards all things shall not be paid by God or man." (British Laws, I, 113).[21]

That is, he would be subjected to a complete social boycott.

This is closely related to the Indian practice of *dhurna* or sitting *dhurna,* described by Shridharani as follows:

> Every so often in the Middle Ages a moneylender, failing to receive his money back in due time, would sit in front of the house of the debtor, refusing to budge from his place or to take any food until the client paid in full. Since the interesting situation always gathered a crowd of idle curious, the debtor would make a supreme effort to pay rather than suffer a long drawn-out siege with its attendant embarrassment. The *Bhat* (bard of the royal court) used a similar method when he wanted his king to "be a man" and fight. When his ruler, out of cowardice or other considerations, refused to meet an invading or offending king in combat, the *Bhat* would sit in the palace gate [way] and start a hunger strike. In most cases, this compelled the king to fight.[22]

There were also a considerable number of Russian hunger strikes, as illustrated by the following examples. Political prisoners in the Peter-Paul Fortress in St. Petersburg went on a long hunger strike during the summer of 1875; following a number of deaths of hunger strikers, the Head of the Third Section (the branch of the police which had a vast network of informers and agents) was assassinated in revenge.[23] In another case, while imprisoned in the dungeon of the Peter-Paul Fortress the notorious revolutionary Sergei Nechaev at about the end of 1877, after four years in solitary confinement, went on a hunger strike to obtain books not in the prison library.[24] In July 1878, reports Peter Kropotkin, six prisoners at Kharkov prison "resolved to starve themselves to death" in an act of opposition against extreme jail conditions. After they had resisted efforts to feed them by injection, officials promised walking exercise for prisoners and the removal of the sick from irons. These promises were not kept, and "only later on, when several had died, and two went mad . . . the prisoners obtained the privilege of sawing some wood in the yard, in company with two Tartars, who understood not a word of Russian."[25] Kropotkin also reports that the right of prisoners in the Peter-Paul Fortress to have visits from relatives every fortnight in 1879 and 1880 was won "by the famous famine strike, during which a number of prisoners in the Trubetskoi bastion refused to take any food for five or six days . . ." and resisted all efforts to feed them by injections.[26]

While confined in Kherson in 1898 the youthful Trotsky persuaded his fellow political prisoners to go on a hunger strike to protest a police proposal that juvenile prisoners be released if their parents promised to give them a thrashing and keep them from political activities; according to Trotsky, this was "an insult to the honor of the juvenile revolutionary."[27] Early in 1922, when two thousand arrested Mensheviks were threatened with administrative mass exile to distant provinces, some of them went on hunger strike, and approximately twelve were eventually allowed to leave the country.[28]

However, the results were very different when similar action was attempted in the autumn of 1936. According to an eyewitness, Boris Podolak, whose testimony was given in 1951, a large, well-organized group of Trotskyist prisoners at Vorkuta, with participation of other political groups, participated in a hunger strike of four hundred prisoners. They remained lying on their bunks and also refused to work. They addressed their declaration to the internal police of the N.K.V.D., denounced the current political system as fascist, and stated demands. Although many of the other prisoners were sympathetic, the number of hunger strikers did not grow, but rather became smaller. After one-and-a-half or two months, most of them could no longer resist forced feeding. Only about forty held out until they died. In the autumn of 1937, the report continues, a special commission arrived from Moscow, and the former strike leaders together with many other prisoners were arrested. After being kept in a barracks, they were moved twenty miles away to an abandoned brickworks "which became a kind of death-isolator." By the end of February 1938 about seven hundred prisoners were being kept there. The first mass executions began the night of May 8-9 and continued. [29]

Hunger strikes have also occurred in the modern Irish nationalist movement. For example, in late September 1917 two Irish nationalists imprisoned for one year at hard labor at Mountjoy Gaol went on hunger strike. They were Thomas Ashe, an Irish Volunteer, and Austin Stack, a Kerry Volunteer, both charged with "attempting to cause disaffection among the civil population." In prison they organized a hunger strike in support of the demand that they be either treated as political prisoners or released. The jail officials, however, force-fed the hunger strikers: after a week of this Ashe collapsed, and within five hours of being hospitalized, died. [30] (A brief account of his funeral is offered in Chapter Three under the method demonstrative funeral.)

The British also applied other measures to deal with hunger strikers including the so-called cat-and-mouse act. This had been used to deal with women suffragists who frequently went on hunger strikes in England. [31] Weakening prisoners on hunger strikes were released, but when they regained their strength they were rearrested. Edgar Holt reports that "it was an effective measure . . . . and there were no more deaths from hunger strikes until 1920."

On Easter Monday, April 5, 1920, some one hundred Sinn Fein prisoners in Mountjoy Gaol began a mass hunger strike, this time demanding either that they be treated as prisoners of war or released. The official British attitude to this challenge was expressed in the House of Commons by Bonar Law, the leader of the House and Lord Privy Seal: "It would be perfectly futile if men are to be released because they choose to refuse food." In Ireland, however, support grew, for members of the Irish Labour Party called for a general strike for April 13 for support of the Mountjoy prisoners, and the Roman Catholic hierarchy publicly declared it to be "their solemn duty to call the attention of everyone to the appalling tragedy that seems imminent in Mountjoy Prison." After ten days, the government released the prisoners unconditionally. [32] One who did not fare so well that same year was the Lord Mayor of Cork, Terence McSweeney, who died after a fast of seventy-four days. [33]

In October 1944 several American conscientious objectors, imprisoned in the federal prison at Lewisburg, who objected to punishment imposed on them for their participation in a work strike against the parole system, organized a "rotation" hunger strike. In this, five men would refuse to eat for a definite but unannounced period, after which five others would take their place as hunger strikers.[34]

In May 1958 nearly thirteen thousand prostitutes in India threatened a mass hunger strike when brothels were closed under an Act prohibiting the letting of houses for prostitution.[35] In a similar case to "sitting *dhurna*" discussed earlier, in August 1959 a factory stoker in New Delhi undertook a fast unto death outside his employer's villa to protest low pay and poor working conditions.[36]

The final type of fast discussed here is the *satyagrahic fast,* predominantly practiced by Gandhi who distinguished his fasts for social objectives from the hunger strike, which he regarded as coercive. Although accused of failing to recognize coercive elements in his own fasts, Gandhi insisted that their objective was to convert. According to him, the *satyagrahi* may fast to "sting" the conscience of the wrongdoer (who may be an individual, a group of people, or even millions) through voluntary suffering only if he has exhausted all other nonviolent means. The satyagrahic fast may be for a set period of time, or unto death if the demand is not granted.

Gandhi sought to establish strict limits on this use of the fast; for example, it should not be applied against just anyone, regardless of the issue. Normally, one would not fast against one's opponent, especially if the opponent were a stranger or not one's friend. Gandhi thought that the wrongdoer and the fasting *satyagrahi* must have been close and have shared mutual affection for this self-imposed form of suffering to be justified and to have the intended conversion effect. Under special circumstances, however, the fast could be applied to others, primarily if the opponent's repression and restrictions closed other avenues of approach. *Satyagrahis* who as prisoners were subjected to inhuman treatment might, for example, fast for the removal of such treatment—though they might not, in Gandhi's view, fast for their release. In either case, the "mistake" of the individual or group against whom the fast is undertaken must have been gross and have moved the *satyagrahi* to the very depth of his being.

Gandhi believed that considerable spiritual preparation and service were necessary before one was justified in undertaking a satyagrahic fast, and that a fast unto death was to be used only when every other form of *satyagraha* had failed. Examples of Gandhi's use of the satyagrahic fast include his fast during the Ahmedabad labor strike in February–March 1918, undertaken to arouse striking workers who had weakened in their resolve to keep their pledges to him to continue the strike until their demands had been granted.[37] His final fast at Delhi in January 1948, for Hindu-Muslim unity in the midst of the riots, is a clearer example of the characteristics he avowed for this instrument.[38] In this Gandhi sought to restore by his fast an awareness of the worth of the lives of all Indians and to arouse feelings of brotherhood between Hindu and Muslim.

160. Reverse trial

Another form of psychological intervention is the reverse trial. Sometimes the combination of circumstances and the behavior during the trial of those prosecuted for political, religious, or other reasons significantly reverses the roles of prosecution and defender in the trial. The defendants become the prosecutors, and the trial is turned into a demonstration against the government and is used by the prosecuted to publicize their beliefs, program and indictment of the established order. This is what we call a reverse trial.

This reversal of roles has taken place in a wide variety of political cases. In Russia, in each of the "great trials of 1877" of revolutionaries the accused were able to conduct themselves in such a way as to arouse public sympathy and support. The first of these, the trial of the demonstrators of the Square of Our Lady of Kazan in St. Petersburg, brought great sympathy for those on trial. In the second trial, of "the fifty" in March in Moscow, observers compared the accused with early Christian martyrs. And in the 1877-78 St Petersburg "trial of the hundred and ninety-three" members of the movement "to go to the people" with the revolutionary message, the events of the trial made an important public impact despite strict censorship. Part of this impact resulted from the speech of Ippolit Nikitch Myshkin, one of the accused, on the ideas and program of socialism. Myshkin, in another speech, also denounced the tribunal itself as "a useless comedy" and "more shameful than a brothel . . ." The revolutionary S.M. Kravchinsky later wrote: "After his words the tribunal was annihilated." [39]

In a very different style, when he was on trial, Gandhi behaved in such a way that even when he pleaded guilty to the charge he gave the impression that he had only been guilty of doing the right thing; this occurred, for example, in 1922, during his trial for writing three seditious articles in his journal, *Young India.* Asking the judge either to resign his post or, if he believed in the system, to give him (Gandhi) the severest penalty possible, Gandhi declared it to be "an honor to be disaffected towards a government which in its totality has done more harm to India than any previous system." [40]

Similarly, Germans prosecuted by the occupation powers during the *Ruhrkampf* used their trials as a means of pointing out the injustice of the French and Belgian seizure of the Ruhr.[41] After the abortive *Putsch* in 1923, Adolph Hitler made the most of his trial, which for the first time gave him an audience outside the frontiers of Bavaria; according to his biographer, Allan Bullock, "in his final speech he established a complete mastery over the court." [42] In the famous *Reichstag* fire trial in Nazi Germany in 1933, one of the accused, the Bulgarian Communist Georgi Dimitroff, served as his own lawyer, cleverly cross-examined Göring himself, taunted him into a rage, and succeeded in obtaining acquittal for himself and three others. [43]

Further examples of reverse trial continue to occur when political and moral issues are involved in the case and when the prosecuted persons are able to regain the initiative against their prosecutors. This method illustrates the potential of simple psychological intervention even when no other types of leverage are at the disposal of the accused.

161. Nonviolent harassment

This method consists of psychological harassment by a combination of actions which concentrate private and public pressures on one or more individuals engaged in activities which are detested. The actions which may be used to produce nonviolent harassment include stronger and more persistent use of "haunting" (constantly remaining physically near the person) and "taunting" (name-calling and accusations)—both of which have been discussed in mild forms as methods of nonviolent protest and persuasion. Nonviolent harassment has also utilized means of public communication such as posters and newspaper advertisements; the use of other such means would fall within this method. The objective of the combination of pressures is to induce the person to halt the behavior or action which is found objectionable; these are not the types of pressures likely to alter the opinion or beliefs of the person against which they are directed. This method has been termed nonviolent harassment by Carleton Mabee in *Black Freedom,* his study of nonviolent opposition to slavery in the United States. [44] The proposal to use this method was worked out in detail by Charles K. Whipple, who had been treasurer of the Nonresistance Society and was a contributor to William Lloyd Garrison's paper, *Liberator.* This method was to be used against slave hunters in Northern states hired to capture and return escaped slaves to their Southern owners. Whipple's proposal drew upon general recommendations by Garrison, Wendell Phillips and the Rhode Island Antislavery Society. The Boston Vigilance Committee debated and partially adopted the proposal, which was published in the *Liberator* and other antislavery papers in 1850-51. The recommendation was this:

As soon as the kidnappers arrived in any town, large handbills should be posted in all the public places, containing their names, with a description of their persons and the business on which they come.

An attempt should be made to induce the landlord of any hotel or boarding-house to which they may go, to refuse them entertainment, on the ground of their being persons infamous by profession, like pickpockets, gamblers, or horse-stealers.

If this proves unsuccessful, some of the committee of attendance should take lodging in the same house with the kidnappers, and take, if possible, sleeping rooms and seats at table directly opposite to them.

The doors of the house should be watched carefully, day and night, and whenever they go out, two resolute, unarmed men should follow each of them wherever he goes, pointing him out from time to time with the word SLAVE-HUNTER. They should follow him into every shop, office, or place of public dwelling, wait outside, watching all the avenues, and ready to renew the attendance when he comes out. If he takes a coach, they should follow in another; if he drives out of town, they should follow; if he takes a seat in a railroad car, they should go with him, and make him known as a slave-hunter to the passengers in the car, and to the people of the town where he stops. He should not have one moment's relief from the feeling that his object is understood, that he cannot act in secret, that he is surrounded by men who loathe his person and detest his purpose, and who have means at hand to prevent the possibility of success.[45]

Mabee reports that on the basis of this and similar proposals nonviolent attempts were made throughout the 1850s to protect fugitive slaves in the North.[46] For example, this method was used in Philadelphia when a Miss Wilson from Maryland arrived to locate her runaway slave. J. Miller McKim, an exponent of nonviolent methods who was in charge of the office of the Pennsylvania Antislavery Society, on hearing of her efforts to hire a local slave catcher, arranged for an abolitionist to pose as one. He was hired and obtained the name of the slave. McKim notified the fugitive, who went into hiding, and then prepared posters about three feet square, headed "BEWARE OF SLAVE-CATCHERS," which were posted about the city. Miss Wilson was named, as well as the slave, whom people were urged to hide, in accordance with a scriptural injunction. When she learned of the posters, Miss Wilson abandoned the hunt and returned to her home in Maryland.[47]

Similarly in Boston, when Charles Hobson from Virginia came to hunt his escaped slave, Henry Langhorn, abolitionists took an advertisement in the newspaper, mimicking the advertisement which Hobson had published seeking his slave; the abolitionists' advertisement described Hobson and stated that he was staying at the Tremont Hotel. They also posted about one hundred placards warning that Hobson was in town to catch a slave.

Unnerved, Hobson hurriedly departed for Virginia without Henry Langhorn.[48]

These cases of nonviolent harassment of slave catchers were not, however, widely imitated, and this method was not applied on a sufficiently large scale to test its potential in that situation.

PHYSICAL INTERVENTION

A second subclass of methods of nonviolent intervention consists of those predominantly characterized by the interference created by people's physical bodies, especially as they enter, or refuse to leave, some place where they are not wanted or from which they have been prohibited.

162. Sit-in

In a sit-in the interventionists occupy certain facilities by sitting on available chairs, stools and occasionally on the floor for a limited or unlimited period, either in a single act or in a series of acts, with the objective of disrupting the normal pattern of activities. The purpose may be to establish a new pattern, such as opening particular facilities to previously excluded persons, or to make a protest which may not be directly connected with the facilities occupied. This method has often been used in the civil rights movement in the United States.

In conception the method is not at all new, however. Mabee reports that as early as 1838 the Antislavery Convention of American Women adopted a comprehensive policy supporting sit-ins and ride-ins, but that there had been no systematic follow-up campaign.[49] Then, during the August 1841 meeting of the Massachusetts Antislavery Society, a "Garrisonian nonviolent actionist," Stephen S. Foster, impatient with regular political methods, moved a resolution which described the basis of sit-ins, ride-ins and related methods: "We recommend to [white] abolitionists as the most consistent and effectual method of abolishing the 'Negro-pew,' to take their seats in it, wherever it may be found, whether in a gentile synagogue [church], a railroad car, a steamboat, or a stage coach."[50] The exponents of nonviolent means within that Society split on the resolution, William Lloyd Garrison himself opposing it, although he personally participated in ride-ins, and the resolution was defeated. Nevertheless, the principle was applied in a series of ride-ins, as will be described under that method.[51]

An early, modified application of the sit-in occurred in Chicago in late 1869 or early 1870. Negro protests had failed to abolish the segregationist

Black Code and segregated education, Negro children being forced to attend the so-called Black School. The Negro parents and children then applied a form of the sit-in; since segregation was then the law, this method also involved civil disobedience. The parents simply sent the children to the school nearest their homes. Although the teachers did not assign the children to classes or give them lessons to do, "The children . . . attended daily, taking their seats in an orderly fashion throughout the controversy that ensued." The school board attempted to compromise by admitting only children with one-eighth Negro ancestry to the regular schools, but the Chicago Negroes invaded the offices of the board and of the Mayor, and the Black School was abolished.[52]

In 1938 Chippewa Indians from a reservation in the Cass Lake region of Minnesota, through their chiefs, had protested against the decision made by Commissioner of Indian Affairs John Collier to move the Bureau of Indian Affairs headquarters from the reservation to Duluth; the chiefs argued that this was a violation of the new United States policy of granting Indian self-government. Agency Superintendent Lewis Balsam, however, proceeded with the moving plans. Then several hundred Chippewa braves, painted and wearing traditional costumes, marched to the headquarters and danced around the building to the beat of drums. A group of Chippewa women followed, entering the office, and Balsam fled. The young braves then moved in, sitting on desks and filing cabinets, while a picket line formed outside. Commissioner Collier still insisted on moving the office to the city, but his superior, Secretary of the Interior Harold L. Ickes, ordered a tribal referendum on the issue, agreeing to accept its results.[53]

In 1960 American Indians of Chrokee ancestry, called Croatans, resorted to a sit-in after six years of unsuccessful efforts to gain admission to Dunn High School, in Dunn, Hartnett County, North Carolina. At the beginning of the 1960–61 school year nine Indian students had attempted to register for school at Dunn but had been refused, being told to attend instead the all-Indian high school, which meant a seventy-mile round-trip each day from Dunn. On August 31 seven Indian youths, accompanied by two adults, began a three day sit-in at Dunn High School. On the third day seven youths and five adults were arrested for trespassing. Promised an Indian school in Dunn by the autumn of 1961, they called off their action. However, in response to protests from across the United States, the local Mayor, G.F. Blalock, insisted that the problem was not the town's fault, and that the local citizens overwhelmingly favored admission of Indian students. In June 1961 the Hartnett County School Board announced that twenty Indians would be allowed to enroll in the Dunn High School during the next school year.[54]

The sit-in has been widely used in the United States to break down racial discrimination in restaurants and lunch counters. In this method the actionists progressively occupy a large number or all of the available seats and refuse to leave until the Afro-American members of the group are served, the restaurant closes, the group arrested, or a certain predetermined period of time elapses.

The Congress of Racial Equality used this method in Northern and border states during the 1940s and 1950s. [55] It first became widely practiced on a large scale in the South in early 1960, with sit-ins in Woolworth's in Greensboro, North Carolina, conducted by students of North Carolina Agricultural and Technical College. Shortly thereafter, high school and college students all over the South began to stage similar sit-ins at lunch counters, and a movement of major proportions developed. [56] The Southern Regional Council reported that within seven months at least 70,000 Negroes and whites had actively participated and 3,600 had been arrested. [57] A U.S. Supreme Court decision on December 11, 1961, outlawed the use of disorderly conduct statutes as grounds for arresting Negroes sitting in to obtain equal service. [58]

The basic principle may also be applied in other situations—for example, to protest segregated housing or to express various political grievances. For example, 801 demonstrators supporting the Free Speech Movement at the University of California at Berkeley were arrested on December 3, 1964, following a sit-in to support their demand for freedom of political action. [59] A student sit-in, called by the Student Council, was held in the administration building of City College in New York City in November 1966 to demand specific measures for increased student participation in administrative decisions for the college. [60] In June 1963 an all-night sit-in was held at the headquarters of the Boston School Committee in protest against the refusal of most of its members to admit the existence of *de facto* segregation in the school system. [61]

In 1964 delegates from the Freedom Democratic Party of Mississippi, which was predominantly Negro, claimed the seats of the regular Democratic Party delegation at the Democratic Party's National Convention, stating that only the Freedom Democratic Party was pledged to support the Democratic Party's national ticket. When their full claim was not granted, the Freedom delegates, aided by sympathetic delegates from other states, entered the convention hall during the evening sessions of August 25 and 26, and the F.D.P. representatives simply sat in the seats for the Mississippi delegation. After a brief attempt to remove them by force, the convention authorities left them alone, and the "regular" white Mississippi delegation had to sit elsewhere. [62]

In addition to student sit-ins in universities in recent years, there have also been sit-ins in mayors' and governors' offices, but these, and suggestions for sit-ins on Capitol Hill and in congressional offices, have been widely condemned and regarded as "the disruption of the governing process itself." [63]

A very different case occurred in Moscow in 1964. Forty-five Moroccan students began a sit-in and twenty-four hour fast at the Moroccan Embassy there on March 19 to protest the death sentences and severe imprisonments of alleged antigovernment plotters in Morocco. At Moroccan request, Soviet authorities expelled them from the Embassy. [64]

163. Stand-in

The stand-in occurs when direct actionists remain standing in an orderly quiet manner at a ticket office, admission entrance, appointment desk, doorway, or the like, as they seek to purchase a ticket, admission, an interview, or whatever when these have been refused to them. This method has been used particularly by civil rights actionists in the United States seeking to obtain equality of service for all potential customers. It has been applied especially in seeking admission to motion picture theaters and swimming pools. When admittance, purchase of a ticket, or the like is refused to the Negro, for example, all the direct actionists, including the person refused admission, wait patiently in line for admittance, refusing to leave until all are granted equal service, a specified period of time has elapsed, the group is arrested, or the facilities are closed. This method may be repeated until the policy is changed to allow all to use the facilities.

The stand-in was used, for example, in 1947 to end discrimination at the swimming pool in the Palisades Amusement Park, New Jersey. On Sundays the interracial Congress of Racial Equality (C.O.R.E.) groups "would remain peacefully lined up in front of the pool's ticket booth after being refused admission." Despite repeated beatings by park guards and police, and arrests, the C.O.R.E. stand-in was continued on Sundays throughout the summer. [65] It has been claimed that the enactment of the New Jersey civil rights bill in 1949 was partly due to the news reports and editorials published in newspapers in northern New Jersey as a result of the beatings and arrests during the summer of 1947. [66]

A different form of the stand-in was urged in 1837 for use in churches where Negroes were admitted but were assigned to segregated seating. In 1837 the periodical *Colored American* told its readers that if they were not allowed to sit where the whites did, they should "stand in the aisles and rather worship God upon your feet than become a party to your own degradation. You must shame your oppressors, and wear out prejudice by this holy policy."[67]

164. Ride-in

The ride-in, popularly known in the United States as the freedom ride, is a type of sit-in adapted to public transportation. It was widely used during the 1960s in the United States against racial segregation on buses, although its earlier use was more diverse. In this method Negroes and whites persist in sitting in sections of buses or other vehicles opposite to those assigned to them. Sometimes such actions have violated company regulations or local and state laws. More recently, since federal rulings have outlawed such segregation, ride-ins were taken to bring local practice into conformity with the law.

In 1841 when the ride-in campaign against frequent, but not universal racial segregation in transportation began in New England, the small minority of Negroes in those states (one percent in Massachusetts and about three percent in Rhode Island, for example) were highly discriminated against. On stagecoaches, Negroes, even in bad weather, might be refused rides completely, or be required to ride on top in the open. On steamboats they might be refused cabins or only be permitted to travel on deck with cattle. The new railroads enforced segregation of free blacks, while allowing slaves to ride with their Southern masters when visiting from the South.[68] The campaign against this discrimination and segregation was led by Garrisonian nonviolent abolitionists, Mabee reports, incuding Garrison himself, John A. Collins, active in the Nonresistance Society, and Frederick Douglass, former slave who became the famous advocate of abolition of slavery.[69]

In June and July 1841, while visiting Massachusetts, the young David Ruggles, a half-blind New York Negro who was very active in the struggle for rights of his people, set a personal example for the ride-ins. He insisted on buying a ticket for first-class accommodation on the steamer for Nantucket, and refused to move from a white car on the New Bedford Railroad. In both cases, he was physically attacked; his nonviolence did not prohibit his taking court action, however. Ruggles based his insistence on equal service on this belief: "While I advocate the principles of equal liberty, it is my duty to practice what I preach, and claim my rights at all times."[70] Following a protest meeting by New Bedford Negroes, chaired by the young Frederick Douglass, Garrison, Douglass and about forty black and white abolitionists boarded a steamer, also for Nantucket. The whole ship was segregated. When the captain refused to sail until the Negroes occupied the upper deck, some of the party left the ship; those remaining, obtained the captain's agreement that the whole group should ride on the upper deck. "As the steamer moved toward Nantucket the abolitionists cheerfully held a meeting . . . to protest the steamship company's already crumbling segregation policy," Mabee reports. [71]

A series of ride-ins on New England railroads took place in 1841. Sometimes whites rode in the Negro car, sometimes unaccompanied Negroes rode in white cars, and sometimes integrated groups or two or three rode in the white cars. Physical assault was commonplace. One of the participants, James N. Buffum, a Quaker, reported his view that the ride-in actions and the reactions of the railroad officials brought new converts to the cause; in Lynn, for example, and "even in Salem, where it has seemed as if nothing short of Almighty judgments could wake them from their guilty slumbers," people were aroused and talking of the "shameful" treatment of the "ride-inners." [72] A boycott of the segregated Massachusetts railroads was organized, people being urged to use unsegregated rail or stage service instead. Mabee writes that "it is doubtful that without the drama of the ride-ins, often heightened by the violence of the conductors, a boycott of significant proportions would have developed." [73] This boycott was strongly supported every week for a year, beginning in April 1842, by Garrison's *Liberator* and by the *American Antislavery Almanac.* [74] The combination of these nonviolent pressures, plus the strong possibility of legislation against such segregation, induced both the New Bedford Railroad and the Eastern Railroad quietly to end segregation. [75] Referring to the ride-ins by Negroes who had entered "the cars intended only for white passengers and allowed ourselves to be beaten and dragged out," Frederick Douglass said in 1849 that this had produced desegregation of the railroads "because the railroad companies became ashamed of their proscription." [76]

A few years later ride-ins were also used on horse-drawn cars in New York City and in Philadelphia. In 1854 and 1855 there were several instances of Negroes insisting on riding on the basis of equality in the horsecars, including members of the congregation of the highly respected Dr. Pennington, the Heidelberg-educated Negro moderator of the Presbyterian Church. Similar action occurred in Philadelphia in 1858 when the well-known Negro poet and Garrisonian Frances Watkins insisted on riding like any other passenger. Similar action occurred during the Civil War when a Negro businessman and his wife insisted on riding inside the car, not on the platform. In that case, in final exasperation the conductor opened all the windows, unhitched the horses, and abandoned the car. [77]

After the Civil War another ride-in was held in Louisville, Kentucky, in 1871, by newly freed Negro slaves who sought the end of segregation on the streetcars of the city. It began in January when Robert Fox paid his fare and insisted on sitting in the white section, refusing to move when ordered and finally being thrown off the car. He won a Federal District Court ruling in his favor, which was, however, ignored by the local street-car company, which continued segregated seating; instead of throwing Negroes bodily out of the cars for refusing to sit where ordered, they simply halted the cars until the Negroes moved. After consultation with local Federal officials and white attorneys, local Negro leaders launched a full-scale ride-in. In May a young Negro boy sitting in the white section was evicted and beaten by a hostile white crowd, then arrested and fined in the city court, with the judge warning against further ride-ins. But the ride-in campaign continued as Negroes in streetcar after streetcar took "white" seats. The drivers then left the cars completely, and occasionally Negroes drove the cars themselves. White violence erupted, and a race riot threatened. Moderate Kentucky newspapers and many community leaders deplored the fighting, and the Republican gubernatorial candidate, John Marshall Harlan—a former slave owner—denounced the segregation policy. National attention grew. There were rumors that President Grant might send in Federal troops. Federal marshals and an attorney for the Federal government backed the Negroes. The streetcar company capitulated, and all city transit companies in Louisville abandoned segregation permanently. [78]

After the 1946 Supreme Court ruling against segregation in interstate travel, George Houser and Bayard Rustin in 1947 organized the first extended freedom ride, the group riding interstate buses throughout the upper South, insisting without violence on their newly awarded constitutional right to be seated without segregation. [79]

The big wave of freedom rides was launched, however, in 1961 under the sponsorship of the Congress of Racial Equality, then a nonviolent group led by James Farmer. On May 4 the interracial group left Washington D.C., originally intending to reach New Orleans. The group was subjected to a long series of arrests, harassments, and white mob violence, though it also gained increased support and wider sponsorship. The freedom ride, however, halted on May 28 in Jackson, Mississippi, where a jail-in campaign developed. At least a dozen of these ride-ins were held during the period, involving over a thousand persons representing four major organizations. Beginning on November 1 all interstate buses were required by federal regulation to display a sign: "Seating aboard this vehicle without regard to race, color, creed, or national origin, by order of the Interstate Commerce Commission." The following year this was also printed on all interstate bus tickets, and terminals for such buses had to post similar signs. [80]

165. Wade-in

The wade-in is a method designed to counter racial discrimination in the use of beaches which are physically accessible to the public (i.e., not surrounded by fences, etc.) and for which tickets are not required. The opponents of racial discrimination simply enter the area and make normal use of the beach and water without regard to restrictive customs or legal prohibition. An interracial group of seventy-five from the Youth Work Committee of the Chicago National Association for the Advancement of Colored People, for example, conducted a wade-in at Rainbow Beach on Lake Michigan, in the South Shore of Chicago, from July 16 to the end of the summer 1961.[81] The principle of such entry and use of facilities may be applicable to other restricted areas which are not fenced in, and is related to, but not identical with, nonviolent invasion, which is described below.

166. Mill-in[82]

In the mill-in the actionists gather in some place of symbolic significance or one which is related to the grievance, such as the offices of the opponent. They then remain there for a certain period, usually determined in advance. But instead of conducting a sit-in or a sit-down, they remain mobile. People may thus move within the building (or other place), and individuals may come and go during the mill-in. This method has been described as capable of achieving the goals of direct confrontation and intervention while being less likely to provoke serious repression than, say, a nonviolent occupation. The presence of a large number of "mill-inners" is likely to impede the normal operations of people who may be working in the building, but deliberate obstruction of their activities is not a part of this method.

The mill-in was used, for example, by the Afro-American Society of Tufts University and its supporters, who sought more minority employment in the construction of a dormitory on the campus at Medford, Massachusetts, in November 1969. After a large police contingent occupied the building site itself, the Afro-American Society held a mill-in at the university administration building, Ballou Hall, on Friday November 7 and again on Monday, November 10. *Criterion,* a Tufts alumni journal, describing the Friday action, reported:

> Approximately 400 students—50 blacks, 350 whites—and a few faculty members—gathered in front of Ballou Hall at 9:00 A.M. for a "mill-in." They divided into four equal groups, each assigned to approach one of four university administrators . . . . The peaceful "mill-in" was al-

lowed by University officials; there were no policemen inside or outside Ballou Hall . . . . Students peacefully occupied administrative offices, querying officials on issues surrounding the situation. A meeting convened around 9:30 A.M. in the Coolidge room of Ballou and was packed with about 300 students. They listened to President Hallowell air the University's position for about one half hour.[83]

Students evacuated the room and building thirty minutes before normal closing time. It is reported that normal administrative work in the building was "either slowed or halted completely" during the mill-in.[84]

167. Pray-in

In the pray-in persons enter, or attempt to enter, a church from which they have been by custom or policy barred, in order to participate equally in the religious services. In cases where admission has been allowed but seating has been segregated, participants in the pray-in sit in the pews reserved for others.

In early 1848 Frederick Douglass urged all Negroes to abandon the separate black churches and instead to attend white ones, in "a massive pray-in," as Mabee calls it. Douglass declared that Negroes "should go in and take seats without regard to their complexion, and allow themselves to be dragged out by the ministers, elders, and deacons. Such a course would very soon settle the question, and in the right way."[85]

This massive action did not occur, but there were a number of individual cases of pray-ins reported from Philadelphia, New York state and parts of New England. The reactions were not always friendly. For example, in Randolph, Massachusetts, sometime before 1835, a Negro family purchased a pew in a white Baptist church; when they discovered one Sunday morning that the pew had been removed, they sat in its place on the floor. The next Sunday, they discovered that even the floorboards had been removed. When visiting the Marlborough Presbyterian church in New York State in 1837, the white abolitionist Lewis Tappan joined with the Negroes, who were served communion last; the minister was startled and later resolved to serve all at the same time.

In 1838 a white minister in Newark, New Jersey, was driven out of his pulpit after he had walked a black woman servant to church and seated her with his wife. The only abolitionist congressman from New York in 1840, Seth Gates, invited a visiting Negro abolitionist to sit with him in his church pew in Genessee County, New York; the local newspaper denounced Gates as an "amalgamator," but he was nonetheless reelected to Congress. A young white Quaker was in 1840 reprimanded for sitting with the blacks in the separate pews assigned to them; the youth was told he was "sitting in judgment" of the Friends who had assigned the pews. The Grimké sisters, Angelina and Sarah, new converts to Quakerism, insisted on sitting with the black women in the Philadelphia Meeting house they attended. Also scolded by the Quakers, the sisters replied: "While you put this badge of degradation on our sisters, we feel it is our duty to share it with them." A predominantly white Baptist church in Newport, Rhode Island, in 1858 refused to renew the lease on the pew of a white lady who had invited a black girl who was a member of the church to sit with her; the white woman brought a camp stool to church and sat in the aisle beside her former pew.[86]

During the civil rights actions of the 1960s, when Negroes sought admission to all-white churches in the South, they frequently knelt at the church entrance; this became known as a kneel-in. For example, one Sunday in February 1961, in Rock Hill, South Carolina, the city's first kneel-ins took place, at the same time that many students were being jailed for participation in sit-ins at lunch counters. The Negroes were admitted to three of the white churches but barred at two others.[87] In Birmingham, Alabama, in 1963 it was announced that part of the current campaign on Easter Sunday, April 14, would include mass attempts to worship at white churches. As had already been done on various occasions, the pattern was that when refused entrance to the churches, the Negroes would kneel on the church steps and pray.[88]

168. Nonviolent raids

In nonviolent raids, volunteers march to certain designated key points of symbolic or strategic importance and demand possession. This method usually involves civil disobedience and the risk of severe repression by police and troops. During the 1930–31 campaign in India, for example, quite a few of the seized Congress offices were reoccupied, and unorganized attempts to occupy government buildings occurred.[89] An even clearer example from that campaign was the effort to "seize" the Dharasana salt depot. Almost every day for a period of weeks volunteers marched in an orderly procession toward the depot and asked possession. Intending to take the salt stored there as an advanced method of defiance of the Salt Act (which was a major point of attack during that campaign), the volunteers met with severe repression.[90]

As the volunteers do not use violent methods of seizing or holding such places, their raids are not conducted with the main intent of actually gaining possession. Rather, nonviolent raids are intended more as a challenge to authority, a symbolic defiance of the established regime, and as a means of bringing into use some of the psychological mechanisms associated with self-suffering. In an extremely advanced stage of a nonviolent revolt, however, large masses of people might conceivably surround such "seized" points and effectively obstruct efforts by officials to recapture them, if helped by restrictions on the means of repression or assistance from the troops or police.

A variation on this method—seeking possession of merchandise rather than of a place—was practiced in Boston, Massachusetts Bay Colony, on January 18, 1770, in an attempt to deal with eight merchants who were violating the nonimportation agreement. The offending merchants had refused to reverse their behavior and to surrender the imported products to the committee of inspection. Arthur Schlesinger reports that:

> The whole body of more than a thousand persons then proceeded, in impressive and orderly array, to the houses or stores of each of these men; and, through William Molineux as spokesman, demanded that the goods, which had once been placed in the store, should be immediately deposited with the committee of inspection. Only Cary made the concession demanded.[91]

169. Nonviolent air raids[92]

Airplanes, balloons, or other air transport may be used to enter the air space of an opponent, without use or threat of any violence or destruction, to bring leaflets, or perhaps food and other gifts, to the population. (Air missions bringing supplies to break blockades are classed separately.) At times such a raid and dropping of leaflets may have an important psychological impact. An example of this occurred in the closing phase of the Kapp *Putsch*. On Tuesday, March 16, an airplane of the German government, which had fled to Stuttgart, appeared over Berlin, held by the putschists, to drop a leaflet, "THE COLLAPSE OF THE MILITARY DICTATORSHIP." Lieutenant-Colonel Goodspeed reports that "even in the fashionable sections of the city, the Berliners eagerly seized the printed sheets and, when they read them, cheered so loudly that officers of the Allied Commission of Control came hurrying to their hotel windows to see what was going on."[93]

Nonviolent air raids have often been small actions in overwhelmingly violent struggles—highly unfavorable conditions in which to produce results. For example, in late July 1965 United States planes dropped toys and clothes over villages near Hanoi in order to impress the civilian population of the good will of the United States.[94] And in South Vietnam U.S. planes some weeks later hovered above National Liberation Front positions, playing tape recordings of typical family noises and sounds. This was followed by a pitiful entreaty intoned by a Vietnamese woman: "Come home." U.S. officials believed this produced many deserters and called it a "humane form of terrorism." [95]

170. Nonviolent invasion

In nonviolent invasion a group of nonviolent volunteers deliberately and openly enter a forbidden area in order to demonstrate their refusal to recognize the right of the controlling regime or agency to exercise sovereignty or control over that area or to use it for a particular purpose. This method entails civil disobedience and the risk of severe repression. The mass nonviolent invasion of Goa in 1955 to defy the right of Portugal to exercise sovereignty over that part of India is perhaps a classic example of nonviolent invasion. [96] Other examples include attempts by pacifists to enter rocket sites near Omaha, Nebraska, in 1959, [97] and attempts to "reclaim" military land in Harrington, England, for peaceful purposes. [98] The attempt, in January 1960, to halt the French atomic test at Reggan, North Africa, by entering the forbidden area was intended to create nonviolent interjection, but as the volunteers did not come close to the actual test site this case was limited to a nonviolent invasion of French-controlled territory. [99] American opponents of nuclear weapons sought to halt Pacific nuclear tests by sailing into the prohibited area in 1958 and 1962. [100]

171. Nonviolent interjection

The method of nonviolent interjection involves placing one's body between a person and the objective of his work or activity, or sometimes between a soldier or a policeman and his opponent, or on other occasions in the path of a vehicle. This action is distinguished from the next method, nonviolent obstruction, in that the interjection does not constitute a sufficiently large or extensive physical obstruction that it cannot be overcome, removed, or surmounted. For example, with nonviolent interjection, persons or vehicles could simply proceed over the bodies, while with nonviolent obstruction they cannot do so. [101] The aim of nonviolent interjection is to persuade or otherwise induce the persons being impeded (soldiers, drivers, etc.) that they should desist from the activity which the actionists regard as immoral or illegitimate, or at least that the activity should not be continued at the price of imposing human suffering on the people who have intervened to bring it to a halt.

Since the possible results of this method are not achieved by imposing an insurmountable physical obstruction, the numbers of actionists are not decisive. A single person or a small group of people may, for example, lie or sit in front of a tank or train carrying war supplies in an effort to induce the driver to refuse to move the vehicle instead of inflicting injury or death on those lying or sitting in front of it. In fact, it has been argued that fewness of numbers increases the psychological or moral impact of the interjection. Bradford Lyttle distinguishes between individual nonviolent interjection (which he sees as running the greatest risk of injury or death because the individual may not be seen or may be thought to be bluffing) and group interjection (in which the risk of suffering or death for each individual taking part is less). Lyttle therefore suggests that individual nonviolent interjection may be more powerful. The examples of nonviolent interjection which are offered here are grouped into three types: intervention in social and employment activities, in actions of police and soldiers, and in halting vehicles.

In a rather atypical case, antiapartheid demonstrators sat down on the tennis court at Madserud Arena, Oslo, on May 13, 1964, to oppose the Davis Cup tennis match between Norway and the all-white South African team.[102] It is more common for this method to be used, however, as interjection between the actionists and the work or other activities of some group. For example, during the 1922 campaign in India, some students sat in the gateways of Calcutta University to block the passage of their fellow students. Urging them to refuse to attend classes, the demonstrators took the risk of being stepped on by those who persisted in entering the university. Similar means were used during the Indian nationalist struggles by women to halt the sale of liquor and by noncooperators to "persuade" government workers still loyal to the British *Raj* to resign their jobs. It is reported that Indian women used this method to induce their husbands working for the British to refuse to cooperate with the regime.[103] In 1957 striking hosiery workers in Reading, Pennsylvania, lay down on the sidewalks at factory gates, forcing the nonstrikers to choose whether they would walk over them in order to enter the factory or stay away from their jobs.[104]

Civil rights demonstrators in the United States have used nonviolent interjection as a strong means of influencing employers to hire more Negroes. In May 1963 Philadelphia chapters of the Congress of Racial Equality and the National Association for the Advancement of Colored People blocked the entry of white workmen at sites of allegedly discriminatory employment—calling this a "job blockade." (In this case there was some violence between the demonstrators and white construction workers.) Similar means were later successfully used in San Francisco to reach agreement from local hotels and car dealers to hire hundreds of Negroes; some demonstrators drew long jail sentences, illustrating that interventionist methods are often met with strong counteraction. The entrance to a New York City plumbers' union headquarters was also blocked, winning an agreement to admit Negro apprentices. [105]

Nonviolent interjection has also been used by white segregationists to block integration in the South; for example, in Greenwood, Mississippi, in the summer of 1964, a Negro couple and their son had been attempting to be served at a local cafe. Undaunted by a lawyer blocking the door one day, they returned the following day carrying a copy of the Civil Rights Act. This time, however, the proprietor herself stood in the door, effectively blocking it, and screaming at them to get out. Later, the couple told civil rights workers that next time they would go somewhere else. [106]

Nonviolent interjectionists have also attempted to interfere with the activities of police or soldiers, especially where they have attempted to arrest persons, or sometimes to prevent fighting. It has also been used to assist the escape of an apprehended Negro who was thought to be an escaped slave. One such example occurred in Boston in 1851, during the period of the Federal Fugitive Slave Law. Shadrach, a waiter in a Boston coffeehouse, had been arrested, Mabee reports, charged as an escaped Virginia slave, and brought to court. A group of from twenty to forty Negroes entered the courtroom and, laughing and jostling, moved about the room, hiding Shadrach among them long enough to rush him out of the room, thus enabling him to start the journey to Canada. Daniel Webster, then Secretary of State, called the rescue treason, and Senator Henry Clay thought the law should be made more severe. The American and Foreign Antislavery Society pointed out, however, that no weapons had been used and no one was injured, while Garrison pronounced this action by "unarmed friends of equal liberty" to be "an uninjurious deliverance of the oppressed out of the hands of the oppressor." [107]

When, in late winter or early spring of 1943, it became known in Bulgaria that the first deportations of Jews were being planned, "revolutionary elements in Sofia" issued an appeal for people to intervene to protect the Jews:

Take your stand before your neighboring Jewish homes and do not let them be led away by force! Hide the children and do not give them to the executioners! Crowd the Jewish quarters and manifest your solidarity with the oppressed Jews! [108]

In the course of rivalries threatening newly independent Algeria with civil war, there were at the end of August and the beginning of September 1962 many instances in which unarmed local inhabitants barred the road between Oran and Constantine with their bodies and challenged the troops to use arms against them if they insisted on advancing toward rival troops. [109] In the Boghari area, south of Algiers, local inhabitants placed themselves between the pro-Ben Bella forces and opposition troops and demonstrated against any resumption in fighting. "Many of them lay down on the road." [110]

In June 1965 opposition Buddhists in Vietnam interjected themselves to prevent troops which were repressing Buddhist resistance from entering a pagoda by sitting in front of the gate of the National Buddhist Institute, Vien Hoa Doa. [111]

Nonviolent interjection has also been used in efforts to stop vehicles, such as automobiles, trucks and trains carrying goods the actionists did not wish to be delivered, construction machinery, and even tanks. On February 11, 1963, students sat on the road outside the Royal College at Nairobi, Kenya, to draw attention to the dangerous road-crossing conditions for undergraduates. [112] Women with baby carriages (prams), some with babies and older children, have often blocked highways and streets in the United States and England in efforts to have traffic lights or other safety devices installed to protect children and others from the traffic. At times this method may be used in a different issue, however, and in association with another method. In connection with the Glasgow school boycott of 1963 described in Chapter Four, against a dangerous unfenced canal, fifty mothers with prams and children blocked the canal bridge to traffic. [113]

In Palermo, Sicily, in 1963, an unemployed bricklayer linked hands with four of his seven children to form a human barrier across a busy street, protesting his being unemployed and "striking" to get a job. [114]

In Bombay, during the 1930–31 campaign a young man, Babu Ganu, attempted to stop a truck carrying boycotted cloth by lying in front of it and was killed when it ran over him. [115] There are several examples of this method in efforts to stop one type of construction or another. For example, in August 1958 at a missile base near Cheyenne, Wyoming, four persons attempted to stop trucks carrying supplies from entering the base; one was seriously injured. [116] Another example took place in England in December 1958 at a rocket site near a town called Swaffham. Direct actionists on two different occasions lay across the road and surrounded equipment in such a way as to force the workmen to choose between halting their work or injuring the demonstrators.[117] There were no serious injuries, the work was temporarily disrupted, and newspaper publicity was often sympathetic.

In 1958, in an effort to block work on a plan of the New York State Power Authority to flood 1,300 acres of Tuscaroras Indian nation land for a storage resevoir while legal action was being taken to stop the seizure of the land, members of this tribe on three separate occasions interjected their persons. Signs such as "WARNING. NO TRESPASSING. INDIAN RESERVE" and "MUST YOU TAKE EVERYTHING WE OWN?" were carried by bands of Tuscaroras in April 1958 as they blocked the entrance of surveyors and trucks by standing or lying down in front of them. State and county police arrested three of the demonstration leaders for unlawful assembly and disorderly conduct. Two of the men were tackled by police and dragged to the police wagon. Some scuffling between the police and Indian women and children occurred, although the interjection itself was nonviolent. In May surveyors again entered the reservation; Tuscaroras stood in front of their instruments to disrupt the survey work. Later, when bulldozers were sent in to clear land, the clearance crew consisting of Tuscaroras men stayed away from the job, and the work was stalled again. In the meantime their attorney, Mr. Grossman, was pursuing the legal battle. Edmund Wilson, in his *Apologies to the Iroquois,* reports that "the practical obstruction by one group of the Indians and the defense of them in their difficulties by Grossman gave pause to the Power Authority and influenced public opinion." In 1959 the Indians won their case when the Federal Power Commission refused to permit the New York Power Authority to build on Indian reservation land.[118]

While demonstrators in Cleveland, Ohio, on April 7, 1964, sought to disrupt construction of a new school in a Negro area—which was seen as an attempt to stop Negroes from attending predominantly white schools and to tighten segregation—the Rev. Bruce William Klunder, twenty-seven, a Presbyterian minister, threw himself on the ground behind a bulldozer which was moving in reverse to avoid three other demonstrators lying in front of it. The driver, not seeing Rev. Klunder, drove over him, and he was crushed to death. Rioting followed.[119]

In one small town in Slovakia during the Nazi occupation all the young men lay down on the railroad tracks to prevent a train from taking away the Jews.[120]

In 1953, when the Russians used tanks in Jena, East Germany, to disperse a crowd of 25,000 persons which were seeking the release of eight demonstrators who had been arrested during the uprising in June, "the crowd refused to budge. Women sat down in rows and forced the drivers to stop," Stefan Brant reports. By this means, and by maneuvering street-cars to block the tanks, the crowd held up the Russians for half an hour, at which time they temporarily withdrew. Eventually, the Russians dispersed the demonstrators by shooting over the heads of the crowd.[121]

172. Nonviolent obstruction

Nonviolent obstruction is similar to nonviolent interjection, except that the human bodies are used not only for psychological intervention but as a physical obstruction.[122] Such physical blocking occurs when the obstruction is undertaken by very large numbers or when the obstructors are so placed that the work, vehicle, police, troops, or the like cannot proceed even though they injure or kill the demonstrators. As in the previous method, the risk of arrest, injury, or death is involved. Such obstruction is unlikely to last very long unless: 1) the numbers are exceedingly large, are maintained over a long period, and are beyond the control of the personnel, equipment, and weaponry which the opponent is able and willing to apply; 2) the opponent is unwilling simply to kill all the obstructors by whatever means may be available; 3) the workers or the enforcement officials, police, or troops are, or become, sympathetic to the demonstrators; or 4) the demonstration of public opposition to the grievance, or to repression of the actionists, is strong enough to induce the opponent to abandon the objectionable activity or halt it for a time.

Various proposals for nonviolent obstruction to protect fugitive slaves in the United States were made between 1850 and 1852. The Rhode Island Antislavery Society, for example, decided that when it was impossible to hide slaves for whom warrants had been issued or to help them escape, "they shall be surrounded by a sufficiently numerous and influential Peace Committee to protect them from assault and capture." Wendell Phillips proposed that in a case where a fugitive was held in a courthouse, "hundreds of thousands" of people should nonviolently surround the building to prevent his return to the South by requiring officials "to walk over our heads." The periodical *National Antislavery Standard* argued that a phalanx of peaceful men, willing to give their lives, could protect an escaped slave even from military forces; it called for men who were ". . . unarmed but determined that no slave shall be taken . . . except over their bodies." This would, it continued, be a "revolution," ". . . the noblest the world ever saw, and it would, we cannot doubt, be effectual. We can hardly believe that armed citizen-soldiers would ride over and cut down their fellow-citizens standing and braving death with calm but desperate resolution lest a man should be taken among them and made a slave." [123]

It is not always easy to find the border-line between nonviolent interjection and nonviolent obstruction, as some of these cases may suggest. In Hungary, in early December 1956, seven hundred unarmed men and women blocked factory gates when police and two truckloads of Hungarian Army officers came to arrest three members of the workers' council at the *Danubia* textile factory. The arresting officers eventually left without the three men. [124] Another case of obstruction took place in Sunakawa, Japan, in 1956, when ten thousand people occupied a site intended for a United States air base; after several days of obstruction, plans for building the air base was abandoned. [125] In Brooklyn, New York, on July 22, 1963, about 1,250 persons took part in an effort to block public construction until more Negroes and Puerto Ricans were hired. More than two hundred obstructors were arrested, including at least ten ministers and church officials. Peter Kihss, of *The New York Times,* reports "In wave after wave for nearly eight hours Negro and white sympathizers darted in front of incoming construction vehicles to sit down or lie down in the roadway. They were picked up and taken away in patrol wagons—a dozen at a time." [126]

In the autumn of 1963, when white segregationist Mississippians feared that governor Ross Barnett might be arrested by federal marshals for contempt of a court order desegregating the University of Mississippi, Waskow reports, thousands of them sat down around the governor's mansion "to interpose their bodies—perhaps intending a 'not-quite-violent' resistance—between him and the forces of law and order." [127]

173. Nonviolent occupation

Nonviolent occupation may be used after a nonviolent invasion or a nonviolent land seizure, or by people who have been ordered to leave their land or building. Thus nonviolent occupation may involve technical trespass and the violation of other laws. Nonviolent occupation was successfully practiced by Bishop Ambrose during Easter week, 385 A.D., when he defied orders of the imperial government of the Roman Empire to surrender one of the larger churches in Milan to the Arian Christians. Although the church was surrounded by troops, Ambrose risked imprisonment and death, and continued to hold masses for five days. Finally the government ordered the troops withdrawn and the fines remitted, and, wrote Ambrose, "as soon as they heard, the troops rushed into the Church to receive the kiss of peace."[128]

During the 1928 Bardoli campaign in India, those peasants whose land was attached because of their refusal to pay taxes either refused to leave the land at all or returned to it. They cultivated it and planted crops, and insisted that whatever the current legal status might be, morally the land remained theirs and that they had a right to use it for constructive purposes.[129]

In August 1957 about two hundred Mohawk Indians, part of the Iroquois Confederacy, settled on the banks of the Schohari Creek, near Fort Hunter, New York; they said that they had been blasted from their homes by the construction of the St. Lawrence Seaway, and that the land they now occupied had belonged to the Mohawks under a treaty made in the 1700s. The Indians built a longhouse—the place of worship of the Handsome Lake religion—and half a dozen cabins. The Mohawks asserted they would recognize no local eviction proceedings, nor would they deal with local or state officials; as they were a nation they would deal only with the Federal government.[130]

The most dramatic nonviolent occupation by American Indians has been that of Alcatraz Island. On November 9, 1969, a few American Indians swam through the waters of San Francisco Bay and landed on the old island prison of Alcatraz, abandoned seven years before by the government. Eleven days later a hundred more joined them, and claimed the site by right of some old treaties that awarded all deserted areas within a tribe's original territory to the original inhabitants. The Indians wanted to make the area into an educational culture center for the American Indian and proved their determination by continued occupation of the island. Power and water were cut off by the authorities, but the inhabitants managed with two malfunctioning generators and the little drinking water that could be carried over in jugs. They were supported from the mainland by both Indians and non-Indians alike, who donated food, clothing and medical supplies. A small school was established, and many families took up permanent residence on "the Rock." It became a central focus of the new Indian movement and a source of pride as a successful intervention to protest the U.S. government's inadequacies in Indian affairs. Alcatraz was held by the Indians until the last fifteen were removed by Federal marshals on June 14, 1971.[131]

With Russian military units outside Czechoslovak government buildings in August 1968, government officials and legislators remained in their buildings and continued to act in their legitimate capacities. For example, in the afternoon of August 24, *Politika* reported:

The Government Presidium building is blockaded, tank guns are aiming at the building from all sides, guns stand in firing positions in the little park at Klarov. The Government Presidium is blockaded, but the Government is functioning. Twenty-two ministers meet, hold discussions, make decisions, report to the parliament on their activity, maintain contact with the new Party leadership. [132]

Politika also reported that the extraordinary twenty-sixth session of the National Assembly had already lasted four days:

The National Assembly building is surrounded by foreign troops, but the deputies are not leaving; they have imposed on themselves a house arrest. Acting on the summons by the Presidium, almost two hundred deputies from all over the Republic have reported in . . . an almost two-thirds majority. . . . On the first night, the deputies slept on the floor of their offices; for the following nights, they were able to get blankets and, more important, field cots for the women. Machine gun salvoes rattle under the windows of the National Assembly building at night. Supplies in the dining room are satisfactory. . . .

Neither the gun barrels aimed at the National Assembly windows nor the threat of arrest will force the deputies to capitulate. The permanent session is to continue until some solution to the aggression is found. [133]

SOCIAL INTERVENTION

Methods which take the form of direct intrusion in social behavior patterns, social occasions and social institutions are grouped as the third subclass of nonviolent intervention. In addition to these seven methods, certain others—such as a sit-in—produce social intervention, even though their dominant form is some other one, such as physical intervention, and hence they are grouped here in another subclass.

174. Establishing new social patterns

While social disobedience, a method of social noncooperation, consists of the refusal to obey various social customs, rules, regulations, practices, and behavior patterns, another method of social intervention consists of new ways of behavior which may positively contribute to the establishment of new social patterns. These may be unplanned actions by individuals or a series of individuals or groups. Or they may be actions planned as organized opposition. A wide variety of social patterns may be involved. It is, however, easily illustrated with behavior which replaces social patterns of inequality, hatred, or avoidance with new relationships of equality and respect. In the 1830s American abolitionists, sometimes naturally and without deliberation, sometimes as a conscious act, associated with Negroes, who even in Northern cities were normally socially boycotted. Mabee reports that on the proposal of Sarah Grimké, a Quaker, the Antislavery Convention of American Women in 1838 adopted a resolution which stated: "It is . . . the duty of abolitionists to identify themselves with these oppressed Americans, by sitting with them in places of worship, by appearing with them in our streets, by giving them our countenance in steamboats and stages, by visiting with them at their homes and encouraging them to visit us, receiving them as we do our white fellow citizens." [134] Some abolitionists did not approve of such practices, however, either because of a fear that they would provoke violence against abolitionists or against Negroes, or because of an opinion that the issues of slavery and racial prejudice should be kept separate. Among abolitionists the issue of public association with persons of another color was so sharp that there was fear in 1836 that the American Antislavery Society would split on it. [135]

Various abolitionists in Boston, Philadelphia, New York City and elsewhere engaged in "walk-alongs" (as Mabee calls them), in which they simply walked in the streets with persons of the other color, and often the other sex, sometimes arm in arm. This often upset people; the mayor of Philadelphia in 1839 urged Lucretia Mott not to do this because it offended the white rabble at a time when an anti-Negro riot was expected. However, she persisted in walking publicly with people regardless of color. After a meeting the Boston physician Dr. Henry Bowditch invited Frederick Douglass to walk home down Washington Street with him to dinner; Dr. Bowditch was afraid he would encounter his friends but Douglass later said that it was the first time a white had treated him as a man. In 1849 Douglass wrote in his periodical, *North Star,* that the way for abolitionists to remove prejudice was "to act as though it didn't exist, and to associate with their fellow creatures irrespective of all complexional differences. We have marked out this path for ourselves, and we mean to pursue it at all hazards." [136]

Mixed dining during the 1840 annual meeting in New York of the American Antislavery Society met with trouble from a mob, but by 1847 and 1858 similar events were not disturbed. [137] Private individuals "interdined," i.e., ate together in violation of taboos against social equality between their groups. To cope with prejudiced Quakers during a Friends Yearly Meeting, the Quaker Isaac Hooper invited his Negro Quaker guests, Mr. and Mrs. David Mapes, to join him for dinner and told the other guests that if they objected to joining them, they could eat later when the first group had finished. None did.[138] Various abolitionists entertained traveling abolitionists of a different color in their homes. However, in Pendleton, Indiana, a Quaker doctor who had been host to Frederick Douglass during his 1843 lecture tour was driven out of town by a mob.[139] Social equality within abolition societies was not fully accepted; about 1835 the Unitarian preacher William Ellery Channing, for example, advised against permitting Negroes to become members of such groups. That advice did not prevail, and Negroes held major offices in the national antislavery societies; but as late as the 1840s and 1850s Negroes sensed that they were not fully accepted.[140]

Interracial marriages occurred among abolitionists. Those marriages clearly set a different social pattern and violated the strong taboo against them. Such marriages were sometimes illegal, as they were in Massachusetts until repeal of the law in 1843. Both men and women married across the racial barrier, sometimes then having to face diverse pressures and sanctions. These included having to move elsewhere, social ostracism, physical assault, and loss of job. Nevertheless, since more male than female fugitive slaves reached Canada, the young men "frequently" married whites; in one year during the Civil War the city of Boston reported that sixteen percent of the Negroes who married that year were marrying whites.[141]

Another variation on this method has been the individual insistence on receiving equal treatment in public facilities, such as restaurants. For example, in 1837 Charles R. Ray and Philip Bell, the general agent and the proprietor of the *Colored American,* traveling up the Hudson on a steamer from New York City refused to have their tea in the kitchen, insisting on service in the dining cabin, even if they had to wait until the whites had had been served. Ray and Bell insisted: ". . . we do not like to be the agents of our own degradation." Similarly, until threatened with physical removal, Frederick Douglass, also on a Hudson River steamer, insisted on taking dinner like the other passengers. In Cleveland in 1857, Susan B. Anthony, the woman suffrage leader, and other delegates to an abolitionist convention refused to enter the dining room until a black abolitionist, William Wells Brown, was permitted to join them; the hotel backed down and provided equal service for the remainder of their stay.[142]

A number of these actions are almost identical with activities which have been undertaken in modern India for the eradication of untouchability and achieving communal unity. "Interdining" by people of various castes, untouchables and members of other religions has frequently occurred. Beginning in the 1930s Gora (born a Brahman), the prominent atheist Gandhian social revolutionary, organized intercaste and interreligious dining on a mass scale in India. Everyone brought his own provisions, and the cooking and dining were done without regard to caste or religious taboos, although intercaste dining was prohibited by orthodox Hindus. Special efforts were sometimes needed to overcome the hesitancy of lower-caste Hindus to eat with groups lower than themselves. Intermarriage has also been practiced and even encouraged as a means of ending untouchability. For example, Gora's children have been encouraged on that basis to marry outside the caste barriers, including with untouchables, and have done so. [143]

175. Overloading of facilities

Overloading facilities involves the deliberate increase of demands for services far beyond their capacity, so that the operation of the institution (government department, business, social service, and so on) is slowed down or paralyzed. Such overloading may be initiated by customers, the public, or employees of the institution. The objectives may vary and may include improved services, wage increases and political ends.

In 1965 at the Los Angeles County Hospital in California, for example, interns protesting pay policies initiated an overloading of facilities by admitting far more patients to the hospital than existing facilities could accommodate—even persons not needing hospitalization were admitted. This was called a heal-in. The interns' aim was to obtain a better bargaining position with the hospital administration. The hospital was filled with patients within four days, and the action cost the city around $250,000 in increased costs. [144]

A similar case occurred in Massachusetts at the Boston City Hospital in 1967, where it was called an "around-the-clock heal-in." This action was begun by 450 residents and interns at Boston City Hospital on Tuesday, May 16, 1967. The purpose of the heal-in was to dramatize salary demands by doctors at Boston teaching hospitals; at that time the take-home salary of an intern was only sixty dollars per week. The doctors felt that it would be in violation of their oaths to go on strike, so they chose instead to practice "ultra-conservative medicine" in order to overcrowd the hospital. Dr. Philip Caper, President of the House Officers' Association, said: "Everyone gets the best of care," which was ensured by having all the interns and residents work twenty-four hours a day. "Every patient who might benefit from hospitalization will be admitted, and no one will be discharged until he is completely well."

The heal-in was patterned after the similar action at the Los Angeles County Hospital eighteen months previously. The Boston City Hospital doctors began their heal-in as an unannounced experiment on Saturday, with 874 patients in the hospital. On Sunday there were 890, on Monday 924, and on Tuesday at 7 A.M. (after the main action was begun) there were 982. An unidentified doctor stated: "With 1,200 or more patients in the hospital the laundry will not be able to keep up, the kitchens will have trouble getting the food out, the X-ray and laboratory departments will be swamped, and people will begin to listen to our demands . . ." By Wednesday morning there were over 1,000 patients, and 1,075 on Thursday. The heal-in was supported by private doctors and house officers at the other major Boston hospitals. Action was taken only at Boston City Hospital because house officers there had full responsibility for medical procedure, unlike the private hospitals.

Countermeasures by the administration began Tuesday afternoon with an announcement that there were no more beds for male patients, which was disproved that evening by the admission of two more patients. They next tried to influence the chiefs of services to override the admittances, which these doctors refused to do on the grounds that these patients were indeed getting the best of care. The administration's final effort was to deny their competence to make salary changes. On the evening of Thursday, May 18, they relented and promised to make salary adjustments. The doctors ended the heal-in voluntarily that night. Observers felt that it was a "safe, effective way of backing up demands for higher wages." [145]

A student version of the method was applied in Japan in 1954. It was the practice in some private universities to admit more students than there were facilities, on the assumption that not all students would attend classes at the same time. The students organized a campaign of "united attendance" as a means of pressure against the university. [146]

176. Stall-in

The stall-in is a method that consists simply of conducting legitimate business as slowly as possible. This differs from stalling and obstruction, described in the previous chapter on political noncooperation, which is action by government employees to delay or prevent the implementation of some policy. The stall-in is undertaken by customers and clients for purposes which are likely to be social, but which may also include economic and political objectives. This method was applied in June 1964 by the Congress of Racial Equality against the Bank of America in San Diego, California, with C.O.R.E. customers taking thirty minutes to transact business normally done in about three. C.O.R.E. was seeking an end to discrimination in the bank's employment practices.[147] In conjunction with the 1938 Harlem Negroes' "black-out boycott" movement (see consumers' boycott above), bill payers by the hundreds went to the electric utilities offices, each paying in nickels and pennies.[148]

177. Speak-in [149]

A special form of nonviolent intervention occurs when actionists interrupt a meeting, church service, or other gathering for the purpose of expressing viewpoints on issues which may or may not be related directly to the occasion. Since the intervention is primarily interference with the social form of the meeting, this method can best be classed as one of social intervention, although it includes psychological and physical aspects also.

This form of action was often used by George Fox and other early Quakers. For example, in his *Journal* George Fox records how one Sunday (First-day) in 1649 he attended the Church of St. Mary in Nottingham, England, (a "steeplehouse," he called it, rather than a church) and was "moved" to speak during the regular service:

> Now as I . . . looked upon the town the greatest steeplehouse struck at my life . . . , a great . . . idolatrous temple. And the Lord said unto me, "Thou must go cry against yonder great idol, and against the worshippers therein." . . . . And when I came there, all the people looked like fallow land, and the priest, like a great lump of earth, stood in his pulpit above. He took for his text these words of Peter, "We have also a more sure word of prophecy, whereunto ye do well that ye take heed. . ." And he told the people that the Scriptures were the touchstone and judge by which they were to try all doctrines, religions, and opinions. . . Now the Lord's power was so mighty upon me . . . that I . . . was made to cry out and say, "Oh, no, it is not the Scriptures," . . . But I told them it was . . . the Holy Spirit, by which the holy men of God gave forth the Scriptures, whereby opinions, religions, and judgements were to be tried. . . . Now as I spoke thus amongst them, the officers came and took me away and put me into prison, a pitiful stinking place . . .[150]

In 1651 at Cranswick, in Yorkshire, one Sunday afternoon, a friend took Fox to meet the local priest, with whom he would talk after the service, which they attended. Fox records what happened:

And he took a text, which was, "Ho, everyone that thirsteth, let him come freely, without money and without price." And so I was moved of the Lord God to say unto him, "Come down, thou deceiver and hireling, for dost thou bid people come freely . . . and yet thou takest three hundred pounds off them for preaching the Scriptures to them. Mayest thou not blush for shame? . . . . And so the priest, like a man amazed, packed away; . . . And so after the priest had left his flock, I had as much time as I could desire to speak to the people, and I directed them to the grace of God that would teach them and bring them salvation. . .[151]

Fox did not always interrupt the regular services but sometimes waited until they had been completed, and then spoke to the priest and the people, as, for example, he did in Doncaster in 1652:

. . . and after the priest had done I spoke to him and the people what the Lord God commanded me, and they were in a great rage and hurried me out and threw me down the stairs, and haled me before the mayor and magistrates . . . and they threatened my life if I ever came there again . . .[152]

During the antislavery campaign in the United States, actionists at times interrupted church services in order to denounce the lack of effective opposition to slaveholding, and also the refusal of many churches to accomodate antislavery meetings. Thus Mabee reports:

One Sunday morning in 1841, a determined young Garrisonian, Stephen S. Foster, entered a Congregational Church in Concord, New Hampshire. In a lull in the service he rose and denounced the church for upholding slavery. The pastor asked Foster to stop speaking, but he continued until some of the congregation took him by the arms and led him out. In the afternoon Foster returned to another service and again spoke without permission. This time some of the congregation threw him down the stairs, and he was arrested for disturbing public worship.[153]

In using this method abolitionists were cautious to attempt a hearing through more agreeable means if possible:

. . . Foster and his team never interrupted a worship service unless they had already tried and failed to win a hearing by permission, including attempts to secure the use of the church building to hold their own meetings.[154]

178. Guerrilla theater [155]

Guerrilla theater, another method of social intervention, means a disruptive skit, dramatic presentation, or similar act. It came to be used in the United States in the late 1960s. The disruption may be of speeches, lectures, or normal proceedings of some group or institution. (The term guerrilla theater is also used for a spontaneous style of stage theater, usually with a political theme.)

Two examples are provided by Jerry Rubin, one of the more dramatic self-styled revolutionaries who emerged in the late 1960s. In late 1967 a conference of college newspaper editors in Washington, D.C., was debating whether or not to take a stand on the Vietnamese conflict:

Someone made a motion to table all resolutions and take no stand. The motion passed. Suddenly the lights went out and across the wall flashed scenes of World War II fighting, burning Vietnamese villages, crying Vietnamese women and napalmed children, image after image. The room echoed with hysterical screams, *"Stop it! Stop it!"*

A voice boomed over a bullhorn: "Attention. This is Sergeant Haggerty of the Washington Police. These films were smuggled illegally into the country from North Vietnam. We have confiscated them and arrested the people who are responsible. Now clear this room! Anyone still here in two minutes will be arrested!"

The editors fell over themselves rushing for the door. . . They believed they were going to be arrested for seeing a . . . film. They believe they live in a Nazi country. They accept it. [156]

Earlier, in August of that year, Rubin and some others had used a similar device to denounce the American preoccupation with money. Rubin and his friends did this at the New York Stock Exchange:

The stock market comes to a complete standstill at our entrance to the top of the balcony. The thousands of brokers stop playing Monopoly and applaud us. What a crazy sight for them—longhaired hippies staring down at them.

We throw dollar bills over the ledge. Floating currency fills the air. Like wild animals, the stockbrokers climb over each other to grab the money.

"This is what it's all about, real live money. Real dollar bills! People are starving in Biafra!" we shout. . .

While throwing the money we spot the cops coming. The cops grab us and throw us off the ledge and into the elevators. The stockbrokers below loudly boo the pigs. [157]

179. Alternative social institutions

One of the forms which nonviolent intervention may take is the building of new institutions. When their creation and growth produces a challenge the previous institutions, the new ones constitute nonviolent intervention. These new institutions intervene in various ways, such as by becoming competitive rivals of the opponent's institutions, by replacing them partly or completely, by providing institutional implementation of the actionists' principles or program, or by increasing the effectiveness of other methods of nonviolent action being used in the struggle. In any of these cases the opponent's institutions will no longer have the field to themselves, and the actionists will have intervened by offering substitute institutions. Alternative economic and political institutions are discussed later in this chapter. The focus here is on social institutions, which of course include educational ones.

It may be useful, however, to note briefly some of the reasons why new institutions may be launched. For example, in a long-term nonviolent struggle a necessary counterpart to noncooperation with certain established institutions may be the building up of alternative institutions, social, economic and political. This is often necessary in order to make noncooperation with institutions controlled by the opponent effective and in order to develop or maintain an alternative social order. Sometimes also this is done in order to prevent "contamination" by the institutions which are opposed, or to fulfill needs neglected by established bodies.

In the nineteenth century, during their resistance to Austrian rule, the Hungarians developed both social and economic institutions to combat the "Austrianization" of Hungary. These included the National Academy of Sciences, the National Museum, and the National Theater, while economic bodies included the Agricultural Union, the National Protective Union, and the Company of Commerce.[158] In 1905 in Ireland, Arthur Griffith developed a comparable Sinn Fein policy of building alternative educational, economic, political and diplomatic institutions for Ireland, built on the Hungarian pattern and designed to restore self-reliance and independence to the country.[159] Gandhi, too, developed the theory of alternative institutions as a crucial part of his constructive program.[160]

Sometimes, however, a resistance movement may select only a few institutions for parallel development. In the nineteenth century the American abolitionists and Negro churchmen, for example, protesting against segregation within the churches, withdrew from them and sometimes established new churches. This is how the African Methodist Episcopal Zion Church was established in 1821. [161]

In addition to privately teaching slaves and free Negroes to read and write, abolitionists and others before the Civil War sometimes established new schools, usually for Negroes but occasionally for an integrated enrollment. In many states both such private instruction and schools were forbidden by law. In breaking up a school for slaves, a grand jury in Lexington, Kentucky, argued that the school would enlighten ". . . the minds of those whose happiness obviously depends on their ignorance." [162] A Negro woman in Savannah, Georgia, taught a black school illegally for over thirty years; in other cases the teacher went to private homes, as in Petersburg, Virginia, where a mulatto secretly went from house to house at night to teach Negroes. In the late 1850s the abolitionist Rev. John G. Fee tried to create integrated schools in Kentucky; after his school building was burned by armed proslavery whites, Fee defiantly returned despite threats. He refused to carry weapons even for self-protection, and although frequently mobbed, he continued to create integrated schools. Catholics, Quakers and Negro church bodies supported several schools for free Negroes in Baltimore and Washington. Mobs broke up furniture and burned these schoolhouses, driving some teachers out of the capital city. After Quakers helped Myrtilla Miner to establish a normal school for Negroes in Washington in the early 1850s, boys on the street tormented the students, and a mob invaded the schoolroom. Miss Miner, however, "laughed them to shame; and when they threatened to burn her [school]house, she told them they could not stop her in that way, as another house, better than the old, would immediately rise from its ashes." A fire was set in 1860, but the building was nevertheless saved. [163]

Schools seem to be one of the most common social institutions for parallel development, for the remaining two examples refer also to them, in very different circumstances. During the German occupation of their country Polish citizens set up an educational system independent of Nazi control. In 1942 in the Warsaw district alone more than 85,000 children were receiving education in small secret sessions in private homes. Over 1,700 had by that date been graduated from high school, receiving innocently worded cards which were after the war to be exchanged for official diplomas. [164]

Alternative private school systems have been created in the U.S. South by prosegregationist whites in efforts to counter Federal court decisions ordering integration in public schools. In Virginia, in the autumn of 1958, for example, state aid to pay tuition for children in private schools was attempted. A Federal court ruling banning publicly paid teachers from operating private segregated schools (along with citizen support for the public schools and other factors) prevented these private schools from re-placing integrated public ones. [165]

180. Alternative communication system [166]

Under political systems which have extensive control or monopoly over systems and media of communication, the creation by opposition groups of substitute systems of communication may constitute nonviolent interven-tion when they disrupt the regime's control or monopoly over the com-munication of information and ideas. This may involve newspapers, radio and even television. Systems for communication between individuals (as substitutes for the controlled postal or telephone system) may also be in-volved. Newspapers themselves, or radio broadcasts, as described in Chap-ter Three, are classed as methods of protest and persuasion; but when these are developed as alternative systems of communication on a suffi-cient scale to challenge the controlled ones, the intervention of these new systems disrupts the opponents control of these media. These new com-munication systems then become powerful tools of the nonviolent action-ists; and, the opponent's control of communication of ideas and informa-tion having been broken, these systems in turn may enable the actionists in the future to resist and intervene in still other ways.

The underground newspaper systems cited in Chapter Three in cer-tain Nazi-occupied countries were on a sufficient scale to constitute an al-ternative news communication system. This was clearly the case in the Netherlands. The very day after the German invasion the first hand-writ-ten underground bulletin appeared, and soon there were more handwritten or typewritten sheets or bulletins, called "snow-ball letters" (which read-ers were expected to copy and to pass on to friends). Major periodicals developed and grew to have very large circulations, especially considering the repressive conditions under which they were edited, published and distributed. *Vrij Nederland* with its local editions reached a circulation in September 1944 of one hundred thousand printed copies. *Het Parool* began as the first printed underground paper with six thousand copies, reaching a circulation of sixty thousand in 1944, and its daily news bul-letins nearly reached a circulation of one hundred thousand. *Je Maintien-drai* grew from a small mimeographed sheet to a weekly which had a cir-culation of forty thousand in 1945. *Trouw* had a basic circulation of sixty thousand, but there were also about sixty local and regional editions; by

January 1945 the total circulation of all its editions and news bulletins was about two million. In 1944 *De Waarheid,* a weekly printed in Amsterdam and Rotterdam, may have reached one hundred thousand copies. *Ons Volk* reached a circulation of 120,000. In addition to these, various other clandestine periodicals and papers were published and circulated, and after confiscation of radios in May 1943 they grew rapidly; 150 separate such titles appeared in 1943, and between September 1944 and January 1945, 350 news bulletins appeared, "reaching a cumulative circulation of millions of copies." [167] With so extensive an alternative system of communication of political ideas, discussion of resistance tactics, and news, the illegal papers clearly rivaled the official ones and prevented the occupation forces from establishing a monopoly for the Nazi-controlled press and censored news reports.

Another type of alternative communication system is more specialized, involving the delivery of information and special messages to particular persons or groups, when the regular media for such communication, like the postal service, telephones and so on, are subject to interception or tapping.

The system of alternative radio broadcasting and television which operated in Czechoslovakia for a full two weeks, described briefly in Chapter Three, is the most advanced development thus far of such an alternative broadcast system operating within an occupied country. It operated longer under those conditions than had been believed possible, but as yet there has been relatively little attention to the technical, organizational and other requirements which might enable such a rival broadcasting system to continue to operate periodically over months or years to assist a resistance movement.

ECONOMIC INTERVENTION

Nonviolent intervention may also take economic forms. [168] The effect of some of the twelve methods in this subclass is, however, primarily psychological, while in other methods it is largely economic, often with political ramifications. Four of these methods are characterized by combined physical and economic characteristics: the reverse strike, the stay-in strike, nonviolent land seizures, and defiance of blockades. Four of these methods are simply disruptive of an opponent's economy, especially that of another country, and these usually involve government action, although they could in special circumstances be carried out by private groups; they are politically motivated counterfeiting, preclusive purchasing, seizure of assets in another country, and dumping of products on the international market to injure or destroy the economy of another country. These methods are far from forms derived from love of one's opponent and indeed have sometimes been used just prior to or during military conflicts by the belligerents themselves. These methods however do fulfill the technical characteristics of this class of methods within the technique of nonviolent action. The last grouping within economic intervention is primarily nongovernmental, and involves the creation, shifting, or increase of alternative purchasing, marketing, transportation and production capacity.

181. Reverse strike

While economic in form, the reverse strike is largely psychological in impact. As far is now known, the reverse strike is a relatively new form of nonviolent action, originating among agricultural workers in Italy around 1950, prior to the well-known use of the reverse strike in Sicily by the Italian exponent of nonviolent social change, Danilo Dolci. In using this method, the agricultural workers worked harder and longer than they were either required or paid to do. They did this to support their demand for pay increases and to place the employer in a difficult position to deny their requests.

The reverse strike has also been used to dramatize the need for jobs for unemployed men. In 1956 unemployed Sicilians led by Danilo Dolci used this method when they voluntarily repaired a public road in order to call attention to the severe unemployment in the area, the government's failure to deal adequately with it, and the constitutional guarantee of the right to work. On this occasion, Dolci and others were arrested.[169]

James Farmer reports that more recently (no date given) in Chicago a Congress of Racial Equality (C.O.R.E.) group organized unemployed Negro youths to work on a slum clean-up campaign and then left a bill at City Hall (which was never paid) enumerating the costs of the effort. They were, as Farmer puts it, "as it were doing public works before they were authorized."[170]

The first Sunday of the Russian occupation of Czechoslovakia, August 25, a majority of workers of the C.K.D., one of the country's largest machinery factories, including office workers, reported for an extra shift of work they called "Dubček's Sunday," to support the Dubček government by building the economy, instead of striking, which would have hurt the country itself, not the Russians. At the compressor plant, however, the instructions for the "Dubček shift" came too late and only about forty percent reported for work.[171]

Although the reverse strike *appears* innocuous and of little threat to the established order, it has at times in Italy been regarded by officials as sufficiently dangerous to merit the arrest, imprisonment and even shooting of reverse strikers by police.[172] Why this is so is difficult to answer unless defiant initiatives and intervention by workers is seen as more perilous than the halting of work by ordinary strikes.

182. Stay-in strike

In the stay-in strike—the term is used by both Peterson and Knowles[173] —the workers halt work but remain at the place of work, such as the factory, and refuse to leave until their demands are granted. This has been more frequently called a sit-down strike, but the term stay-in strike is recommended here as a more accurate (for the workers do not literally remain sitting down), and in order to avoid confusion with the sit-down described in Chapter Seven. When used by miners, this has been called a stay-down strike, since they remain down in the mines for its duration.

The stay-in strike has a number of advantages for the strikers: it leaves them in control of the means of production; it reduces the chances of strikebreakers being used to keep production going; and unless the stay-in strikers are attacked by police or troops, the chances of violence and sabotage in the strike are lessened.[174]

Joseph G. Rayback, in his *A History of American Labor,* reports that "women in the needle trades had engaged in at least one sit-down strike in the nineteenth century" and says that the method had been used in Poland and France, but that these cases were not remembered by the American trade unionists in the mid-1930s.[175] Although it is by no means clear, there is some evidence that the development of this method in the United States was influenced by the Gandhian struggles in India.[176]

Stay-in strikes were widely used in Europe and the United States during the 1930s. Rubber workers in Akron, Ohio, in 1936 conducted the first major American sit-down strike,[177] and the same year Cleveland auto workers conducted another.[178] In October 1936 the stay-in strike was used against the speedup at the General Motors plant in Anderson, Indiana,[179] and on November 13, the same year, it was used against the firing of union men at General Motors' Chevrolet plant in Flint, Michigan.[180]

It was, however, the strike by the United Automobile Workers against General Motors at Flint which made the stay-in, or sit-down, strike famous, Rayback reports. "The strike was something new because workers instead of walking out of the plant just sat at their workbenches . . . . The sit-down proved highly effective." The action was denounced by General Motors as an unlawful invasion of property rights and ejection of the workers was demanded. The company cut off heat in the plants, but the workers remained. Two waves of attack by Flint city police were repulsed violently by the strikers, first with coffee mugs, soft drink bottles, iron bolts and hinges, and then, against tear gas bombs, by fire hoses. Governor Frank Murphy refused to use the state militia to expel the strikers. The workers defied a court order for evacuation, saying that they were seeking to make General Motors "obey the law and engage in collective bargaining"; in defiance of the Wagner Act, the company had refused to discuss either union recognition or collective bargaining. On February 4, President Franklin D. Roosevelt requested that negotiations be resumed, and a week later an agreement was reached whereby the company recognized the union, dropped the injunction, and agreed not to discriminate against union members.

In April 1937 a short stay-in strike forced the Chrysler Corporation to come to terms, Rayback also reports. The strike innovation spread widely, so that between September 1936 and June 1937 almost five hundred thousand workers took part in stay-in strikes in rubber, textile, glass and many other industries. This type of action produced a strong reaction, however, from employers, newspapers, sections of the public, the United States Senate, and finally the American Federation of Labor (A.F.L.). The Congress of Industrial Organizations (C.I.O.) had primarily used it against companies which ignored or defied orders of the National Labor Relations Board; in the summer of 1937 the C.I.O. decided that the stay-in strike "was both unnecessary and impolitic," writes Rayback, and it was quietly abandoned. In 1939 the United States Supreme Court virtually outlawed this type of strike as trespass on private property. [181]

Whereas the stay-in strike in America was used only to press for particular demands concerning wages, working conditions and union recognition, the use of the method in Italy before Mussolini's rise to power was revolutionary—the workers hoped to take over the factories and run them themselves. [182] These cases were sometimes combined with violence.

There are a number of examples of the stay-down strike by miners. In 1934 the miners of Pecs, Hungary, conducted a combined stay-down and hunger strike in the mines. [183] The stay-down strike has also been used by coal miners in Poland and Wales, [184] including two cases of eight miners in September 1959 at the Great Mountain Colliery, Tumble, near Llanelly, South Wales, [185] and thirty-seven men at Groesfaen Colliery, Glamorgan, Wales in March 1960. [186]

In Bitterfeld during the East German Rising in June 1953, the stay-in strike was used as a method of nonviolent struggle which would be effective while keeping people off the streets and avoiding mass confrontations with Russian and East German police and troops. The head of the local strike committee later declared: "We appealed to the workers over the city radio to return to their firms but not to resume work." [187] Evaluating the general use of this method in that revolt, Rainer Hildebrandt writes: ". . . [in] some factories . . . the sit-down strike lasted several days, sustained no casualties and even got some workmates released who had been arrested for striking." [188]

183. Nonviolent land seizure

Another method of economic intervention occurs when people nonviolently expropriate and utilize land which by statute has belonged to someone else, with the intent of producing a *de facto* change of ownership and control. They hope that it will be recognized as a *de jure* change of ownership as well. Usually such land seizures are carried out by landless peasants against large landowners, frequently the same ones on whose land the peasants have previously worked. On other occasions, the seized land may be owned by the government, or may recently have been confiscated as punishment for popular antigovernment resistance, such as tax refusal.

The conditions under which nonviolent land seizures occur differ widely, sometimes even being undertaken with the approval of the government in power or with the encouragement of powerful groups in the society. It seems that the social and political situation is always complicated. They have occurred in diverse parts of the world, only a few examples of which are cited here.

The accounts of land seizures which are readily available are, as is the cases with many other methods, written with a focus which makes it difficult to determine whether the particular seizure was completely nonviolent, largely so, or mixed with significant violence; further research on such illustrative cases as are listed here might therefore require some modification in their descriptions.

As a few examples, we may cite peasant land seizures which occurred in Central and Southern Italy and in Sicily in 1919 and 1920. Christopher Seton-Watson reports that peasant land seizures began in August 1919 in the Roman Campagna.

Columns would set out at dawn from the villages, with banners and martial music, march to the selected estate, mark out the uncultivated land in strips or plots, and at once begin to dig or plough, to establish ownership. Often the land selected for seizure had been the object of bitter disputes for decades and was regarded by the peasants as rightfully theirs.[189] In September the government authorized the prefects to requisition uncultivated land; it was to be distributed to needy claimants if they organized themselves into cooperatives. In the spring of 1920 Catholic peasant leagues, frequently encouraged by parish priests, organized larger land seizures in Sicily. The government then said that only peasants capable of efficient farming would have their claims recognized. The total amount of land which permanently changed hands by land seizures was small.[190]

A large number of cases of land seizure have occurred in South America, especially in Colombia, Bolivia, Peru, Venezuela and Brazil. In Colombia peasant leagues in 1929 used land seizures and apparently defensive violence in Cundinamarca, Tolima and Valle and maintained on the former Viotá estates, in a mountainous area of over five hundred square kilometers, an independent communist republic for over twenty years. In 1933 the peasants took advantage of a Colombian law which made the landlord financially obligated to his tenants for improvements they made on his land. With and without permission, tenants planted coffee trees, making repossession by the landlord impossible without payment to the tenants. In the area of Cundinamarca these peasant actions were successful, and they kept the land. Somewhat later the Colombian Congress passed the Law 200, known as the López land reform.[191] The *Caja Agraria,* agricultural credit bank, legalized the seizure of various *haciendas* by buying them from the original owners and selling them on long-term credit back to the peasants who had occupied them; this would not have happened except for the peasants' action.[192]

About 1961 between five and six hundred peasant families invaded and seized the large abandoned *haciendas* of the area of Cunday. In this and two other areas the government's Land Reform Institute then divided the estates among a large number of peasant families.[193]

Miguel Urrutia reports that around 1967 land seizures were still being organized by peasant unions and that the Roman Catholic-oriented *Federación Agraria Nacional* (affiliated with the *Unión de Trabadores de Colombia)* had organized land seizures which had given *de facto* property rights to thousands of peasants. Such seizures have often been approved by Church advisors and led by priests. Nonviolent seizures were in some cases made legal by sales on credit by the landowner to the peasants, while in other instances the government's Land Reform Institute declares the invaded land a "land reform" area. In other cases, says Urrutia, "the peasants keep their land through force." [194]

Major land seizures have also occurred in Bolivia, often with government encouragement. In 1945 at a national congress of *campesinos* the Indians were urged by officials of the revolutionary nationalist government to strengthen their organizations as a step toward future actions to expropriate the *latifundios*—the large estates. However, later under a conservative government when Indians invaded the *haciendas* of the plateau they were cruelly repressed, Eduardo Arze-Loureiro reports. [195]

In 1952, after the elected Nationalistic Revolutionary Movement gained government power, the N.R.M. and government together set about urging the Indians to occupy the land. With help, agricultural unions were established, and land was distributed into family plots and collective fields.

> With surprising rapidity the land was taken and distributed, without violence, even before the promulgation of the Agrarian Reform Decree. The process took place almost simultaneously throughout the vast zone which is inhabited by 80 percent of the national population, and this with all its amplitude and with a stability that precluded the necessity for subsequent revisions. [196]

The feudal divisions of land use, between family plots and the landowners, were kept, but ownership was transferred to the family groups and the community respectively. "It has been a peaceful process," writes Arze-Loureiro, "although one of transcendent importance, because it has eliminated one rural social class, that of the *latifundistas,* and has converted the serf into the owner of his parcel and a member of an institution with common possessions and interests." [197] The large landowners retreated to the cities, where they turned to gaining control of the State apparatus by means of the *coup d'etat.*

Huntington reports that peasant land seizures in the Cuzco area of Peru and the growing strength of peasant organizations contributed to the passage of the 1960 land reform law in that country; [198] it is also reported that President Belaunde Terry had "encouraged landless Indians to seize untilled latifundios so as to force through Congress his land reform bill." [199] In 1962-63 in Peru a syndicate movement grew in the departments of Junin and Pasco in the Central Sierra. Doreen Warriner reports that these groups organized "numerous seizures or invasions of *haciendas* which had taken land from the Indians. ('Invasion' means that the Indians drive their cattle onto the disputed land, build huts and live there.)" [200]

After President Rómulo Betancourt of Venezuela returned to power in 1959, his government immediately began to distribute public lands and to approve of land seizures which had been organized by the syndicates. The 1960 Agrarian Reform Law, writes Warriner, "did not really initiate the reform: it regularized the preceding take-overs of land by the syndicates, and provided a mechanism by which syndicates could, in future, petition the National Agrarian Institute for the expropriation of estates." [201] She also reports that "Venezuela is the only country where a trade union movement has carried out a land reform . . ." [202]

In 1963-64 land invasions occurred in Brazil, especially of abandoned and uninhabited estates where opposition was unlikely. The Paraiba Valley was the scene of many of the land seizures. Police threw the invaders out most of the time but not always, as Warriner reports: "In one case where the invaders were backed by the railway workers' syndicate which threatened a railway strike if the invaders were expelled, the state government purchased the estate and handed it over to the invaders." [203] The Brazilian government agency *Superintendencia da Politica de Reforma Agraria* did expropriate some properties where land seizures had been attempted or had been successful. [204] The government of President Goulart was ousted by a *coup d'etat* in April 1964. Landowners' fear of a general upheaval is reported as one factor in its overthrow. Leaders of the syndicate movement were then imprisoned. [205]

184. Defiance of blockades [206]

In the course of international conflict, nations may attempt to exert political pressure by blockading opponents, to exclude certain "strategic goods" of a military nature or to cut off food and other necessary supplies, or both. Defying the blockade without the threat or use of military action, in order to bring food and related necessities to the cut-off population, then constitutes a method of economic intervention which third parties may use to support the besieged country. Such defiance may be made by both private and governmental bodies. Where governmental action is involved, there is always the possibility that even when there is no intent to threaten or use military support, the opponent may perceive this to be a possibility if he interferes with the defiance of the blockade. Also, as in the case of embargoes, there may be an implicit possibility of violent action by the government to support a method which is by itself nonviolent. These background conditions may have been present in the best-known example of blockade defiance, the Berlin Airlift of 1948-49. In it British and United States planes airlifted into Berlin food, fuel and other necessary supplies after the Soviet Union had imposed a blockade, which began on June 24, 1948, and continued until May 12, 1949. There does not, however, appear to have been an explicit threat of Western military action by the British or Americans, nor apparently were the supply planes armed. This case thus meets the criteria for classification as nonviolent action as well as do embargoes. Further study of this type of phenomenon is needed.

In addition to the Allied airlift, Germans themselves brought supplies to Berlin for several months. W. Phillips Davidson writes in his book *The Berlin Blockade* that owing to the currency reform it was profitable for West German farmers to increase production and to try to keep Berlin as a market.

> Enterprising truckers managed to evade Soviet controls and spirit produce from West Germany [across East Germany] to West Berlin, where it would command slightly higher prices. During the summer there were some days when fresh vegetables smuggled in from the west zones were available at such reasonable prices that the Magistrat [the executive branch of the Berlin city government] was hard pressed to dispose of those marketed through the usual channels.
>
> In addition, throughout the summer West Berliners were able to obtain a limited quantity of food and other supplies from the Soviet zone. Trucks drove out daily into the surrounding country-side and came back with vegetables. Individuals returned by boat, train, subway, or bicycle with wood, coal briquettes, potatoes, and sundries. [207]

In the autumn of 1948 Soviet officials moved to seal these holes in the blockade.

The vast bulk of supplies, however, were brought in by air; these included not only vast quantities of food, but even coal, machinery and electrical generating equipment. The record was set on April 16, 1949, when 12,490 tons were airlifted in twenty-four hours. Tonnage airlifted for the month of April alone was 235,000. [208]

185. Politically motivated counterfeiting

Politically motivated counterfeiting involves the deliberate distribution in one country of counterfeit money and other documents of economic importance by a hostile country. "It might be done either to disrupt the economy by monetary means," writes Professor Thomas C. Schelling, "or to create such a prevalence of counterfeit as to cause loss of confidence in the currency." [209] Murray Teich Bloom reports that "counterfeiting an enemy's coinage or currency has been a tactic of most wars since 1470 when the wily Duke Galeazzo Sforza of Milan used it against Venice." [210]

President Franklin D. Roosevelt is reported to have asked the British to consider counterfeiting German currency, but they refused, though they did make good facsimiles of Nazi ration stamps, which were air-dropped in 1940. Counterfeit postage stamps for Germany and occupied France were also made, and used by secret agents and for mailing propaganda within these countries. It is also reported by Bloom (and denied by the former director of the Office for Stategic Services) that the United States made and distributed counterfeit Japanese currency. [211]

After 1943 the Germans circulated counterfeit British notes of various denominations. The very best quality notes were used in neutral countries and by German spies in enemy countries, the second best for paying off collaborators and Quislings in occupied countries, and notes of the third quality were to be dropped over England by plane to disrupt the British banking system. Others were unusable. The counterfeit money was distributed widely in North Africa after the Allied invasion, and in Portugal and Spain, among other places. The Bank of England suspected the scheme in April 1943. In 1944 alone the Nazis produced usable British currency worth about $277,500,000. Only a very few U.S. one hundred dollar bills were produced early in 1945. [212]

186. Preclusive purchasing

Preclusive purchasing is a intervention which involves "buying strategic commodities in world markets for the purpose of making them unavailable to the enemy." [213] During World War II, for example, the United States bought various minerals in Spain, Portugal and Turkey in order to ensure that they did not become available to the Axis powers. [214]

187. Seizure of assets

Another method of economic intervention involves the impounding or confiscating of assets, including "blocking the use of bank accounts, or of securities in brokerage accounts; preventing the payment of interest or dividends to enemy countries; abrogating patent or royalty rights and so forth." [215]

All Japanese assets in the United States were ordered frozen on July 25, 1941, and Britain and the Netherlands took similar action. Japan had signed a treaty with Axis powers in September 1940, and a treaty of neutrality with the Soviet Union in April 1941; after the German attack in June on Russia, Japan had made demands on the Vichy French government for still more bases in Indochina. Embargoes on shipment of various war materials to Japan had already been declared; petroleum supplies were particularly short. "In these circumstances," writes Thomas A. Bailey, "the Big Freeze was a blow hardly less jarring to the Japanese than their later assault on Pearl Harbor was to the Americans."[216] During World War II the freezing of assets of enemy countries was a standard practice.[217]

Following the nationalization of the Anglo-Iranian Oil Co. by the government of Iran under Mossadegh in 1951, one of Britain's actions was to freeze all Iranian deposits in British banks, thus bringing all of Iran's foreign trade to a standstill.[218]

188. Dumping

This is, writes Professor Schelling, the "deliberate sale [at below standard prices] of a commodity on world markets to depress price and reduce the earnings of another country."[219] It is, he writes, "most uncommon," partly because it is very expensive. The threat to dump agricultural products may be a very serious threat against countries whose economies are highly dependent on export of such products. When the Russians in the early 1950s sought to sell oil abroad, they were wrongly thought to be aiming at disrupting the oil market, and some also thought that the 1953-54 Russian gold sales were intended to cause confusion in foreign financial circles.[220]

Such examples involve government action which is likely to make possible faster and more complete results. However, there has been at least one abortive and somewhat ambitious attempt by private groups to undermine an economic system by dumping on the international market. This complex plan to end slavery in the United States by dumping cotton on the international market was developed, St. Clair Drake reports, by physician Martin R. Delaney and minister Henry Highland Garnet, founders of the African Civilization Society. Under a mandate by the Emigration Convention of 1854, Delaney went to Africa and signed an agreement with the rulers of Yoruba (now part of Nigeria) to allocate land for settlement by Negro freedmen from the United States. The plan was that these ex-slaves would teach Africans how to grow cotton. It would then be dumped on the world market at such a low price as to destroy the economic basis of the Southern plantation system. The result would be freedom for the slaves, cheaper cloth, and skills and prosperity for the Africans. The plans, and British financial support, ended with the outbreak of the Civil War.[221]

189. Selective patronage

As mentioned in the discussion of consumers' boycotts in Chapter Five, nonviolent campaigners in the United States have sometimes urged patronage of named firms, instead of boycott of others, in order to bypass anti-boycott laws in some states. Selective patronage campaigns have, however, been used more widely, and with other motives, than those cases suggest. This method has been used in order to reward financially businesses which have pursued an approved policy, especially at times when such a policy was regarded by some as an economic risk.

Garrison and a group of abolitionists in 1834 deliberately chose to patronize a steamboat on the Delaware River which was not segregated, as some were; the route was slower and less direct, but they preferred to encourage the integration policy, and told the captain that because of it he had gained twenty-seven dollars worth of business. *The Liberator* reported their view that if the refusal to use segregated transportation, and the choice of integrated transportation, were "extensively imitated by anti-slavery men . . . every barrier of caste will soon be overthrown." [222]

When the people of one country are engaged in a struggle to attain independence from another country which has been ruling them, the economic means of action used often include campaigns to purchase the products grown or made in the dependent country. This is often the counterpart of an economic boycott, but in important ways differs from it. The object with a program of selective patronage of a county's own products is not simply to hurt the opponent country economically (which would be compatible with buying the boycotted products from other countries instead), but to build up the dependent country economically. This is sometimes seen as a necessary step toward full independence.

This was an important component of American colonial struggles before 1775. As resistance was organized in 1765 against the Stamp Act, for example, a campaign was launched to promote and develop alternative American products. [223] Although the policy did not originate with him, this movement was given impetus by a pamphlet by Daniel Dulany, who wrote: "By a vigorous Application to Manufactures, the Consequence of Oppression in the Colonies to the Inhabitants of Great Britain would strike Home and immediately . . ." [224] Various societies were organized to promote the manufacture and use of American products in preference to English ones, and descriptions of the domestic products were publicized in the newspapers. These American-made items included scythes, spades, shovels, wallpaper, liquors, cordials, cloth and clothing. The colonial production campaign included the promotion of American linen, made of native-grown-and-spun flax. Factory production of linen grew in Philadelphia and New York, while in Rhode Island women turned to spinning flax in their homes. A variety of American substitutes for tea—sage, sassafras and balm—were promoted as more healthful, and the eating of lamb was abandoned in order not to interfere with the production of American wool.[225]

During the Gandhian struggles against the British rule of India, an important component of the Indian means of action was the movement to increase Indian production and use of her own products. This was called *swadeshi,* and it had a philosophical as well as economic and political ramifications. Gandhi often preferred *swadeshi* to an economic boycott movement which he sometimes, especially earlier in his career, regarded as vindictive. *Swadeshi,* however, positively built up India's economy and independence, and reduced economic dependence on all foreign countries.[226]

Trade unions in the United States have often urged the purchase of products bearing the union label, as a means of supporting higher wages and improved working conditions. Myers and Laidler defined the union label as "a device which organized labor has developed to encourage the purchase of goods made under union conditions."[227] Looking something like trademarks, insignia, coats of arms, and the like, the union label is attached directly to the product where possible, or displayed where the item is sold, or shown on the packaging. Its presence shows that the article has been "produced by union labor under conditions required of union shops."[228] Trade unionists have been especially urged to purchase products bearing the union label, and conventions in the 1930s in the United States used to have a "union-label roll call" in which delegates using particular union-made items were asked to stand as the list of products was called. The union label began in 1875 among cigar factory workers in California and was originally used to identify cigars made by white workers.[229] One of the departments created in the merged A.F.L.-C.I.O. was a Union Label Department, in Washington, D.C., which provides lists of union-label products.[230] After the grape growers of California began signing union contracts with the United Farm Workers in 1970, the union label on boxes of grapes sold throughout the country became very important in determining which grapes should be purchased by supporters of the grape workers and which should still be boycotted.

190. Alternative markets[231]

Illegal or "black" markets, especially in wartime or during occupations, are usually associated with exploitative prices and selfish objectives.

In some cases, however, alternative illegal channels of buying and selling food and various other supplies may be created as a form of economic intervention. Apart from helping to meet needs of the populace and keeping goods out of the enemy's hands, there may be a wider political significance in such action. Against a totalitarian regime's attempts to control all economic life, thwarting that control by the maintainance of independent channels of distribution may become an important resistance objective.

This method has been used at least once in a struggle during an occupation, the German occupation of Norway. A.K. Jameson reports:

> The high moral tone of the whole movement is clearly shown in the way the black market was run. Producers of foodstuffs were supposed to hand over all their produce to government distributing agencies, but in fact they succeeded in keeping back quite a lot. In contrast to what happened elsewhere, however, this store was sold secretly at prices very little higher than those officially fixed and much of it was bought up by employers for the benefit of employees and by individuals for the maintainance of those hiding from the authorities. Practically no private profit was made from these transactions and hence the market had not the same demoralizing effects as it had in other occupied countries, and it ceased the moment the occupation was over. [232]

It is difficult without detailed research to judge whether this report may be too sweeping, although in any case it illustrates the potential of this method. In a wider discussion of production during this period, not limited to foodstuffs, Professor Erling Petersen points out that while many products were saved for the Norwegian economy by withholding them from the regular market, "in many cases" the main consideration was to get the high prices of the black market, with the "moral excuse" of keeping the products out of German hands. [233]

191. Alternative transportation system

Side by side with the boycott of a public transportation system, a parallel substitute system has occasionally been improvised. This occurred in the Montgomery, Alabama, bus boycott, already described in detail, almost immediately after its beginning. "In the early stages of the protest the problem of transportation demanded most of our attention," Dr. Martin Luther King, Jr., later wrote. For the first few days Negro taxi companies followed an agreement to carry passengers for the ten cent bus fare, but a law which set a minimum taxi fare of forty-five cents required that other arrangements be made. Drawing on experience during an earlier bus boycott in Baton Rouge, Louisiana, the Montgomery group quickly decided to set up a volunteer private car pool. The new transportation system established forty-eight dispatch and forty-two pick-up stations by December 13. Dr. King reports: "In a few days this system was working astonishingly well" and even impressed the white segregationists. During the next year fifteen new station wagons were purchased for the transport system.

The parallel transportation system was clearly seen by the Montgomery city officials and the bus company as a serious problem in itself. Four times the insurance on the vehicles was canceled and under the administration of Mayor Gayle the city's legal department took court action to ban the motor pool. But the United States Supreme Court decision that Alabama's state and local bus segregation laws were unconstitutional came before the local court's temporary injunction against the motor pool. [234]

192. Alternative economic institutions [235]

Although not all economic institutions created or used by nonviolent actionists constitute economic intervention, they do so when the economic institution is itself used in a conflict situation as a method of wielding power or influence. These new institutions may be concerned with production, ownership, or distribution of economic goods. The objectives may not only be economic but also be social and political.

For example, when consumers' or producers' cooperatives are engaged in conflict with capitalist or State industries, or when the cooperatives are being deliberately developed and expanded to replace the existing economic system, or part of it, they constitute economic intervention. For example, after the turn of the century the Swedish cooperative society *Kooperativa Förbundet,* having failed to lower the price of margarine by boycotting the products of the margarine cartel factories, purchased a small margarine factory, and later built a larger one, in order to enter the market itself at lower prices. The result was a sixty percent cut in the price of margerine, which saved Swedish consumers about two million dollars annually. [236] During the 1920s and 1930s K.F. bought or built plants for making other products, including light bulbs, tires, fertilizers, pottery and building materials. Usually when they captured fifteen to twenty-five percent of the market monopoly prices were broken. [237]

In Italy after 1890 the "Charity and Christian Economy" branch of the Roman Catholic activist organization *Opera dei Congressi* attempted to build up "a network of cooperatives, peasant unions, friendly societies, insurance and rural credit institutions." With continued expansion, these had the potential of becoming "the framework, prefabricated and tested by experience, of a new Catholic state, rising from the ruins of liberalism." [238] By 1912 this branch had 360,000 members.

The Southwest Alabama Farmers Cooperative Association, organized in 1967 by veterans of the Selma civil rights march, arranged for marketing of produce through cooperative channels. This, writes Michael Miles in the *New Republic,* "disrupted the system of exploitation of the black farmer, which depends on the identification of each farmer's cotton at the warehouse so that it can immediately be appropriated by his creditors . . ." [239] Other Southern black organizations attempting economic intervention include the Poor People's Corp., (Jackson, Mississippi), the Federation of Southern Cooperatives, and Crawfordville (Florida) Enterprises. [240] Such organizations have often encountered strong opposition but nevertheless increased the economic well-being and self-determination of their members.

POLITICAL INTERVENTION

This last subclass of methods of nonviolent intervention includes seven which are clearly political in form. The first five of these are acts by citizens, individually or in small or large groups, who attempt to intervene by disrupting the administrative or enforcement agencies of the government. The sixth method, work-on without collaboration, is undertaken by the government employees and officials, while the last one, dual sovereignty and parallel government, involves the shift of loyalties by citizens to a new rival government. All of these, in differing degrees and ways, intervene to disturb the working of the opponent's government and even to challenge its existence.

193. Overloading of administrative systems [241]

Administrative systems of governments may be overloaded by excessive compliance in providing them with diverse types of information which may be directly or indirectly related to their responsibilities, or in making an excessive number of enquiries of them, or by providing them with excessive numbers of suggestions, protests or statements. The resulting overloading of the administrative system may make the continuance of operations difficult or may slow its capacity to deal with its normal activities. This type of action is particularly likely to happen where the law or regulations which the administrative unit is implementing require frequent revision of data concerning personnel or other matters, or when complex systems of rules and regulations to be followed are subject to frequent change.

This method—called the comply-in—was applied in the United States in the spring of 1970 by the antiwar movement, as people were urged to comply with all the usually neglected provisions of the law concerning personal information. The *New York Times* quoted Mrs. Trudi Young, spokesman for the New Mobilization Committee to End the War in Vietnam, to this effect: "The [Selective Service] law also requires registrants to inform the draft boards within ten days of any change in address or status. This means changes in religion, mental attitude and everything else." Although almost entirely ignored by the Selective Service System itself, the law applies its regulations to all males born after August 30, 1922, not just to those up to twenty-five years of age. Mrs. Young continued:

> We want everyone to take this law so seriously that they inform their board of every single change, even if they're over age or have already completed their service. This means wives, mothers, and friends as well. They should submit documents attesting to any change in the status of a registrant. The Selective Service just cannot stand up, administratively, to absolute obedience to the draft law.

The paper quoted a Selective Service spokesman as saying that if thousands of overage men followed the law to the letter, "Lord help us." [242] This type of action is closely related to the "working-to-rule" strike described in Chapter Six.

In Massachusetts in June 1970, following the invasion of Cambodia by United States forces and the resultant protests, Colonel Paul Feeney of the Selective Service System in the state in an interview described the flood of mail which had poured into their offices:

> Some of the mail says "I've changed my status, I've moved from the first floor to the third floor." Or we'll get a letter saying, "I'm going to Europe." A few days later we'll get another letter saying, "I've changed my mind. I am not going to Europe."

One official estimated that perhaps a thousand man-hours had been lost by handling the excess mail. Officials ordered seven hundred thousand postcards which could quickly, yet legally, be used to respond to the increased quantity of mail. [243]

194. Disclosing identities of secret agents[244]

Where secret police and undercover political agents are employed, one means of dealing with them when they are discovered has been to publish their names, perhaps with other details, photographs and the like; this has the effect of making it extraordinarily difficult for those particular persons to continue their activities as secret agents. This may be applied to political agents which have infiltrated, or have attempted to infiltrate, resistance organizations, and may constitute an alternative to murdering them, a frequent practice by resistance movements in Nazi-occupied countries during World War II.

The publication of names and descriptions of slaveowners seeking their runaway slaves, described earlier in this chapter under nonviolent harassment, is very close to this method. In other cases the various other described forms of personal harassment were not used but placards were posted describing paid slave hunters; these instances are clearly within this method. Such a case occurred in Boston in 1850 when two slave hunters arrived to seize William and Ellen Craft; with the identities and objective of the hunters openly revealed, their effectiveness was reduced, and this helped to induce the slave hunters to leave town.[245]

In 1969 the *Los Angeles Free Press,* which opposed imprisonment for the use of nonaddictive drugs, published the names of over fifty state narcotics agents with their addresses and telephone numbers. The newspaper saw this as a political act, although officials took a different view. The California Attorney General then obtained an injunction against publication of more "confidential" documents of the state Justice Department, and the exposed agents as a group filed a suit for $25,000,000 against the newspaper, while the Attorney General filed another damage suit for the state.[246]

195. Seeking imprisonment

Imprisonment in civil disobedience is normally a secondary consequence of the peaceful breaking of a law or regulation, which act is seen to be of much greater importance than the imprisonment. However, on occasion imprisonment may be sought by the nonviolent actionists as a *primary* objective, especially when this is done in very large numbers. Actionists may deliberately disobey a particular regulation in order to be imprisoned, and may ask to be arrested even though police select others for arrest or even though the persons were not present on the original occasion. At times the objective is to fill the jails; that is called a jail-in.

Requests to be arrested usually occur as an expression of solidarity with associates already under arrest, but the intent may also be to demonstrate a lack of fear of arrest, to obtain the release of those already arrested, to clog the courts or fill the prisons, or to obtain wider publicity and increased resistance. During the Norwegian teachers' noncooperation struggle in 1942, the day after Quisling had personally stormed and raged at the teachers in the Stabekk school and ordered their arrest, teachers who had that day been absent went to the prison and demanded to be arrested also.[247]

In January 1959 women supporters of Dr. Banda and the Nyasaland African Congress rejected police orders to disperse as they marched toward the Zomba Government House to hear the results of talks between Dr. Banda and the Governor. An initial advance was followed by a clash and beatings of the women, and finally another advance;

> . . . in the end, the police arrested a few of them. The remainder protested. They began to protest physically and insisted that if some are arrested, then all must be arrested. . . So the police arrested them —36 in all.[248]

In France in 1959 a group under the auspices of *Action Civique Nonviolent* went to the Thol detainee camp, where North Africans were held without trial or hearing, and requested that they, too, be placed in the camp as witnesses against the flagrant miscarriage of justice.[249]

In 1961, in connection with a wave of freedom rides against racial segregation on buses, C.O.R.E. members, together with many volunteers, began to fill Mississippi jails—the jail-in being "aimed at making segregationist practices so expensive and inconvenient as to become unfeasible." The flood of prisoners cost the city of Jackson, Mississippi, alone over a million dollars in increased enforcement and imprisonment bills.[250] James Peck, a veteran of many nonviolent civil rights struggles, reports that the term jail-in was coined by newspapermen in February 1961 to refer to the increasing number of antisegregation Southern nonviolent student actionists who "to emphasize the injustice of being arrested for protesting racial descrimination, chose to remain in jail rather than pay fines or go out on bail."[251]

On March 25, 1960, four days after the shootings at Sharpeville, Philip Kgosana, a young Pan-Africanist leader led a march of 1,500 Africans from Langa location to the police station in nearby Capetown and demanded their arrest for refusing to carry the required passes. The police chief, however, turned them away, and they went home in an orderly manner.[252]

At the time of the arrest and trial of six members of the Committee of 100 in Britain in 1962, several other members of the Committee offered themselves for arrest as being equally guilty.[253]

In February 1964 Southern Rhodesian African women protested the lack of government action in providing roads, bridges and schools in the Tanda reserve by refusing to dip their cattle as required. Of the 172 women arrested, 150 refused to pay the imposed fine, choosing instead to serve the prison sentence. Another group of 158 was remanded for later sentencing. Three hundred more women also marched to the Meyo Court demanding to be placed under arrest. They were reinforced by still another angry group of 300 women, who arrived later with the same demand.[254]

196. Civil disobedience of "neutral" laws

Although civil disobedience is usually the disobedience of laws which are regarded as inherently immoral or otherwise illegitimate, at times nonviolent actionists may disobey or ignore laws and regulations which are regarded as morally "neutral." This is most likely to occur in the advanced stages of a nonviolent revolutionary movement (as in India under the British), or in cases where the nature of modern government, or of the issue itself, makes it difficult to noncooperate with or to disobey a law directly related to the grievance. An example of this was the issue of nuclear weapons in Britain in 1962.

In all modern States there are laws which exist simply to help the government exercise its authority, regulate the citizenry, and carry out its functions, but which neither prohibit people from committing some "inhuman" or "immoral" act, nor are themselves regarded as unjust or oppressive. These "neutral" laws are often of a regulatory character. While disobedience of laws which prohibit infliction of harm on other people does not fall within civil disobedience of any type, these "neutral" laws are violated in this extreme type of civil disobedience. The point then is not that the disobeyed law is itself wrong, but that the actionists have either rebelled against the government, or have found no other strong way to express their grievance.

Gandhi regarded this type of civil disobedience as justified at times, but as "a most dangerous weapon." It should be postponed, he maintained, when the opponent is in difficulties; at such times the *satyagrahi* ought not to harass him but rather seek to convert him. However, when the government is regarded as having become so unjust as to have forfeited all obligation to obedience, and the intention has become to destroy the government by noncooperation and disobedience, this type of civil disobedience may be justified. Gandhi believed that then the breach of such laws would not harm the people, but would merely make it more difficult for the government to carry out its administration, and that, when undertaken on a mass scale, such a breach would contribute to the government's dissolution. [255] This stage has thus far rarely been reached in actual campaigns, but during the 1930-31 Indian campaign it was closely approximated on several occasions. [256]

197. Work-on without collaboration

This method involves determined persistence by civil servants, government officials, and ordinary citizens in carrying out the legally established policies, programs and duties in indifference to, or defiance of, contrary measures from a usurping regime, which has seized the State apparatus in either a *coup d'etat* or a foreign invasion. This method thus differs from a selective refusal of assistance by government aides, a method of political noncooperation, which is a refusal to carry out particular instructions or orders, though the two methods may be related. The emphasis here is on the deliberate continuation of legitimate duties and tasks.

The clearest theoretical presentations of this method have been made by Dr. Theodor Ebert in discussion of the strategic problems of civilian defense—i.e., the prepared use of nonviolent action for purposes of national defense. Ebert writes: "Everyone should remain at his job and do his duty under the law and in the tradition of his country until physically removed by the occupation power." This would involve, Ebert writes:

> . . . a strict refusal at all levels to recognize the usurper's legality and to obey his orders. The constitution and the laws of the land should be defended as legitimate, and the occupiers regarded as unauthorized private persons whose orders must be ignored. Every member of parliament, minister, civil servant and ordinary citizen would become, in the event of occupation, a soldier on guard at his place of work. *In general, the emphasis should be more on a determined continuation of the existing social and political system, than on resignations and strikes* [italics added].

This method would thus involve "the deliberate continuation of ordinary social roles according to one's legal status . . ." [257]

> Dismissals by the new authorities are to be ignored and people are to attend to their work until physically restrained from so doing. When a leader is removed, his legitimate representative should take his place; and where no such person is available, the subordinates and

assistants are to act on their own responsibility, the usurper's appointees being ignored. [258]

Ebert argues that this method would cause the usurper "more technical and psychological difficulties than a strike or voluntary resignations," reduce opportunities for collaboration, force the opponent to leave legitimate holders of positions alone or face the difficult task of replacing an entire administration (especially difficult on the local level), reduce the risk of social and industrial chaos which is run in a prolonged general strike, and, finally, by the continuing struggle illustrate the objective of the conflict: "to ensure a society's right to order its affairs free from outside coercion." [259]

One interpretation of official policy which is very close to the work-on but not identical with it was issued in May 1943 in the occupied Netherlands. This was written by Bosch Ridder van Rosenthal, former Comissioner of the Queen for the province of Utrecht and a leading resistance leader. Rosenthal wrote a "Commentary," which was published in the underground press on the "Directives of 1937," issued by the Colijn government; Warmbrunn describes these as "a set of somewhat vague secret instructions for the conduct of civil servants in the event of a military occupation." He summarized them as instructing civil servants to continue their work if their service to the Netherlands population was greater than to the enemy; otherwise they should resign. The "Directive of 1937" assumed, however, that the occupier would respect the rules of the Hague Convention, and were so vague that decisions were left to each individual. [260] Also these directives were kept so secret that Prime Minister Gerbrandy (with the exile government in London) apparently did not learn of them until 1943! [261]

However, in addition to urging officials to refuse to carry out actions which conflicted with the interests of the population, Rosenthal's "Commentary" urged them not to resign but "to wait for possible dismissal for their failure to implement 'illegal' German orders." "The assumption was that the German authorities might not dismiss all officials practicing such passive resistance." The "Commentary" also emphasized that the legal government of the Netherlands was the one in exile in London, and it was to it that loyalty was due. Specific impermissible types of assistance by civil servants to the Germans were also enumerated. [262]

On a minor scale many of the Norwegian teachers in the case described in Chapter Two conducted a work-on wthout collaboration; those who were not arrested when they returned to their schools repudiated membership in the fascist teachers' organization, explained to their classes their higher responsibilities, and continued to teach without regard to new fascist "obligations." [263]

198. Dual sovereignty and parallel government

This method involves the creation of a new government, or continued loyalty to an existing rival government to that of the opponent. If the parallel government receives overwhelming support from the populace, it may replace the opponent's established government. This extreme development of alternative political institutions has only rarely been deliberately initiated and developed; more commonly it has been an unanticipated product of a massive resistance or revolutionary struggle. Although the examples here refer to this type of situation, comparable cases of parallel government may also occur when the population of an occupied country continues to obey the legal government deposed by the invader and to deny the legitimacy of the invader's regime and hence disobey it.

When a nonviolent revolutionary movement seeking the abolition, not reform, of a regime, and possessing extensive popular support, reaches an advanced stage, it threatens the stability of the old regime by depriving it of the obedience and cooperation of the populace. At this point, the shifting of loyalty to a new authority and the creation, or acceptance, of some type of a parallel government is a necessary next step if the movement is to prove successful. This is both a logical consequence of the cooperation which has developed among the resisters themselves, and a step taken to maximize the impact of noncooperation and defiance against the old regime. A new sovereignty thus begins to replace the established one and a new political structure evolves to claim the support and allegiance of the populace. Although this tendency may be present without conscious intent, the resisters often deliberately attempt to establish a parallel structure to advance their policies. [264] A parallel government with widespread popular support can take over the governmental functions and eventually squeeze the tottering regime out of existence. [265]

This general phenomenon has occurred in a variety of situations and is by no means a product of twentieth century revolutions. Important elements of a parallel government emerged in 1575-77, for example, during the Netherlands' struggle against the Spanish king. [266] The characteristics of parallel government often occur during struggles of national liberation (especially at the time of a declaration of independence), and in domestic revolutions against a dictatorship or social system. As Crane Brinton has pointed out: "This is at once an institution and a process; or better, a process that works through a very similar set of institutions."

When another and conflicting chain of institutions provides another and conflicting set of decisions, then you have a dual sovereignty. Within the same society, two sets of institutions, leaders, and laws demand obedience, not in one single respect, but in the whole interwoven series of actions which make up life for the average man.

. . . the legal government finds opposed to it, once the first steps in actual revolution have been taken, not merely hostile individuals and parties—this any government finds—but a rival government, better organized, better staffed, better obeyed. . . . At a given revolutionary crisis they step naturally and easily into the place of the defeated government. [267]

The outcome of a contest between rival governments in ultimate terms is usually determined by their relative ability to procure the necessary support and obedience from the populace. This contest for obedience occurred, for example, when both the Japanese and the "Border Government" were trying to rule in North China in the late 1930s:

In this extraordinary situation there is a sense in which the rival govments were concerned . . . more with the problem of creating new bases for political authority, new concepts of political obligation, new relations between government and people, than with the mere exercise of authority. [268]

Parallel government may develop in revolutions in which violence plays an important role, as well as in conflicts in which violence is noticeably absent. Although the new government may continue to use violence after its victory, the emergence of dual sovereignty and parallel government is *not* intrinsically associated with violence and in fact depends almost entirely on the voluntary withdrawal of authority, support and obedience from the old regime and their award to a new body. Dual sovereignty and parallel government may thus be classified as a method of nonviolent action and occur in revolutionary struggles in which violence is largely or entirely absent.

Professor Brinton notes that the general phenomenon occurred in England in the conflict between Charles and the Long Parliament (albeit in the context of a civil war) during the 1640s. He mentions also the struggle of the American colonists, both before and after 1776, and the rival groupings of the French Revolution. [269]

Various organs of parallel government were of extreme importance in the American colonists' struggle. The Continental Association—the program of organized nonviolent resistance adopted by the First Continental Congress in the autumn of 1774, which its authors described as "a nonimportation, non-consumption, and non-exportation agreement"[270] illustrated this development well, while parallel government found also organizational expression in a variety of alternative quasi-governmental bodies. Gipson writes:

> Although the First Continental Congress was dissolved on October 26, 1774, the measures it had adopted were held by the patriots to be nothing less than the supreme law of the land, taking precedence over any measure or pronouncement of the individual colonial assemblies, not to mention the laws of Parliament relating to America. Therefore, it was not surprising that the Association adopted by the Congress was entered into and enforced with a high degree of unanimity.[271]

The extremity of the collapse of British colonial power at least in certain colonies *before* the War of Independence is testified to by two British governors. Governor Dunmore of Virginia wrote to Lord Dartmouth on December 24, 1774, that the Continental Association was being enforced "with the greatest rigour" and that "the Laws of Congress" (i.e., the First Continental Congress) were given by Virginians "marks of reverence which they never bestowed on their legal Government, or the Laws proceeding from it." Dunmore added:

> I have discovered no instance where the interposition of Government, in the feeble state to which it is reduced, could serve any other purpose than to suffer the disgrace of a disappointment, and thereby afford matter of great exultation to its enemies and increase their influence over the minds of the people.[272]

On September 23, 1775, Governor Wright of Georgia wrote in similar but more extreme terms, complaining also of intimidation and threats of destruction of property: "Government totally Annihilated, and Assumed by Congresses, Councils and Committees, and the greatest Acts of Tyranny, Oppression, Gross Insults &c &c &c committed, and not the least means of Protection, Support, or even Personal Safety . . ." Wright added on October 14: "The poison has Infected the whole Province, and neither Law, Government, or Regular Authority have any Weight or are at all attended to."[273] In some cases existing legal organs of local or provincial government *under* the British system were turned into parts of a system of parallel government *against* the British system, and in other cases new bodies helped serve this role, representative ones (such as certain provincial assemblies and the Continental Congresses) or self-selected ones (for example, the Sons of Liberty).[274]

Usually parallel government has been but one of many methods and types of action which emerge in the course of a very large struggle. There is at least one instance, however, in which during a significant period of a struggle this method became the predominant method of action relied upon by those opposed to the established order. This was in Rhode Island in 1841-42, during what became known as "Dorr's Rebellion," or, far less accurately, as "Dorr's War." [275]

In 1841 Rhode Island's government was still operating under the Charter granted by King Charles II in 1663. Under that Charter, representation in the legislature took no account of the shifts of population and the growth of certain cities; even more seriously, built-in property qualifications for voting disenfranchised three of every five adult white males (to say nothing of anyone else). From 1796 on, repeated attempts had been made to obtain a new constitution, or reapportionment in the legislature, or an extension of the suffrage, if not to all adult white citizens, at least to a few more. All these efforts had been defeated, obstructed or ignored by the legislature or the property-owning voters (called "freemen"). In January 1841 the General Assembly passed over the call to expand the suffrage and responded favorably to an appeal for a constitutional convention—but the delegates to it were apportioned exactly like the existing General Assembly, and existing restrictions on who could vote applied also to election of the delegates. Thus two of the main grievances were built into the convention, and power was clearly intended to be kept in the same hands.

In April, May and July mass meetings of suffragists were held in Providence and Newport. At the Providence meeting on July 5 a resolution was passed demanding a constitutional convention and expressing determination to put into effect a new constitution. On July 20 it was announced that on August 28 delegates to such a convention would be elected by all adult male citizens resident in the state; the constitutional convention would meet at Providence on October 4. Over 7,500 of over 25,000 potential voters—which included resident adult male citizens whether or not franchised under the constitution—participated in the election of delegates. The new constitution—called the "People's Constitution"—was completed by the Convention in mid-November; it extended voting to all adult resident white male citizens, reapportioned representation in the General Assembly, increased the separation between the legislative and judicial branches, and made certain other changes. In December 1841, in a referendum in which all resident adult white male citizens could take part, the new constitution was ratified by a vote of nearly 14,000 to 52 (with more than 10,000 potential voters not participating).

But this was not the whole story, for another convention which had been called by the legislature in January—the "Freemen's Convention"—had also met in November; finally in mid-February 1842 it completed its new draft constitution. This also extended the suffrage to adult white male resident citizens but only reapportioned seats in the House of Representatives. A few weeks before, however, on January 12, the People's Convention had reassembled and declared its "People's Constitution" to be in force. Under attack by extremists on both sides, the "Freemen's Constitution," with the same enlarged electorate as had voted in the other referendum, was narrowly defeated by less than 700 votes of a total of about 16,700. The state Supreme Court unofficially denounced the "People's Constitution" as illegal, and in March a repressive "Algerine Law" was passed. This law imposed severe penalties, including the charge of treason, for people who participated in any elections not in accordance with previous statutes; even persons voting in elections held under the "People's Constitution" were to be punished.

Claiming popular sovereignty in a republic, the suffragists argued that their constitution was legal. Governor Samuel King of Rhode Island appealed to President Tyler, who replied on April 11 that he could not anticipate a revolutionary movement but that should an actual insurrection take place, Federal aid would be forthcoming; he also denied his right to judge on the merits of the conflict in the state, but added that he would continue to recognize the established government until advised that another had legally and peaceably been adopted by both the authorities and the people of the state.[276]

On April 18 elections were held for state offices under the "People's Constitution," including for members of both houses of the new legislature; all candidates were elected unanimously, but the leader of the movement, Harvard graduate Thomas Wilson Dorr, received only a little over 6,300 votes for governor, which did not help establish his authority. President Tyler's letter, the repressive Algerine Law, and perhaps other factors had caused many persons who were undecided to shift over to the "law and order" party. Many suffragists also weakened in their determination to go through with the new substitute constitution and government, and several of the earlier nominees of the suffragists for that election had even withdrawn.

On April 20, two days after the "People's Election," the regular election according to the regular Charter took place, and Governor King defeated his challenger, General Carpenter, who was originally to have been the candidate on the "People's ticket" by a margin of a little more than two to one. About seven thousand property-owning "freemen" had voted.

Despite the severity of the challenge by the new constitution and the elected substitute government, the established government was cautious in repressing the rival group for, as A.M. Mowry points out, they would have been acting against 180 of the state's most prominent citizens, backed by at least a large minority of the citizens of Rhode Island, over six thousand of whom had also laid themselves open to prosecution by voting in the "People's Election."[277] The Charter government was not certain that the state militia would come to its aid.[278] The situation was clearly regarded by both sides as grave, and there were signs both sides were preparing for military action.

On May 3, 1842, after Thomas Dorr and elected members of the new General Assembly paraded through the streets of Providence with a militia escort, they were inaugurated, and the Assembly received an inaugural address from Governor Dorr. The new officials, however, did not even attempt to gain access to and control of the State House, or to install a new judiciary. In his history Mowry says that it would have been "a peaceful, as well as an easy, task" to take possession of the State House, but instead of doing so the new legislature met in an empty foundry building, and after two days of action adjourned for two months. They had requested Governor Dorr to make known to the President, Houses of Congress, and governors of the states those changes which had taken place: they proclaimed the new government as duly organized, called for obedience, and repealed the Algerine Law and various other acts. Dorr later wrote that the failure to replace the old government by occupying the State House was "fatal." Mowry writes that "the old charter government had lost its force, and could accomplish little; the new charter government had yet to organize; and the charter officials were at Newport."[279]

However, on May 4, at Newport, the government elected under the old Charter met and organized, and passed a resolution against the new constitution and government under Governor Dorr; they particularly called attention to "the strong military force" supporting Dorr (the fairly small militia escort at the inauguration, which body had pledged obedience to Dorr as the state commander-in-chief). On this basis, the Charter legislature declared that an "insurrection" existed in Rhode Island and called for Federal intervention.[280]

Governor King sent a delegation to see President Tyler. Governor Dorr also sent various documents to President Tyler. Tyler, however, did not wish to intervene at the moment. On May 7, Dorr, wanted for arrest by the rival government, secretly left for Washington, D.C., to plead the case of the People's government in person, leaving his government in Rhode Island without effective leadership. During the brief stay of

Dorr and his colleagues in Washington, they scored no tangible successes with either executive or congressional officials.

In Rhode Island, within a week of the adjournment of the General Assembly under the People's Constitution, the new rival government was in a state of collapse. Arrests and resignations depleted its ranks.

There seems to have been no consideration given, either at an earlier or at this critical stage, to a campaign of noncooperation with the Charter government and persistent obedience to the People's government. Nor apparently was there any consideration of the possible negative effects that even the appearance of military action might have on many Rhode Islanders, or on Federal intervention (as President Tyler had already indicated). Instead, on his return from Washington, Governor Dorr sought support from the Democrats of Tammany Hall, and while in New York he explored the possibilities of military assistance from other states. He received offers from two commanders of regiments of New York state militia, and wrote the governors of Connecticut and Maine for military aid in case of Federal intervention. [281]

Arriving in Providence on May 16, Governor Dorr was welcomed by a crowd of about 1,200 persons, a quarter of whom were armed. The outcome of the contest was still unsettled, and even the loyalty of the militia was undetermined. There were no attempts to arrest Dorr on the sixteenth or seventeenth. Dorr then clearly shifted to military action, even if it was slightly comic. In a swift move, two field pieces were seized without a fight, but his men forgot to take the balls and shot for the cannons. The Charter government called the militia of Providence to readiness and summoned other outside companies to report to the city. Dorr determined to seize first the arsenal, then several other buildings and armories; otherwise, he thought, the whole campaign was lost.

About midnight on the seventeenth, with about 230 men and two cannons, Dorr's forces set out for the city arsenal in the midst of great confusion and a heavy fog, with many people flooding the streets, bells ringing, and uncertainty as to who was friend and who foe. When the arsenal commander refused to surrender, Dorr ordered the cannons fired, but either someone had tampered with them or the damp from the fog was as effective, and they only flashed twice but did not fire. Had they worked, and had troops in the well-armed stone arsenal returned fire, the attackers would quite probably have been annihilated. As the night went on, Dorr's volunteers melted away until by daylight not more than fifty remained. At about eight o'clock Dorr was given a letter stating that all the officers of his government who lived in Providence had resigned. Dorr was advised to flee and this he did, though later he reportedly regretted having done so. Members of the People's legislature repudiated the military actions. After a brief rally of his forces in Glocester late in June, Dorr escaped to New Hampshire.

While the tide of reaction was still strong, a new constitutional convention for Rhode Island was assembled that November. The Charter General Assembly authorized increased representation for Providence and Smithfield, and permitted all native-born adult male citizens to vote for delegates. The new constitution, with limited reapportionment, and a somewhat expanded but complicated system of suffrage rights, was adopted in November and went into effect in May 1843. Dorr's supporters boycotted the referendum, while many diehard supporters of the Charter opposed the constitution as too liberal. About 7,000 men, of a voters' list of over 25,000, voted in the referendum. Dorr returned to Providence to surrender in October 1843 and was sentenced to life imprisonment. After one year the new governor signed a bill releasing him, and in 1851 the General Assembly restored his civil and political rights. Despite the state Supreme Court's protest, the General Assembly in 1854 reversed his conviction for treason.

From the perspective of nonviolent action, this case illustrates the deliberate development of a parallel government by popular assembly and referendum and also its initial operation, although the events do not show how the later struggle might have been conducted nonviolently. The introduction of military action to defend the new constitution and government, and Dorr's appeals for Federal support, seem to have been remarkably ineffective. The events even suggest that the threat and use of military action were counterproductive. They may have caused those people who were wavering in loyalty to support the Charter government, and may also have caused even existing supporters of the People's government to withdraw, leaving it still weaker.

Some other very clear examples of parallel government occur in the Russian 1905 Revolution and in the 1917 Russian Revolution prior to the Bolshevik seizure of power from both the Provisional Government and the independent *soviets*. [282] The most famous such organ of the 1905 Revolution was the Council of Workingmen's Deputies of St. Petersburg, "at once general strike Committee, communal administration, organizer of nationwide revolt, temporary parliament of labor in particular and the Russian people in general, rival governmental power." [283]

For the St. Petersburg Soviet had astonishingly maintained itself as in some sort a rival authority to the government. It was to the soviet that the working population turned for advice or aid in the chaotic conditions in the capital; it was the soviet which gave instructions in the workers' quarters. Its executive committee negotiated directly with Prime Minister Witte on problems of transport and food supplies. The government's orders to the postal and telegraph workers could be issued only through the soviet. Even the city duma was obliged to carry out the instructions of the soviet, most conspicuously in allocating funds for the relief of the strikers' families.

For the time being at least the government could not but acquiesce. But so paralysing a form of dual power in the capital could not continue indefinitely.[284]

On trial for his role in the revolution, Trotsky told the court that the Council of Workingmen's Deputies "was neither more nor less than the self-governing organ of the revolutionary masses, *an organ of state power . . .*"[285]

This was by no means the only expression of parallel government during that revolution, however, as the Bureau of *Zemstvo* Congresses also exercised considerable authority at one time.[286] Entire districts established their own administrations independent of the central government,[287] especially certain nationalities as happened in Georgia, where the parallel government was maintained into 1906,[288] and the Mongol government which was elected and obeyed for some months toward the end of 1905.[289] Prior to these events, Marxist thought had given relatively little attention to this method as a means of carrying out a revolution, despite an early comment by Marx[290] and some significant discussion by the Menshevik Axélrod just prior to the 1905 revolution.[291]

Strong tendencies to develop alternative sovereignty and parallel government have emerged, unanticipated and unplanned, during large-scale nonviolent struggles, such as Western general strikes and Indian independence movements. Hiller, for example, noted the development of control organizations among strikers and wrote:

> Control organizations, whether representing attempts to assert authority and enforce it by physical coercion or to "maintain order" while practicing economic non-participation, constitute usurpation of governmental functions. For example, the enrolling of an independent police force responsible to an upstart authority is a revolutionary act, and, if community-wide and permanent, constitutes an actual revolution. It signifies a new integration of society around the competing center of dominance in the social body.[292]

Crook points out that during the 1919 general strike in Winnipeg, Canada, a citizens' committee of one thousand ran the fire, water and police services, which is evidence that it had some of the qualities of a parallel government.[293] Hiller cites further examples of this kind of development during the general strikes in Seattle and the Italian general strike of 1904.[294]

Although the British General Strike of 1926 was not intended or pursued as a revolutionary strike for overthrowing the government, W.H. Crook concludes that:

> There can be just as little question that the *orders* of the General Council, as interpreted by the various strike committees throughout the nation and as put into practice by them, did logically constitute an attempt to set up a rival authority to that of the local and national governing bodies. This is particularly evident in the matter of *permits*. The General Council had apparently intended that the workers themselves should carry on, if not actually organize, the distribution of food and absolute essentials of life . . . . The Government, through Mr. Churchill, had tendered an emphatic refusal to enter "into partnership with a rival Government."[295]

The nascent forms of a parallel government were nearly or actually reached on several occasions in local situations during the Indian struggles, especially the 1930–31 campaign. In late April 1930, after the refusal of two platoons of the Garhwali Regiment to support the police against the nonviolent volunteers, troops were removed from Peshawar city completely. The Congress Committee then assumed virtual control of the city, including issuing instructions and patrolling the streets at night, for nine days. A contemporary British report also described the success of the local Muslim nonviolence organization, the Khudai Khidmatgar, in collecting land revenue owed to the government.[296] The authority of the old *panchayats* was restored in many places to replace the British judicial system. A program of "national education" was intended to replace the British schools.[297] In some cities volunteer corps were organized to direct traffic and to act as policemen. The Bombay Congress Committee worked out its own system of taxation for those citizens who would cooperate, and in a few instances even fined financial interests when they diverged from Congress policies.

Speaking of Bombay during the early period of the 1930 struggle, an eyewitness, H.N. Brailsford, wrote:

Bombay, one soon perceived, had two governments. To the British Government, with all its apparatus of legality and power, there still were loyal the European population, the Indian sepoys who wore its uniform, and the elder generation of the Moslem minority. The rest of Bombay had transferred its allegiance to one of His Majesty's too numerous prisoners. In Mahatma Gandhi's name Congress ruled this city. Its lightest nod was obeyed. It could fill the streets, when it pleased, and as often as it pleased, with tens of thousands of men and women, who shouted its watchwords. It could with a word close the shutters of every shop in the bazaar. When it proclaimed a *hartal* (a day of mourning), which it did all but every week, by way of protest against some act of the other government, silence descended upon the streets, and even the factories closed their doors. Only with its printed permit on a scrap of coloured paper, dare a driver urge his bullocks and his bales past its uniformed sentries, who kept watch, day and night, in every lane and alley of the business quarter. They had their guardrooms. Their inspectors entered every warehouse and shop, and watched every cotton-press. They would even confiscate forbidden goods, which a merchant had tried to smuggle past their patrols.[298]

At such points the program of building alternative institutions may culminate in a major challenge to the existence of the old institutions. In Gandhi's view this did not necessarily mean violence, for he repeatedly emphasized that any parallel government ought not rely on the usual governmental coercive powers but upon strictly nonviolent methods and popular support of the populace.[299]

In the relative absence of theoretical foundations and studies of the strategic role of parallel government in nonviolent struggle, these various developments may be highly significant. Parallel government in the context of nonviolent struggle may point to a type of institutional change which differs sharply from the *coup d'etat* on the one hand and the abortive collapse of the resistance movement on the other.

CONCLUSION

Any future revision of the listing in these past six chapters is certain to lead to considerable expansion. This listing itself has increased by one quarter since the 1968 version, and that had more than doubled in length since the author's first version, prepared in 1960;[300] the latter was itself vastly longer than any previous integrated list.[301] Future research should also produce further examples of the listed methods, which would make the illustrations more representative historically, geographically and politically.

These methods have all occurred spontaneously, or have been consciously invented, to meet the needs of an immediate conflict situation. They have then spread by imitation, perhaps being modified in the process to suit new circumstances. To my knowledge, however, no one has tried to compile as many *new,* previously unused, methods as possible which conceivably could be applied in future conflicts. This task is a logical next step in the conscious development of the technique of nonviolent action which has now begun. It may be particularly important in the possible extension of its applicability to new political situations and conditions.

These six chapters, which have examined minutely many specific methods at the disposal of the practitioner of nonviolent action, present a one-sided and somewhat static view of the conflict situation in which (at least) one side is using this technique. These many methods can be viewed as limited implementations of the theory of power presented in Chapter One —that all governments and hierarchical systems depend on the obedience, assistance and cooperation of the people which they rule and that these people have the capacity of limiting or withholding their contributions and obedience to the system. According to that theory, if the withholding is undertaken by enough people for a long enough period of time, then the regime will have to come to terms or it will be collapsed.

But of course only very rarely, if ever, do governments and other hierarchical systems face the extreme alternatives of complete support or none. Most frequently they receive partial support. Even when, in the end, the regime is destroyed by disobedience, noncooperation and defiance, this may follow only after a severe struggle in which the regime was supported sufficiently and long enough to inflict brutal repression against the nonviolent actionists. The simple enumeration of specific methods of this technique and exploration of their characteristics and application give less than one side of this picture. This is so because even that does not explore the psychological forces which may operate in these conflict situations nor does it take into consideration the extreme and often quick shifts in power relations which occur between the contesting groups.

Except for an introductory discussion in Chapter Two, what has been missing thus far in our examination of the basic nature and characteristics of the technique of nonviolent action has been an exploration of how it operates in struggle against a violent opponent and the several ways in which changes are finally produced. That is, we have not yet examined the technique's dynamics in struggle, its mechanisms of change, the specific factors which determine whether a given campaign will be a success or a failure or something in between. It is to these vital aspects of our subject which we now turn: how does nonviolent action work in struggle?

NOTES

1. Ch'ien Yung, *Li-yüan ts'ung hua*, chapt. 1, p. 11a-11b. I am grateful to Professor Wolfram Eberhard for both the example and the translation from the original Chinese text.
2. Personal letter, 19 November 1966.
3. Leon Trotsky, **My Life** (New York: Grosset & Dunlap, Universal Library, 1960), p. 25.
4. *Peace News*, 4 and 25 May, 24 August, 26 October and 14 December 1962, and 4 January, 29 March and 20 December 1963. For a Canadian example, see *ibid.*, 15 June 1962.
5. Whitley Stokes, ed., **Tripartite Life of St. Patrick** (London: H.M. Stationary Office, by Eyre and Spottiswoode, 1887), CLXXVII, pp. 219, 417 and 419.
6. Gipson, **The British Empire Before the American Revolution**, vol. XII, **The Triumphant Empire, Britain Sails into the Storm, 1770-1776**, pp. 240-241.
7. Paul Leicester Ford, ed., **The Works of Thomas Jefferson**, vol. II, pp. 9-10.
8. *Ibid.*, p. 10, n. 1.
9. B. O. Flower, "Jefferson's Service to Civilization During Founding of the Republic," in Andrew A. Lipscome, editor-in-chief, **The Writings of Thomas Jefferson** (Washington, D.C.: The Thomas Jefferson Memorial Association of the United States, 1903), vol. VII, p. vii.
10. Ford, ed., **The Works of Thomas Jefferson**, vol. II, pp. 10-11.
11. *Ibid.*, p. 11. n. 1.
12. Flower, "Jefferson's Service to Civilization During the Founding of the Republic," p. viii.
13. Ford, ed., **The Works of Thomas Jefferson**, vol. II, p. 12.
14. Gipson, **The British Empire . . .** , vol. XII, p. 233.
15. *Ibid.*, pp. 316-317 and Trevelyan, **The American Revolution** (New York: Longmans, Green & Co., 1908), p. 277.
16. *Peace News*, 20 April 1962.
17. *Ibid.*, 8 and 15 June 1962.
18. Giovanni Pioli, *Peace News*, 16 March 1956 and Mary Taylor, ed., **Community Development in Western Sicily** (duplicated; *Partinico: Centro studi e iniziative*

per la piena occupazione, 1963), pp. 5-6.

19. Helen Mayer, *Peace News,* 4 February 1966.
20. Hanh, "Love in Action," p. 12.
21. Patrick Joyce, **A Social History of Ancient Ireland** (London: Longmans, Green, 1903) vol. I, pp. 204-205.
22. Shridharani, **War Without Violence** (U.S. ed.: pp. 19-20; Br. ed.: p. 85.)
23. Seton-Watson, **The Decline of Imperial Russia,** pp. 68-69.
24. Prawdin, **The Unmentionable Nechaev,** p. 102.
25. P. Kropotkine (sic), **In Russian and French Prisons** (London: Ward and Downey, 1887), p. 76.
26. *Ibid.,* p. 101.
27. Issac Deutscher, **The Prophet Armed: Trotsky: 1879-1921** (New York and London: Oxford University Press, 1963), pp. 40-41.
28. Schapiro, **The Origin of the Communist Autocracy,** p. 205. See also I.N. Steinberg, **In the Workshop of the Revolution** (New York: Rhinehart & Co., 1953), pp. 167-172. (Cited by Miller, **Nonviolence,** pp. 174-175.)
29. Paul Barton, "The Strike Mechanism in Soviet Concentration Camps," in *Monthly Information Bulletin,* International Commission Against Concentration Camp Practices, no. 4, (Aug.-Nov., 1955) pp. 25-26.
30. Holt, **Protest in Arms,** p. 145. I am grateful to William Hamilton for this and certain other examples.
31. Bernard, **Social Control in its Sociological Aspects,** pp. 396-397; and S.K. Ratcliffe, "Hunger Strike," **Encyclopedia of the Social Sciences** (New York: Macmillan, 1935), vol. VII, pp. 532-533.
32. *Ibid.,* pp. 206-07.
33. Ratcliffe, "Hunger Strike," p. 533.
34. Mulford Sibley and Asa Wardlaw, "Conscientious Objectors in Prison," p. 304, in Lynd, ed., **Nonviolence in America.**
35. *The Times,* 2 May 1958.
36. *Observer,* 9 August 1959.
37. Louis Fischer, **The Life of Mahatma Gandhi,** (New York: Harpers, 1950), pp. 154-157 and Erik Erikson, **Gandhi's Truth: On the Origins of Militant Nonviolence** (New York: W.W. Norton & Co., 1969), pp. 255-392.
38. Sharp, **Gandhi Wields the Weapon of Moral Power,** pp. 227-289.
39. Venturi, **Roots of Revolution,** pp. 585-590.
40. Louis Fischer, **The Life of Mahatma Gandhi** (New York: Harpers, 1950), p. 203.
41. Sternstein, "The *Ruhrkampf* of 1923," p. 114.
42. Bullock, **Hitler,** p. 117.
43. Delarue, **The Gestapo,** pp. 38-39.
44. Mabee, **Black Freedom,** p. 301.
45. *Ibid.,* p. 302.
46. *Ibid.*
47. *Ibid.,* pp. 303-304.
48. *Ibid.,* p. 204. See also p. 311.
49. *Ibid.,* p. 115.
50. *Ibid.*

51. *Ibid.*, pp. 115-116.
52. From the account of a "Colored Old Settler," quoted by St. Clair Drake and Horace R. Cayton, **Black Metropolis: A Study of Negro Life in a Northern City** (New York: Harcourt, Brace, 1945), p. 44.
53. DeMarco, "The Use of Non-violent Direct Action Tactics and Strategy by American Indians,". MS. p. 6; her source is John R. Covert, "Indians Win Sit-Down Strike," *Philadelphia Evening Bulletin,* 19 April 1938.
54. DeMarco, *ibid.,* pp. 14-15. Her sources are the *Philadelphia Bulletin,* 7 September 1960 and the *New York Times,* 1 September 1961, p. 18.
55. See George Houser, **Erasing the Color Line** (Rev. ed., pamphlet; New York: Congress of Racial Equality, 1948); Farmer, **Freedom—When?**, pp. 61-62; and Peck, **Freedom Ride**, pp. 45-50, for descriptions of the 1942 Chicago restaurant sit-in—probably the first of its kind.
56. Patrick O'Donovan, *Observer,* 20 March 1960; and Jim Peck, *Peace News,* 4 March 1960. Merrill Proudfoot's **Diary of a Sit-in** (Chapel Hill, N.C.: University of North Carolina Press, 1962) contains a detailed account—from a religious perspective—of the campaign for the integration of lunch counters in Knoxville, Tennessee in July 1960. See also C. Eric Lincoln, "The Sit-in Comes to Atlanta," in Westin, ed., **Freedom Now**, pp. 259-265. On other cases see Peck, **Freedom Ride**, pp. 73-79 and 82-88.
57. Claude Sitton, "A Chronology of the New Civil-Rights Protest, 1960-1963," in Westin, ed., **Freedom Now**, p. 81.
58. Peck, **Freedom Ride**, p. 89.
59. *Peace News,* 11 December 1964.
60. *New York Times,* 10 and 12 November 1966.
61. Hentoff, **The New Equality**, p. 204.
62. Waskow, **From Race Riot to Sit-in**, pp. 267-275.
63. *Ibid.*, pp. 243-244.
64. *Peace News,* 3 April 1964.
65. James Peck, **Freedom Ride**, pp. 23-29. For another case see p. 44.
66. *Ibid.*, pp. 34-35.
67. Mabee, **Black Freedom**, pp. 127-38.
68. *Ibid.*, pp. 112-13.
69. *Ibid.*, p. 112.
70. *Ibid.*, p. 114.
71. *Ibid.*, p. 115.
72. *Ibid.*, p. 121.
73. *Ibid.*, p. 122.
74. *Ibid.*, pp. 123-24.
75. *Ibid.*, p. 125.
76. *Ibid.*, p. 126.
77. *Ibid.*, pp. 202-203.
78. Westin, "Ride-in's and Sit-in's of the 1870's," in Westin, ed., **Freedom Now**, pp. 69-70.
79. For an account, see Peck, **Freedom Ride**, pp. 14-27.
80. Lomax, **The Negro Revolt**, pp. 145-156, Miller, **Nonviolence**, pp. 313-316, and Peck, **Freedom Ride**.

81. *New York Times*, 9, 16, 23 and 24 July 1961
82. This section is based on a draft by Michael Schulter.
83. **Criterion,** November 1969, p. 4.
84. *Ibid.*, p. 1.
85. Mabee, **Black Freedom,** p. 128.
86. *Ibid.*, pp. 128-130.
87. Peck, **Freedom Ride,** p. 98.
88. Anthony Lewis and *The New York Times,* **Portrait of a Decade: The Second American Revolution** (New York: Random House, 1964) p. 177.
89. Sharp, **Gandhi Wields . . .** , p. 177 and Shridharani, **War Without Violence,** U.S. ed., pp. 41-42; Br. ed., p. 57.
90. Sharp, **Gandhi Wields . . .** , pp. 132-151.
91. Schlesinger, **The Colonial Merchants and the American Revolution,** p. 176.
92. This section, and the Vietnamese examples, have been suggested by Michael Schulter.
93. Goodspeed, **The Conspirators,** p. 134.
94. *Newsweek*, 2 Aug. 1965, p. 10.
95. *Ibid.*, 4 October 1965, p. 40.
96. *The Times*, 19 and 20 May and 16 June 1955.
97. *Peace News*, 22 May, 10, 17, 24 and 31 July 1959.
98. *Ibid.*, 27 November and 4 December 1959, and 2 and 15 January, and 18 March 1960.
99. *Ibid.*, 2, 9 and 23 October, 13 and 27 November, 18 and 25 December 1959, 1 and 22 January and 10 June 1960.
100. *Peace News*, 20 June 1958, and 13 and 20 July 1962.
101. This definition is based upon a terminological refinement by Bradford Lyttle, **Essays on Nonviolent Action** (mimeo; Chicago, The Author, 1959), pp. 31-32.
102. *Peace News*, 22 May 1964.
103. Shridharani, **War Without Violence,** U.S. ed. p. 21; Br. ed., p. 41.
104. Myers and Laidler, **What Do You Know About Labor?,** p. 76.
105. Waskow, **From Race Riot to Sit-in,** p. 242.
106. Belfrage, **Freedom Summer,** p. 184.
107. Mabee, **Black Freedom,** p. 307.
108. Matei Yulzari, "The Bulgarian Jews in the Resistance Movement," in Suhl, ed., **They Fought Back,** p. 277.
109. *Guardian*, 1 September 1962.
110. *Ibid.*, 3 September 1962.
111. *Peace News*, 2 July 1965.
112. *Peace News*, 1 March 1963.
113. Isobel Lindsay, *Peace News*, 29 November 1963.
114. *Peace News*, 12 April 1963.
115. Sharp, **Gandhi Wields . . .** , pp. 166-167.
116. Lyttle, **Essays on Non-violent Action,** p. 34, and *Peace News*, 22 and 29 August 1958.
117. *The Times*, 8 December 1958, *Manchester Guardian*, 8 December 1958,

Observer, 21 December 1958, *The Times*, 22 December 1958 and *Manchester Guardian*, 22 December 1958.

118. This account is based on student paper by Margaret DeMarco, "The Use of Non-violent Direct Action Tactics and Strategy by American Indians," MS. pp. 15-17. Her sources are Edmund Wilson, **Apologies to the Iroquois** (New York: Farrar, Straus and Cudahy, 1960), the quotation being from p. 143, and the *Philadelphia Evening Bulletin*, 7 May 1958.

119. Benjamin Muse, **The American Negro Revolution: From Nonviolence to Black Power 1963-1967** (Bloomington and London: Indiana University Press, 1968), pp. 111-12.

120. Friedman, "Jewish Resistance to Nazism," in **European Resistance Movements**, p. 204.

121. Brant, **The East German Rising**, pp. 111-112.

122. Lyttle, **Essays on Non-violent Action**, p. 32.

123. Mabee, **Black Freedom**, pp. 300-301.

124. *Daily Mirror* (London), 7 December 1956.

125. *Peace News*, 26 October 1956 and 1 March 1957.

126. Peter Kihss, "Blockades in New York," in Westin, ed., **Freedom Now**, pp. 275-276.

127. Waskow, **From Race Riot to Sit-in**, p. 279.

128. John Morris, "Early Christian Civil Disobedience," in *Peace News*, 5 January 1962. This article contains a translation of Ambrose's letter to his sister describing the events.

129. Bondurant, **Conquest of Violence**, p. 57 and Desai, **The Story of Bardoli**, pp. 172 and 186.

130. *New York Times*, 17 August 1957, p. 17. This account is based on Margaret DeMarco's unpublished paper, "The Use of Non-violent Direct Action Tactics and Strategy by American Indians," MS. pp. 7-8.

131. This account has been prepared by Katherine Preston. For some coverage of the occupation at Alcatraz consult **Akwesasne Notes**, a resume of Indian affairs available from Mohawk Nation, via Roosevelttown, New York, 13683, and also **The Warpath**, published by the United Native Americans, Inc., P. O. Box 26149, San Francisco, California, 94126. Details of final removal are from *New York Times*, 14 June 1971.

132. Littell, ed., **The Czech Black Book**, p. 142.

133. *Ibid.*, pp. 147-48. See also pp. 164, 198, 204, 208, 223, 224 and 249.

134. Mabee, **Black Freedom**, pp. 91-92.

135. *Ibid.*, p. 93.

136. *Ibid.*, pp. 93-94.

137. *Ibid.*, p. 104.

138. *Ibid.*, p. 105.

139. *Ibid.*, p. 104.

140. *Ibid.*, p. 106.

141. *Ibid.*, pp. 107-09.

142. *Ibid.*, pp. 95-97.

143. G. S. Rao, **Gora—An Atheist** (Vijayawada, India: Atheistic Centre, 1970), pp. 4, 13-14, and 16; and personal conversations with Lavanam, one of the sons, in

1968, and Gora himself in 1970.

144. James Q. Wilson, "The Negro in Politics," in *Daedalus*, vol. 94, no. 4 (Fall, 1965), p. 973, n. 29. No other details are given.

145. This account has been drafted by Ronald McCarthy on the basis of reports in the *Boston Globe*, 16-19 May 1967. The quotations are respectively from the following issues: 16 May (morn. edition), 16 May (eve. ed.), 16 May (morn. ed.), *ibid.*, 18 May (eve. ed.), and 16 May (eve. ed.).

146. Shimbori, "Zengakuren", in *Sociology of Education*, vol. 37, no. 3 (Spring 1964), p. 247.

147. Michael Parkhouse, *Peace News*, 10 July 1964.

148. Botemps, **100 Years of Negro Freedom**, p. 254.

149. This section is based on a draft prepared by Michael Schulter.

150. John L. Nickalls, ed., **The Journal of George Fox** (Cambridge: [Cambridge] University Press, 1952), pp. 39-40.

151. *Ibid.*, p. 76.

152. *Ibid.*, p. 98.

153. Mabee, **Black Freedom**, p. 205.

154. *Ibid.*, p. 208.

155. This section is based on a draft by Michael Schulter.

156. Jerry Rubin, **Do It!** (New York: Simon and Schuster, 1970), pp. 133-135.

157. *Ibid.*, pp. 117-118.

158. Griffith, **The Resurrection of Hungary**, pp. xx, xxvi-xxvii, 7 and 170.

159. *Ibid.*, pp. 139-163.

160. Gandhi, **The Constructive Programme**.

161. Mabee, **Black Freedom**, pp. 127 and 133-135.

162. *Ibid.*, p. 140.

163. *Ibid.*, pp. 139-142. See also p. 149.

164. Karski, **The Story of a Secret State**, pp. 304-305 and 308.

165. Muse, **Virginia's Massive Resistance**, pp. 8, 15, 76-79, 111-118, and 148-159.

166. This section has been suggested by Michael Schulter.

167. Warmbrunn, **The Dutch Under the German Occupation 1940-1945**, pp. 221-258. The quotation is from p. 244.

168. My earlier drafts of discussions of nonviolent intervention did not include economic intervention as a distinct class within it. A student and friend at Harvard, Robert Reitherman, argued that this was unfortunate, and produced an independent study paper, "Nonviolent Economic 'Intervention' ", 15 pp., in March 1970, which was convincing.

169. Pioli, *Peace News*, 16 March 1956.

170. Farmer, **Freedom—When?** p. 105. No date is given for this example.

171. Littell, ed., **The Czech Black Book**, pp. 162 and 191. CKD, as it is now known under State ownership, was originally founded as a private firm *českomolavska-Kolben-Daněk*.

172. *Peace News*, 20 April 1956.

173. Peterson, **American Labor Unions**, p. 30, and Knowles, **Strikes**, pp. 10-11.

174. For further discussion of the sit-down strike, see Ligt, **The Conquest of Violence**, pp. 144 and 167; Edward Levinson, "Sit-down Strike," in E. Wight

Bakke and Charles Kerr, **Unions, Management and the Public** (New York: Harcourt and Brace, 1948), pp. 410-412; Coleman, **Men and Coal**, p. 164; Howe and Widick, **The U.A.W. and Walter Reuther**, pp. 47-65; Herbert Harris, **American Labor** (New Haven: Yale University Press, 1938); Peterson, **American Labor Unions**, pp. 222-225 and 268.

175. Joseph G. Rayback, **A History of American Labor**, p. 353.

176. Peterson, **American Labor Unions**, p. 223.

177. Peterson, **American Labor Unions**, p. 217 and *Newsweek*, vol. VII, no. 13 (28 March 1936), pp. 13-14.

178. Rayback, **A History of American Labor**, p. 353.

179. Levinson, "Sit-Down Strike," p. 410.

180. *Ibid.*

181. Rayback, **A History of American Labor**, p. 355 and Solomon Barkin, "Labor Unions and Workers' Rights in Jobs," p. 127, in Arthur Kornhauser, Robert Dubin and Arthur M. Ross, eds., **Industrial Conflict** (New York: McGraw-Hill, 1954) and references cited in n. 92.

182. Harris, **American Labor**, p. 294.

183. Ligt, **The Conquest of Violence**, p. 144.

184. Peterson, **American Labor Unions**, p. 223.

185. *Observer*, 6 September 1959.

186. *Ibid.*, 13 March 1960.

187. Quoted by Theodor Ebert, "Nonviolent Resistance Against Communist Regimes?" in Roberts, ed., **Civilian Resistance as a National Defence**, p. 193; Br. ed.: **The Strategy of Civilian Defence**, p. 193.

188. Rainer Hildebrandt, *Was lehrte der 17 Juni*, p. 7 (Berlin: the author, 1954), quoted by Ebert, *op. cit.*, p. 193.

189. Christopher Seton-Watson, **Italy From Liberalism to Fascism 1870-1925** (New York: Barnes and Noble, 1967, and London: Methuen, 1967), p. 521.

190. *Ibid.*, p. 522.

191. Miguel Urrutia, **The Development of the Colombian Labor Movement** (New Haven and London: Yale University Press, 1969), pp. 130-131. On the Viotá case, Urrutia cites José Gutiérrez, *LaReveldia Colombiana* (Bogotá: Tercer Mundo, 1962), pp. 83-96. From Urrutia's account it is difficult to determine the extent of violence in this case as his conception of violence (p. 128) includes the general strike and the "sit-in strike."

192. Samuel Huntington writes that Colombia's agrarian reform law of the 1930s was "primarily designed to legitimize peasant land seizures which had already occurred." Samuel P. Huntington, **Political Order in Changing Societies** (New Haven and London: Yale University Press, 1968), p. 393. See also p. 358.

193. Urrutia, **The Development of the Colombian Labor Movement**, p. 135.

194. *Ibid.*, p. 133.

195. Eduardo Arze-Loureiro, "The Process of Agrarian Reform in Bolivia, in T. Lynn Smith, ed., **Agrarian Reform in Latin America** (New York: Alfred A. Knopf, 1965), p. 133.

196. *Ibid.*, p. 136.

197. *Ibid.*

198. Huntington, **Political Order in Changing Societies**, p. 393.

199. John Gerassi, **Great Fear in Latin America** (New York: Collier, 1965), p. 139. I am grateful to Bob Reitherman for this reference.

200. Doreen Warriner, **Land Reform in Principle and Practice** (Oxford: Clarendon Press, 1969), p. 259. I am grateful to Jeffrey B. Peters for these references, and for encouraging the expansion of the discussion of nonviolent land seizures.

201. *Ibid.*, p. 353.

202. *Ibid.*, p. 351.

203. *Ibid.*, p. 289.

204. *Ibid.*, p. 290.

205. *Ibid.*, pp. 290-291.

206. This method has been suggested by Michael Schulter.

207. W. Phillips Davidson, **The Berlin Blockade** (Princeton, N.J.; Princeton University Press, 1958), p. 196.

208. *Ibid.*, p. 261.

209. Thomas C. Schelling, **International Economics**, p. 488.

210. Murray Teigh Bloom, "The World's Greatest Counterfeiters," *Harpers Magazine*, vol. 240, no. 1436 (July 1957), p. 47.

211. *Ibid.*

212. *Ibid.*, pp. 50-52.

213. Schelling, **International Economics**, p. 488.

214. *Ibid.*, p. 489.

215. *Ibid.*, p. 488.

216. Bailey, **A Diplomatic History of the American People**, p. 734.

217. Schelling, **International Economics**, pp. 488-489.

218. Nirumand, **Iran**, p. 55.

219. Schelling, **International Economics**, p. 488.

220. *Ibid.*, p. 489.

221. St. Clair Drake, "Negro Americans and the Africa Interest," in John P. Davis, **The American Negro Reference Book** (Englewood Cliffs, N.J.: Prentice-Hall, Inc., 1966), p. 675, n. 23. I am grateful to Robert Reitherman for this reference.

222. Mabee, **Black Freedom**, p. 99.

223. Morgan and Morgan, **The Stamp Act Crisis**, pp. 49-50; and Gipson, **The British Empire Before the American Revolution**, vol. X, **The Triumphant Empire: Thunder-Clouds Gather in the West, 1763-1766**, p. 361.

224. Gipson, *op. cit.*, p. 363.

225. Schlesinger, **The Colonial Merchants . . .** , p. 77.

226. See M. K. Gandhi, **Economics of Khadi** (Ahmedabad, India: Navajivan, 1941), esp. pp. 3-20, 26-29, 108-109, and 369-372; and Bondurant, **Conquest of Violence**, pp. 106-107, 126-127, and 180.

227. Myers and Laidler, **What Do You Know About Labor**?, p. 186.

228. Dale Yoder, **Labor Economics and Labor Problems** (New York and London: McGraw-Hill Co., 1939), p. 509.

229. *Ibid.*, pp. 309-310.

230. Myers and Laidler, **What Do You Know About Labor**?, pp. 32 and 187n.

231. This section is based on a draft by Michael Schulter.

232. A.K. Jameson, **A New Way In Norway** (pamphlet; London: *Peace News*, 1946 or 1947 [?]; also quoted in Mulford Q. Sibley ed., **The Quiet Battle** (Boston: Beacon Press, 1968), pp. 168-169.

233. Professor Erling Petersen, *"Økonomiske Forhold,"* in Steen, gen. ed., **Norges Krig**, vol. III, pp. 524-26.

234. King, **Stride Towards Freedom**, pp. 69-74 and 151-154.

235. This section draws heavily on Bob Reitherman's unpublished student independent study paper "Nonviolent Economic 'Intervention'," Harvard University, March 1970.

236. Wilfred Fleischer, **Sweden: The Welfare State** (New York: John Day, 1956), p. 76.

237. *Ibid.*

238. Seton-Watson, **Italy: From Liberalism to Fascism**, pp. 228-29 and 302.

239. Michael Miles, "Black Cooperatives," *New Republic*, vol. 159, no. 2 (21 September 1968), p. 22.

240. Art Goldberg, "Negro Self-Help," *New Republic*, vol. 156, no. 239 (10 June 1967), pp. 21-23.

241. This section is based on suggestions by Robin Remington and Michael Schulter.

242. *New York Times*, 3 March 1970, I am grateful to Robin Remington for this reference.

243. Interview with Colonel Paul Feeney, *Record American* (Boston), 27 June 1970.

244. This section is based on a proposal by Michael Schulter.

245. Mabee, **Black Freedom**, pp. 302-303.

246. *New York Times*, 13 August 1969, p. 39.

247. Sharp, **Tyranny Could Not Quell Them.**

248. Letter from H.B. Chipembere to M.W.K. Chiume, Appendix I, p. 145, **Report of the Nyasaland Commission of Inquiry.** See also p. 53.

249. *Peace News*, 6 May 1960.

250. Farmer, **Freedom—When?**, pp. 70-72.

251. Peck, **Freedom Ride**, p. 94.

252. Miller, **Nonviolence**, p. 280.

253. *Peace News*, 16 February 1962.

254. *Ibid.*, 6 March 1964.

255. Gandhi, **Non-violent Resistance**, p. 265; Ind. ed., *Satyagraha*, p. 265.

256. Sharp, **Gandhi Wields . . . ,** pp. 152, 182, and 187-189.

257. Theodor Ebert, "Organization in Civilian Defence," in Roberts, ed., **Civilian Resistance as a National Defence**, p. 258; **The Strategy of Civilian Defence**, p. 258.

258. *Ibid.*, p. 262

259. *Ibid.*, pp. 260-261.

260. Warmbrunn, **The Dutch . . . ,** p. 121.

261. *Ibid.*, p. 298. n. 4.

262. *Ibid.*, pp. 121-122.

263. Sharp, **Tyranny Could Not Quell Them**.

264. Bernard, **Social Control . . . ,** pp. 126 and 186.

265. Shridharani, **War Without Violence**, U.S. ed., p. 42; Br. ed., p. 58.

266. Geyl, **The Revolt of the Netherlands 1555-1609**, pp. 138-139, 147-148, and 154.

267. Crane Brinton, **The Anatomy of Revolution**, pp. 139-141.

268. Taylor, **The Struggle for North China**, p. 199.

269. Brinton, **The Anatomy of Revolution**, pp. 142-143.

270. The full text is published in Schlesinger, **The Colonial Merchants . . .** , pp. 607-613.

271. Gipson, **The British Empire . . .** , vol. XII, p. 313.

272. Schlesinger, **The Colonial Merchants . . .** , p. 519.

273. *Ibid.*, pp. 551-552.

274. See *ibid.*, p. 136, 148-149, 428, 435-436, 452, 483-484, 494, 505, 509, 519, 522-523, 528-529, 549, 551, 563, and 580-581; Trevelyan, **The American Revolution**, pp. 270-271; Gipson, **The Coming of the American Revolution**, pp. 103, 180-181, 203, 222-223, and 228-230; Gipson, **The British Empire Before the American Revolution**, vol. XI, **The Triumphant Empire, The Rumbling of the Coming Storm 1766-1770**, p. 513; and *ibid.*, vol. XII, pp. 157, 160, 216-217, 222, 313, 315-316, 324 and 349.

275. I am grateful to Dennis Brady for calling my attention to this case. This account is based primarily on Irving Berdine Richman, **Rhode Island: A Study in Separatism** (Boston and New York: Houghton Mifflin Co., 1905), pp. 285-307, and Arthur May Mowry, **The Dorr War or The Constitutional Struggle in Rhode Island** (Providence, R.I.: Preston & Rounds, 1901), pp. 98-198 and 286-306, and also on Peter J. Coleman, **The Transformation of Rhode Island 1790-1860** (Providence, R.I.: American History Research Center, Brown University Press, 1963), pp. 255-294. See also, e.g., Dan King, **The Life and Times of Thomas Wilson Dorr with Outlines of the Political History of Rhode Island** (Boston: the Author, 1859) and "A Rhode Islander," **Might and Right** (Providence: A.H. Stillwell, 1844). A larger literature is available.

276. Mowry, **The Dorr War**, p. 143.

277. *Ibid.*, p. 139.

278. *Ibid.*, p. 140.

279. *Ibid.*, p. 155.

280. *Ibid.*, p. 157.

281. *Ibid.*, p. 172.

282. See Charques, **The Twilight of Imperial Russia**, p. 243, Deutcher, **Stalin**, pp. 130, 134, 160-161, and 193, and Schapiro, **The Communist Party of the Soviet Union**, pp. 154, 159, 162 and 166.

283. Wolfe, **Three Who Made A Revolution**, p. 319.

284. Charques, **The Twilight . . .** , p. 134. See also Seton-Watson, **The Decline of Imperial Russia**, p. 227, and Harcave, **First Blood**, pp. 187-189, 195, 212-214 and 236.

285. Wolfe, **Three Who Made a Revolution**, p. 333.

286. Keep, **The Rise of Social Democracy in Russia**, p. 162.

287. Schapiro, **The Communist Party . . .** , p. 66.

288. Seton-Watson, **The Decline . . .** , p. 240, and Keep, **The Rise . . .** , p. 160.

289. Seton-Watson, **The Decline . . .** , p. 241.

290. Wolfe, **Three Who Made a Revolution**, p. 493.

291. Schapiro, **The Communist Party . . .** , p. 67, and Keep, **The Rise . . .**, p. 214.

292. Hiller, The Strike, p. 246.

293. Crook, "General Strike," p. 610.

294. Hiller, The Strike, pp. 244-249.

295. Crook, The General Strike, p. 402. See also Symons, The General Strike, pp. 89, 93, 118, 124-125, 138, 144, and 158-159.

296. Bondurant, Conquest of Violence, p. 137.

297. Sharp, Gandhi Wields . . . , p. 152.

298. H.N. Brailsford, Rebel India (New York: New Republic, Inc., 1931; and London: Leonard Stein [with Victor Gollancz], 1931) U.S. ed., pp. 4-5; Br. ed., p. 13.

299. See Pyarelal (Nayar), "Gandhiji Discusses Another 1942 Issue: Non-violent Technique and Parallel Government," reprinted from *Harijan*, in *The Independent* (Bombay), 25 March 1946.

300. Sharp, "The Methods of Nonviolent Resistance and Direct Action;" duplicated, 68 pp.; Oslo: Institute for Social Research, 1960). That paper contained sixty-three methods.

301. Indeed, some additional methods have already been suggested which have not been included here for one reason or another. These are: circulation of hostile rumours and jokes, the "rally" (which might possibly be classified separately from "assemblies of protest or support" and "protest meetings"), hoarding (under certain political and economic conditions), a noisy claque pro or con some cause involved in a meeting, packing a meeting with sympathizers, clogging the channels of justice (which here might be a part of "seeking imprisonment"), over-use of certain technical or mechanical (as distinct from social) facilities (as clogging a telephone switchboard with masses of calls), inviting martyrdom (if one separates the extreme forms— as daring soldiers or police to shoot one—from the general phénomenon which may occur with various methods), aesthetic display (art, music, poetry, drama) not itself containing protest but performed *in the name* of protest, subtle protest through artistic performance (as a few lines in a play). These have been suggested by John L. Sorenson while at the Defense Research Corporation; he also called my attention to several others which are included in the present classification.

Acknowledgments

Appreciation is gratefully acknowledged to the authors and publishers whose works are quoted in this volume. Complete publication details are provided in the footnotes and bibliography.

Aptheker, Herbert, *American Negro Slave Revolts.* Copyright © 1963 by International Publishers, Inc. New York: International Publishers, 1964. Permission courtesy of International Publishers, Inc.

Bailey, Thomas A., *A Diplomatic History of the American People.* Sixth edition. Copyrighted. New York: Appleton-Century-Crofts, 1958. Permission courtesy of Appleton-Century-Crofts.

Bauer, Raymond A. and Alice H. Bauer, "Day to Day Resistance to Slavery," *Journal of Negro History*, vol. XXVII, no. 4 (Oct. 1942), pp. 388-419. Copyright © 1942 by the Association for the Study of African-American Life and History, Inc. Permission courtesy The Association for the Study of African-American Life and History, Inc., and Raymond A. and Alice H. Bauer.

Blum, Robert, *The United States and China in World Affairs.* ed. by A. Doak Barnett. Copyright © 1966 by the Council on Foreign Relations. New York: McGraw-Hill (for the Council on Foreign Relations), 1966. Permission courtesy McGraw-Hill Book Co.

Bondurant, Joan V., *Conquest of Violence: The Gandhian Philosophy of*

Conflict. Copyright © 1958 by Princeton University Press. Princeton, New Jersey: Princeton University Press. London: Oxford University Press, 1958. Passages reprinted by permission of Princeton University Press.

Borton, Hugh, *Peasant Uprisings in Japan of the Tokugawa Period.* Second Edition. New York: Paragon Book Reprint Corp., 1968. First published in *The Transactions of the Asiatic Society of Japan* (Second Series), vol. XVI, 1939. Passage reprinted courtesy of Paragon Book Reprint Corp.

Brant, Stefan, *The East German Rising.* Translated and adapted by Charles Wheeler. Copyright © 1955 by Stefan Brant. New York: Frederick A. Praeger, 1957. London: Thames and Hudson, 1955. Permission courtesy of Praeger Publishers, Inc.

Brinton, Crane, *The Anatomy of Revolution.* Copyright © Prentice-Hall Inc. Englewood Cliffs, N.J. New York: Vintage Books, 1962. Passages reprinted with permission of Prentice-Hall, Inc.

Case, Clarence Marsh, *Nonviolent Coercion: A Study in Methods of Social Pressure.* Copyright 1923. New York: The Century Co., 1923. Permission courtesy of Appleton-Century-Crofts, Inc.

Charques, Richard, *Twilight of Imperial Russia.* Copyright © 1958 by Richard Charques. Fair Lawn, N. J.: Essential Books, 1959. London: Phoenix House, 1958. Permission courtesy of Dorothy Charques.

Clark, Evans, ed., *Boycotts and Peace.* New York and London: Harper & Bros., 1932. Permission courtesy Harper & Row Publishers, Inc.

Crankshaw, Edward, *Gestapo: Instrument of Tyranny.* Copyright 1956. New York: Viking Press, 1956. London: Putnam, 1956. Permission courtesy of Edward Crankshaw.

Crook, Wilfrid H., *The General Strike: A Study of Labor's Tragic Weapon in Theory and Practice.* Chapel Hill: University of North Carolina Press, 1931. Passages reprinted by permission of the Shoe String Press, Inc., present copyright owner.

Dallin, Alexander, *German Rule in Russia, 1941-1945: A Study of Occupation Policies.* Copyright 1957. New York: St. Martin's Press, 1957. London: Macmillan, 1957. Permission courtesy of St. Martin's Press and Macmillan, London and Basingstoke.

Daniels, Jonathan, *Frontiers on the Potomac.* New York: Macmillan, 1946. Permission courtesy of Brandt & Brandt.

Davison, W. Phillips, *The Berlin Blockade: A Study in Cold War Politics.* Copyright © 1958 by the Rand Corporation. Princeton, N. J.: Princeton University Press, 1958. Passage reprinted by permission of Princeton University Press.

Deanesly, Margaret, *A History of the Medieval Church, 590-1500.* London: Methuen & Co., 1965. Permission courtesy of Associated Book Publishers Ltd.

Delarue, Jacques, *The Gestapo: A History of Horror.* New York: William Morrow, 1964. Passages reprinted courtesy of Macdonald & Co. (Publishers) Ltd.

Ebert, Theodor, "Theory and Practice of Nonviolent Resistance," unpublished English translation of a doctoral thesis presented at the University of Erlangen, Germany, 1965. Permission courtesy of Theodor Ebert.

Eyck, Erich, *A History of the Weimar Republic,* Vol. I. *From the Collapse of the Empire to Hindenburg's Election.* Copyright © 1962 by the President and Fellows of Harvard College. Cambridge, Mass.: Harvard University Press, 1962. Permission courtesy of Harvard University Press.

Farmer, James, *Freedom—When?* Copyright © 1965 by the Congress of Racial Equality, Inc. New York: Random House, 1965. Permission courtesy of James Farmer and Random House.

Faulkner, William, *A Fable.* Copyright © 1950, 1954 by William Faulkner. New York: Random House, 1954. Permission courtesy of Random House, Inc.

Fogg, Richard W., "Jazz Under the Nazis," in *Music 66, "down beat's* Annual," 1966, pp. 97-99. Copyright © 1966 by *down beat,* 1966. Permission courtesy of *down beat.*

Frank, Jerome D., *Sanity and Survival: Psychological Aspects of War and Peace.* Copyright © 1967 by Jerome D. Frank. New York: Random House and Vintage Books, 1968. Permission courtesy of Jerome D. Frank.

Friedrich, Carl J., ed., *Totalitarianism.* Copyright © 1954 by President and Fellows of Harvard College. Cambridge, Mass.: Harvard University Press, 1954. Permission courtesy of Harvard University Press.

Gandhi, M. K., *An Autobiography, The Constructive Programme, Economics of Khadi, Hind Swaraj, Non-violence in Peace and War,* Two vols., *Satyagraha, Satyagraha in South Africa, Young India,* Vol. I; publication details as cited in the bibliography; Gandhi's works are copyrighted by Navajivan Trust, Ahmedabad, India, and the passages reproduced in this volume are reprinted with the permission and courtesy of Navajivan Trust.

Gipson, Lawrence Henry, *The British Empire Before the American Revolution,* vols. X, XI and XII (see Bibliography). Copyright © by Alfred A. Knopf, 1961, 1965 and 1965 respectively. New York: Alfred A. Knopf, 1961-1965. Permission courtesy of Alfred A. Knopf, Inc.

———, *The Coming of the Revolution, 1763-1775.* Copyright © 1954 by Harper and Brothers. New York and Evanston: Harper Torchbooks, 1962. Permission courtesy of Harper & Row, Publishers, Inc.

Goodspeed, D. J., *The Conspirators: A Study of the Coup d'Etat.* Copyright © 1962 by D. J. Goodspeed, 1962. New York: Viking Press, 1962. Toronto: Macmillan Co. of Canada, 1962. Permission courtesy of Viking Press and of Macmillan (London and Basingstoke).

Gopal, S., *The Viceroyalty of Lord Irwin, 1926-1931.* Copyright 1957. London: Oxford University Press, 1957. Permission courtesy of Oxford University Press.

Görlitz, Walter, ed., *The Memoirs of Field-Marshal Keitel.* Trans. by David Irving. Copyright © 1965 by William Kimber and Co., Ltd. Passages reprinted with permission of William Kimber and Co., Ltd., and Stein and Day Publishers.

Gregg, Richard B., *The Power of Nonviolence.* Second revised edition. Copyright © 1935, 1959, 1966 by Richard B. Gregg. New York: Schocken, 1966. London: James Clarke & Co., 1960. Permission courtesy Schocken Books Inc. for Richard B. Gregg.

Halberstam, David, *The Making of a Quagmire.* Copyright © 1964, 1965 by David Halberstam. New York: Random House, 1965. London: The Bodley Head, 1965. Permission courtesy of Random House.

Halperin, S. William, *Germany Tried Democracy: A Political History of the*

Reich from 1918 to 1933. Copyright © 1946 by Thomas Y. Crowell Co. Hamden, Conn. and London: Archon Books, 1963 [1946]. Used with permission of Thomas Y. Crowell Co.

Harcave, Sidney, *First Blood: The Russian Revolution of 1905.* Copyright © 1964 by The Macmillan Co. New York: Macmillan, 1964. London: Collier-Macmillan, 1964. Permission courtesy of The Macmillan Co.

Harris, Errol E., "Political Power," *Ethics,* vol.XLVIII, no. 1 (Oct. 1957), pp. 1-10. Copyright © 1957 by the University of Chicago Press. Permission courtesy of University of Chicago Press.

Hentoff, Nat, *The New Equality.* New Edition. Copyright © 1964 by Nat Hentoff. New York: Viking Press, 1965. Permission courtesy of Nat Hentoff.

Hiller, E. T., *The Strike: A Study in Collective Action.* Copyright © 1928 by University of Chicago Press. Chicago: University of Chicago Press, 1928. Permission courtesy of University of Chicago Press.

Hsiao, Kung-ch,üan, *Rural China: Imperial Control in the Nineteenth Century.* Copyright © 1960 by University of Washington Press. Seattle: University of Washington Press, 1960. Permission courtesy of University of Washington Press.

Janis, Irving L. and Daniel Katz, "The Reduction of Intergroup Hostility: Research Problems and Hypotheses," in *Journal of Conflict Resolution,* vol. III, no. 1 (March 1959), pp. 85-100. Excerpts are reprinted by permission of the present publisher, Sage Publications Co., Inc. and the authors.

Karski, Jan, *Story of a Secret State.* Boston: Houghton Mifflin, 1944. Permission courtesy Houghton Mifflin Co.

Katkov, George, *Russia 1917: The February Revolution.* Copyright © 1967 by George Katkov. New York: Harper & Row, 1967. Permission courtesy of George Katkov.

Keep, J. H. L., *The Rise of Social Democracy in Russia.* Copyright © 1963 Oxford University Press. Oxford: Clarendon Press, 1963. Permission courtesy of the Clarendon Press.

King, Martin Luther, Jr., *Stride Toward Freedom: The Montgomery Story.* Copyright © 1958 by Martin Luther King, Jr. New York: Harper & Row and Ballentine Books, 1958. London: Victor Gollancz, 1959. Permission courtesy of Harper & Row, Publishers.

———, *Why We Can't Wait.* Copyright © 1963, 1964 by Martin Luther King, Jr. New York: Signet Books of The New American Library, 1964. Permission courtesy of Harper & Row, Publishers, publishers of the hardcover edition.

Knapp, Wilfrid F., *A History of War and Peace: 1939-1965.* Copyright © 1967 by Royal Institute of International Affairs. London, New York and Toronto: Oxford University Press (issued under the auspices of the Royal Institute of International Affairs), 1967. Permission courtesy of Wilfrid F. Knapp.

Koestler, Arthur, *Reflections on Hanging.* Copyright © 1957 by The Macmillan Co. New York: Macmillan, 1967. Permission courtesy of The Macmillan Co.

Korbel, Josef, *The Communist Subversion of Czechoslovakia, 1938-1948: The Failure of Coexistence.* Copyright © 1959 by Princeton University Press, 1959. Excerpts reprinted by permission of Princeton University

Press and Oxford University Press.

Kuper, Leo, *Passive Resistance in South Africa.* New Haven, Conn.: Yale University Press, 1957. London: Jonathan Cape, 1956. Permission courtesy of Yale University Press and Leo Kuper.

Lasswell, Harold D., *Power and Personality.* Copyright © 1948 by W. W. Norton & Co., Inc. New York: W. W. Norton & Co., 1948. Permission courtesy W. W. Norton & Co., Inc.

Lenin, V. I., *Selected Works in Three Volumes.* English language translations copyrighted. New York: International Publishers, and Moscow: Progress Publishers, 1967. Passages reprinted with permission of International Publishers, Inc.

Liddell Hart, Sir Basil, *Strategy: The Indirect Approach.* Coprighted. New York: Frederick A. Praeger, 1954. London: Faber & Faber, 1954. Permission courtesy of Lady Kathleen Liddell Hart.

Littell, Robert, ed., *The Czech Black Book: Prepared by the Institute of History of the Czechoslovak Academy of Sciences.* Copyright © 1969 by Praeger Publishers, Inc., New York. New York, Washington and London: Frederick A. Praeger, 1969.

Lochner, Louis P., ed., *The Goebbels Diaries, 1942-1943.* Copyright © 1948 by the Fireside Press, Inc. Garden City, New York: Doubleday & Co., 1948. Permission courtesy of Doubleday & Co., Inc.

Loh, Robert (as told to Humphrey Evans), *Escape from Red China.* Copyright © 1962 by Robert Loh and Humphrey Evans. New York: Coward-McCann, 1962. Passages reprinted by permission of Coward, McCann and Geoghegan, Inc.

Luthuli, Albert, *Let My People Go: An Autobiography.* Copyright © 1962 by Albert Luthuli. New York: McGraw-Hill Book Co., Inc., 1962. London: Collins, 1962. Used with permission of McGraw-Hill Book Co., Inc.

Mabee, Carleton, *Black Freedom: The Nonviolent Abolitionists from 1830 Through the Civil War.* Copyright © 1970 by Carleton Mabee. New York: Macmillan, 1970. Toronto: Macmillan, 1970. London: Collier-Macmillan, 1970. Permission courtesy of The Macmillan Co.

MacIver, R. M., *The Web of Government.* Copyright © 1947, 1965 by Robert MacIver. New York: Macmillan, 1947.

Miller, William Robert, *Nonviolence: A Christian Interpretation.* Copyright © 1964 by National Board of Young Men's Christian Association. New York: Association Press, 1964. Permission courtesy of Association Press.

Morgan, Edmund S. and Helen M., *The Stamp Act Crisis: Prologue to Revolution.* New, revised edition. Copyright © 1953 by the University of North Carolina Press; Copyright © 1962 by Edmund S. Morgan. New York: Collier Books, 1963. Permission courtesy of Edmund S. Morgan, the University of North Carolina Press and the Institute of Early American History and Culture, Williamsburg.

Mosca, Gaetano, *The Ruling Class.* Introduction by Arthur Livingstone. Copyright © 1939 by McGraw-Hill. New York and London: McGraw-Hill, 1939. Permission courtesy McGraw-Hill Book Co.

Jawaharlal Nehru, *An Autobiography* (sometimes cited as *Jawaharlal Nehru. An Autobiography*). New edition. London: The Bodley Head, 1953. Excerpts quoted with permission of The Bodley Head and the John Day Company. U.S. copyright: Copyright © 1941, The John Day Company

Renewed 1968 by Indira Gandhi.

———, *Toward Freedom: The Autobiography of Jawaharlal Nehru.* Revised edition. Copyright 1941, The John Day Company, New York: John Day Co., 1942. Permission courtesy of The John Day Co., Ind., publishers.

Neumann, Franz, *Behemoth: The Structure and Practice of National Socialism, 1933-1944.* Copyright © 1942, 1944 by Oxford University Press, New York. New York: Octagon Books, 1963. Passages reprinted courtesy of Farrar, Straus & Giroux, Inc.

Neustadt, Richard E., *Presidential Power: The Politics of Leadership.* Copyright © 1960, 1964 by John Wiley & Sons, Inc. New York and London: John Wiley and Sons, 1960. Permission courtesy John Wiley & Sons, Inc.

Nicholson, Harold, *Diplomacy.* Second edition. Copyrighted 1950, 1960. London, New York and Toronto: Oxford University Press, 1960 [1950]. Permission courtesy of Oxford University Press.

Nickalls, John L., ed., *The Journals of George Fox.* Cambridge: University Press, 1952. Quotations reprinted by permission of Cambridge University Press.

Oppenheimer, Martin and George Lakey, *A Manual for Direct Action.* Copyright © 1964, 1965 by Martin Oppenheimer, George Lakey, and the Friends Peace Committee. Chicago: Quadrangle Books, 1965. Permission courtesy of Quadrangle Books.

Peace News (London), passage from issue of July 2, 1965. Permission courtesy of Peace News Ltd.

Peck, Graham, *Two Kinds of Time.* Copyright © 1950 by Graham Peck. Houghton Mifflin, 1950. Permission courtesy of Houghton Mifflin Co.

Peck, James, *Freedom Ride.* Copyright © 1962 by James Peck. New York: Simon & Schuster, 1962. Permission courtesy Simon & Schuster.

The Pentagon Papers as published by "The New York Times", Copyright © 1971 by The New York Times Company. New York, Toronto and London: Bantam Books, 1971. Permission courtesy of *The New York Times.*

Prawdin, Michael, **The Unmentionable Nechaev: A Key to Bolshevism.** Copyright 1961. London: Allen and Unwin, 1961. Permission courtesy of Reneé C. Prawdin.

Rayback, Joseph G., *A History of American Labor.* Copyright © 1959, 1965 by Joseph G. Rayback. New York, Macmillan, 1964. Permission courtesy of The Macmillan Co.

Révész, Imre, *History of the Hungarian Reformed Church.* Washington, D.C.: Hungarian Reformed Federation of America, 1956. Passage reprinted from p. 128. Courtesy of the Hungarian Reformed Federation of America.

Reynolds, Lloyd G., *Labor Economics and Labor Relations.* Copyright © 1949 by Prentice-Hall, Inc. Englewood Cliffs, New Jersey: Prentice-Hall, 1959. Permission courtesy of Prentice-Hall, Inc.

Roberts, Adam, "Buddhism and Politics in South Vietnam," in *The World Today* (London), vol. 21, no. 6 (June 1965), pp. 240-250. Permission courtesy of Adam Roberts.

———, *Civilian Resistance as a National Defence.* Harrisburg, Pa., Stackpole Books, 1968. Original British edition: *The Strategy of Civilian Defence.* Copyright © 1967 by Adam Roberts, 1967. London: Faber & Faber, 1967. Permission courtesy of Adam Roberts.

Rosenthal, Mario, *Guatemala: The Story of an Emergent Latin American Democracy.* Copyrighted, New York: Twayne Publishers, 1962. Permission courtesy of Twayne Publishers, Inc.

Rostovtzeff, M., *The Social and Economic History of the Roman Empire*, Vol. I. Second edition revised by P. M. Frazer. Copyright © 1957 by Oxford Universtiy Press. Oxford: Clarendon Press, 1956. Permission courtesy of Clarendon Press.

Rubin, Jerry, *Do It!* New York: Simon and Schuster, 1970. Permission courtesy of Jerry Rubin.

Schapiro, Leonard, *The Communist Party of the Soviet Union.* Copyright © 1960, 1971 by Leonard Schapiro. New York: Random House, 1960. London: Eyre & Spottiswoode, 1960. Permission courtesy of Leonard B. Schapiro.

Schelling, Thomas C., *International Economics.* Copyright © 1958 by Allyn and Bacon, Inc. Boston: Allyn and Bacon, 1958.

Seifert, Harvey, *Conquest by Suffering: The Process and Prospects of Non-violent Resistance.* Copyright © 1965 by W. L. Jenkins. Philadelphia: Westminster Press, 1965. Permission courtesy of the Westminster Press.

Seton-Watson, Christopher, *Italy From Liberalism to Fascism, 1870-1925.* Copyright © 1967 by Christopher Seton-Watson. New York: Barnes and Noble, 1967. London: Methuen, 1967. Permission courtesy of Christopher Seton-Watson.

Shirer, William L., *The Rise and Fall of the Third Reich.* Copyright © 1959, 1960 by William L. Shirer. New York: Simon and Schuster, 1960. London: Secker and Warburg, 1962. Permission courtesy of Simon and Schuster.

Shridharani, Krishnalal, *War Without Violence: A Study of Gandhi's Method and Its Accomplishments.* New York: Harcourt Brace and Co., 1939. London: Victor Gollancz, 1939. Permission courtesy of S. K. Shridharani.

Soloman, Frederic and Jacob R. Fishman, "The Psychosocial Meaning of Nonviolence in Student Civil Rights Activities", *Psychiatry*, vol. XXVII, No. 2 (May 1964), pp. 91-99. Permission courtesy of *Psychiatry: A Publication.*

Steiner, Stan, *The New Indians.* Copyright © 1968 by Stan Steiner, 1968. New York: Harper & Row, 1968. Permission courtesy of Stan Steiner and Harper & Row.

Suhl, Yuri, *They Fought Back: The Story of Jewish Resistance in Nazi Europe.* New York: Crown Publishers, 1967. London: MacGibbon and Kee, 1968. Permission courtesy of Yuri Suhl.

Sunday Times (London), a passage from the issue of March 19, 1967. Permission courtesy of the *Sunday Times.*

Symons, Julian, *The General Strike: A Historical Portrait.* Copyright © 1957 by Julian Symons. London: The Cresset Press. 1957. Permission courtesy of the Cresset Press, and Julian Symons.

Tabor, Robert, *M-26: Biography of a Revolution.* Copyrighted 1961. New York: Lyle Stuart, 1961. Permission courtesy of Lyle Stuart, Inc.

Taylor, George R., *The Struggle for North China.* Copyright © 1940 by the Secretariat, Institute of Pacific Relations. New York: Institute of Pacific Relations, 1940. Permission courtesy of William L. Holland, Editor, *Pacific Affairs.*

Ullstein, Heinz, *Spielplatz meines Lebens: Erinnerungen.* Copyright © 1961 by Kindler Verlag München. Munich: Kindler Verlag, 1961. Permission courtesy of Kindler Verlag. English translation in text by Hilda von

Klenze Morris.

Vassilyev, A. T., *The Ochrana: The Russian Secret Police.* Edited and with an Introduction by Rene Fülöp-Miller. Copyright © 1930 by J. B. Lippincott Co. Philadelphia and London: J. B. Lippincott Co., 1930. Passage reprinted by permission of J. B. Lippincott Company.

Warmbrunn, Werner, *The Dutch under German Occupation 1940-1945.* Copyright © 1963 by Board of Trustees of the Leland Standford Junior University. Stanford, California: Stanford University Press, 1963. London: Oxford University Press, 1963. Passages reprinted with permission of Stanford University Press.

Warriner, Doreen, *Land Reform in Principle and Practice.* Copyright © 1969 by Oxford University Press. Oxford: Clarendon Press, 1969. Permission courtesy of Clarendon Press.

Waskow, Arthur I., *From Race Riot to Sit-in: 1919 and the 1960s.* Copyright © 1966 by Doubleday and Co., Inc. Garden City, N. Y.: Doubleday, 1966. Permission courtesy of Doubleday & Co.

Wheeler-Bennett, Sir John W., *The Nemesis of Power: The Germany Army in Politics, 1918-1945.* New York: St. Martin's Press, 1953. London: Macmillan, 1953. Permission courtesy of Sir John Wheeler-Bennett.

Williams, Robin M., *The Reduction of Intergroup Tensions.* New York: Social Science Research Council, 1947. Permission courtesy of Robin M. Williams.

Wolfe, Bertram D., *Three who Made a Revolution.* Copyrighted. New York: Dial Press, 1948. London: Thames and Hudson, 1956. Permission courtesy of Bertram D. Wolfe.

Zinn, Howard, *Albany.* Atlanta: Southern Regional Council, 1962. Permission courtesy of Howard Zinn.

NOTES

NOTES

NOTES

Write for complete catalogue

EXTENDING HORIZONS BOOKS

Porter Sargent Publisher
11 Beacon St., Boston, Ma. 02108